After the French Revolution

New York University Studies in
French Culture and Civilization

General Editors:
Tom Bishop and Nicholas Wahl

Under the Sign of Ambiguity: Saint-John Perse/Alexis Leger
Erika Ostrovsky

The State and the Market Economy: Industrial Patriotism and
Economic Intervention in France
Jack Hayward

The Trouble with France
Alain Peyrefitte

Medieval Narrative and Narratology: Subjects and Objects of
Desire
Evelyn Birge Vitz

Poetics of the Literary Self-Portrait
Michel Beaujour

After the French Revolution

Six critics of democracy and nationalism

Jack Hayward

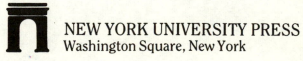

NEW YORK UNIVERSITY PRESS
Washington Square, New York

First published in the U.S.A. in 1991 by
NEW YORK UNIVERSITY PRESS
Washington Square
New York, NY 10003

Printed in Great Britain

Library of Congress Cataloging-in-Publication Data

Hayward. Jack Ernest Shalom.
    After the French Revolution : six critics of democracy and
nationalism / Jack Hayward.
        p.   cm.
    Includes index.
    ISBN 0-8147-3480-4
    1. France--Politics and government. 2. Democracy--France-
-History. 3. Nationalism--France--History. I. Title.
JN2451.H38   1991   91-29800
320.5'0944--dc20   CIP

CONTENTS

PREFACE

This book originated in a series of Tagore Lectures which I was invited to deliver at the University of Baroda in 1984 by the Vice-Chancellor Professor Bhikhu Parekh. So it has been several years in gestation, six lectures expanding into a nine-chapter volume. It has represented a return to an old interest of mine in the history of political ideas.

I would like to thank the Rockefeller Foundation Bellagio Center for allowing me to start writing this book during an unforgettable month's residence at the Villa Serbelloni in 1986. I also wish to thank the University of Hull for allowing me two separate terms of leave, in 1986 and again in 1989, to complete the research and writing.

I am grateful to Dr Cecil Courtney (Christ's College, Cambridge) for his detailed comments on the chapter on Benjamin Constant, and to Dr Vincent Wright (Nuffield College, Oxford) for general comments on the initial draft. Finally, I wish to express my gratitude to Janet Braim and to Enid Tracy for the patience with which they translated my handwriting into typescript.

The substance of this book formed the basis of the lectures I delivered in 1990–1 as the holder of the Elie Halévy Visiting Professorship at the Paris *Institut d'Etudes Politiques*. So it both began and ended as a set of lectures, undergoing a transmutation in the intervening years.

Jack Hayward
Paris, November 1990

INTRODUCTION

Why did it take France almost two hundred years to recover its equilibrium after seeking simultaneously to reconstruct its political system around a unitary national community and a democratic decision-making process? Why did it take two monarchies, two empires, the Vichy regime and five republics (to mention only the main constitutional experiments) before France was able to reconstitute a government capable of giving democratic leadership through an elected head of state? Why did the urge to create national unity seem to require the subordination of a plurality of identities to conform with a centralized uniformity? Why did a movement to liberate individuals from the grip of past intolerance and arbitrary power itself become systematically oppressive and intolerant, acting in the name of the sovereign people? How did the seemingly unending process of revolution and reaction resolve itself into a sufficient measure of agreement about institutional fundamentals for unavoidable ideological, social and economic disputes to become the subject of dedramatized debate and general acquiescence in the decisions made?

The argument presented in the chapters that follow attempts to show that even though the French revolutionary impetus has not spent itself, the historical vicissitudes to which it has been subjected and the intellectual criticisms to which it has been exposed permit us to understand more clearly how it has been domesticated. Self-destructive religious, social, industrial and political dissension has been increasingly channelled into a general acceptance that gradualist, incremental reform allows a shifting balance to be struck between desirable continuities and changes. What unites is widely regarded as usually more important than what divides, even if some backward-looking zealots strive to resurrect passions that seem to have been irretrievably dissipated. Yet the Revolution's unfinished agenda precludes the comfort of quietism. It beckons French leaders to the restless pursuit of aspirations which can never be wholly attained.

The questions posed can be elucidated in a variety of ways. They will be explored here mainly through the interaction between political history and political theorizing. This initially takes the form of an investigation of the sources from which the founding myth of a liberal, democratic and national Revolution emerged to legitimize the modern state. The liberal 'English' path, as reflected notably in the writings of Montesquieu, is considered because it remained for two centuries both an attractive and repellent alternative to the one chosen in France. There, the predominant view did not follow Locke's French or American protagonists. Instead, it turned above all to Rousseau as its guide, in an attempt to free France from the unenlightened practices of what in retrospect came to be known as the Old Regime. The revolutionary experience itself is considered primarily to show the way in which popular sovereignty, as embodied in the French nation, acquired its symbols, practices and protagonists. The founding myth was manipulated, especially by Robespierre and Napoleon, to establish a patriotic revolutionary dictatorship and then an imperial populist despotism which temporarily achieved national reconciliation at the price of international aggrandizement.

Repeated and explicit attempts to 'end the Revolution' for the next century and a half both inspired and were inspired by numerous and contrasting interpretations of what the French experience meant. They ranged from ultra-reactionary efforts to restore and stabilize the past to hyper-revolutionary endeavours to push the changes to a futuristic conclusion. While it is somewhat arbitrary to give pride of place to six personalities, they are representative and remarkable individuals. Each of them played an active as well as speculative part in trying to understand and remedy the consequences of the upheaval that threatened to make inherited ways of thinking and acting comprehensively obsolete. While the lives of Maistre, Saint-Simon and Constant were directly disrupted by the French Revolution (they died in the decade 1821–30), Tocqueville, Proudhon and Blanqui were most immediately affected by the subsequent Revolutions of 1830 and 1848.

Maistre and Saint-Simon both represent the counter-revolutionary Right, but whereas Maistre was the ultimate and uncompromising reactionary, Saint-Simon placed his faith in progress through science and industry, managed by a trained élite, rather than monarchical and papal autocracy. While all six analysts of the revolutionary phenomenon were conscious of the importance – positive or negative – of religion in creating a stable post-revolutionary society, Maistre's traditionalist catholicism and Saint-Simon's New Christianity made the most explicit appeal to religious belief as the indispensable foundation of political order. Constant's individualistic and protestant liberalism placed much greater trust in constitutional forms as a guarantee against the propensity of the democratic revolution to degenerate into tyranny, while his fellow liberal Tocqueville's pluralistic and fatalistic liberalism relied upon socio-cultural practices that were less susceptible to legal ingenuity and human will. Unlike Saint-Simon, Constant regarded modern industrial and commercial society as a powerful force for human liberation, whereas Tocqueville was more inclined to fear it as a disruptive factor promoting class conflict. The latter view was a natural response to the emergence of socialism, of which Proudhon and Blanqui represent highly contrasting proponents. Although they shared a hatred of inequality, Proudhon always placed liberty first – as in the revolutionary trilogy – and was above all else fearful of the power of the state as an instrument of oppression. Industrial democracy – however desirable – must come from the voluntary and decentralized actions of individuals. Blanqui believed that state power had to be seized and used dictatorially to bring about the social changes that would otherwise not occur. Far from revolution being a Proudhonian pervasive, permanent process that would never be complete, Blanqui thought that carefully planned insurrection could ensure an eternity of social justice: a revolution to end revolutions.

These alternative paths to a consensual order capable of withstanding the polarizing pressures of dynamic modernity offered the French people a bewilderingly diverse set of answers to the predicaments posed by the French Revolution. They all attracted ardent supporters, which contributed to a prolonged inability to secure a minimal consensus. By the mid-nineteenth century, the major choices – each with variants – had been forcefully formulated. However, it took another century for their implications to be evaluated in the context of an evolution from a rural–agricultural to an urban–industrial society. By the second half of the twentieth century, with catholicism and communism in precipitate decline as political forces, the authoritarian extremes of Right and Left had lost their ideological underpinning. There remained the liberal critiques of democracy and nationalism, flanked by the vision of a meritocratically managed industrial society and the moralistic defence of the rights of those who were managed freely to mind their own affairs.

If the Revolution can in some sense be said to have ended, this is due to the socio-economic modernization of France, which happened less through the impersonal market processes envisaged by Constant than by the élite-led technobureaucratic organization propounded by Saint-Simon. The shift from French nationalism to a European internationalism similarly has been less the consequence of free trade than the need for large-scale collective organization for security and prosperity. However, Constant's *revanche* came with the 1980s shift from technocratic public management to market forces, the consumer becoming more important than the voter, although the central place of the firm and the business entrepreneur is something of which both Constant and Saint-Simon would have approved. Both would also have wholeheartedly endorsed the shift from a Europe ravaged by war to one in which commerce would be the concomitant of international peace. The end of the cold war, the collapse of the Communist political and economic alternative to liberal democracy and market capitalism, have powerfully reinforced this trend by extending it from the Atlantic to the Pacific. However, while Saint-Simon did at one stage link economic and political liberalism, he ultimately placed his faith in a technocratic élite which alone had the scientific knowledge to manage an advanced industrial society. Liberal democracy has had intractable problems in accommodating such economic and political managerialism.

The British model of parliamentary government exercised a powerful influence in French liberal circles throughout the nineteenth century, and on no one more than Constant. However, the inability to develop a British-style two-party system proved a major handicap, as France lurched between an anarchic multifaction government by Assembly and the appeal to one-man rule. Constant had hoped to develop an approximation to the British system through constitutional proposals that allowed the head of state – whether constitutional monarch or president of the republic – to play an active if 'neutral' role. The July Monarchy did not fulfil his hopes and the Second Republic – in whose constitution-making Tocqueville played a leading role – looked to a directly elected president to fulfil this function. However, an untutored universal suffrage proved more inclined towards the populistic Caesarism of Louis Napoleon than to liberal democracy. The subsequent abolition of the Second Republic with popular approval bequeathed a legacy of hostility to 'personal power' in the hands of the executive that bedevilled French politics for another hundred years. It was de Gaulle's Fifth Republic which at last achieved a reconciliation between effective representative government through direct election of the president and a representative parliament as legislature. Its Constitutional Council has developed into a powerful legal check upon attempts to infringe the liberal principles enshrined notably in the 1789 Declaration of the Rights of Man.

Before France could feel that it had acquired stable and acceptable political institutions, these had to be accepted by liberal Socialists as well as by liberal conservatives. While the Socialist tradition in France included leaders like Louis Blanc who continued to look to Robespierre as a model and others like Blanqui who explicitly favoured dictatorship, Proudhon combined a profound indifference to constitutions with an implacable hostility to the state. Torn between authoritarians (who predominated in the Socialist and Communist Parties) and libertarians (who were more influential in the trade union movement), it was the emergence under Mitterrand of a Socialist Party willing to accept the Fifth Republic that not only made it fit for office but also ended the long-standing dispute over the regime. By accepting the constitution that de Gaulle had instituted as a latter day lawgiver in the Montesquieu and Rousseau manner, Mitterrand retrospectively made the will of the General into the general will.

Having spent decades in opposition, the Socialists – despite the influence of Jacobinism within their political culture – came to give much more importance to decentralization, of which Tocqueville and Proudhon had been such ardent advocates. Just as the nation-state needed to be transcended by wider European loyalties, so the smaller subnational communities should acquire a genuine autonomy. Rather than transferring sovereignty from the king to the people and to 'its' government, power should be dispersed to a plurality of supra- and subnational authorities, with a preference for the communes where those citizens who wished to play an active part would have most scope to do so. While Proudhon would have been far from content with the 1980s shift of emphasis from centre to periphery, he would have to acknowledge that France has been moving in the 'Girondin' direction.

With the benefit of hindsight we shall try to show how complex a phenomenon 'the French Revolution' was, involving stubborn continuities as well as momentous discontinuities. The diversity of the responses it prompted at the time and during its extended aftermath can only be partially reflected in the political analysts considered here. Three of the six (Maistre, Saint-Simon and Tocqueville) were aristocrats, coming from a class which had contributed most to the Revolution, both by seeking to preserve its privileges and by undermining their legitimacy. Two of them (Constant and Blanqui) were from the rising middle classes, who profited much more from the Revolution than they contributed to its advent. Neither was truly representative of the bourgeoisie, if only because Constant's spendthrift habits prevented him from becoming a *nouveau riche*, while Blanqui deliberately identified downwards and sought the status of *déclassé*. Only one, Proudhon, came from the working classes, to whom he remained loyal even when he ceased to be a printer and became a journalist and writer. In no case can their views be 'reduced' to their origins. In two cases (Maistre and Constant) they were not French by birth. Three of them (Maistre, Constant and Proudhon) spent extended periods in involuntary exile and four of them (Saint-Simon, Tocqueville, Proudhon and particularly Blanqui) were incarcerated in French prisons for their political activities. Three of them (Constant, Tocqueville and, briefly, Proudhon) were members of Parliament. Faced with a society shattered by the impact of the French Revolution, their attempts to grapple with its consequences have much to teach us about how democracy and nationality can cease to be forces for destruction. While France is their focus, the portent of their intellectual efforts is universal.

Our six critics of democracy and nationalism range from the extreme Right to the extreme Left. Maistre's criticisms were both powerful and influential but did not provide the constructive sources for a modern élitist and internationalist order. This required a republicanized version of the science-based industrialism of Saint-Simon and Comte, which provided the impetus for technology-driven society controlled by meritocratic managers. Yet, in a liberalized form, the appeal to a catholic model of political leadership triumphed with de Gaulle, even though in its reactionary form it had failed under Pétain. The centre of our spectrum is occupied by Constant and Tocqueville, who provided a corrective to the neglect of the international market economy, stressing the need to protect individual rights and to avoid the abuse of centralized bureaucratic power. With an initial surge in the early years of the Third Republic, their ideas were to be much more fully accepted in the 1980s of the Fifth Republic. Ironically, this occurred under the aegis of the Socialists, who have in practice adopted a very liberalized form of socialism, rather than the nominal conservative champions of liberalism. The Communist inheritors of Blanquist revolutionary dictatorship have not been able to find acceptance for their programme within the context of a liberal democracy. Their guilt by association with a foreign, Soviet nationalism and opposition to West European unity has furthermore condemned them, like the reactionary Right, to a role of marginalized irritant. Eliminating the extremes, France has turned from introspective recrimination towards a reformism made possible by reconciliation over fundamentals. How has it reached this haven?

CHAPTER ONE

THE FOUNDING MYTH:
THE IDEOLOGICAL PRECURSORS

What is a revolution? The rhetoric and the reality

We must begin with the notion of beginning. Paradoxically, it is difficult to innovate in an unprecedented way. It is precisely when a society is embarked on what it conceives as forward-looking changes that it consciously or unconsciously adopts a backward-looking model that restores continuity with the past. Fascinated yet frightened by the thought of starting afresh, a foundation myth or legend often provides the more or less plausible reassurance during the journey into the unknown. One may be making a leap in the dark but at least the darkness of the absolute, original point of departure is given a resplendent if mysterious illumination. Subsequently, innovation can be disguised as a restoration of the original, mythical state, so that it appears to be a counter-revolution rather than a revolution.

Prior to the French Revolution, the term revolution was traditionally used in the astronomic sense of a recurring rotation and the revolutionaries themselves were not conscious that they were embarking upon a new political beginning. Hannah Arendt has reminded us that the mid-seventeenth-century English Revolution, the 'first modern revolution, was officially understood as a restoration', although Guizot set the fashion of using the analogy with the French Revolution to curb its propensity to radicalization. The subsequent 1688 '"Glorious Revolution", the event through which very paradoxically the term found its definite place in political and historical language, was not thought of as a revolution at all, but as a restoration of monarchical power . . . . The revolutions of the seventeenth and eighteenth centuries, which to us appear to show all evidence of a new spirit, the spirit of the modern age, were intended to be restorations.'[1] Alexis de Tocqueville, whose knowledge of English constitutional history and its American variant contributed to his emphasis upon the fundamental continuity rather than rupture between the Old Regime and the Revolution, explicitly argued: 'It almost seemed as if the object of the impending revolution was not to destroy but to restore the old regime.'[2]

A great gap usually yawns between what it is intended to 'restore' and the state of affairs that is actually brought about by revolutionary activity. Although Saint-Just had proclaimed – in the rhetoric of civic humanism that was widely accepted if usually expressed with less eloquence – 'The world has been empty since the Romans, their memory is now our only prophecy of freedom', the stable authority based upon a republican alliance between patricians and plebians was not to be established by the Jacobins. The aspiration to imitate the Roman Republic instead degenerated under Napoleon into what Tocqueville – living resentfully under the democratic despotism of Louis-Napoleon – polemically dubbed 'a minor copy of the gigantic and despicable Roman Empire.'[3] Although at times Tocqueville writes of the French Revolution as a spectacular sequence of events – 'The spectacle was short but it was one of incomparable grandeur' – François Furet has emphasized that contrary to the revolutionaries' self-perception, Tocqueville correctly conceived of them as the instruments of a continuous process in which 'the Revolution changed everything but by preserving everything.'[4] While such an emphasis upon the Revolution's dynamic conservatism is excessive, it is an indispensable corrective to the usual tendency to exaggerate the break with the past.

Nothing perhaps so exemplifies the desire to symbolize such a rupture as the replacement of the Gregorian calendar of 1582, which treated Christ's death as the turning point from which time could be counted both backward and forward. Attacks upon the ecclesiastical basis of the Gregorian calendar – used in France for two centuries – developed in the years immediately preceding the Revolution, but on 5 October 1793 the Convention abolished the Christian calendar and declared that Year One began on 22 September 1792 because the proclamation of the Republic had been the true turning point in human history. After all, the Roman Republic had its own calendar, one which admittedly had been modified by Julius Caesar. Space was republicanized with the creation of the new *départements*, as was measuring and counting through the metric and decimal systems, but time proved more resistant to change. When Napoleon restored the Gregorian calendar as from 1 January 1806, little more than a dozen years later, it seemed that 'the Revolution was reintegrated, as it were, into the historical process with its twofold extension towards infinity. It was as though it was conceded that not even the Revolution . . . contained sufficient independent meaning in itself to begin a new historical process . . . a repudiation of the Roman faith in the sacredness of foundations with the accompanying custom of numbering time from the foundation date.'[5] However, just as we should beware of assuming that one can simply make a new start, we should also avoid the notion that the process of change can simply be halted or reversed.

The problem with this sort of dual circumspection is that the revolutionary phenomenon is in danger of being relativized out of existence or at least diffused to such an extent as to rob it of identity. Of the many attempts to characterize revolutions in general, the one that seems to provide the most useful conceptual framework – because it avoids excessive abstraction without retreating into barefoot empiricism – is that offered by Charles Tilly. Treating revolutions not as peculiar phenomena but as 'an extreme condition of the normal political process', Tilly expands Trotsky's notion of dual sovereignty into that of 'multiple sovereignty' as their salient feature. 'A revolution begins when a government previously under the control of a single sovereign polity becomes the object of effective, competing, mutually exclusive claims on the part of two or more distinct polities; it ends when a single sovereign polity regains control over the government.'[6] It is essential to emphasize the mutually *exclusive* nature of the claims made to sovereignty; otherwise pluralism would imply permanent revolution. If the claims can be accommodated and power shared, a revolutionary situation can be avoided. It is the failure to recognize this distinction that has led authoritarians to see the only choice as between absolutism and anarchy.

Whereas most analysts of revolution stress such features as the transfer of power from one ruling class to another, the large amount of violence employed, the massive political involvement of the oppressed, the emergence and popularity of a visionary new society, and the spread of extensive structural, social, economic and political changes, Tilly argues that they do not clearly and unambiguously distinguish revolutions from routine political activity. Instead, he propounds four pre-conditions of revolution: the appearance of (coalitions of) new contenders for governmental power; active support of a 'significant (unspecified) segment of the subject population'; normally a coalition between insider contenders and outsider challengers for power; and the government's inability or unwillingness to suppress the threat to its monopoly of power.[7] The rules that habitually regulate political life are suspended.

The government's inability to assert its authority effectively may be due to an insufficiency of coercive resources, inefficiency in enforcing coercion or inhibition in its application, usually because it has lost control of the armed forces. Tilly goes on to set out an ideal but probabilistic sequence in the revolutionary process, warning against the tendency to regard a mass of antecedent events as causes and almost all subsequent events as effects. The

revolutionary process starts with the mobilization of traditionally inert social forces into active contenders for power, making unacceptable demands
for control over government. Unsuccessful efforts by the government to
accommodate or suppress these demands result in the achievement by the
contending coalition of control over some part of the territory, functional
apparatus or government personnel. Subsequent struggles lead to the re-
establishment of sovereign control over the polity either by the victory of
the revolutionary coalition or through its fragmentation and defeat, ending
with the reimposition of routine government control. Tilly concludes that
the correct 'revolutionary strategy therefore is to mobilize new contenders
with exclusive claims to control of the government, encourage acceptance
of these claims by people outside the contenders, form coalitions with established members of the polity and neutralize the government's repressive
capacity. That . . . is more or less what effective revolutionaries have been
doing all along.'[8] In the ideological terms of making a complete break with
the pre-revolutionary past defined as the 'Old Regime', the need to change
the conception of the political community and of its political institutions
was seen as irreconcilably adversarial. This meant demolishing the founding
myths of the old order and replacing them with new ones.

While Tilly's model will be used to locate the core of the prolonged
revolutionary process, we shall adopt a broader view in which sovereign
control of government comes after the impact of selected preparatory factors that are often not fully appreciated until after the event, and before
the diffusion of the selected effects throughout society expends its initial
impetus. We must bear in mind his warning not to confuse antecedent and
subsequent events with causes and consequences of revolution, keeping
our focus upon the nation as the political community and democracy as
the way in which it takes its political decisions. Nevertheless, the general
point that the historian–politician Guizot made remains valid: 'We have
to date revolutions from the day they break out. It is the only precise
date we can assign them but it is not the one from which they start.
The jolts called revolutions are less the symptom of something beginning
than the affirmation of what has happened.'[9] Krishan Kumar has taken the
same point further. Revolution is not an event but a process: 'In most
cases the opening stages of the classic Revolutions are the final stages
of the revolutions proper, the revolutionary period . . . that process of
the disintegration of political authority which essentially constituted the
revolution, and to which the occurrence of the Revolution so-called appears
as a coda, concluding a much longer period of revolutionary activity.'[10]

Because political revolution is synonymous with the breakdown of sovereignty, the historic function of the successful revolution is to re-establish

sovereignty. In this sense, a revolution is more a restoration than an inno-vation, although in the process the causes of the breakdown of authority – whether they derive from divisions among the state rulers or challenges from society – will be dealt with by strengthening the government. This will involve eliminating its internal dissensions as well as reducing the autonomy of potential challengers to its authority by centralization. In France it took nearly a century and only the Third Republic was able to start to formalize the process of bringing the Revolution to 'completion' with an improvised constitution that secured an acceptable institutional compromise. It reconstituted what the Old Regime was unable to achieve and the intervening political regimes failed to secure. It gave the ruled the feeling that they were also the rulers, to the minimal extent that they thought this to be necessary. The 1789–90 municipal revolutions, 'spon-taneously transforming France into a federation of communes', doubtless required the full countervailing power of a unitary and indivisible sover-eignty to restore authority and crush the danger that continuous popular participation would lead to a destabilizing permanent revolution.[11] It also necessitated the liberal toleration of diversity alongside the drive towards democratic uniformity. The revolutionary controversies over sovereignty dissipated themselves as France regained its equilibrium during the late-nineteenth-century period of socio-political stalemate, preparatory to en-gaging in a process of modernization from the mid-twentieth century that has taken revolution off the Fifth Republic's political agenda. In its place, an increasing acceptance of pluralism has dissipated the fratricidal assertion of mutually exclusive claims to sovereignty into a piecemeal reformism. Not 'fraternity or death' but a dispassionate willingness to reach uninspiring compromises is the reality 200 years after the event.

The Old Regime

Hannah Arendt has argued in relation to both the French and Russian Revolutions that 'Nothing, indeed, seems more natural than that a revo-lution should be predetermined by the type of government it overthrows; nothing, therefore, appears more plausible than to explain the new absolute, the absolute revolution, by the absolute monarchy which preceded it, and to conclude that the more absolute the ruler, the more absolute the revolution will be which replaced him.'[12] Let us therefore consider the salient charac-teristics of the paternalist, divine right, absolute monarchy with its reliance upon religious and *raison d'état* sanctions, to see whether what seems natural was actually the case. 'At the close of the seventeenth century, by the efficiency of its administrative and governmental structure, France was in advance of every other country in Europe.' However, Alfred Cobban went on to show, 'It was in France that the great edifice that towered over Europe was erected in the seventeenth century and it was in France that the principle of Divine Right was to receive its death-blow.'[13] Despite ups and downs, there was a secular trend away from medieval constitutionalism starting in the fifteenth century. The judicial *Parlements* as well as the Estates-General and Provincial Estates – required for consent to taxation – were weakened or eliminated in favour of royal sovereignty until the revival of the *Parlements* after the death of Louis XIV and of the Estates-General just before the Revolution. 'French constitutionalism, from its medieval origins into the eighteenth century, was a distinctive blend of legalism, pluralism and historicism. It was a theory of a complex polity, centred around a monarch whose power was formally absolute, but making room for effective sharing in power by other bodies in the state, especially the judges, the assemblies of the nobility and the clergy.'[14] The king was subject to the supposedly immemorial fundamental laws covering the legitimate extent and proper users of state power, of which the *Parlements* were the judicial guardians.

In the context of late-sixteenth-century religious wars, the Estates lost the battle for an English-style parliamentary system because they were associated with the catholic extremists and the Huguenots. The king, assisted by the *Parlements*, defeated the attempt to revive the Estates and instead asserted a Roman law, imperial role as defender of the common interest and a godlike supremacy in place of the feudal 'suzerain of suzerains' status. Jean Bodin, who was a Third Estate delegate to the 1576 Estates General, by his exclusion of both *Parlements* and Estates from a share in legislative sovereignty, conceived of as enforceable commands, reinforced royal absolutism, although he regarded the king as limited by natural law, the fundamental laws of the realm and private property rights. Despite these restrictions, Nannerl Keohane argues that 'because of this potent concept of lawmaking, Bodin was able to present a novel picture of the sovereign as a creative, innovative force within the state rather than the . . . maintainer of an established equilibrium.'[15] The state's interests came to be synonymous with that of the sovereign. In particular, 'Richelieu was responsible for making the notion of *raison d'état* acceptable as an approach to governance. He authorized writers to expound the concept and sought to legitimize its precepts', notably in his *Testament politique*.[16] The mid-seventeenth-century judicial and *parlementaire Fronde* ineffectually aimed at a return to the old semi-pluralistic medieval constitution with taxation by consent, involving a curb on the power of usurping cardinals and interventionist *Intendants*. Its failure prevented the emergence of an English-style constitutional monarchy in France and instead consolidated royal absolutism. It is not by chance that Hobbes – who had formulated the absolutist ideas of the *Leviathan* during his French exile – attracted more contemporary attention in France than in England.

Nevertheless, although Louis XIV and his political cardinals appeared to have perfected royal absolutism, their legacy carried with it ominous consequences. It mobilized rival contenders for power and proved incapable of preserving its monopoly of power. As Cobban put it, 'By completing the elimination of all rival authorities from the Government, Louis XIV had put on the monarchy the burden of total responsibility, but at the same time without endowing it with total power. He had gone either too far or not far enough ... he had left the higher orders of the State – clergy, *noblesse* and *parlements* – sufficiently independent to oppose the will of the king, hamper the work of the bureaucracy and stand in the way of efficient government.'[17] Frequent wars and an inability to reform the tax system led to persistent and ultimately fatal financial difficulties both with the aristocracy and with the Church. Furthermore, the divine right monarch lacked indispensable support from a divided Church: divided between an aristocratic, worldly, upper clergy and a mass of poor parish priests, attracted to the view that the Church should itself be organized on the lines of a constitutional and not an absolute monarchy. Persecution of Jansenists and Protestants was a constant source of controversy, while the pro-Gallican *Parlement* of Paris was able to secure in 1762 the expulsion of the Jesuit Order, which had assisted the rise of royal absolutism. Unwilling to replace its reliance upon the nobility by the bourgeoisie, divine right monarchy was also unable to curb the Church's privileges, because its support was necessary to maintain a cultural hegemony that was increasingly threatened – at least among the influential educated minority – by the critique of the *philosophes*.

The reformist re-emergence of constitutionalism: liberalism and democracy

Madame de Staël, in posing the question of whether France had a constitution prior to the Revolution, answered that 'France had been governed by customs, often by caprices and never by laws.'[18] This was because there had been a prolonged struggle by the aristocracy to preserve its privileges, by the people to acquire rights and by the kings to secure absolute power. A fellow liberal, Alexis de Tocqueville, expresses the somewhat confused but comprehensive intellectual reaction against the Old Regime that long preceded the Revolution. 'All over the Continent that instinctive attachment and involuntary respect which men of all ages and nations are wont to feel for their own institutions, for their traditional customs, and for the wisdom or the virtues of their forefathers had almost ceased to exist among the educated classes . . . . Hence that universal desire for change, flooding every mind, though no one knew as yet how that change could be brought about.'[19] The sunrise of the *Roi Soleil* proved to be much more resplendent than his sunset. Royal absolutism's apogee had already passed by the beginning of the eighteenth century and the constitutionalist counter-attack began in earnest. A number of practitioners of what they termed the 'science of government' or 'political science', such as the Abbé de St-Pierre, the Comte de Boulainvilliers and the Marquis d'Argenson, proposed more or less radical reforms, to be followed by more famous forerunners of the French Revolution: Montesquieu, Rousseau, Condorcet and Sieyès.

The Abbé de St-Pierre's ardent advocacy of a utilitarian applied master science of politics in the early eighteenth century is of more interest because of his influence on others than for the cogency of his own voluminous writings. D'Argenson was his protégé, while Rousseau was selected to edit his manuscripts for posthumous publication. Although he worked on them between 1754 and 1756, when he was preparing to embark upon his epoch-making *Social Contract*, Rousseau abandoned the idea for fear that St-Pierre's heterodox views would land him in serious political trouble. Nevertheless, he did bring out abridged editions of *Perpetual Peace* (the advocacy of federal European unity) and the *Polysynodie* (a defence against one-man rule of government by committee, as it was tried and failed during the post-Louis XIV Regency), incorporating some of his own ideas in the process. However, the Abbé's biographer concludes that 'If St-Pierre anticipates ideas of the *Contrat Social* early in the eighteenth century, it is impossible to delimit any area in which he alone exerts an influence on Rousseau.'[20] Rousseau may nevertheless have taken over from St-Pierre the view that the public interest emerges from the clash and mutual destruction of private interests, as well as both the contractual and the democratic basis of the political community.

The Marquis d'Argenson – whose *Jusques où la démocratie peut être admise dans le gouvernement monarchique* also influenced Rousseau's *Social Contract* – was unlike his patron St-Pierre, who had written and published much and was ridiculed for his pains. D'Argenson wrote a great deal and prudently published little under the absolute monarchy. Unfortunately much of his unpublished work was consumed by fire during the Paris Commune, making him a belated victim of the revolutionary movement of which he was a forerunner. He had the advantage over St-Pierre of administrative and political experience: as an *Intendant* (predecessor of the Prefect), which persuaded him of the need for *laissez-faire*, a slogan he coined in 1751, counsellor to the *Parlement de Paris*, Counsellor of State and Minister of Foreign Affairs. D'Argenson's biographer wrote: 'His ideal was a version of Bodin's model in which absolute monarchy as a form of government is combined with an administration in which democratic elements are prominent.'[21] 'D'Argenson's definition of the democracy that progresses in history is close to that of Tocqueville: equality of all citizens and participation in local government.'[22] Acton argued that d'Argenson was 'the earliest writer from whom we can extract the system of 1789 . . . . Although the science of politics was in its infancy . . . . He is eager to change everything, except the monarchy which alone can change all else . . . . D'Argenson saw so little that was worthy to be preserved that he did not shrink from sweeping judgements and abstract propositions. By his rationalism and his indifference to the prejudice of custom and the claim of possession; by his maxim that every man may be presumed to understand the things in which his own interest and responsibility are involved; by his zeal for democracy, equality and simplicity, and his dislike of intermediate authorities, he belongs to a generation later than his own. He heralded events without preparing them',[23] though the failure to effect an orderly revolution from above meant that France experienced a series of disorderly revolutions from below.

D'Argenson shared with Montesquieu and Rousseau the conviction that small size was essential to good government in general and republican government in particular. In d'Argenson's case, it was based upon a comparative study of nineteen contemporary European governments, including Switzerland, Rousseau's homeland. Montesquieu was more inclined to look to classical examples, with the decline of the Roman Republic being an inevitable consequence of its vast increase in size. However, his comparative concerns led him, through a study of the corrupt modern Italian and Dutch republics, to be pessimistic about substituting a republic for monarchy, a constitutional monarchy being in practice the best form of modern government. It was natural that Montesquieu's *Considerations on the Causes of Roman Greatness and Decline* should be the model for Tocqueville's *Old Régime and the Revolution* because they were both members of a legal aristocracy seeking to promote constitutional constraints upon government, whether monarchical or democratic. The title of Montesquieu's much-quoted masterpiece, *The Spirit of the Laws*, was probably borrowed from the great Jansenist seventeenth-century lawyer Jean Domat, Montesquieu's link with the pioneer early-sixteenth-century

constitutionalism of Claude de Seyssel. However, Montesquieu's backward-
looking appeal to France's ancient Gothic government owed two important
debts to the Comte de Boulainvilliers. Firstly, his defence of the Estates
and *Parlements*, the mediating bodies of nobility and clergy between king
and people, led to the conclusion that if power was not shared it would be
abused and absolutism would become indistinguishable from despotism.
Secondly, Boulainvilliers proposed the English system of government as
a model, which Montesquieu observed closely during his extended visit to
England from 1729 to 1731. Thanks to the 'Glorious Revolution' of 1688,
'A novelty that defied the wisdom of centuries had made good its footing,
and revolution had become a principle of stability more sure than tradition.'[24] When such views spread and took hold, political change assumed
the reassuring appearance of constitutional monarchy.

The most immediate influences upon Montesquieu's theory of the separation of powers – conceived as the institutional instrument of English
constitutional liberty – formulated in an essay after his return from England
and only published fifteen years later in *The Spirit of the Laws*, were Locke
and Bolingbroke. Both of them emphasized the separation of executive and
legislative powers to the neglect of judicial power. Although it was the Whig
view that prevailed in Britain, symbolized by the sovereignty of the King-in-
Parliament, Montesquieu elevated and broadened Bolingbroke's advocacy of
a 'mixed state' balancing the powers of King, Lords and Commons into a
liberal formula that became embalmed in the American Constitution. However, it was not implemented by the French Revolution, despite its initial
influence during the phase of constitutional monarchy from 1789 to 1791.
As Melvin Richter has put it, 'although he thought that England offered
the best single case of constitutional liberty, Montesquieu believed that the
English constitution had evolved without plan or conscious construction.
By attempting to make explicit its principles, Montesquieu opened the way
to the deliberate construction of constitutions. Probably he came closest
to this notion when he spoke of the classical persona of the "legislator",
a person called in to construct a scheme of government for a state' (a
notion to which Rousseau was to appeal in the *Social Contract*). 'When
the American and French Revolutions occurred, Montesquieu's theories
received the closest attention of those engaged in debating the details of
the new constitutions being drawn up . . . . Montesquieu made perhaps the
single and most important statement of eighteenth century constitutional
theory prior to these actual cases of revolution and reconstruction which
he thus influenced without having anticipated.'[25]

Montesquieu's pessimistic judgement that despotism was the most normal form of government was to prove accurate, not merely in the particular

case of Revolutionary France but in most of the numerous states that secured independence and the right to self-misgovernment. Yet, had England's political history been studied more carefully, the lesson of its one and only written constitution, Cromwell's 1653 Instrument of Government, would have shown the fragility of attempts to reconstitute stable and free institutions after periods of royal and parliamentary tyranny. It put forward a paper separation of powers between the executive Lord Protector and the parliamentary legislature to avoid the undivided despotism of either the king or 'government by assembly' of the Long Parliament. The desperate attempt to avoid a reversion to despotism by broadening the duality of power into a threefold separation of power, as advocated by Lilburne and the Levellers, suggested the emergence of the judiciary as an institutionally separate authority.[26] The death-throes of the Protectorate and the Restoration supervened and England took the road of parliamentary sovereignty. It was left to the United States to build upon Montesquieu's theory and to make judicial review the arbiter of executive and legislative acts within a federal system. The greatest analyst of American democracy, Tocqueville, who like Montesquieu hated despotism above all else, subsequently deplored the impetuous French Revolutionaries' urge to sweep aside Montesquieu's rejection of sovereignty in favour of the separation of powers. They 'rushed towards unlimited democracy. At first Montesquieu was most frequently quoted; in the end no one was cited but Rousseau.'[27]

It has been said of those who wrote about politics in the 1780s and who were to play an active part in the French Revolution: 'Everyone drew his inspiration from Montesquieu or Rousseau or, more often, from both'; they 'were quoted, paraphrased and misunderstood by everyone', despite their diametrically opposed standpoints based respectively on the *esprit général* and the *volonté générale*, because 'the men of 1789 tried to have the best of both worlds, to achieve Rousseau's regenerative ends by Montesquieu's libertarian means.'[28] Montesquieu's greatest legacy to nineteenth-century liberalism was his insight that whereas the location of power had preoccupied political thinkers since Aristotle, it was the conditions under which power was exercised that were of prime importance. Not *who* but *how* was the vital question if one's primordial concern was defending liberty and preventing despotism. Rousseau's priorities were different, and it was *his* remains that the Revolutionary Convention decreed in April 1794 should be buried in the Pantheon.

It was a version of Rousseau's views that was to prevail and with it came the revival of absolutist theories of sovereignty, although supreme power was now confided not to a hereditary monarch ruling by divine right but to the people. For, while Rousseau had declared that only gods were fit to rule democratically, the French Revolutionary leaders were to see themselves as godlike. They confused Rousseau's view that sovereignty belonged only to the general will of the legislator with the notion (which he specifically rejected) that sovereignty could be wielded by a representative assembly, much less by its executive arm, the Committee of Public Safety. He prophetically wrote: 'Public safety is non-existent if all individuals are not secure',[29] but such moments of practical wisdom were overlaid in the minds of those who misread him by the a priori abstractions of his *Social Contract*. There, Rousseau deified popular sovereignty because as the exponent of the general will it was by definition incapable of willing evil. He was expressing an idealization of the classic Greek vision of a political community embodying law and religion, entitled to make total demands on its citizens, in which state and society were fused. A civil religion was essential to ensure national cohesion, an idea that was to commend itself not merely to revolutionaries like Robespierre but also, in the more general form of the social indispensability of religion, to protagonists as different as Maistre and Saint-Simon, Constant and Tocqueville.

Politics as consensus was all-pervasive but as controversy it was eliminated from Rousseau's imaginary reconstruction of his beloved Sparta and Republican Rome. Seeing himself as an inspired lawgiver in the manner of Moses, Solon and Lycurgus, Rousseau scorned modern governments, offering direct democracy as his model of the only legitimate form of polity. (De Gaulle was to play this law-giving role in 1958, see Chapter 9, pp. 292–3.) The representative government which Montesquieu and his disciples advocated, along with the English example, were dismissed by Rousseau as the offspring of absurd feudal government, in which the people's nominal representatives became their masters. Rousseau was closer to d'Argenson's idea of a 'marriage of absolute sovereignty and extensive popular participation', in which a French monarch was superimposed upon little republics in each town.[30] Rousseau himself recognized that the participant democracy he admired had only been possible in small-scale city-states in which slavery had afforded the leisured class of citizens the freedom to preoccupy themselves with public affairs. In his proposals for Corsica, the suffrage was confined to property owners. However, the French Revolutionaries who purported to realize his ideal retained the attribution of absolute legitimate power without conforming to its express preconditions. In particular, they quickly abandoned his advocacy of a confederation of direct democracies,[31] although the initial impetus of the French Revolution was decentralist. The centralizing impulse of state sovereignty proved to be too powerful.

Rousseau asserted that the only limitation upon sovereign power was the public interest as conceived by the sovereign. What gave it revolutionary implications was Rousseau's claim that the democratic republic was the only legitimate polity. From Hobbes and the natural law theorists Grotius and Pufendorf, Rousseau retrieved the idea of sovereignty, which had been used in the service of absolute monarchy in its struggle against the rival power of the Church, saying that they had 'stripped the people of all their rights to clothe the kings'.[32] Of those like Pufendorf, who summarized his views in a book entitled *The Duties of Man and the Citizen*, Rousseau declared: 'They either do not dare or do not wish to say what they should to those that command, being *paid by the strong to preach to the weak*, so that they only speak to the latter of their duties and to the former of their rights.'[33] (On 4 August 1789, the proposal that a 'Declaration of Duties' should be added to the *Declaration of the Rights of Man and the Citizen* was voted down by 570 votes to 533.) However, while Rousseau presented the social contract as basing political obligation upon voluntary association, in practice the sovereign power to which it gave birth amounted to the 'pact of submission' of the earlier absolutist theorists, with obedience becoming the worm within the fruit of freedom. So the artifice by which Rousseau justifies the abandonment of all individual rights – that the general will provides people with protection as members of a democratic community such that they could not possibly be harmed – would in practice differ from earlier advocates of autocracy only in that popular sovereignty is not merely the source of power; the people actually wield legislative power.

Because the people can only make general rules, the actual work of government decision-making is conceded to an executive which exercises power, so that no constitutional limits can be placed upon a popular sovereignty that is inalienable, indivisible, incommunicable. . .but also impracticable. Rousseau echoed Hobbes in proclaiming: 'In every political state there must be a supreme power, a centre on which everything converges, a principle from which all derives, a sovereign who can do everything.'[34] Consequently, in his desire to reconcile the people's freedom with the unity of political authority, Rousseau transferred absolute power intact from the monarch to the people's 'general will'. In the absence of any effective embodiment of that will and despite recourse to a succession of constitutions, which Rousseau had rejected as unacceptable constraints upon popular sovereignty, the people in 1789, having reclaimed power from the king, almost immediately lost it. The people's will was to be successively usurped by representative assemblies, the Jacobin Club, the Directory oligarchy and Bonaparte from 1789 to 1799; all would have been anathema to Rousseau. He had presciently warned that such usurpations of sovereignty were inevitable,[35] which makes it the more ironic that he is often saddled with the responsibility for them.

After all the diatribes of which he has been a victim in the last two centuries, it is surely time to agree with a recent commentator who is not especially well disposed to Rousseau. 'One thing is certain: the historic Rousseau, the authentic Rousseau has little in common with the revolutionary democrat of the Jacobins, or the pretotalitarian thinker imagined by his adversaries.'[36] However, the 'posthumous Rousseau' has been unwittingly held responsible for those who have read into his concern to establish political authority on firm and legitimate foundations a prescription for the unmitigated abuses of power in the name of the people which have occurred since the French Revolution. Rousseau cannot be exonerated from all responsibility because he helped discredit all sources of political legitimacy other than the direct expression of the people's general will. His support for the strict theory of the mandate and of representatives reporting back regularly to their constituents[37] did provide a method of partially legitimizing the principle of representation which he did so much to undermine, but the delegitimization of parliament was a destabilizing legacy. Furthermore, the notion that the people should periodically explicitly reconsider whether they wished to preserve the existing form of government[38] imparted an additional precariousness to the very institutions upon which people relied to provide the minimum stability necessary to social life. When coupled with Rousseau's scathing egalitarian critique of private property through which the rich exploited the poor (which had more impact than its rehabilitation by him in practice) and his evocation of the absolute and impersonal political power of the people, this heralded an eruption into the political process of hitherto excluded popular forces, to which others such as Robespierre and Babeuf were to give forceful practical application.

The explosive effect of his populist message was multiplied by his eulogy of 'patriotic intoxication that alone can raise men above themselves' and his recommendation to Poland that 'The nation also must become a total, monolithic and closed collectivity in which the individual is absorbed body and soul, in a state of permanent exaltation, "patriotic drunkness'.[39] Developing the classical idea of patriotism as republican civic virtue, which he shared notably with Montesquieu, Rousseau through the notion of the general will expressed the idea of the members of a community having a common national consciousness. This general will, based upon shared institutions and a way of life, not only 'spelt the doom of the *ancien régime*, but also prophesied the national state of the future which would take its place.'[40] Such incitement to nationalism – French and foreign – which was an extrapolation from classical civic fraternity, was never corrected by the treatise on confederations that was to form the sequel to the *Social*

Contract. So instead of providing a peaceful link between the federalist vision of St-Pierre and that of Proudhon, Rousseau fired the particularist passions that were such a potent if disruptive force in post-Revolutionary European politics.

The last two ideological precursors of the French Revolution whom we shall consider, the Marquis de Condorcet and the Abbé Sieyès, both played an active and influential part in the Revolution. They in fact collaborated closely at times in the attempt to restrain its rapid radicalization, as well as to persuade the newly enfranchised people of the need for constitutional representative government. Condorcet was the last of the eighteenth-century *philosophes* and the first of the nineteenth-century *idéologues*, regarding people as essentially reasonable yet compelled by revolutionary experience into 'forcing them to become reasonable so that they want to obey the laws'.[41] As permanent secretary from 1776 of the Academy of Sciences, Condorcet used his position as the leading spokesman of the science establishment to champion rational decision-making under the guidance of a scientific élite, in which power would be allied to knowledge. As the protégé of the Encyclopaedist d'Alembert and the biographer of the reforming technocrat Turgot, Condorcet was concerned to apply his skills as a mathematician to the solution of social problems in the context of a centralizing and bureaucratic absolutism that was embroiled in conflict with the feudal vestiges of the old order. This work on a probabilistic 'political arithmetic' led him to embark upon a heroic but 'self-defeating attempt to compute a form of decision-making that would ensure the collective discovery of truth',[42] a struggle in which some political scientists are still engaged.

While Condorcet admired 'the luminous principles which shine in the work of Montesquieu and Rousseau', he took issue with both of them at crucial points. In his posthumously published observations on the twenty-ninth chapter of the *Esprit des Lois*, his mathematician's impatience with Montesquieu's relativist emphasis upon differences and his defeatist determinism is clear; but what irritated him even more was Montesquieu's reliance upon aristocratic privileges to check the danger of a royalist revolution from above. In his 1788 *Essai sur la Constitution*, Condorcet rationalistically argued that Montesquieu would have modified his view 'if he had been able to reflect more on the nature and effects of truly representative constitutions; if he had not been more concerned with finding the reasons for that which is, rather than discovering that which should be; with perceiving how abuses counterbalance abuses, rather than examining the means of enveloping them all in the same destruction; finally, with examining the combinations of laws proper to each kind of constitution, to each climate, to each national character, rather than seeking the principles according to which one can find just and reasonable laws suitable for all men.'[43] This was the authentic voice of those who on the eve of the Revolution were to believe that a Declaration of the Rights of Man deduced from rational first principles would be an effective safeguard against the arbitrariness, anarchy and authoritarianism that were to be unleashed.

Condorcet's anxiety at the unpreparedness of his fellow countrymen for the daunting task of founding new political constitutions is evident, however, in his postscript to the *Essai*; they relied upon 'a few maxims taken from the *Esprit des Lois* that are more ingenious than solid, more dangerous than useful, and an admiration for the English constitution that is more passionate than enlightened.'[44] However, Condorcet's own breathtakingly naive view that a constitution and legislation were simply matters of translating the self-evident truths of natural law into positive law was explained by him when, in hiding and under the shadow of the guillotine, he wrote: 'I believed that a constitution, in which all the laws prepared by a small number of men chosen by all citizens, would subsequently be presented for their ratification, in which government action, restricted to the utmost simplicity and confined to a very few economic acts, was the goal towards which all political institutions should strive, and that one could attain it more quickly to the extent that the whole mass of peoples were more enlightened. I thought that all laws should be the obvious consequences of natural law, so that all that would be left to opinion or the will of the legislator would be purely practical or formal matters of application, in which even anything of an arbitrary nature that they involved would gradually disappear.'[45] The repeated rewriting of the constitution made it clear that far from stopping the Revolution, the insecure location of sovereignty in practice underlined that revolution could be defined as a shift in sovereignty.[46]

While, with Montesquieu and Rousseau, Condorcet took the view that France was not yet fit for pure democracy, he noted that d'Argenson had not regarded democracy as dangerous to monarchy. To reconcile the principle of the natural equality of men, which implied that all should share in making the laws they were all expected to obey, with the patent differences in knowledge and ability among them, Condorcet sought – against Rousseau – to justify representative institutions. He used his expertise in probability theory to demonstrate that the unenlightened and unrepresented many might be induced to accept the decisions of the enlightened few if they were given 'a mathematical guarantee of the rationality of the political decisions taken on their behalf.'[47] In asking whether the general will could err, Rousseau had offered – in an obscure formula – a mathematical guarantee that the common interest would prevail because private interests would cancel each other out. Although Condorcet was to rely upon a complicated system of assemblies and special majorities to ensure that the decisions taken would most probably be correct, it has been persuasively argued that 'In submitting himself to a law contrary to his own opinion, the dissenting citizen of Rousseau and the represented citizen of Condorcet are both following the same reasoning.'[48] To avoid having to rely, like Montesquieu, upon aristocratic liberal élitism or on the unenlightened mass of the people as required by Rousseau's popular sovereignty, Condorcet concocted 'one of the most tortuously complicated constitutional schemes ever devised by an enlightened mind.'[49] He followed Turgot in restricting the franchise to property owners who alone had a sufficient 'interest in the common prosperity' and were capable of 'free, reasonable and uncorrupted opinion'; even accepting Turgot's distinction between propertied 'full citizens' and unpropertied 'fractional citizens', almost conceiving the state as a joint-stock company.[50] This attempt to restrict the vote to those who by virtue of owning property could be deemed to act rationally was a forerunner of Sieyès' distinction between 'active' and 'passive' citizens, while Condorcet's fear that assemblies were unlikely to take decisions rationally may have influenced Sieyès' strange 1799 parliamentary institutions where some were only entitled to speak and others only to vote.

Baker argues that the 'attempt to reconcile scientific élitism and democratic liberalism lay at the heart of Condorcet's conception of social science. It was also its weakest point'; and 'the events of the Revolution were to place increasing strain on precisely this aspect of Condorcet's thinking.'[51] He first collaborated with the moderates Lafayette and Sieyès in the 'Society of 1789' which sought to rival the Jacobin Club. (Condorcet had dedicated a 1786 essay *De l'influence de la Révolution de l'Amérique sur l'Europe* to Lafayette, regarded as a potential French Washington, suggesting that America was the democratic model of what Europe would become,[52] a view that Tocqueville would closely scrutinize half a century later.) However, after the king's flight in 1791, Condorcet became a republican, while Lafayette deserted to the royalists. On his election to the Legislative Assembly he played the key part in drafting the Girondin Constitution of 1793, embodying the principle of male suffrage (Condorcet would have wished to include women) while retaining his fear that the people were too ignorant to use their votes wisely in advance of the education which they had not yet received. He wrote in the 1793 prospectus to a short-lived periodical, *Journal d'Instruction Sociale*, edited jointly with Sieyès, that 'The equality of stupidity is not equality at all, for it does not exist between cheats and their dupes, and every society which is not enlightened by philosophers is deceived by charlatans.'[53] He was forced into hiding in July 1793 when his Girondin political friends were swept from power and sentenced to death. In the eight months of life that remained, Condorcet – in a final affirmation of his belief that democratic politics could be made rational and rational politics could become democratic – wrote the *Esquisse d'un tableau historique des progrès de l'esprit humain*. It was not only to be adopted as the doctrine of the *idéologues* (who were the official philosophers of the Directory); it also inspired the writings of Saint-Simon and Comte (see Chapter 4). Arrested in March 1794 for continuing to speak out during the Terror, Condorcet died in prison, being less fortunate than his fellow moderate Sieyès, whose prudent silence meant that he survived not merely the Terror but lived to die peacefully of old age more than forty years and several regimes later.

Much more directly than Rousseau, the Abbé Sieyès was the propagandist *par excellence* of democratic nationalism, so it was singularly appropriate that he would play a pre-eminent part both in the onset of the Revolution in 1789 and in its provisional mastery by Bonaparte in 1799.[54] (That he has not received due acknowledgement may be due to the fact that he upset the Right by his revolutionary role in 1789 and the Left by his counter-revolutionary role in 1799.) A reluctant member of the clergy (in 1789 he was elected by the Third Estate and not as a clergyman), he played an active role in pre-revolutionary agitation and his *What is the Third Estate?* was the pamphlet that had the most pervasive impact upon opinion and events of the thousands that were published at the time. This prompt manufacturer of constitutions was frequently described as a French Solon or Lycurgus, a title to which he aspired and believed himself fitted. Sieyès would more modestly have been described as a crudely prescriptive rationalist who sought to apply the Cartesian method of *tabula rasa* to politics. Like Rousseau, he was contemptuous of the empirical historical record and wrote in 1772: 'Enough people have been concerned to formulate *servile* ideas, always in accord with events. When one thinks about them, motivated solely by the public interest, one is compelled to acknowledge that healthy politics is not the science of *what is* but of *what ought to be*. Perhaps they will one day be united and then it will be possible to distinguish the history of human follies from political science.'[55] Although indebted in particular to Locke and Rousseau, Sieyès was rather dismissive of all predecessors and boasted that 'Politics is a science which I believe I have brought to completion.'[56] This prescriptive political science took the form of numerous attempts at constitution-making in the decade 1789–99, all of which quickly came to grief. The sceptical Burke, who considered that the 'science of government' should be a matter of trial and error, not a priori reason, savagely ridiculed such pretension: 'The Abbé Sieyès has pigeonholes full of ready-made constitutions, labelled, sorted and numbered, suitable for all seasons and all tastes . . . some the colour of blood, others that of Paris mud. . .'; while Sieyès himself said of his proposal to deport most of the nobility: 'You have asked me for a new suit; I have provided you with one; if it seems too long, shorten it; if it seems too wide, take it in', indicative of his instrumental, bespoke approach to politics.[57]

Sieyès was the theoretician who above all projected the inordinate demands of the propertied middle classes, although he stressed capability rather than property itself in principle, while accepting property as an indication of political capacity in practice. In words that go beyond Saint-Simon's distinction between the producers and the idle, he declared: 'A noble is not of my species; he is a wolf and I shoot.'[58] With his predilection for the arresting formula, he began his 1789 pamphlet with the question: '1) What is the Third Estate? *Everything.* 2) What has it been until now in the political order? *Nothing.*'[59] Anticipating Adam Smith's labour theory of value and following Chastellux, Sieyès found in Smith's division of labour the basis for his view that in politics specialization took the form of representation. Conceiving the political system as an 'immense workshop', all those who worked were entitled to participate equally in making the laws which they were required to obey. However, as direct democracy was neither possible nor desirable, it was necessary that the 'uneducated multitude' should 'nominate representatives more capable than themselves of knowing the general interest' and it was this leisured class that would legislate on their behalf. So, while work provided the legitimate basis of citizenship, it was only the leisured class that was fit to exercise the specialized political skills indispensable to achieving both liberty and prosperity.[60] This appeal to functional expertise as a curb on democracy anticipates a Saint-Simonian line of argument that was to be developed in relation to professionalized, technocratic administration rather than a political class of legislators.

Sieyès proposed and secured in 1789 the adoption of the title of National Assembly (borrowed from Voltaire and proposed in *What is the Third Estate?*) for the unicameral representative body which was to give democratic expression to national unity. While ridiculing those who wished to imitate British institutions, especially that 'monument to gothic superstition' the House of Lords,[61] Sieyès sought to give practical expression to a domesticated and indirect form of popular sovereignty, with the non-taxpaying 'inactive citizens' as he called them excluded from voting. However, he resisted the attempt of the aristocracy to entrench their privileged position in the Second Chamber, declaring that second chambers were obnoxious if they disagreed with the first chamber or superfluous if they agreed with it. (Bicameralism was rejected in the Constituent Assembly by almost 10:1 on the specious ground that the supposed unity of the nation required representation through a single chamber.) His ingenious way of avoiding the concentration of sovereign power was to propose in 1795 the creation of a 'constitutional jury', a sort of supreme court that would preserve the rights and restrictions embodied in the constitution.[62] In this anticipation of the Fifth Republic's Constitutional Council, Sieyès was closer to the concern to limit sovereignty which preoccupied his liberal disciple Constant, than in his rejection of decentralization. Sieyès not only imparted to France the ideology of democratic nationalism, proudly proclaiming that he coined the slogan: *Vive la Nation*.[63] He also played a large part in devising the structure of centralized local government, through the demarcation of rationalistic *départements* in place of the historic provinces, intended to ensure the artificial creation of national unity by state institutions. He said, in justification of his aim of making France a *'single whole*, uniformly submitted in all its parts to the same legislation and a common administration': 'I know of no better means to make all parts of France into a unit and all the peoples that divide it into a single nation.'[64]

Although an inactive member of the Jacobin Club and more inclined in his moderation to the Girondins, Sieyès prudently took a back seat as the Revolution rapidly accelerated beyond the constitutional monarchy which he initially supported. A regicide who narrowly escaped the guillotine, he was able laconically to reply to the question about what he had done during the Terror: 'I survived.' Quite early on in the revolutionary process he became disillusioned, saying 'If I had known how the Revolution would turn out, I would never have got involved with it.'[65] In the 18 Brumaire *coup* of 1799, as we shall see, he played a key role in temporarily mastering the revolutionary process, with his own elimination from the political scene as an unforeseen consequence. However, it is first necessary to examine how the reformist constitutionalism of the likes of Sieyès gave way first to patriotic revolutionary dictatorship and then Napoleonic despotism. In the process, an Old Regime without a clear doctrine – which was only formulated after its demise – was displaced by a regime based upon the old doctrine of natural law. What astounded the world was the French revolutionaries' attempt to implement old ideals in new positive laws. The ensuing proclamation of the primacy of rights over facts was to lead to an explosive encounter between theory and practice in which appeals to democracy and nationality were to play a decisive part. As the prospectus for the *idéologue* periodical *La Décade Philosophique, Politique et Littéraire* clinically put it in the twilight of the Terror in 1794: 'The French Revolution might be described as the first experiment performed on the grand scale on a whole nation.'[66] It is with the conclusions drawn from the results of that uncontrolled experiment that we shall be concerned hereafter, once the constituent elements have been identified and their interactions analyzed.

CHAPTER TWO

THE FOUNDING MYTH:
THE PROTAGONISTS

The revolutionary emergence of the people: democracy displaces liberalism

Considered broadly and with the benefit of hindsight, a striking feature of the extraordinary sequence of events that constitute 'the' French Revolution is the disproportion between its many and varied purported antecedents and its momentous effects. While our main concern is with the reactions to these effects, it is important to avoid reducing them to the level of the sometimes prosaic contributory causes of these events. In the concern to demythologize the French Revolution, one should beware of explaining it away. The problem begins with circumscribing the phenomenon in time because there is no agreement either on when it started or on when it could be said to have ended. In any case, it is usually regarded less as a continuous process than as a series of discontinuous events. Each of the great interpreters of these events saw them in terms of their own post-revolutionary historical context: Thiers as an opponent of the Bourbon Restoration, Tocqueville against the Second Empire and Taine against the 1871 Paris Commune. At the end of the nineteenth century, while Aulard could regard the Third Republic as the final achievement of the French Revolution's objectives, Jaurès would emphasize its unfinished, socialist purposes. As Cobban put it: 'To each terminal date corresponds a different interpretation. . . . The Revolution has ceased to be a revolution and become a series of revolutions. . . . The French Revolution is in fact a name we give to a long series of events. What it means depends on the light in which we see the connection between these events. In this sense the French Revolution, if not a myth, is a theory, or rather a number of rival theories.'[1]

The Revolution was in appearance abrupt but in practice a complex and indecisive process of conflict. It lasted at least a century, during which a decadent royal sovereignty, which despite its claim to absolute power was proving increasingly incapable of asserting itself, was replaced by a popular or democratic sovereignty. We shall argue in the concluding chapter that what Stanley Hoffmann has called the 'Republican synthesis' – which he dates from 1878 – may for all practical purposes have begun to bring the revolutionary process to an end in France, although it was not until a century after that date that François Furet could plausibly claim that 'The French Revolution is over.'[2] While its reverberations have continued around the world, latterly in the Communist world, in France itself the original democratic impetus had largely ceased to be a dynamic force. Instead, it became the increasingly accepted new legitimacy. The unitary sovereignty of the legal, constitutional authorities was able to provide the focus of a stable political system, although it was to experience searing residual vicissitudes well into the third quarter of the twentieth century. The belief that 'the people' could seize power by storming the Bastille provides an excellent symbolic rallying point for the celebration of national consensus, as it does on every 14 July. Reconstituting on new foundations the political authority violently overthrown proved a long and tortuous process, with many false starts and illusory finishes. Having considered in what sense it could be said to be a revolution, let us turn to some of the explanations offered to account for it, bearing in mind Cobban's cautionary comment that 'All through the Revolution we find that theory plays little part in determining policies, though it has played much in their subsequent interpretation.'[3]

Since Tocqueville, the more sophisticated interpreters of the French Revolution have seen it more in terms of a transition from rather than a break with the past. Yet despite those, such as Burke, who from the very start deplored France's failure to engage in a process of incremental and gradual change which would have reflected the continuity with its past, France instead embarked upon a 'new experimental government'.[4] Why did the transfer of sovereignty from the king nominally to the people and in practice to the representative government which acted in their name precipitate a revolution and why were piecemeal reforms submerged in an attempt at comprehensive revolution? If one sets aside the circumstances of the moment, such as mass hunger, the crushing burden of debt incurred mainly in foreign wars or the inability to rely upon the armed forces, three pairs of rivals can be selected for brief treatment: ideology versus interests as motivation; the business bourgeoisie versus state élites as the driving force; conspiratorial discontinuity versus deterministic continuity as characterizing the process of revolution.

For much of the nineteenth century the notion that ideas are forces that shape events inspired not only idealist historians such as Michelet but even such circumspect writers as Tocqueville. 'Never forget the ideological character of the French Revolution: its principal *characteristic,* though a *transitory* one.'5 Madame de Staël went further, roundly declaring that 'It was the philosophers who made the Revolution, they will end it.'6 A more earthy, self-interested view would stress the ambitions of the legally trained juridico-administrative officials who played so prominent a part in the revolutionary assemblies. If inflation is sometimes oversimplified as 'too much money chasing too few goods', revolution on this view might be simplified as too many ambitious people pursuing too few prominent jobs. This careerist, *arriviste* view, favoured by Thiers and to some extent even Tocqueville, not only establishes a more realistic motivation for those who actually engaged in the revolutionary power struggles; it also plausibly explains that these talented careerists saw themselves as the new élites, with a vested interest in the survival of the Revolution's rejection of Old Regime privileges.7

The emergence of these new political élites can no longer be convincingly construed as the advent of a new ruling class. The capitalist bourgeoisie could not have overthrown a functionless feudalism, as it had already largely disappeared. This is partly because 'the bourgeoisie' and nobility were not initially divided by economic interests and partly because they were themselves subdivided in ways which prevented them adopting common political strategies once regal sovereignty was overthrown. Such a revisionist interpretation began to be dealt with by neo-Marxist advocates of the bourgeois revolution thesis such as Barrington Moore. His successors, notably Theda Skocpol, have sought explicitly to reconcile it with 'a more state-centred approach' which considers the French Revolution in its processes and outcomes to be 'as much or more a bureaucratic, mass-incorporating and state-strengthening revolution as it was (in any sense) a bourgeois revolution.'8 However, this partial switch of emphasis from social to political and administrative interpretations of the French Revolution does not go far enough in making the acquisition of sovereign political power the focus of the revolutionary process, with the result that it blurs the picture without really rescuing the Marxist interpretation.

The theory that the French Revolution was the achievement of the bourgeoisie was part of a wider attempt to find an impersonal, deterministic explanation to replace that propounded by the conspiracy theorists, who portrayed it as a succession of subversive *coups d'état.* It might be a beneficent or maleficent conspiracy of the Enlightenment thinkers and their successors, secret societies like the Freemasons or the clubs, of which the most famous was to become the Jacobin Club.[9] Burke had given eloquent expression to the conspiracy theory put about by the *émigrés,* with religion and landed property as the targets. In addition, he offered the paper-money-promoted financial oligarchy or monied interest profiteers from public debt – what some Marxists would call a fraction of capital. Had he developed it further, this could have become a basis for the theory of bourgeois revolution discussed earlier.[10] A more serene historian of the Revolution's administrative, social, economic and political antecedents, Tocqueville offered an outright determinist analysis, while acknowledging the leading role played by 'men of letters'.[11] Those who took a more long-term view of the forces that had brought about the Revolution, such as Madame de Staël, sagely warned that conspiracy theorists 'confuse the actors with the play'.[12] This is our cue for considering the play of events that form the immediate prelude to our study proper.

The disintegration of monarchical sovereignty

We mentioned earlier that an important precipitant of the French Revolution was the inability of successive governments to deal with the burden of debt. At the eve of the Revolution this was so great that the interest payments alone absorbed nearly half the government's current expenditure. The major cause of this accumulated debt was the French monarchy's foreign wars, including ironically support given to the American Revolution. For just as the outcry against taxation without representation had been a potent slogan in the prelude to the English and American Revolutions, so the breakdown of monarchical sovereignty in France was accelerated by a loss of confidence owing to the government's inability to borrow, following the *parlements'* struggle to impose the rule of law upon royal rapacity. It was their opposition to absolutism which spearheaded the 'revolution of the notables' who, in Tocqueville's words, were 'capable of inciting the people; they were incapable of directing it'; so that by 1787 'the hatred of arbitrary power seemed to have become the sole passion of Frenchmen, the government the common enemy.'[13] Although the *parlements* had been accustomed to thunder vainly against the sovereign's abuse of power, that power had now become too weak to withstand challenges to the legitimacy of the state's authority. This was partly because the challenge to royal authority had been generalized from specific fiscal and religious grievances through the emergence of public opinion as an alternative system of authority. 'Construed as rational, universal, impersonal, unitary', public opinion ominously 'took on many attributes of the absolute authority it was displacing, just as it prefigured many ambiguities of the revolutionary power to which it gave rise.'[14] Tocqueville detected a decisive shift from 'rights to be acquired' towards mass 'wants to be satisfied' in the *cahiers de doléances,* a medieval precedure revived in a radical and unprecedented form. The result was that when the Estates General met at Versailles in 1789, inordinate expectations were aroused indicative of comprehensive change rather than piecemeal reform. 'Nobles, clergy, bourgeois alike now clearly saw that the object was not to modify this or that law but to remodel them all. . . . No one knew exactly what would be destroyed or what would be created but everyone felt that immense demolitions would take place and immense structures would rise.'[15]

For those liberal successors of Montesquieu who regarded constitutional monarchy as the best modern form of government, 1789 was a sublime interregnum even if the great revolutionary enterprise that started under such exhilarating auspices was to go badly astray. The members of the Constituent Assembly – formed by the doubling of the Third Estate's representation and amalgamation with of the nobility and clergy, as advocated by Sieyès – achieved what Tocqueville called the 'sudden transfer of total power to new hands. It meant the surrender of the direction of affairs to a single passion, to a single interest, to a single idea. This led not to Reform but to Revolution.'[16] This ephemeral period, when the educated classes 'had ceased to fear the power of the Crown, though they had not yet learned to tremble before the power of the people', was nevertheless crucial because 'little of what had been achieved by 1791 was to be lost, and most of what was done subsequently was to be undone.'[17] The Declaration of the Rights of Man and the Citizen, which became the Preamble to the 1791 Constitution, has been given legally enforceable status under the Fifth Republic. It is pre-eminently a permanent legacy, not merely to its country of origin – as were the British and American Bills of Rights – but to the world, even though Lafayette's drafts were inspired by American models. It asserted (Article 2) that the purpose of political association was the preservation of the natural rights of liberty, property, security and resistance to oppression; that sovereignty belonged to the nation, from which all exercising authority must emanate (Article 3); that liberty could only be circumscribed by law (Article 4) which expressed the general will of the citizen, directly or through representatives (Article 6); but that the separation of powers (Article 16) was essential, involving – along with representation – another Montesquieu-derived corrective to the antithetical principles inspired by Rousseau.[18]

Although Article 10 of the Declaration protected freedom of opinion in general and religious beliefs specifically, provided public order was not disturbed, the subsequent seizure of Church property to meet desperate financial needs and the institution of the Civil Constitution of the Church contributed substantially to developing the mass counter-revolutionary movements that radicalized the Revolution and deprived it of public support. Although Robespierre never made this mistake, the anticlerical revolutionaries – among whom Bishop Talleyrand and the Abbé Sieyès were prominent – in their onslaught on the Church as a political institution, ignored the historical evidence that, as Tocqueville later observed, 'in all periods the religious instinct has had its most abiding home in the hearts of the common people.'[19] To harness religion to public purposes, the clergy became elected civil servants and were required to swear an oath of loyalty to the Civil Constitution. The significance of this in shaping French political behaviour for nearly the next two centuries is the broad coincidence between those areas of the country where priests refused the oath and subsequent right wing voting, while acceptance correlated subsequent dechristianization with voting for the Left (and with the spread of birth control).[20] The encouragement to provincial royalism that resulted from religious persecution was a powerful centralizing force and undermined the promising decentralization of power that marked the municipal revolutionary period of 1790–1.

Although misleadingly identified especially with the Girondins, when the idea of federalism was treated by the Jacobins as counter-revolutionary during the infighting between the revolutionaries, it was natural that the initial tendency of the anti-absolutist Revolution should be decentralist. Their first inclination was to retrieve the medieval right to elect their own municipalities, lost in 1692, until when 'some towns were still to all intents and purposes small democratic republics, their officials being elected by the townsfolk and answerable to them alone.'[21] However, the autonomy won by the revolutionary municipalities quickly led to fears that, as the constitutional monarchist Mounier put it (since oft repeated), 'It would be too dangerous to create states within the State and to multiply sovereignties.'[22] Such expectations were shared by anti-revolutionaries like Burke, who predicted that 'When they framed democratic governments, they had virtually dismembered their country' into a confederation or 'collection of republics', although he also pointed to the domination of Paris.[23] Sieyès – who with Thouret was the main architect of the centralist division of France into an approximation to 'geometrical' departments, although he failed in an attempt to reduce the number of communes from 44,000 to 720 – likewise feared the threat to national sovereignty and the fissiparous power of local notables.[24] So the Revolution continued rather than reversed the centralizing work of the monarchy. Ironically, the constitutional monarchy was itself to be abolished in 1792, following the attempted flight of Louis XVI, which brought to an end a compromise regime that tried simultaneously to be too republican and too monarchical.[25]

The eruption of the patriotic revolutionary dictatorship

The ground for ending the identification of the state with the monarch and his replacement by the nation had been prepared by various champions of constitutional monarchy, so that it seemed natural that the Constituent Assembly should decree that the royal title describe Louis XVI as 'King of the French', long before Louis-Philippe enthusiastically adopted this style in 1830. As Cobban has argued, 'During the eighteenth century the impersonal conception of the state had been growing fast. Loyalty was passing into patriotism. The idea of the *patrie* was possibly the dominant, as it was certainly the commonest, idea of all political thinkers in eighteenth century France. And what was the *patrie*? Once the mainly territorial conception of the community had declined . . . the *patrie*, or the state, came to mean primarily the inhabitants, that is, the people. The substitution of the sovereignty of the people for the sovereignty of the monarch was a natural conclusion.'[26] However, whereas before the Revolution a 'patriot' meant a humanitarian who loved liberty, thereafter it quickly became a synonym for aggressive chauvinism. The *levée en masse* decreed by the Convention in 1793 was turned by Carnot into a devastating new model, military mass mobilization for war. 'When governments become the people's governments, their wars become the people's wars and their armies the armies of the nation.'[27] Yet despite impassioned calls for mass conscription of the 'people in arms' to save the 'country in danger' from civil and foreign wars, the premature nature of such attempts at mass participation and mobilization is evident from the widespread resistance to enrolment and the frequency of desertion. 'The truth is that there was very little patriotism in France in 1793.'[28] Exhortation to self-sacrificing patriotism in the manner of Sparta was actually indicative of its absence, just as the repeated invocations of national unity reflected the bitterness and depth of divisions.

To risk dying for your country is a big demand, so what about the modest demand of voting for your country's legislature? Insurrection rather than election having been given pride of place in revolutionary history, turnout has not hitherto been a prime concern. Furthermore, it is extremely difficult to evaluate because even if one knows accurately the number who actually voted, there is great uncertainty about the number of those entitled to vote. It has been estimated that between 10 and 20 per cent voted in Paris for the Constituent Assembly of 1789, with a much higher but very variable turnout in the provinces, although the real turnout will never be known. The turnout of even those entitled to vote (the 'active citizens') for the Legislative Assembly in 1791 was less than one in four and in Paris voter turnout dropped to 10 per cent, despite hectic press propaganda.[29] While it is not surprising that those who receive the vote for the first time do not appreciate its significance, it is important to note that even on a restricted suffrage, the vast majority of the people were unready for democratic participation. It is only in this context that the imperious recourse to patriotic revolutionary dictatorship by the virtuous but unrepresentative few can be understood.

The most ardent champion of universal suffrage as well as the most exemplary personification of revolutionary dictatorship was Maximilien Robespierre, who as a fervent disciple of Rousseau and a leader of the Jacobins placed the sovereignty of the people on the agenda of history, not merely of France but of the whole world. The enduring fascination he exercises is due to the fact that in his tormented attempt to reconcile his theoretical convictions and practical predicaments, we can observe popular sovereignty being rapidly transformed from a liberating into a tyrannical principle, in which all opposition to an infallible people's will became intolerable. The fundamental problem was that popular sovereignty was still sovereignty, with the added legitimacy over monarchy that it derived from the people, so that the revolutionaries were condemned to perpetuate royal despotism rather than to replace it. While Robespierre could not have repeated Louis XV's claim that 'sovereign power is located in my person alone . . . to me alone belongs legislative power, independent and unshared . . . all public order derives from me', he declared that as lawmaker the nation's will was above the law, that the rule of law became synonymous with the day-to-day decrees of the people's sovereign will, of which he was the spokesman.[30] In reducing the Declaration of Rights simply to the equality of rights and the sovereignty of the people, the displacement of pluralistic liberalism by monolithic democracy is clear in Robespierre as early as 1791[31] and the way was open to a centralizing dictatorship in the name of the people for which Marat had been calling since 1790. In terms of how the revolutionary government was meant to work during the period 1793–4, in which the Committee of Public Safety ruled on behalf of the Convention, the continuity with the pre-1789 royal absolutism and post-1799 Napoleonic absolutism is as significant as the contrast with the Revolution's initial decentralizing liberalism.[32]

Robespierre justified his switch from a Montesquieu-inspired liberalism to a Rousseau-inspired authoritarianism with the formula: 'The aim of constitutional government is to preserve the Republic. The aim of revolutionary government is to found it'; and to achieve this end he was prepared to use methods as 'illegal as the revolution, the fall of the throne and of the Bastille, as illegal as liberty itself. . . . Do you want a revolution without revolution?'[33] As one of the rival leaders of a small revolutionary vanguard that had lost touch with the people generally and even with the Paris activists, he was driven to what he hoped was only temporary terrorism to dissuade the counter-revolutionary, conspiratorial 'enemies of the people'. Far from being guilty of totalitarianism – an anachronistic accusation because no pre-twentieth-century regime was *capable* of such comprehensive control – and despite the ideological rhetoric intended to create an illusion of integration, Robespierre lacked the support of a disciplined revolutionary party such as Lenin was to forge. Consequently, Revolutionary France was increasingly 'governed by a minority many times sub-divided. . . . A Republic so conceived must remain at war with a large part of its own population.'[34] Setting aside the rhetoric and summing up the period of Jacobin dictatorship (which together with the Babeuf Conspiracy of the Equals in 1796 was to provide a precedent for Auguste Blanqui, as well as an anti-model for all the others we shall be considering), Palmer wrote: 'As in the name of liberty France now possessed the most dictatorial government it had ever known, so, in the name of the people, it had the political system which, of all systems in its history, probably the fewest people really liked. The ruling group knew that in a free election it would not be supported. It knew that it did not represent, in the sense of reflecting, the actual wishes of actual men and women. It claimed to represent, in the sense of standing for, the real will of the real people, the fundamental, unrealized, inarticulate, ultimate desires, the true welfare, of Frenchmen and of mankind, present and future. This was the Revolutionary faith.'[35]

Robespierre, an enemy of the death penalty, was to use decapitation – an aristocratic form of execution which the Revolution had democratized – for a long list of political crimes, following a mere appearance at show trials and without legal protection, before a Revolutionary Tribunal. Political disagreement had sunk to the level of a bloody life and death struggle, in which Robespierre was himself to perish on 27 July 1794. This was exactly a year after he entered the Committee of Public Safety, which Cobban has called 'a government of perhaps the ablest and most determined men who have ever held power in France.'[36] A sanguinary experiment in democracy without enough democrats had come to an end for the reason that Saint-Just explained in 1794: 'A revolution has taken place within the government; it has not yet penetrated civil society.'[37] It was time for society to reassert its primacy over government. Only in the nineteenth century would it be appreciated that far from democracy being a threat to the status quo, it might more often be a bulwark against revolutionary minorities led by the would-be successors of Robespierre and Babeuf.

An ephemeral bourgeois republic

Barrington Moore has argued that both in revolutions and in counter-revolutions, 'A new crime becomes a new legality.'[38] While some would claim that the fall of Robespierre marked the end of the Revolution, we have already agreed with Cobban that such a view tells us more about its author's interpretation than about the Revolution itself. Elsewhere, Cobban himself asserts that Thermidor 'ended the Revolution', declaring less controversially that its offspring, the Directory, 'had been brought to birth by a *coup d'état*, it was to live by *coups d'état* and to die by a *coup d'état.*'[39] While the general view, especially of left wing historians, has tended to be that the Revolution did end in 1794, this is paradoxical because it is precisely in the five years of the Directory that France may be regarded as coming closest to the apotheosis of a bourgeois revolution. This is exemplified in a book by Madame de Staël, published more than a century after it was written, with the significant title: *On the present circumstances that can end the Revolution and the principles on which the Republic should be founded in France.* With impeccable bourgeois credentials as the daughter of the Swiss banker Necker – whose assistance Louis XVI had secured in his attempts to solve the monarchy's financial difficulties and who is regarded as the man who did most to destroy the Old Regime – Madame de Staël was searching for a tolerant ideological consensus and secure constitutional framework that would protect freedom and property by avoiding both revolutionary despotism and royalist reaction.

She started with the heartrending question: 'Will the French Revolution end in our time?'[40] which made clear that she knew in 1798 that the Revolution was not yet over. She deplored the fact that constitutional monarchy on the English model had not been given a chance. If it had endured long enough (she says ten years at one point, fifty at another) a republic could have been established by consent, without the traumas of the Terror and the Directory's own unscrupulous and frequent indulgence in institutionalized and improvised illegality to prevent both royalists and

Jacobins from overthrowing it. The reign of political expediency after that of political fanaticism led her to bewail the fate of a country which was being 'saved' every day. The great political achievement of the Revolution having been the elimination of hereditary privilege in favour of election (not merely of politicians, but judges and even priests), the Directory had, notably through restricted suffrage and bicameralism, placed power in the hands of property owners who were also assumed to be the best educated. She went on to assert what Michels was to call 'the iron law of oligarchy', though she gave it a strong meritocratic twist. 'Strictly speaking, there is no democracy in the French constitution. It is natural aristocracy, in opposition to artificial aristocracy; it should be government by the best people; it is always and unavoidably the power of all placed in the hands of a few. So it is essential to study the principles of this type of government . . . it is an entirely new kind of political system and it should not be confused with democracy. . .'[41]

Madame de Staël's conception of 'government by the best people' was very close to that of her friend Boissy d'Anglas (who with the *idéologue* Daunou was the main architect of the 1795 Constitution). The bourgeois élite was to be a combination of meritocracy and plutocracy, identified with property ownership.[42] Unfortunately, the 'Bourgeois Republic', dedicated to prevent the resurgence of both anarchy and dictatorship, was to lead first to the one and then to the other, with Madame de Staël's closest political friends bringing about the final *coup d'état* that appeared to end the Revolution but instead eliminated for half a century both the Republic and many precious liberties that had been won. The middle-class notables on which the Directory, like the July Monarchy, relied were too concerned with the pursuit of their own pecuniary self-interest to provide that force for unity within the political community which their protagonists, since Aristotle, had attributed to them. They were moderate even in their support for the very regimes dedicated to the promotion of their collective interest.

Before exile dispersed and prudence silenced most of the *idéologues*, these disciples of Condorcet (with whom Madame de Staël and Benjamin Constant were fellow-travelling associates in the Directory and Consulate) were the principal protagonists of moderate revolutionary principles. Who were these links between the eighteenth-century Enlightenment and nineteenth-century liberalism and positivism, who in seeking to perpetuate and stabilize the Revolution earned the hostility in turn of Robespierre and Napoleon? Grouped around the salons of Madame Helvétius, Madame Condorcet and to a lesser extent Madame de Staël, with *La Décade philosophique, politique et littéraire* as their propaganda periodical from 1794 to 1807 and the *Institut National* (especially its innovative 'Moral and political sciences' section from 1795 to 1803) as their official forum, they were the exponents of a 'scientific' solution to the revolutionary crisis. Condorcet was the revered forerunner, his principal disciple and literary executor the physician and physiologist Cabanis having provided him with the poison that probably allowed him to commit suicide in prison during the Terror. The ex-*Abbés* Sieyès and Daunou, the great constitutional drafters of 1789–99, were associated with the *idéologues*, as were Pierre-Louis Roederer and Jean-Baptiste Say in political economy, but the one who gave them their name in 1797 and became their exemplary exponent was Destutt de Tracy. He had been a member of the liberal nobility who sided with the Third Estate in the Constituent Assembly; commanded the cavalry in Lafayette's Revolutionary army but refused to join him in exile; survived imprisonment during the Terror to become the champion of educational reform under the Directory, to impart – even indoctrinate – the principles of political science on which government should be founded; refused Napoleon his support and retreated into the scholarly critique of Montesquieu and the writing of *Eléments d'Idéologie*. He re-emerged as a life peer during the Restoration and was carried, almost blind in his old age, to the barricades during the 1830 July Revolution to demonstrate his loyalty to the principles of his youth.

The *idéologues* were torn between their desire to guide the Revolution intellectually while actively participating in it. They proved incapable of controlling it, even during the Directory when they were at their most influential. Daunou's 1795 constitution (adopted by referendum with a mere 915,000 'yes' votes and 42,000 against) marked the attempt to reverse the first five years of revolutionary radicalization and signalled five years of revolutionary retreat. It was characterized by the desire to constrain rather than increase popular control, government becoming the preserve of the propertied and the enlightened. Freedom was increasingly feared as a threat to public order. Despite the persisting political crisis and instability, the reaction against Jacobin concentration of power led to the rigid separation of power. It was above all this deliberate creation of a weak state that led to the demand for a reconcentration and recentralization of power and paved the way for Napoleon. The people having persistently voted 'badly', Cabanis advocated a top-down decision process and the deliberate elimination of popular participation. This distinguished scientist peremptorily dogmatized: 'Choices must be made not at the bottom, where they are necessarily made badly, but at the top where they are necessarily made well.'[43]

Cabanis welcomed the advent of Napoleon, whom the *idéologues* thought would save *their* Revolution and *their* Republic. Condorcet had argued that the enlightened few must act on behalf of the masses who were susceptible to the machinations of agitators and charlatans. His disciple Cabanis proclaimed that with the Sieyès–Napoleon 18 Brumaire *coup,* 'democracy' had been purged of 'all its disadvantages . . . the ignorant class no longer exercises any influence either on the legislature or on the government; consequently no more demagogues. All is done for the people and in the name of the people; nothing is done by it under its unthinking guidance.' The people would live peacefully, 'its industry would be exercised and extended without obstacles . . . guaranteed by a government strong enough always to be its protector.'[44] Daunou, the main author of the 1795 constitution, later criticized the separation of powers and along with Cabanis and Roederer reversed Condorcet's commitment to decentralization, demanding that all French political and administrative authority be centralized in Paris and imposed upon the whole country. When this system was established by Napoleon, with Roederer playing a part in the creation of the prefectoral system, many of the *idéologues* became critical and were excluded in 1802 from the pseudo-parliamentary *Tribunat* for their pains. Daunou and Say notably, along with Constant, were purged for their opposition to illiberal, retrograde legislation, such as the abolition of the jury system and restoration of slavery in the colonies. Roederer himself was later dismissed as a 'metaphysician' when he refused to be a mere instrument of the despot's will. Others, like Cabanis and Destutt de Tracy, continued to sit in the Senate but they were generally reluctant to become servile members of the new meritocratic Napoleonic nobility, provoking Napoleon into popularizing the term 'ideologist' as a term of abuse. As Picavet put it, 'Bonaparte upset the hopes of both the *Idéologues* who hoped for a Washington, and those of the royalists who saw him as a Monk', ready to restore the monarchy like his English counterpart in 1660.[45]

The *idéologue* cultural revolution bequeathed a dual legacy: the liberal elements were championed more consistently by Benjamin Constant, while the social scientism was developed by Saint-Simon and August Comte. In addition to the creation of the institutional base of the new technocratic élite through the establishment of the *Ecole Polytechnique* in 1794 (it acquired this name in 1795), the *idéologues'* most important instrument of cultural policy was the *Institut National* whose function was to formulate a new orthodoxy. Taking on the unfinished work of the *philosophes' Encyclopédie,* it was to end the revolutionary intellectual crisis and bring about national unity. Daunou, who extended Condorcet's work on behalf of a centralized and standardized educational system with a Cabanis-inspired emphasis upon technical education to equip the 'industrial class' to apply the results of science, proclaimed the Institute's task: 'to finish the Revolution it has begun, to extinguish all dissent. . .'[46]

This illiberal objective was motivated in part by Daunou's indictment, when imprisoned during the Terror, of Robespierre with having equated the 'people' with the least educated and having adopted the view that *'no one had the right to be wiser* than the people.'[47] Fearing, from experience, the premature involvement of the uneducated masses in political decision-making, the *idéologues* retreated from Condorcet's acceptance of universal suffrage. They accentuated his advocacy of the primacy of a pedagogic scientific élite over the demagogic political élite of lawyers that had predominated at the most turbulent periods of the French Revolution. This onslaught on the lawyers and eulogy of the scientists was to be revived as part of a systematic reform programme by Saint-Simon and Comte, to accomplish the objective of ending the Revolution. They were to draw the conclusion that the reorganization of society through the reorganization of the state had proved illusory and that it was cultural and socio-economic reorganization and not political revolution that was the answer. The influence of the *idéologue* Jean Baptiste Say, who separated economics from politics, was to play an important part in this process. As early as 1799 he declared that 'The greatest revolutions are not political revolutions' because 'Authority changes hands but the nation stays the same'; while Roederer and Say stressed the importance of 'work' and the need to eliminate 'idlers',[48] a pivotal Saint-Simon theme as we shall see in Chapter 4. Meanwhile, the ideologist Roederer, who had been Sieyès' 'disciple' and aide in the Constituent Assembly, worked closely with him in 1799 to bring Napoleon to power, the nascent principles of social science being sacrificed to the imperious requirements of political expediency. Roederer was subsequently to boast of his part in 1792 and 1799: 'I spent the last night of his reign with Louis XVI and the first night of his reign with Bonaparte.'[49]

Repeated purges of the most dynamic and idealistic revolutionary activists meant that an enfeebled regicide Directory could not establish the rule of law and moderation but fought a losing battle against uncompromising extremists to its Right and Left, depending ever more on the army to keep it in power. The debasement of the electoral process inaugurated an enduring French tradition that those in power are entitled to manipulate elections, while recourse to massive invalidations of elected opposition candidates discredited the regime and deprived it of representative legitimacy.[50] In a scathing denunciation of the 'tottering' Directory, Tocqueville described it as 'anarchy tempered by force. It was not expected to endure by any one of its supporters.'[51] They proceeded from 1797 to plot its demise. Ironically, given her subsequent hatred of Bonaparte, it was friends of the Directory like Madame de Staël and Sieyès, who became its leader in 1799, that brought about its overthrow, with Madame de Staël's present and former lovers Benjamin Constant and Talleyrand serving as intermediaries between Sieyès and Bonaparte. Sieyès had hoped that General Joubert would be the 'sword' at his disposal but he was killed in battle. Sieyès then said to Joseph Bonaparte (Napoleon's brother): 'I will march with General Bonaparte, because he is the most civil of the military men.'[52] However, Sieyès' plan to establish a senatorial republic, headed by a strong executive, with him pulling the strings in the background, predictably evaporated when the conspirators combined the water of civil power with the fire of military power. Robespierre had ended his speech on 8 Thermidor, just before the *coup* that overthrew him, by warning the Convention: 'If you leave the reins of revolution slack for a moment, military despotism will seize hold of them.'[53] Sieyès' riding lessons in the Luxembourg Gardens to prepare for the 18 Brumaire *coup* did not suffice to equip him to play the part of the man on horseback in the 'military republic' that from the start Burke had predicted was likely to emerge as the dominant force in France.[54]

The triumph of force over anarchy: the napoleonic despotism

A Sieyès biographer explains his conduct in 1799 by the desire to bring the revolutionary process to an end at any cost and by any means, euphemistically declaring: 'He wanted to ensure through irregular methods the final attainment of the permanence of rules.'[55] With a critical eye on the comparable development in the mid-nineteenth century, the Second Empire of Louis-Napoleon which was intended to end the 1848 Revolution, Tocqueville – in his notes for the never-to-be-completed second volume of his study of the Revolution – similarly observed: 'For the sake of rest and order, the nation throws itself into the arms of a man who is believed sufficiently strong to arrest the Revolution and sufficiently generous to consolidate its gains.'[56] Three weeks after the *coup d'état*, the Consuls – Bonaparte, Sieyès and Ducos – proclaimed the Constitution (which was such a travesty of Sieyès' draft that he said it was no longer a constitution) even before the improvised plebiscite that was to impart it with a democratic but non-liberal legitimacy. 'Citizens, the Revolution is established upon the principles which began it: It is ended.'[57] In fact the plebiscite results were fraudulently inflated, systematically and massively, by the new dictator's brother, Minister of the Interior Lucien Bonaparte, misrepresenting mass acquiescence as popular enthusiasm. Napoleon Bonaparte in any case did not share Sieyès' liberal conception of constitutional constraint, being much closer to the cynical scepticism of a Burke or a Maistre: 'The belief that a sheet of paper can be of any value unless it is supported by force has been one of the cardinal mistakes of the Revolution.' 'A constitution ought to be made so that it does not impede the action of government.'[58] So the Revolution was to create a more arbitrary tyranny than it had displaced. The replacement of elected local government by prefects, the re-establishment of slavery in the colonies, the reconciliation with the Catholic Church prior to its subordination to the state, were some of the ways in which the purported end of the Revolution made itself felt.

Tocqueville depicted the Napoleonic empire as 'the despotism of a single person resting on a democratic basis', partly analogous to the Roman Empire which had replaced the Republic. 'The same procedures: to govern in the name of the people; to represent the masses . . . through the abolition of all those intermediary orders which had humiliated them; thus satisfaction is given to the passions of envy and to the sentiments of equality in their grossest forms (i.e. everyone reduced to the same level of servitude). At the same time satisfaction given to the rich by assuring their material order, the tranquil possession of their goods, by continued well-being, of opportunities of enrichment through official positions.'[59] The ennobled and enriched élite that Napoleon ensconced in power combined those sections of the middle classes that had acquired administrative or military posts with the survivors of the old landed socio-economic élite. What they shared, in Tocqueville's bitter words, was a plutocratic readiness 'to give up the liberty which the Revolution had merely promised, in order finally to enjoy the profits that it had brought.'[60] Once again, a triumph of the *grande bourgeoisie* was concomitant with an attempt to halt the Revolution but the new sovereignty was to prove ephemeral and the revolutionary process was to recover its interrupted momentum. Napoleon was part of the continuing Revolution as well as an attempt to subordinate it to an illiberal authority enjoying popular support.

Fictions with a future: the revolutionary legacy

Before turning to our six critics of nationality and democracy, ranging from the extreme Right to the extreme Left, let us consider how these normative innovations became the test of the legitimacy of the scope of the political community and its mode of government, not merely in France but universally. Even when they have been violated, as they often are in practice, it has been essential to appear to respect and identify with them. In this pervasive sense, it was impossible to 'halt the Revolution'. By fusing political power and a particular people in the concept of popular sovereignty, these new values unleashed disruptive forces which throughout the nineteenth and twentieth centuries were to be domesticated only with the greatest difficulty. As we shall argue in the final chapter, it was almost two centuries after the Revolution that national integration, socio-economic modernization and mass politicization might be said to have proceeded sufficiently for it to be plausibly claimed that the Revolution had become a spent force, supporting the political order rather than destabilizing it.

In a classic 1862 essay on 'Nationality', Lord Acton referred to 'that absolute right of national unity which is the product of democracy' in France because 'the theory of nationality is involved in the democratic theory of the sovereignty of the general will. . . . To have a collective will, unity is necessary, and independence is necessary to assert it.'[61] State boundaries had hitherto been the non-national product of war and dynastic marriages. Tyranny had been defined as infidelity to the ancient laws and customs. With the Revolution it became non-conformity with the people's will. Sieyès was the most forthright exponent of nationhood as the self-evident attribute of any association of people who choose to be governed within a political community by laws passed by a representative legislature. Sovereignty belonged to the national will. 'The nation is prior to everything. It is the source of everything. Its will is always legal; indeed it is the law itself.' 'Not only is the nation not subject to a constitution but it *cannot* be and it *must not* be' because 'its will is always the supreme law.'[62] Sieyès used the substitution of 'nation' for 'people' to transmute Rousseau's notion of popular sovereignty into national sovereignty – aimed against both royal and popular power – which denied the people any direct say and could be exercised only by their parliamentary representatives.[63] Because fraternity was quickly circumscribed to one's fellow countrymen, the Revolutionary trilogy was in effect Liberty, Equality, Nationality.

The contrast between French and English conceptions of constitutionalism brings out another fiction with a future: the French Revolution's anti-traditionalist repudiation of the past and the belief that a new form of legitimate government could be produced by human will and artifice. Like his Anglophil French political friends the *monarchiens,* Burke hoped that France would restore its ancient constitution, embodying the hidden truths of an empirical historical legacy from which royal absolutism had been an aberration. However, France was not to follow the Whig path of a reliance upon the peculiarly English Common Law liberties and feudal constraints; rather it was to reject the Old Regime as synonymous with arbitrary absolutism and the lack of a constitution. Unable to restore a non-existent libertarian past, France was compelled to proclaim as natural, rational and universal the Rights of Man that marked the decisive break with its past. As Rabaut St-Etienne declared: 'Our history is not our code.'[64]

The new basis of government was willed in a social contract in which the nation as the constituting power would, through a modern constituent National Assembly rather than Rousseau's archaic Legislator, establish legitimate political authority. The defeat in the 1789 debate on the royal veto of those, like Mirabeau, Lally-Tollendal and Mounier, who sought a 'balanced' constitution on English lines, marked the decisive shift to power concentrated in the hands of the people's representatives, government by assembly. Burke's attempt to show that the web of hallowed prejudices and pluralistic interests was the best bulwark against the illiberalism of unbounded democracy based upon popular sovereignty was treated with scorn. In the wake of Sieyès, France embarked upon 170 years of constitutional experiment in search of the stable legal norms that the English piecemeal, shifting and irrational reliance upon custom and pre-cedent seemed incapable of offering. The revolutionary democratic tradition became both the foundation of political authority and the origin of repeated challenges to that authority, so that French liberals, lacking a Whig past *à la* 1688, had to rely upon 1789.

A further fiction, that partisan political differences, whether ideological or organizational, could be reduced to the duality of Right and Left, is also directly derived from 1789. While it may have been indirectly inspired by the fact that in the House of Commons the government and its supporters always sit to the Speaker's right and its opponents sit to his left, they changed sides after electoral victory and defeat, so the terms were not identified with a specific party or ideology. It was from the constitutional debate over the issue of royal power from 28 August to 11 September 1789 that this dichotomy can be dated. It was born on 11 September 1789 at a meeting of the Estates General transmuted into a National Assembly. This feudal institution had not met for 175 years but was on that day discussing whether the king should have a veto over the decisions of the people's representatives. The nobility were seated on the left side of the chamber, the commoners or Third Estate in the middle and the clergy on the right side. When it came to the vote on the issue of the royal veto, the commoners voted against and the clergy in favour, with the nobility split. To simplify counting votes (which was done by members standing and sitting) the nobility who favoured the king's veto crossed the floor to sit on the right with the clergy, while the commoners and anti-veto nobility grouped themselves on the left.[65] In the subsequent revolutionary legislature, this Right–Left split was not perpetuated in the seating arrangements of the Constituent and National Assemblies. The 'Left' sat on the upper seats and were known as the 'Mountain', while the 'Right' sat on the lower seats. Nevertheless, the revival of parliament during the Restoration resurrected the Left–Right political dichotomy and with it a continuing reference back to the legitimizing myths of the 1789 Revolution. The Left became identified in France with hostility to a head of the executive, even President of the Republic, an attitude reinforced by its disastrous experience with the directly elected President Louis-Napoleon in the Second Republic. While it failed to abolish the office during the Third Republic, it managed to weaken it with the result that until the Left's reluctant acceptance of the Fifth Republic, republicanism came to be identified on the Left with government by assembly.

Mass democracy was the implicit rather than explicit ideology that the French Revolution provided as the new source of legitimacy for a sovereign state that had proved incapable of governing. It was through an appeal to democracy that 'the Revolution mobilized society and disarmed that state.'[66] The overt appeal to democracy did not come until the Revolution was radicalized because at first the intention was to secure a compromise between a constitutional authority that came from above and a legitimacy that came from below.

Representative élitism proved too weak a bulwark in support of the liberal, reforming consensus that united a majority of politically conscious people in 1789. However, it emerged from the subsequent conflicts as the main principle of political organization, while an emphasis upon the ownership of property played the pivotal part in establishing a new basis of legitimate authority. 'The principle that was revolutionary, in France at least, was that the community of propertied men should not only dominate society, but exercised everyday control of government, too, through representative institutions. . . . It was the crown's decision to hold elections that first admitted the bourgeoisie to the political nation; and in this sense the fundamental social decision of eighteenth century French history was taken not by the Revolution, but by the old order. By calling the bourgeoisie into political activity, the monarchy, in its last positive act, created the élite of social "notables", a blend of noble and non-noble property owners, that was to govern the country far into the next century.'[67] This was not the modernizing business bourgeoisie – to whom liberal economists and managerialists like Saint-Simon looked to substitute peaceful production for political controversy – but the non-commercial lawyer and rentier bourgeoisie, which had been aroused by the class-conscious pamphleteering of Sieyès and others. The concern of the new notables to circumscribe who would be eligible to vote and be elected, as well as the reluctance of many of the newly enfranchised either to vote at all or to overcome their traditional deference, was to defuse much of the latently explosive potential of mass democracy.

Although the Convention was elected in 1792 nominally on the basis of manhood suffrage, this was vitiated by the exclusion of royalists and domestic servants, Sieyès having justified the exclusion of servants and the very poor on the ground that 'in every country in the world, the rabble belong to the aristocracy' in the sense of being subject to their influence.[68] In fact, throughout the revolutionary period suffrage was both indirect and in practice restricted. Sieyès had persuaded the Constituent Assembly of 1789 to adopt a most significant distinction between all citizens enjoying 'passive' civil rights and 'active' citizens who received the political right to vote. Suffrage was confined to men of at least 25 years of age, who had lived in the same canton for at least one year, were not domestic servants, bankrupts or waiting trial and paid direct taxes amounting in value to at least three days' wages of an unskilled worker. The number of seats allocated to each *département* was weighted according to three criteria: one-third of the seats to be allocated equally (three each) between *départements* on the criterion of size; one-third proportionate to the population; one-third proportionate to the contribution to tax revenue. This electoral law, more restrictive than that for the Estates General of 1789 – which had accorded virtual male suffrage – was even more exclusive regarding those who could be chosen to select deputies in primary assemblies at the second stage of the indirect electoral process. For these primary delegates, a property qualification was fixed amounting in value from 100 to 400 days' wages according to the size of the commune. 'It was estimated that out of about 7,000,000 adult males, 4,300,000 qualified as active citizens and fewer than 50,000 as potential delegates', with great variations between urban and rural areas and between *départements*.[69]

The distrust of mass democracy and the desire to favour the propertied middle classes was mercilessly mocked by Burke as inconsistent with egalitarian revolutionary principles. Having shown that indirect elections meant that representatives would paradoxically not come into contact with their constituents, he turned to the restriction of the vote to taxpayers. 'What! a qualification on the indefeasible rights of men? Yes; but it shall be a very small qualification. Our injustice shall be very little oppressive; only the valuation of three days labour paid to the public. Why, this is not much, I readily admit, for anything but the utter subversion of your equalising principle ... on your ideas, it excludes from a vote the man of all others whose equality stands the most in need of protection and defence; I mean the man who has nothing else but his natural equality to guard him.'[70] Burke proceeds to pillory the revolutionaries for forcing the people to buy their natural rights and imposing property qualifications which showed 'how much they were embarrassed by their contradictory ideas of rights of men and the privileges of riches.'[71]

The abortive 1793 constitution, in addition to instituting direct elections in single member constituencies and reducing the voting age to 21, included a significant element of direct democracy. It was ratified by a referendum (in which those who abstained outnumbered those who voted by more than two to one) and provided for referendums to ratify legislation if a tenth of the primary assemblies in over half the *départements* objected. However, the 1795 Directory constitution reverted to the practice of indirect elections and exclusive suffrage, with the number of direct electors falling to about 30,000. Although it did not revive the odious distinction between active and passive citizens, it did envisage the subsequent adoption of a literacy electoral test. It is notorious for the massive resort to the invalidation of elections whose results the Directors did not welcome in nearly half the *départements* in 1797 and nearly a third in 1798.[72] Thus the reactionary revolutionaries of the Directory made more of a farce of representative democracy than perhaps even Burke had anticipated and prepared the way for the plebiscitary Napoleonic dictatorship, which despite all the associated electoral manipulations won fewer votes than abstentions. Damning evidence that meaningful participatory mass democracy in the 1790s was at least premature is provided by the very low figures of electoral turnout, which declined from under a quarter of active citizens (Cobban's estimate was that only 7.5 per cent of the electoral chose the 1792 Convention) until the fraudulent plebiscites under Napoleon cynically and spuriously elevated electoral turnout.[73] Revolutionary democracy could not overcome the passivity of even its active citizens.

The final fiction with a future was that of the unfinished revolution, subject to counter-revolutionary setbacks but a permanent revolution condemned never to achieve political stability. Furet controversially ended a lecture on 'The French Revolution revisited' with the claim that Bonaparte had put an end to the Revolution by personifying mass democracy, but the implications of the very different remarks he made at the start are more to our purpose. He drew attention to 'the long survival of the revolutionary phenomenon', 'perpetually enacting the same historical drama', so that 'the Frenchmen of the nineteenth century felt that they were living in a sort of indefinitely prolonged French Revolution. . .'[74] No one saw this more clearly than Tocqueville, that acute observer of underlying French continuity. 'Often during the course of the Revolution, the French thought that they were on the point of finding a solution to this great crisis' but 'all these attempts had been in vain. The march of the Revolution was not arrested.' He went on in the late 1850s to describe the French Revolution as 'that strange drama whose end is not yet in sight.'[75] It was precisely because Napoleon Bonaparte had failed to devise an enduring formula which could reconcile all Frenchmen that the search for harmonizing myths – France, the People, the Republic, the Revolution – vainly continued through the nineteenth century.[76] Consequently, in considering how the Revolution's national and democratic bequests were challenged in the century before France attained stalemate if not stability, it is desirable to represent the full range of responses from farthest Right to farthest Left, before we consider in what sense the irresistible movement inaugurated by the French Revolution may be said to have spent itself in the democratic nation-state.

CHAPTER THREE

MAISTRE: THE COMPLEAT COUNTER-REVOLUTIONARY?

In Joseph de Maistre, the French Revolution met its intellectual match. Suffering almost unendurably, both in his private and his public life, the disruptive and devastating consequences of the Revolution, Maistre's ideological response was intended to be comparably devastating. This truculent free-thinker became the supremely splenetic apologist of uncompromising and all-consuming reaction. He developed his case with determinist logic but his passions were as transparent and as irrepressible as an alpine torrent. 'Every new doctrine since the ages of faith is torn to shreds with ferocious skill and malice.' Isaiah Berlin goes on to claim that Maistre's 'armoury of weapons against liberal and humanitarian doctrines is the most effective ever assembled'. However, he was more an anti-revolutionary than a counter-revolutionary because he thought that attempting to reverse the Revolution 'was as if one had been invited to drain the Lake of Geneva by bottling its waters in a wine cellar.'[1] More monarchist than the monarch and more papist than the Pope, Maistre was to deploy his sardonic shrewdness and mordant wit in a lifelong forlorn battle that led a contemporary Catholic philosopher, Ballanche, to dub him the 'prophet of the past'.[2]

Maistre burst on to the European scene in 1797 with the anonymous publication of his *Considerations on France*. It was described by the poet–politician Lamartine – to whom he was related by marriage – as 'thought out by an exterminating mind and written in blood. . . . This succinct, lively and lucid style, with its denuded sentences and robust limbs, had nothing of eighteenth century flabbiness . . . he was bitter and savage; he had no respect for human beings, he conveyed a sense of solitude.'[3] It would be wrong, of course, to regard him as an intellectually isolated figure because he became the leading light in the Catholic Royalist school of thought. Among them, he was the supreme polemicist on behalf of papacy and monarchy. However, he was more feared than loved, more suspected than trusted, more admired than emulated. So, in another sense, he was always a solitary, having too astringent and trenchant a mind to allow even those he supported to feel secure. While Bonald, Ballanche and the younger Lamennais were eloquent exponents of political catholicism, they seldom attained his capacity to dominate the past, present and future, using an inimitable combination of capacities for analytical dissection, withering irony and verbal *coup de grâce*.

Before the Revolution

Maistre added to an incisive vehemence a profound grasp of the ideas he was fighting precisely because he had originally shared many of them. In a sense, he retained a respect and even sympathy for pre-revolutionary aspirations, although he had come to judge their practical consequences to be subversive. Near the end of a life whose best years were spent in unremitting anti-revolutionary speculation and action, Maistre wrote to his fellow combatant Ballanche: 'If you consider the expression *Revolutionary Spirit* rather distasteful, you would be making a great mistake, because we all derive from it. Some more and some less, no doubt, but there are few minds that have not been affected by it in one way or another; and even I have often asked myself whether I do not derive from it. . . .'[4] Maistre's hatred of the Revolution was rooted in an early love for the liberal ideas that led up to it, which requires us to touch on the pre-revolutionary prologue which extended over nearly the first forty years of his life.

Maistre was born on April Fool's Day 1753 at Chambéry, capital of the French-speaking province of Savoy, governed from across the Alps in Turin by officials of the King of Sardinia. Given the importance that Maistre was to attach to language, notably as the indicator of national identity, he was inclined to identify with France, even claiming that his family originally came from Languedoc. In fact they came from Nice – then Italian, although like Savoy it was to be annexed by France – so that the French Revolution was ironically to make of Maistre an *ex post facto* Frenchman. He was the eldest son of a prominent Chambéry magistrate, who was later made a count. Maistre was to follow in his father's footsteps in both capacities. After attending a Jesuit school, Maistre acquired a doctorate in law and his first judicial post before the age of 20.

Prior to the Revolution, he shared the anti-absolutist and anti-clerical ideas fashionable in his milieu, which had much in common with those of the French *parlementaires* and British Whigs. The future advocate of absolute sovereign power was, in his early writings, a champion of a sort of separation of powers in which religion ensured social cohesion. The king exercised political authority on the advice of the lawyers, thereby establishing an arbitrating but non-arbitrary monarchy. By settling social conflict on behalf of the king, 'The judge was the man who stopped revolutions'; 'the supreme art of the judge is to use royal and ecclesiastical power to check each other, so as to acquire the role of arbitrator.'[5] In 1788, Maistre argued that all power was 'limited by nature or law', the judges being mediators between the king and the people, but he also argued that France should have a Parliament on the British model to mediate politically.[6] So, despite his hesitancy on the score of whether it was the judiciary or representative parliamentary assembly that should curb royal absolutism, Maistre was clearly swimming in the mainstream of reformist liberal ideology at the onset of the French Revolution. As it developed, he became convinced that the admirable British model could not be exported.

Maistre suffered all his life for the extravagant reputation he then acquired with the Turin authorities as a 'Jacobin'. This was due to his ardent and precocious sympathy with the threatening new liberal ideas, the forthright and caustic way in which he expressed himself and his active role in Freemasonry. While Freemasonry had been condemned by the Pope in 1738, Maistre was at this stage of his life a Gallican – asserting the independence of the French Church against the ultramontane pretensions of the papacy – as became a free-thinking inhabitant of the French side of the Alps. As far as its character as an international secret society is concerned, the revolutionary role of Freemasonry has been dismissed as a conspiratorial myth. An authority on the subject states judiciously that Maistre himself subsequently presented Freemasonry as 'an association of clubs, many of whose members sympathised with the Revolution [though this was not a function of their Masonry]. They were therefore likely to use the organisation to which they belonged as a natural channel or framework for their activity in forming revolutionary clubs. This commonsense view corresponds, in fact, to what is now the accepted view of the masonic role in 1789 and the early Revolution.'[7] Nevertheless, although Maistre served the Sardinian monarchy for the whole of his life, he remained tainted by his early liberalism and Freemasonry, which persisted during the initial phase of Revolution.

'Just before the Revolution, Maistre who is almost forty years of age, is mature but unknown, dissatisfied with his career as a judge; a man who sees in freemasonry – to which he has belonged for fifteen years – a way of expressing his personality and corresponding to his purely political conception of the state; a man who ultimately subordinates religion to politics, who dreams of action, hopes for profound changes and does not despair of one day carrying them out as a prominent adviser of the government, which would be a sort of English-style monarchy, as remote from despotism as from democracy.'[8] This able summary of Maistre's frame of mind in the late 1780s can be supported with plenty of evidence. A letter of 1785, in which Maistre approved Necker's policy of reform, must suffice to convey both Maistre's gradualism and his radicalism at this time. 'Great revolutions in domestic policy are like disharmonies in music.' Then, changing the simile, Maistre continues, 'Every old institution has sent down deep roots that usually extend further than one expects. It must not be uprooted before all these long tendrils have been cut, one after the other and if possible quietly, so that when one strikes the great blow, no vast turmoil or ruptures result.'[9] As we are about to bid farewell to Maistre the tough-minded, enlightened Whig, let us do so with a remark he made in his early post-revolutionary writings, which reflects a nostalgia for the type of ordered free society that he no longer believed possible. 'Nothing can equal the great days of republics but they vanish in a flash.'[10] Such retrospective reflections would soon give way to the remorseless fury of the embittered reformer in troubled times.

The impact of the Revolution

Maistre's reaction to the impact of the French Revolution in his *Considerations* permeated everything he subsequently wrote. While there is general agreement with the judgement of Sainte-Beuve that 'The French Revolution was the great moment of his life, his attainment of maturity and clearsighted initiation', there is some disagreement about the alacrity with which Maistre chose the anti-revolutionary camp.[11] After some hesitancy in 1789–90, he abandoned his earlier liberal attitudes in the winter of 1790–1 under the pressure of events in Paris – the increasing extremism of the revolutionaries – and his reading, notably of Burke's *Reflections on the Revolution in France* in September 1791. A more direct and decisive determinant was the pro-Revolutionary riots in Chambéry with which Maistre had to deal as a judge early in 1791. It was no longer possible to adopt the judicious role of intermediary between the king and the 'people'. Maistre sided with the king and adopted a repressive role. In September 1792 Savoy was invaded and enthusiastically accepted the French army as liberators. It was subsequently annexed, Maistre going into exile with his family for almost the rest of his life, losing his property and becoming wholly dependent on the fickle favour of the Sardinian monarch. The traumatic effect of his experience marked him indelibly but his description of the conquest shows his capacity to sublimate it into the inspiration of his apocalyptic political analysis. 'This sudden and terrible disintegration of all the authorities, a sort of agony preceding death . . . this sinister wreckage of all the pillars of government, simultaneously submerging under the *tricolore* flag' was the cataclysm that henceforth rendered objectivity and tolerance impossible.[12] The virulence of his onslaught on the French Revolution was that of a detached observer – born outside France and never having visited it until almost the end of his life in 1817 – condemned to the half-life of an exile and so deprived of the serenity that is usually associated with detachment. His personal tragedy was exacerbated by the fact that his role as the leading anti-revolutionary propagandist never earned him due recognition from the Sardinian king whom he served. (He was even reduced to organizing Sardinian spying in Savoy in 1793–4.) Many years later, writing from a remote St Petersburg embassy, he complained with pardonable exaggeration: 'I was the knight errant of a power that wanted to have nothing to do with me. . . .'[13]

Although Maistre's method was to start empirically from political events, he placed them in a metaphysical and theocentric context, using this to interpret the political facts. He acknowledged that the person who most helped him to make the transition from his pre-Revolution traditionalist liberalism to his post-Revolution ultra-traditionalist illiberalism was 'the admirable Burke . . . I cannot possibly tell you how much he has reinforced my anti-democratic and anti-Gallican ideas.'[14] The French Revolution had forced Burke to offer a theoretical explanation of these momentous political events, but the old Whig was never to go to the extremes attained by Maistre in his frenzied animosity towards incarnate evil. Like Burke, Maistre – in the guise of historical relativism but in fact adopting a profoundly anti-historical idealization in the wake of Blackstone and de Lolme – believed that the lesson of British constitutional history was that there had not been an a priori attempt to establish a rational constitution from first principles. Historic circumstances had created the constitution piecemeal, 'had finally produced, after many centuries, the most complex unity and the best balance between political forces that the world has ever seen.'[15] Far from constitutions being capable of creation a priori, he quotes the more circumspect Hume in support of his extravagant view that 'The real *English constitution* is this admirable, unique, infallible (*sic*) public spirit which is beyond all praise, which guides everything and saves everything. What is written is of no account whatsoever.'[16]

The only exception to the rule that no legitimate and durable constitution could be written was the Mosaic law, because it was divinely inspired.

(Charles de Rémusat subsequently mocked Maistre's obsessive hostility towards written constitutions, remarking that he chose to ignore both the Church's reliance upon scripture and the durability of the Roman legal codes.) Maistre sweepingly dismissed the eighteenth century's institutional engineering proclivities, arguing that all man-made institutions were bound to fail. 'If the foundation is purely human, the building cannot stand; the more men who have been involved in its construction, the more deliberation, science and *especially writing* they have devoted to it . . . the more will the institution be fragile.'[17] Burke was Maistre's anti-Rousseau, inspiring his attack on the abstractions of reason, individualism and natural rights, as well as the democracy that was derived from them. Like Burke, Maistre had sympathized with the American Revolution because, unlike the French, the Americans did not start afresh but built on the English constitutional tradition. Oversimplifying drastically an important truth, Maistre wrote: 'The Americans did not commit the extravagance of destroying a political system from top to bottom to create a new one. . . . Used to the English form of government, the Republic kept to its fundamentals.'[18]

Maistre's 'anti-Gallican' debt to the Anglican Burke may at first sight seem more paradoxical but it went to the heart of his conversion into the arch-advocate of papal theocracy. The 1790 Civil Constitution of the Church, with its split between priests loyal to the Pope and those loyal to the state, opened up a cleavage that made stable authority a fitful phenomenon. It impelled Maistre into hostility towards the Revolution. Burke's conception of man as a religious animal and the interdependence of politics and religion led Maistre to his pivotal belief that to reconstitute an unquestionable authority it was necessary to place temporal monarchical power under the spiritual protection of an infallible papacy. This was to go far beyond anything that the impassioned but fundamentally moderate Burke would have envisaged. Maistre was driven to go wider, deeper and further than Burke because he was concerned not simply to react against the Revolution as an incomprehensible monstrosity. Rather, it was essential to learn the lessons that Providence was teaching mankind through the punishment being inflicted upon it and to build a new conservative order capable of withstanding future revolutionary onslaughts. Maistre's anti-Gallicanism was an integral part of his anti-nationalist search for a universal spiritual authority. Napoleon's humiliation of the papacy and ruthless subordination of it to the secular power of the French state discredited the Gallicanism favoured by Bonald, Maistre's fellow protagonist of political catholicism, preparing the way for the subsequent assertion of papal infallibility by the First Vatican Council in 1870.

The stimulus to Maistre writing his sensational *Considerations on France* was the urge to counteract the immense success to the polemical pamphlet improvised by Benjamin Constant in defence of the post-Thermidorian Directory. (Constant was then profitably currying favour with the ineffectual Directors, who were trying to retreat from revolutionary excesses with a semblance of good order.) Maistre was acquainted with Constant because they frequented the same Lausanne salons, together with Madame de Staël – Constant's mistress – and her father Necker, whom Maistre – in his liberal phase – had admired when he was Louis XVI's finance minister. They appear even to have courted the same lady, Harriet Trevor, wife of the British ambassador to Turin, which could well account for the asperity in Maistre's comments on *'ce petit drôle de Constant'*, accused of 'lacking virility, at least in his books'.[19] We must postpone a discussion of Constant's *De la force du gouvernement actuel et de la nécessité de s'y rallier*, except to say that it championed moderate republicanism and that Chapter four of Maistre's book is a direct attempt to refute Constant's claim that (as against the classic view advocated by Rousseau) large countries could be republics. Maistre was able to dash his diatribe off quickly, using an unpublished manuscript *Treatise on Sovereignty* which was mainly an attack on Rousseau. While the work was published anonymously, Maistre received a letter of thanks from the future Louis XVIII, though after this leaked out it harmed his 'Sardinian' career. When republished in 1814, it also frustrated his hopes of a career with the restored Bourbon monarchy, Louis XVIII now regarding Maistre's extremism as an unwelcome criticism of his own expedient attempt to establish a constitutional monarchy.

The enduring Revolution

Unlike most anti-revolutionaries, who allowed their repugnance to distort their judgement, Maistre quickly grasped that far from being an ephemeral phenomenon the French Revolution had permanently transformed the context of politics. The intellectual independence he had demonstrated in the pre-revolutionary years equipped him to appreciate by 1794 that absolute monarchy had no future and that a theocratic basis had to be instituted, which would come about through the cosmic determinism of Providence. (This was a sheer piece of mystical effrontery.) Before the Revolution, Maistre had believed in the freedom of political action but by 1794 he began to formulate what he called an 'experimental politics' in which experience was reduced to history and history to the will of God. 'The political world is as ordered as the physical world; but because human freedom plays a certain part, we end up believing that it can control everything.'[20] With the publication of his *Considerations*, Maistre is asserting that counter-revolution is inevitable because it is in the historic nature of things. Yet how could the French Revolution be the product of conditions preceding it, yet involve a fundamental break with them? Maistre's method was to treat the Revolution not as an event but as a self-liquidating part of a historic process which would inevitably engender its counter-revolutionary antidote.

To explain the extraordinary disproportion between the enormity of the Revolution's consequences and what Maistre regarded as the mediocrity of most of the revolutionary leaders as well as their propensity to mutual destruction, he hypostasized the Revolution as a providential force almost separate from its agents. This idea was quite common in contemporary *émigré* circles and Bonald independently arrived at the same view in his 1796 *Théorie du Pouvoir Civil*. With his gift for the telling phrase Maistre put it better: 'It is not men who lead the revolution but the revolution who uses men.'[21] Both Maistre and Bonald had been anticipated by the theosophist Saint-Martin, whom Maistre knew and admired. However, Maistre went much further in extending the Revolution in space – it was becoming universal – and in time: not only backward to the sixteenth century Reformation but also into the future. Far from being defeated with the death of that satanic genius Robespierre and the crowning of Napoleon, the revolutionary process was being further extended. Napoleon's historic function was to regenerate an effete monarchy. Napoleon – who probably read Maistre's *Considerations* while campaigning in Milan – later returned the compliment, recognizing the utility of the Catholic religion as an instrument of social control. 'I have seen Godless man at work since 1793. One cannot govern such a man, one can only shoot him.' Referring to bishops as his 'purple prefects' and priests as his 'sacred gendarmes', Napoleon cynically justified his 1801 Concordat with the Church: 'I do not see in religion the mystery of Incarnation but of social order', which would have pleased Maistre, who made repeated attempts to arrange a meeting with Napoleon in 1807.[22]

Even after the Restoration of the Bourbons, Maistre warned the royalists in the preface to *Du Pape* that 'the height of folly would be for them to believe that the Revolution was over', arrestingly adding in a letter of 1819: 'the Revolution is without doubt still standing, not only is it standing, it is walking, it is running, it is lashing out.'[23] After all, the Charter which Louis XVIII adopted in 1814 resembled the 1791 Constitution. It proved that the 'Restoration' had not reversed the revolutionary process. To understand its enduring impact, we must briefly consider what were the causes to which Maistre attributed the coming of the Revolution.

Maistre did not attach prime importance to the proximate factors, such as the moral degeneration of the nobility and clergy, nor did he go into the Revolution's economic causes. In trying to explain the childlike revolutionary mentality which treated government like a mechanical toy which could be broken to discover how it worked, Maistre isolated three crucial fallacies. Firstly, there was the fallacy of abstraction, which started with the *tabula rasa* of words and ended with actions, believing this to be the ideal instrument for effecting change – only to discover that it was easier to change words than things. The Rights of 'Man' and the incantatory revolutionary trinity of 'Liberty, Equality, Fraternity' were mere words, as their subsequent failure to become realities clearly demonstrated. (Ominously, the Latin word for man – *homo* – originally meant a rightless person or slave, nothing but a man. Although the first three were not attained, the last word of the revolutionary slogan – 'Liberty, Equality, Fraternity or Death' – most certainly was and this reality shaped Maistre's analysis as well as his prophetic legacy.) Maistre unmercifully teased the protagonists of an abstract humanity, declaring: 'The 1795 Constitution, like its predecessors, is made for *man* but there is no *man* in the world. In my life I have seen Frenchmen, Italians, Russians and so forth, I even know thanks to Montesquieu *that one can be a Persian;* but as for *man,* I affirm that I have never in my life met him; if he exists, I am unaware of the fact.'[24]

Secondly, the Rousseau-inspired fallacies of the social contract and popular sovereignty – to whose refutation Maistre devoted much of his posthumously published *Study of Sovereignty* of 1794 – abstracted society from its reality as an involuntary, natural fact and erected upon it the sovereignty of another abstraction, the people. Thirdly, there was the fallacy of the indivisibility of the republic. While all power was indivisible, only small states could be republics – a point on which he was happy to agree with Rousseau.

Maistre attributes the responsibility for these nefarious ideas to the corrupting and disintegrating effects of the heresies propagated by the Protestant sects, assisted by Jansenism and Gallicanism, as well as by such philosophers as Bacon, Locke, Voltaire, Rousseau and Kant. (Maistre's contempt for Protestantism is revealed in his terse response to the attempt by the Protestant Anglophil Madame de Staël to persuade him of the attractions of Anglicanism, which he dismissed as 'the ecclesiastical equivalent of the orang-outang amongst the monkeys'.[25]) However, before we discuss the polemical papism which embodies his cure for the malady, we must first examine his onslaught on the political weakness of the revolutionary *volontarisme* which believed that all was possible if enough willpower was exerted.

Sovereignty versus democracy

Far from rejecting the Jacobin's conception of the indivisibility of political power, Maistre parted company with them from the neo-feudal champions of a separation of powers like Montesquieu and Burke, reviving the conception of *raison d'état* that Richelieu had personified. He harked back to the sixteenth- and seventeenth-century absolutist exponents of 'royal science' or 'political science', Louis Le Caron and Charles Loyseau, the latter arguing that the state was synonymous with royal sovereignty and that 'the public power of the state resides perfectly and entirely in sovereign princes.'[26] Louis XIV's court theologian Bossuet, Bishop of Meaux, had deployed biblical support for the doctrine that no people can exist without God – given unlimited kingly sovereignty – in his *Politique tiré des propres paroles de l'Ecriture sainte.*

However, Bossuet's serene rhetoric had to be bolstered by new arguments. Britain had demonstrated the dispensability of written constitutions; its history embodied its constitution and its unity derived from the existence of a sovereignty that, far from originating from the people, was above and beyond its reach. Yet the Jacobin constitution of 1793 – drafted in eight days by Hérault de Séchelles (because he closely followed Condorcet's Girondin constitution) and never implemented – could be lauded to the Convention by two of the leading members of the Committee of Public Safety in the following dithyrambic rhetoric. Barère asserted: 'In a few days we have reaped the enlightenment of all the ages'; while Robespierre, not to be outdone, declaimed: 'We can now present to the universe a constitutional code, infinitely superior to all moral and political institutions . . . the essential basis of public happiness, offering a sublime and majestic picture of French regeneration.'[27] Maistre had a field day turning the arguments and experience of the revolutionaries against the Revolution in his long, ironic 1795 pamphlet, *Bienfaits de la Révolution française*, trampling in the process his earlier liberal ideas. However, in the exuberance of scoring facile rhetorical points – 'In the place of the abuse of grandeur, [the Revolution] has put the grandeur of abuse'[28] – Maistre missed the significance of the move from political to social revolution.

In the constitutional debate mentioned earlier, a member of the Convention, Chabot, was applauded when he lodged an objection to the draft: 'It fails to assure bread to those who have none. It fails to banish beggary from the Republic.' Less than three months later, following the invasion of the Convention by the Paris Commune on 5 September 1793 which – in the context of a food shortage verging upon famine – marked the beginning of institutionalized Terror, its spokesman Chaumette declared: 'This is the open war of the rich against the poor.' He added later, 'If we do not beat them, they will beat us. Let us throw between us and them the barrier of eternity.'[29] The leaders were unwilling to call an election to implement the new, democratic constitution. 'A new election would be risky for regicides. A free election would represent the country only too accurately, representing it in all its appalling dissensions, bring into the centre of government the yawning fissures and irreconcilable estrangements left by five years of revolutionary change. There was not in France in 1793 a true majority for anything'[30] and so no short-term hope for political democracy.

Before turning to Maistre's devastating onslaught upon the actual prac-tice as well as the fundamental principle of democracy, let us consider, with the help of twentieth-century hindsight, the Jacobin failure to found the stable republic upon which they had set their hearts and in aid of which they bent every muscle of their being. Hannah Arendt has persuasively argued that 'every revolution must go through two stages, the stage of liberation – from poverty [which is a liberation from necessity], or from political domination, foreign or domestic [which is a liberation from force] – and the stage of foundation, the constitution of a new body politic or a new form of government. In terms of historical processes, these two belong together, but as political phenomena, they are very different matters and must be kept distinct.' She goes on to argue that liberation takes priority over foundation and that the revolutionary failure to liberate by abolishing poverty doomed the French Revolution and most of its successors to fiasco once the revolutionaries recognized the previously latent 'enormous power inherent in wretchedness, once this *malheur* has come out into the open and has made its voice heard in public. This happened for the first time in the French Revolution, and it has happened time and again since.'[31] One may quibble about Roman precedents or about whether the twentieth century has given us the technical capacity to abolish poverty and thereby prevent the political inability to 'liberate' from leading to the failure to 'found' a new form of government. Nevertheless, Arendt's analysis clearly takes us in a direction that Maistre never explored but with which others, as we shall see, were to concern themselves.

In demonstrating that full democracy was for all practical purposes impossible, Maistre was able to make use of the arguments advanced by Montesquieu and Rousseau that 'true' or 'pure' democracy had never existed; Rousseau having added for good measure that democracy was too perfect a political regime for imperfect man. Recalling the notion of 'isonomy' which since Herodotus had signified a condition of 'no rule', no separation between the rulers and the ruled, Maistre defined democracy as a voluntary 'human association without sovereignty', which as such could not endure.[32] He ridiculed the idea of representatives speaking for the nation, as favoured not merely by his adversary Sieyès but by his much admired fellow scourge of the French Revolution, Edmund Burke. 'What does this empty benefit of representation mean for the nation when it is involved so indirectly and when millions of individuals will never participate? Are sovereignty and government any less alien to them?' Maistre proceeds to rub salt in the wound of the body democratic: 'It is a pity, but the people count for nothing in revolutions, or at least they play a part only as a passive instrument.' More generally, he hammers home the crucial point about the impotence of the people: 'In a republic the right to vote gives neither prestige nor power.' Despite Rousseau's laughable pretensions to the contrary, 'the simple citizen counts for nothing.' Maistre presses his attack on the self-contradictions of democracy even further by ridiculing the key principle of popular sovereignty. 'It is said that the people are sovereign; but over whom? – over themselves apparently. The people are thus subject. . . . The people are a sovereign who cannot exercise sovereignty.'[33] It is only those of noble birth and family ties, wealth and talent who have influence in democracies.

Maistre is exposing the fundamental flaw in classical democratic theory, of which Rousseau was the most forceful modern exponent: if power is shared by the whole people, *nobody is powerless and nobody is powerful.* Yet Maistre is conducting his case by a priori argument. He is scornful of the American democracy that was to become the subject of a searching vindication by Tocqueville some forty years later. 'America is often cited to us: I know nothing so provoking as the praise showered on this babe-in-arms: let it grow.' Maistre even ventured confidently to predict that its new purpose-built capital – a typical example of rationalist folly – would never materialize: 'It is 1000 to one that the town will not be built, or that it will not be called *Washington,* or that Congress will not sit there.'[34] He was of course wrong on all three counts, which simply goes to show that reactionary sceptics can sometimes be as disastrously misguided as can optimistic innovators. Since Washington there have been other examples of man-made capital cities, notably in federal states, which are a monstrosity to absolutist champions of sovereignty such as Maistre although he was to recommend one – under the Pope – for Italy. Perhaps as a providential punishment for making rash predictions, Maistre was to begin, in 1803, a fourteen-year term as ambassador in St Petersburg, the purpose-built capital whose creation was begun by Peter the Great exactly a century earlier in 1703.

Maistre was joined by his fellow Catholic royalist protagonists in attacking democracy. Lamennais in particular – before his subsequent conversion to democracy – regarded it as synonymous with agitation, instability, corruption, materialism, atheism and despotism. Bonald similarly castigated democracy but unlike his co-critics he championed decentralization, which Tocqueville was later to praise as a corrective to some of the defects of democracy.[35] However, Maistre could not tolerate such restraints on central omnipotence, defining sovereignty with a forthright brutality that neither Napoleon nor de Gaulle was to surpass. 'Every species of sovereignty is absolute of its nature . . . *despotic* in the full sense of the term. . . . However sovereignty is defined and vested, it is always one, inviolable and absolute.'[36] Here we see the uninhibited reassertion of the authoritarian French conception of political power, which has been shared by the mainstream parts of the Right and the Left.

Maistre understood why the French Jacobins were condemned to resort massively to the guillotine to preserve their hold on power during the Terror of 1793–4. Far from seeing this as an aberration, he did not squeamishly hesitate to generalize it into a universal principle. No stable authority was possible in a wicked world without the aid of the God-sanctioned author of social order: the executioner. What makes us obey – the efficient, shameful secret of power revealed by Hobbes – is the fear of death, so 'all grandeur, all power, all subordination rests on the executioner: he is the horror and the bond of human association. Remove this incomprehensible agent from the world, and at that very moment order gives way to chaos, thrones topple, and society disappears. God, who is the author of sovereignty, is the author also of chastisement.'[37] This dread, apocalyptic vision proved in France as elsewhere to be a mere nightmare when, in 1981, one of the first acts of President Mitterand was to abolish capital punishment. Though petty, non-capital crime continued to increase, notably crimes motivated by cupidity and the desire for wealth without work, no threat to social order emerged when the public executioner went into permanent retirement.

The dogmatist of infallible theocracy

If we are to understand what at first sight seem such astounding statements as Maistre's assertion that 'the scaffold is an altar', we must place them in the context of the post-revolutionary need to secure spiritual support for an ineffective temporal authority. Hereditary monarchy was ceasing to be an unquestioned source of political legitimacy. The sceptical relativism induced by the *philosophes* was not capable of coping with the need for a secure foundation for government once it came under subversive challenge. Before Maistre's theocratic advocacy of papal infallibility, Robespierre's demand for an 'Immortal Legislator', which was associated with the deistic cult of the Supreme Being, had already reflected the enduring hankering after a religious sanction for law. Robespierre needed the law to be based not just upon the people's will but also on divine command. 'In terms of the French Revolution, he needed an ever-present transcendant source of authority that could not be identified with the general will of either the nation or the Revolution itself, so that an absolute sovereignty . . . might bestow sovereignty upon the nation . . . some permanence and stability to the republic, and, finally, that some absolute Authority might function as the fountainhead of justice from which the laws of the new body politic could derive their legitimacy.'[38]

The nineteenth century was to witness a long struggle to separate Church and state, politics and religion in France, precisely because as the revolutionary process developed each ruling group turned to spiritual sanctions to support their challenged secular authority. As Tocqueville was able to discern in mid-century, 'Religion regains its influence in each class when that class becomes imperilled by revolution – first the upper classes turn to religion in 1793, then the middle classes in 1848 . . .'[39] The recourse to new pseudo-religions, such as 'Theophilanthropy', which one of the post-Thermidor Directors, La Révellière-Lépeaux, sought vainly to popularize after the downfall of Robespierre, were feeble potions compared with the potent holy wine of theocracy which Maistre dispensed. Scientism was to emerge as a partial substitute for religion, with the triumph of Enlightenment theophobia.

French history demonstrated, claimed Maistre with no little oversimplification, that the bishops had built up the monarchy, so that French government had deep theocratic roots. As he wrote in 1814 with remorseless dogmatic logic to Count de Blacas, in what was virtually a deductive summary of his future theocratic masterpiece, *Du Pape*: 'There is no public morality or national character without religion, no European religion without Christianity, no Christianity without Catholicism, no Catholicism without the Pope, no Pope without his supremacy.'[40] Following the Revolution's early annexation of Avignon, which envenomed relations with the papacy, and despite Napoleon's 1806 abolition of the Holy Roman Empire, his absorption of the papal states and abduction of Pope Pius VII in 1809, the attempt at Caesaropapism – united spiritual and temporal power under the temporal authority of the French emperor – collapsed. The Pope's restoration led to a reinvigoration of the Vatican praetorianism of the theocrats, although there was no revival of the Holy Inquisition, which Maistre believed might have prevented the Revolution had it not been abolished.[41]

It seems that Maistre was hoping to receive a high Vatican position in recognition of his championship of papal infallibility, but *Du Pape* was received with circumspect suspicion by Pius VII, who wished to avoid trouble with Gallicans. Furthermore, Maistre as a lawyer was offering the Pope not so much infallibility as 'inappelability': the Pope's pronouncements were presented not as ecclesiastically true (a master of controversy) but as final (a practical, judicial matter of fact).[42] Pius VII did not find this to his taste and may also have been disturbed at the advocacy of a Christianity without Christ. However, the infallibility that Pius VII was unwilling to claim was proclaimed in 1870 by Pius IX. Hobbes may have mocked the papacy as being merely the 'ghost of the Holy Roman Empire sitting crowned upon the ruins thereof', but his successor as the champion of sovereign power, elevated into its theocratic equivalent of papal infallibility, enjoyed the last laugh. Had not Maistre proclaimed with his characteristically intimidating, God-intoxicated logic: 'There can be no human society without government, no government without sovereignty, no sovereignty without infallibility'?[43] Thanks to the allegiance of all Catholics to an infallible Pope, conflicts between nations would be transcended by a Rome-centred ideological internationalism; a conception with close analogies to the so-called 'proletarian internationalism' that Moscow – and more particularly the ex-seminarist Stalin – sought to enforce through the Comintern a century after the publication of *Du Pape*.

Attempts have been made to argue that Maistre was an advocate of nationalism and even a precursor of the Risorgimento, rather than adopting a patrimonial view of the relationship of the nation and the monarch. Both these views are oversimplifications. Maistre regarded nations as 'natural' phenomena, and governments were no more the creation of the nation – as the French revolutionaries proclaimed – than was its language. He was only too aware that linguistic nations and states were far from identical, being born in French-speaking Savoy, administered from Italian Turin and under the authority of the King of Sardinia, at a time when Italy was split into thirteen separate political units. The proximity of multilingual Switzerland, in which he spent some of the early years of his exile, would have reinforced this perception.

Maistre adopted a sceptical attitude towards the idea of nationhood, stating that the nation is 'a splendid and extremely convenient word since one can make of it what one wishes.'[44] At times he explicitly adopts the historical relativism of Montesquieu, considering that each nation has the particular characteristics and form of government appropriate to it, and uses this as an argument against Rousseau's 'ridiculous' appeal to social contract. At others, he adopts a providential and apocalyptic view in which nations have an unconscious, God-given mission; and once they have fulfilled it they go into irretrievable decline, to be replaced by others as 'God's instruments'. Seventeenth-century France, 'Louis XIV's century', was the culmination of French perfection in all spheres, including that of its language. A crisis might lead to the emergence of new nations and for the purposes of counter-revolutionary convenience, Maistre asserted in 1794 that 'the Vendée is a nation.'[45] In 1814, he appears to have called upon Victor Emmanuel I of Piedmont-Sardinia to become the 'leader of the Italians', advice that was not accepted, although Victor Emmanuel II subsequently followed similar advice from Cavour. In *Du Pape,* a few years later, Maistre advocated a federation of Italian states under the Pope – a rather curious suggestion for a champion of sovereignty – but he had no more success with this proposal, although it was vainly resuscitated in 1848.

Maistre wielded his pen with mastery but his performance as a man of action led to a series of fiascos. For much of the crucial quarter of a century following the French invasion of Savoy and then Piedmont, Maistre's master was 'a dispossessed king who lived in Rome on subsidies from the British government and the Tsar.'[46] Although Victor Emmanuel I was initially well disposed to Maistre, following the publication of *Consideration on France,* the suspicion that he had switched his loyalties to the French pretender led to renewed coolness and his eventual despatch in 1800 to remote Cagliari in Sardinia, where he occupied the senior judicial post of regent. However, his blunt and dogmatic assertiveness continued to render him *persona non grata* to those in authority and he was sent as far away as possible – as ambassador to St Petersburg – in 1803.

He did not endear himself to his foreign ministry by despatching elaborate philosophic statements of the principles that should inspire a diplomatic strategy of world counter-revolution to combat world revolution. Thus in an 1809 report setting out his ten strategic principles, the first two were: 'If there is something that is unfortunately obvious, it is that the contemporary revolution has no limits other than the whole world. Secondly, this revolution cannot end with a return to the former state of things, which seems impossible, but by a rectification of the state into which we have fallen . . .' Such missives provoked the exasperation of recipients whose horizons were more limited. One of them wrote: 'In God's name, ask the Count to write despatches and not dissertations.'[47] Even though he was at times close to Tsar Alexander I, whom he cast in the role of champion of the counter-revolution, the anti-Catholic advocate of the 'Holy Alliance' of conservative monarchs eventually asked for the recall of Maistre in 1817, who was suspected of promoting Jesuit propaganda in Russia. Maistre departed sadly, not to the post that he coveted at the Court of the restored Bourbons in France or in the Vatican, but to head the judiciary in Turin – which enabled him to resist all attempts to establish a Piedmont Sardinian constitution.

Although the Count d'Artois, the extremist brother of Louis XVIII and future undertaker of Bourbon legitimism as Charles X, was married to a daughter of the Sardinian royal family, Maistre got into trouble for appearing to have divided loyalties, being branded with the nickname *il Francese*. At the request of the future Louis XVIII he redrafted a declaration against Napoleon's usurpatory proclamation as emperor in 1804, but his version was not accepted. Louis XVIII's restoration in 1814 resulted in Maistre's aspirations turning again to the legitimate monarch. However, his hopes of a career in France were destroyed by Bonald's publication of a work Maistre had written in 1809, *Essai sur le principe générateur des constitutions,* which was read as an attack on the conception of constitutional monarchy that Louis XVIII had adopted in the 1814 *Charte.* The success of this demonstration of the futility of constitutions, despite the disapproval of the censorship, meant that Maistre – Louis XVIII's former champion of 1797 in the *Considerations* – was received coldly by the restored king in 1817.

Maistre had, in an 1816 letter to the king's favourite from 1810, the Comte de Blacas, described the *Charte* as a 'soapbubble' because, as he had written in 1814, Louis XVIII did not really sit on the throne of his ancestors when he promulgated the charter of constitutional monarchy. 'We are far from having attained stability. The Revolution was at first democratic, then oligarchic. Today it is royal; but it still retains its impetus.'[48] Once again the perspicacity of the blunt theoretician, who combined an incisive style with a systematic and consistent doctrine, had blocked the advancement of the would-be confidant of the powerful. He seemed congenitally incapable of acquiring the supple ability of the successful *arriviste* who effortlessly adapts to circumstances. However, by 1817 he could cynically write to his brother: 'You made me burst out laughing with the description you gave me of the *French Charter.* If some fools believed in it or still believe in it, too bad for them. The king, however, may well have done the right thing . . . It is necessary to do many things in politics for *the crowd* . . . .'49

Maistre's impact: the meaning of his legacy

Those who, like Madame de Staël, were ardent advocates of constitutional monarchy on the British pattern attributed the stability and liberty of that country partly to its Protestantism. By contrast, in her posthumously published chapter entitled 'Are the French capable of freedom?', she argued that in France a major problem was 'catholicism, which decides everything by authority and considers kings to be as infallible as Popes, unless the Popes are at war with the kings.'50 Maistre was undoubtedly one of the targets of this criticism, which was subsequently to be a leitmotif of the battle against clericalism, although only a minority were to commend Protestantism as the antidote to intolerant and authoritarian catholicism. The clerical extremism of the Restoration undoubtedly contributed, by its comprehensive attempt to reverse the legacy of the Revolution, to a perpetuation within French political culture of an enduring polarization that, until the latter half of the twentieth century, has had even more powerful effects than the post-industrial cleavage between social classes. In fact, the post-1789 reactionaries attempted to go further than simply return to the pre-1789 status quo ante. For royalism had then been characterized by a measure of the ambient eighteenth-century rationalism and reformism. These became anathema to the post-revolutionary reactionaries, because they were seen as key causes of the Revolution and consequently had to be extirpated, root and branch.

Although it purported to introduce British-style constitutionalism, under the polarizing pressures of reactionary ultras and revolutionary liberals, the 1814 charter became an unstable compromise between Divine Right and the Rights of Man. Article 5 proclaimed Roman Catholicism to be the state religion but Maistre's hope that religious authority would be the rock on which sovereignty could be built proved illusory when that very authority was bitterly contested. Even when the papacy acquired infallibility, it was circumscribed in ways which ensured that it was incapable of playing the *political* role Maistre had ascribed to it. The liberal and social catholicism advanced after 1830 by Maistre's former admirer, the unfrocked priest Lamennais, has become in the latter half of the twentieth century the predominant view among bishops and priests (if not the laity), conscious that true believers are now only a relatively small minority in France. Agreement about fundamentals in an idealized, united Christendom has gone for good. Nevertheless, the constituency to which Maistre gave vehement expression has not disappeared. In contemporary France, if you wish to know how people will vote, it is more important to know whether they attend mass and confession than whether they are manual workers or bourgeois. The Socialist Government of 1984 learnt to its cost that to threaten the autonomy of Church-organized schools was capable of arousing and successfully mobilizing over a million demonstrators in the streets of Paris, although whether Maistre and his successors Montalembert and Veuillot would have been unreservedly pleased at the recourse to such mass pressure is open to doubt. Clearly, despite increasing dechristianization, the clerical constituency continues to exist as a powerful political force in French society, although it has so far been a source of political contention rather than of consensus.

Maistre's legacy can be traced clearly to positivism, of which Auguste Comte was the chief intellectual exponent and Charles Maurras the foremost political propagandist. So high an opinion did Comte have of the theocrat that he declared: 'Maistre has for me the peculiar property of helping me to estimate the philosophical capacity of people by the repute in which they hold him.'[51] The 'New Christianity' which the mainstream disciples of Saint-Simon (in connection with whom we shall discuss Comte in the next chapter) embraced explicity owed a great deal to Maistre's theocratic ideas, although he would have hoped for a more orthodox progeny when predicting a religious revival. In particular, in the seventh of his *Lettres sur la Religion et la Politique,* Saint-Simon's disciple Eugène Rodrigues asserted: 'There is, as Maistre says, a natural affinity between science and religion', while in the eighth letter, after long quotations from *Du Pape,* he adds: 'The State and the Church are united; because henceforth religion embraces the whole of society.'[52]

This identification of religion, science and politics took, in the case of the Saint-Simonians, the form of international peace, a rather paradoxical prediction to place under Maistre's patronage. Rodrigues first quotes the *Soirées de St. Petersbourg*: 'How could God, the author of a *society of individuals* allow man ... not even to attempt to rise to the *society of nations*? All the imaginable reasons to prove that such a society is impossible could be used *against the society of individuals.*' He then comments: 'Let us say with Maistre, we need to rise to the society *of nations* ... attain the unity of *temporal* religious society. Only then will *nations* disappear to be replaced by UNIVERSAL *society.*'[53] The contrast could not be greater with the *Action Française* nationalism of Charles Maurras, disciple of both Maistre and Comte, whose anti-German and anti-Semitic monarchism was to end up during the Second World War in support of the collaborationist

Vichy Regime. He has claim to be the most vitriolic of twentieth-century counter-revolutionaries, combining pseudo-scientism and traditionalism through rhetorical skill rather than rational argument.[54]

However, whereas Maurras was a fanatical decentralist and convinced atheist, Maistre was an ultra-centralist and had a God-centred conception of nature, society and history. Divorced from God, man can only destroy and so the Revolution, incapable of creating, pulverized political order. The last words of Maistre's unfinished and posthumously published 'Study on sovereignty' were; 'Everything brings us back to the author of all things. Power comes from him, obedience comes from him; everything comes from him, except evil . . .'[55] but although the great antitheist Proudhon was happy to agree that the power and obedience he abominated came from God, he *therefore* regarded the divinity as evil incarnate. Proudhon arrived at his personification of evil in God in contradistinction to Maistre, who had identified evil with the French Revolution – perceptively declaring in *De la Justice dans la Révolution et dans l'Eglise* that the counter-revolutionary thinkers 'copy the Revolution while contradicting it' and that the 'whole genius of de Maistre is the antithesis to the Revolution.'[56] Proudhon learnt a great deal from the counter-revolutionaries and held these adversaries in high regard. 'When, fifty or sixty years ago, catholic and monarchist absolutism was about to descend into the tomb, it made a supreme effort. It was then that it produced its most illustrious apologists, de Maistre, Bonald, Chateaubriand and Lamennais.'[57]

Maistre's popularity in the nineteenth century is evidenced by the frequent republication of his works – *Considerations* being reprinted fourteen times between 1843 and 1868, while *Du Pape* went through 40 reprints in France and was translated into English, German and Spanish.

We know from Proudhon's unpublished notebooks that he devoured these writers attentively and that he had the highest opinion of Maistre, whom he read carefully in 1829, 1839–40 and 1844, taking notes from *Considerations on France,* the *Soirées* and *Du Pape.* After reading *Du Pape,* Proudhon noted: 'Curious book, full of verve, wit and malice, perfectly logical; veritable code of the protagonists of authority. De Maistre shows himself to be a genius.'[58] Like the Saint-Simonians, as well as Comte and Le Play, Proudhon learnt from Maistre the crucial role of the Church in preserving social cohesion. However, unlike these conservative successors of the great theocrat, Proudhon repudiated with contumely the old authoritarian alliance of altar and throne, particularly since it had been replaced by the new authoritarian alliance of altar and bank vault, which sanctified capitalism. In a brief 1852 correspondence, on Proudhon's emergence from three years in prison, Comte sought to win his support for positivism, 'the only faith capable of ending the western revolution', but was peremptorily dismissed for making 'war on *socialism* in the name of sociology; a perpetual counterfeit of theocracy', which Proudhon had earlier described as a reactionary 'perpetuation of catholicism'.[59] Comte was roundly condemned for combining the new technocratic authoritarianism with scientized old theocracy; 'He ruins his case in damning the Revolution . . . he only required a little more consistency to reconstruct the whole of catholicism.'[60]

Proudhon learned from Maistre the pervasiveness of contradiction, conflict and war, not merely as an evil but as an ineradicable presence in human development. In their common rejection of the Rousseau-inspired Revolutionary import into politics of pity, hitherto confined by Christianity to the extra-political realm, they paradoxically sought to curb what Hannah Arendt has called 'the most powerful and perhaps the most devastating passion motivating revolutions, the passion of compassion . . . . If Rousseau had introduced compassion into political theory, it was Robespierre who brought it into the market-place with the vehemence of his great revolutionary oratory' and since then 'the passion of compassion has haunted and driven the best men of all revolutions.'[61] Because the misery to be alleviated was so immense, the people's protagonists had to be heartless in using, when necessary, violent methods against the people's inhuman enemies, who could therefore be deprived of human rights. So the arbitrary power of despotism could be justified and so too could mass murder, internally and externally in worldwide war. Maistre, the prophet of pervasive evil, was – alas – not as Ballanche described him a retrospective 'prophet of the past' but a prophet of one side of the irrational, satanic, terror-ridden and tormented twentieth century, a prophet of the future. The failure to create either a new consensus or an agreement to differ has led to the 'established disorder' of selfless strife and 'compassionate' repression.

Ironically, the last words Maistre spoke were: 'Let me die in peace.'[62] Yet, within two weeks of his death in Turin in 1821 a *Carbonari* insurrection had led to the king's abdication in the same town. (This link between the ultimate reactionary and Blanqui who, as *Carbonaro* and professional revolutionary, would have been sovereignly repugnant to Maistre, brings us full circle from extreme Right to extreme Left, an aspect of the continuing Revolution to which we will return in Chapter 8.) Because the Church could not defeat the legacy of the French Revolution, it rallied to it in late-nineteenth-century France in an attempt to build a new consensus. The supreme irony is that in the twentieth century, the Catholic Church has often sided with those who are in revolt against the government, particularly in the Communist and Third World countries, on behalf of democracy and nationalism.

CHAPTER FOUR

SAINT-SIMON AND THE INDUSTRIAL COUNTER-REVOLUTION

The road to the golden age

In the wake of the French Revolution an acute sense of crisis obsessed thinking people of all shades of opinion. The apparent demise of God left people disorientated, lacking a stable and accepted order, exposed to an anarchy of opinions and interests. Of the many proponents of a new universal system to replace the irretrievably damaged old order which Maistre and his fellow aaanti-revolutionaries were desperately seeking to shore up, one of the least original but most influential was Henri Saint-Simon. His most perceptive biographer has stated the problem of finding a panacea to deal with a cataclysm that had swept away the traditional spiritual and temporal authorities in arresting if somewhat sweeping terms. 'For a thousand years mankind had lived with unquestioning faith in the existence of a unifying principle in the world. The first full understanding of its destruction gave birth to scores of artificially and highly self-conscious attempts to substitute for the old religion a scientific principle or a moral principle or an emotional principle dressed up as God. The throne of the absolute could not be left untenanted.'[1]

From the 1802 'Religion of Newton' – a naive aspiration to generalize Newtonian gravitation into a theory of universal unity which he shared with many others – to the pseudo-religion of 'New Christianity' at the end of his life in 1825, Saint-Simon made repeated pseudo-scientific attempts to formulate a 'science of man' equipped with a new clergy appropriate to the post-theological and post-metaphysical, positive era. In contrast to the atheistic *philosophe* view that religion was an unnatural, unreasonable and absurd tissue of errors, Saint-Simon followed Dupuis in his partial rehabilitation of the religious past. In the throes of the revolutionary convulsions (1795, Year III of the Republic), François Dupuis' *Origine de tous les cultes ou religion universelle* explained that religions had, at least in part, been pre-scientific forms of knowledge, appropriate to their time.[2] Saint-Simon's life's work was to build upon the historically indispensable demolition work of the eighteenth-century Encyclopaedia by constructing an irrefutable new dogma based upon an ideology masquerading as science. In the social science propounded by Auguste Comte and his disciples, this dogma became positivism, although for Saint-Simon and most of his business disciples the ideology was that of industrialism.

Despite the force of many of the criticisms levelled by Maistre at the manifestations of modernity – rationalism, secularism, liberalism and nationalism – their impact was blunted by an anachronistic idealization of the pre-revolutionary regime and an incapacity to acknowledge the widespread support for many of the revolutionary changes. As former *Abbé* Daunou, revolutionary drafter of the 1795 constitution and Restoration Liberal put it, Maistre's advocacy of papal power was predicated on a spurious characterization of medieval Europe as unified and the Old Regime as stable, whereas they were both subject to frequent disorder and upheaval. Far from reducing the Revolution to a conspiracy, it had to be seen as the product of an emerging society.[3] It was Daunou's fellow *idéologue* Destutt de Tracy who, along with their common master Condorcet, paved the way for one of Saint-Simon's most celebrated pronouncements, when he wrote in *Elémens d'Idéologie:* 'The highly praised golden age was the time of suffering and destitution.'[4] Unlike Condorcet, who castigated the medieval period as a retrogression from classical excellence, and Maistre who pilloried post-Reformation retrogression from medieval high culture, Saint-Simon's unilinear conception of progress was nevertheless much closer to Condorcet than Maistre. In 'New Christianity' – which was more novel than Christian – Saint-Simon indicted the papacy as anti-Christ because it put superstitious dogma in the service of secular power instead of seeking to improve the lot of the most numerous and poorest people.

In the perfectibilist spirit of Condorcet's *Sketch of the Progress of the Human Mind*, Saint-Simon's criteria of human progress were the increasing happiness of the majority, increasing upward mobility of the meritorious and increasing technical and scientific achievement. In his 1814 *Plan for the Reorganisation of European Society*, two decades after Condorcet's testament and at the end of twenty years of bitter strife, Saint-Simon delivered his secular providentialist counterblast to Maistre's eschatological pessimism and to Rousseau's resurrection of Sparta's regimented unanimism. 'Poetic imagination has identified the golden age with the infancy of the human species, amidst the ignorance and coarseness of the earliest times. Rather, it was the iron age. The golden age of humanity is not behind us, it is before us, in the perfection of the social order. Our forefathers did not witness it, our offspring will attain it one day. It is up to us to clear the way for them.'[5]

Saint-Simon before the Revolution

Despite his spurious claims to have been descended from Charlemagne, Count Henri de Saint-Simon was undoubtedly a member of France's most distinguished aristocracy, being related to the celebrated memorialist of the Court of Louis XIV, the Duc de Saint-Simon. Saint-Simon received little formal education and at 17 he was commissioned in the army. At 19 he took part in Lafayette's expeditionary force supporting the American colonists in their war of independence, being in charge of an artillery battery at the decisive battle of Yorktown. He was subsequently wounded and this early military experience seems to have left him with a disgust for war and led him to abandon his military career. With hindsight, in his 1817 'Letters to an American', he claimed that in America 'I occupied myself much more with political science than with military tactics. . . .Above all, I applied myself to studying the likely consequences for my own country. I now saw that the American Revolution marked the beginning of a new political era . . . . I studied carefully the circumstances of the inhabitants of America, and compared them with those prevailing in the Old World. I realised that they were essentially different, and I concluded from this that civilisation would not follow the same course in the two hemispheres'.[6]

While these retrospective reflections are misleading in relation to Saint-Simon's thoughts in 1783, they are instructive about his state of mind during the early Restoration and anticipate in a superficial way Tocqueville's much more profound analysis. He went on to observe that America was characterized by religious tolerance and the absence of a dominant religion; no privileged nobility; no monopoly of state power; peace-loving people, industriously concentrating upon economic activity. 'I concluded from these observations that the Americans would establish for themselves a regime infinitely more liberal and more democratic than the one under which the peoples of Europe lived', devoted to commerce rather than war.[7] As we shall see, this retrospective rewriting of his pre-revolutionary views represented only one – the American – model of liberalism which attracted Saint-Simon. The other – the English model – whose principal exponent was to be Benjamin Constant, also won his support and was more capable of assimilation in Restoration France.

Prior to the Revolution, Saint-Simon proposed two highly speculative engineering schemes: the building of a Panama canal and later a canal from Madrid to Spain's Atlantic coast. This not only anticipated the ambitious public works programmes that his disciples were to carry out during the Second Empire, as well as inspiring the de Lesseps construction of the Suez canal; Manuel persuasively argues that Saint-Simon's collaboration on the Madrid canal scheme with Count Caburrús provided him with 'the prototype of the grand projector whom Saint-Simon. . .later elevated to the apex of the new industrial system – the banker who utilised the credit system to inaugurate vast enterprises which energized the whole social organism'.[8]

Despite his rank as colonel in the Royal Army, Saint-Simon avoided doing military service during the revolutionary period. He did not merely survive the period of revolutionary turbulence; he prospered. Both before and after incarceration during the Terror, he made a small fortune by speculation in the 'national property' seized from the Church and *émigré* nobility, being, along with Constant, an early profiteer from privatization. Balzac's *Comédie Humaine* novels are replete with 'bourgeois predators feeding off the corpse of the *ancien régime*[9] – acquisition of national property for a mere one-twelfth down payment in the rapidly depreciating *assignat* paper currency being the road to quick profits, social status and in some cases political power during the Empire and Restoration periods. Despite having renounced his title and even his name – 'citizen' was now a safer title than 'count' – Saint-Simon spent November 1793 to August 1794 in prison. Manuel comments: 'The astounding circumstance in Saint-Simon's revolutionary fortunes is not that he was apprehended, whether or not by mistake, but that a speculator, a former noble, a man involved in the society of Palais Royal intriguers, a relative of notorious *émigrés*, a business partner of a Prussian Ambassador (to London), managed to escape death when he was already lodged in the prison of the Terror.'[10]

From his experience during the Revolution, Saint-Simon along with many others acquired both a fear and a hatred of the puritanical Robespierrist reign of virtue. He became an exultant participator in the subsequent uninhibited sexual and speculative spree of the Directory, including the enthusiasm for scientific speculation. He was in his element in a socially mobile society in which the talented and unscrupulous could rise quickly, a situation that he sought to institutionalize in his attempt to 'end the Revolution' by building upon its most positive achievements. Meanwhile, he dabbled in politics, becoming involved in the 1797 abortive secret negotiations to secure peace between France and Britain and in the attempts to strengthen the Directory executive. Saint-Simon actually discussed his proposed constitutional reforms with Napoleon Bonaparte prior to his seizure of power in 1799.[11] Having quarrelled in 1798 with his

Prussian associate in speculation, Saint-Simon proceeded to squander his ill-gotten fortune through lavish entertainment of the most distinguished natural scientists and by financing science courses for the public. Lodged opposite the *Ecole Polytechnique* the better to sample its intellectual fare, Saint-Simon acquired not only a dilettante smattering of scientific knowledge but, more important, an extravagant conception of the role that science could play in the management of society. At this time he became friendly with Lazare Carnot – 'organizer of national victory' as a member of the Committee of Public Safety – but whom Saint Simon admired more for his role as champion of applied science who founded the technocratic *Ecole Polytechnique* during the Directory.

What was the significance of the French Revolution for Saint-Simon? With the help of his two remarkable secretaries, the historian Augustin Thierry and the sociologist Auguste Comte, Saint-Simon saw the Revolution as a deep-seated movement, not a spectacular event or even a series of events. It was the greatest revolution in human history because it marked the transition from the theological–military past to the scientific–industrial future, even though as an ultra-ambitious attempt at social engineering it went badly wrong because political power was in the hands of lawyers and metaphysicians. 'If one must absolutely assign an origin to the French Revolution, it should be dated from the emancipation of the communes and the study of the sciences of observation in Western Europe.'[12] Saint-Simon supplemented this with a political economy explanation of the failure of the productive classes of society to displace the unproductive ones, associated with a change of power holders rather than the creation of a socio-economic organization that would render the old forms of political power redundant. Priding himself on having played no part in the Revolution's demolition work, Saint-Simon was to offer h i s services in the task of constructing the new order. As Guizot (who had his own conservative formula for this ambitious task) put it in 1818: 'As far as destruction is concerned, the Revolution is finished, we do not need to repeat it; as far as founding a new order is concerned, it is only starting.'[13]

The formative influences

While Saint-Simon's disordered thoughts were opportunistically adapted to circumstances in their presentation over the quarter-century during which he launched out on what he called his 'physico-political career', in their fundamentals they stayed the same. His strength lay in his intuitive grasp of new insights that had been formulated by others.[14] Gouhier says that Madame de Staël's remark about Rousseau could more appropriately be applied to Saint-Simon: 'He discovered nothing but he set everything alight.'[15] So, rather than treat his ideas chronologically, we shall focus on the enduring impact of his work as a whole, diffuse in its unity, disseminated the more readily because of its diverse borrowings and arresting simplifications. This eclecticism requires us to go on what may at first seem to be a long detour.

While the Abbé de St-Pierre had provided an early-eighteenth-century formulation of scientific politics based upon an enlightened 'technocratic absolutism' and a belief in human progress which placed the golden age at the end of human history, it was from Turgot and especially from Condorcet that Saint-Simon drew his inspiration. Concluding his biography of Turgot, Condorcet expressed his mentor's faith in 'what reason would dictate for the happiness of humanity. Why should politics, based like all the other sciences on observation and reason, not be perfected in the measure that one brings to observations more subtlety and exactitude, to reasoning more precision, profundity and good judgement?'[16] While the statistical subtleties of Condorcet's political arithmetic did not catch on, his *Sketch of the Progress of the Human Mind* was 'officially adopted as the philosophical manifesto of post-Thermidorian reconstruction', being 'Propagated by the Ideologues as the authentic testament of the Enlightenment' against the anti-secularist attacks of Bonald and Malthus.[17] Saint-Simon's profusely annotated copy of the *Sketch* is eloquent testimony to his intellectual debt but he is closer still to Condorcet's posthumous *Fragment on Atlantis*, in which the aspiration for unity through scientific certainty during the supreme arbitrariness of the Terror seems to threaten to submerge freedom and democracy. However, Condorcet did not confuse management of society with the management of the state. The spiritual–scientific power, embodied in a world scientific organization, and the democratic temporal power, embodied in the nation-state, were kept separate, so that truth and freedom could be achieved separately, whereas Saint-Simon wanted to revive Bacon's *New Atlantis* rule by a sacerdocy of scientists.[18]

Saint-Simon characteristically oversimplified and exaggerated one side of Condorcet's complex blend of élitist rationalism and egalitarian democracy. 'Condorcet signalled the danger of the establishment of an exclusive intellectual elite for scientific and social advance; Saint-Simon maintained that unless the bearers of scientific knowledge constitute a socially organized elite within the hierarchy of society there can be no social stability. Condorcet had been concerned to reconcile scientific elitism with the principle of democratic control in politics; Saint-Simon expected political choice to give way to scientific administration. . . .Deriving these powerful reinterpretations from the *Esquisse* by fusing Condorcet's conception of historical progress with the organic social theory of the theocrats, Saint-Simon constructed a view of history as a succession of discrete social systems each based on a systematic philosophy, represented in social terms by the dominance of a particular elite associated with it.'[19] So, whereas Condorcet had believed that with science as the handmaiden of democracy, a social harmony of interests could be achieved, Saint-Simon saw class conflict as an unavoidable feature of the critical revolutionary period, with harmony reserved to the post-revolutionary organic period of history.

Saint-Simon also partially rejected Condorcet's view of religion as a relic of past barbarism, following up Dupuis' study of comparative religion which purported to show that each religion reflected the contemporary state of science. Saint-Simon combined this historicist relativism with the Bonald–Maistre stress upon religion's indispensability to social unity. In his 1807–8 *Introduction to the Scientific Studies of the Nineteenth Century*, he claimed that 'the idea of universal gravitation should serve as the basis of the new scientific system, and *consequently of the new religious system. . . .Religion is the collection of applications of general science by means of which enlightened men rule the ignorant. . . .*I believe in the necessity of a religion for the maintenance of the social order. I believe that deism is outworn, but that physicism is not sufficiently developed to serve as the basis of the religion. I believe that there have to be two distinct doctrines: physicism for educated men and deism for the ignorant.'[20] The élitist twist he imparted to the new religion of science was combined with a monistic obsession: the unity of all science.[21]

Saint-Simon's urge to systematize all the natural and social sciences into a universal system put off many of the genuine scientists to whom he appealed. Concerned with careful, specialized analysis, they regarded his rush to premature generalized synthesis as the fanciful ravings of a crackpot; and in fact Saint-Simon had intermittent bouts of mental disorder in the decade preceding 1814, marked by a 'trail of unfinished brochures'.[22] It is hard to resist the view that Saint-Simon's obsession with systematic organization was psychologically characteristic of a disordered personality fascinated by the qualities it lacks.

More generally, Saint-Simon owed an intellectual debt to the *idéologues* and Madame de Staël, who after Condorcet's death popularized his social scientism and accentuated his élitism. Saint-Simon was very enthusiastic about her *De la Littérature* of 1800, with its advocacy of positive science generally and political science in particular. He is said to have vainly proposed marriage to Madam de Staël on the ground that he and she were the most extraordinary man and woman of their time.[23] More circumspect than Saint-Simon, while Madam de Staël sought to abolish political conflict through Condorcet-inspired mathematical calculation, she recognized the need to counteract the a priorist 'Newtonian' tendency towards political Utopia with a healthy dose of Montesquieu's pragmatic 'historiography of chance'.[24] As for the *idéologues*, who institutionalized the social sciences in the years from 1795 to 1803 (when Napoleon abolished as subversive the separate 'Class of Moral and Political Sciences' in the Institute), they not only spread the Condorcet scientific aspiration. Destutt de Tracy modified Condorcet's conception of the progress of civilization into a clear forerunner of the Saint-Simon-Comte 'Law of the Three Stages'. Tracy defined the level of civilization by the level of culture and type of government. Primitive societies were characterized by direct democracy or simple monarchy; the second stage was characterized by the predominance of religion, metaphysics and aristocracy; while the third stage, nowhere as yet fully achieved, was based upon rational philosophy, positive science and representative government.[25] However, it was through the pioneer physiologists Bichat and Cabanis and the pioneer political economist Jean-Baptiste Say that the main influence of the *idéologues* on Saint-Simon was transmitted.

Carried along by the spurt of scientific creativity that marked the revolutionary period, Saint-Simon was impatient to extrapolate from the supposed certitudes of the findings of the natural sciences to a total systematization of all knowledge. This implied that the methods of the natural sciences were applicable to the social sciences, and like subsequent positivists Saint-Simon operated on this assumption. While at first attracted by Condorcet's advocacy of mathematics as the model, Saint-Simon switched to the life sciences and physiology in particular under the influence of Condorcet's disciple Cabanis. Although reluctant to abandon his master's ideal of progress towards increasing equality, Cabanis undermined the assumption of natural equality that had been shared by eighteenth-century *philosophes* in the wake of John Locke. Condorcet had restricted equality to legal status and rights but he envisaged progress as a process by which natural inequalities would be gradually reduced, until the ultimate achievement of actual equality. Cabanis' attack upon the physiological and psychological uniformity of the human species switched the direction of the biological and social sciences towards a stress upon the functional specialization of organically related unequal parts.

While Saint-Simon knew and frequently entertained the physician Dr Cabanis to dinner in an endeavour to pick his brains, it was as a patron of Dr Burdin (a friend of Bichat) that Saint-Simon attributed his first appreciation of the importance of physiology.[26] On Saint-Simon's own testimony, the source of his 'law' of functionally specialized, mutually exclusive capacities as the basis of human organization was the 'immortal physiologist' Bichat, although it had echoes of Plato's *Republic*. This was achieved by transposing Bichat's conception of three complementary faculties into a social classification in which the predominance of the brain was found in scientists; of the sensory capacity in artists and men of religion; of the motor capacity in all those involved in industry, from entrepreneurs to manual workers. Because these capacities were complementary, mutual aid rather than conflict between these three classes would result, each contributing to the collective good according to their own capacity. 'In Saint-Simon's doctrine, the scientific elite of Condorcet, the findings of the new physiology of Bichat, the new psychology of Cabanis coalesced with an appreciation of the organic order of the theocrats', to lay the basis for the scientific–industrial management of inegalitarian post-revolutionary society.[27]

For his inspiration in the élitist critique of liberal democracy and the foundation of a self-managed liberal economy based upon the leadership of entrepreneurs, which dominated his thought during the Restoration, Saint-Simon turned to the *idéologues* Destutt de Tracy and especially Jean-Baptiste Say. Their essential work was done during the Directory and the Consulate, before Napoleon wound up the Second Class of the Institute concerned with the moral and political sciences, which had been their springboard for organizing all knowledge to ensure the wise use of power. Modelling themselves on the First Class of Physical and Mathematical Sciences and retaining the scientific faith of their martyred mentor Condorcet, 'the "ideologists" of the Institute's Second Class still believed in a unitary scientific method that eventually would unlock the mysteries of both the physical and social universe'.[28] However, as Cabanis ironically had predicted in 1796: 'The instinct of despots, who encourage the mathematical and physical sciences, literature and the arts, has always made them fear the moral and political sciences.'[29]

This perspicacity did not prevent him, with other *idéologues*, from actively participating in the pre-Brumaire 1799 plots that put Bonaparte in power, in their desperate search for an authority that would avoid reverting to either royalist or Jacobin absolutism. The ambitious general cultivated their illusion that he shared their wish for a scientific basis for political power and would be guided by them. Had not Condorcet as early as 1782 sketched out the programme of a comparative political science on behalf of the French Academy of Sciences, destined for the guidance of the future Czar Paul I of Russia?[30] Because the Directors, whom the *idéologues* supported, had been forced into repeated illegality in order to survive threats from the royalist Right and Jacobin Left, Cabanis defended such expedients: 'The Constitution (of 1795) has not been violated an instant except to conserve it.' Cheryl Welch comments that while 'The search for a stable liberal government was a central preoccupation of the Ideologues during the Directory years. . .the lasting significance of this work lies in the way in which it at once undermines the existing epistemological bases of liberalism and yet affirms the value of liberal procedures and institutions.[31]

Victims who were fortunate enough to have survived the revolutionary Terror, the *idéologues* reacted against the excessive mass expectations aroused by rhetorical appeals to natural rights and popular sovereignty. 'Certainty in method and precision in expression were to be the fundamental goals of an ideologist.'[32] Tracy coined the term 'ideology' to signify an analytic social science of ideas, based upon psychological sense data, whose purpose would be to give a scientific basis to the liberal reform programme. Whereas Condorcet and Sieyès had sought to justify the constitutional rule of law and civil liberties by appealing to the natural and absolute rights of man, the *idéologues* – in the wake of revolutionary experience – regarded these rights as relative to circumstances. Say went so far as to object to including a declaration of rights as a preamble to the 1795 constitution on the grounds that the constitution 'must necessarily restrain them'.[33] Popular sovereignty and absolute rights had led to absolute arbitrariness and popular insecurity, so it was vital to see political participation not as a metaphysical right but as a function, in which a propertied, secularly educated élite would govern in rational and scientific ways. The Convention had envisaged in the Education Law of 25 October 1795 the creation of an *Ecole des Sciences Politiques*, which Tracy thought should be modelled on the recently established *Ecole Polytechnique*. 'From it will come the teachers, the diplomats and senior officials'[34] – an anticipation of the National School of Administration that was born in 1945 after a false start in 1848 under the son of the *Polytechnique's* founder, Lazare Carnot. Whereas the working classes were to receive a general elementary education, the élite were to be educated in the political science of ideology.

Postponing for the present the momentous impact which *idéologue* political economy had upon Saint-Simon, let us conclude this discussion of Saint-Simon's forerunners with Thomas Kaiser's verdict that 'Many if not all the Positivist themes were given wide currency by the Ideologues before 1800 – the general incompetence of the masses, the fear of anarchy and disorder, the necessity of rule by an elite of talent and wealth, the division of society into sectors derived from the division of labour, the need for organization, centralization and repression, the helplessness and moral inferiority of a social man. . . . Ideology may be properly considered an intermediary between the Enlightenment and Positivism. . . .It was Saint-Simon and Comte who would carry on the work of Ideology as a whole, extending it, shifting its focus, altering its methods in the process. . . .Saint-Simon and Comte would work to make the social philosophy of the Ideologues more consistent, to juxtapose the various theoretical fragments left by the Ideologues and to combine them along with other elements to form a synthesis at which the Ideologues aimed but never achieved.'[35] However, before we discuss Saint-Simon's own industrial ideology, we must consider to what extent it can be disentangled from the contributions of two crucial collaborators, Thierry and Comte.

Henri Gouhier, who systematically played down what he regarded as the excessively favourable treatment of Saint-Simon not merely by his disciples but by historians like Michelet, described his writings up to 1813 as 'a synthesis achieved by the reduction of the complex to the oversimplified through the use of ideas that reveal a beatific innocence of scientific knowledge.'[36] Suddenly, in 1814, Saint-Simon authored a properly structured book on the *Reorganization of European Society* from which pseudo-scientific elucubrations about universal gravitation had disappeared. Although he claimed that only those who worked usefully should be rewarded, 'Saint-Simon was incapable of carrying any enterprise through to a successful conclusion or even to live from his work. . . .He was incapable of directing, foreseeing or acting methodically. Saint-Simon was only ever able to organize the future.'[37] As an aristocrat, he may never really have been capable of managing mundane matters without assistance. In any event, from 1814 onwards he had the benefit of a series of exceptionally gifted collaborators who not merely presented his ideas methodically but infused them with their own views, so that it became virtually impossible to detect what belongs to each. Nor is this a matter of prime concern to us once it is accepted, as even Gouhier accepts, that Comte is interpreting and developing Saint-Simon's intuitions and formulas that antedate their first encounter.[38]

His first 'secretary' was Augustin Thierry who, with François Guizot during the Restoration, pioneered nineteenth-century French history as a 'science', just as Say developed a 'science' of economics and Comte a 'science' of sociology. His arrival in 1814 coincided with the phase of political liberalism in Saint-Simon's outpourings. Proud of his status as a commoner, Thierry saw French history as the advance of the bourgeoisie of the communes to achieve the freedom to find fulfilment through work. In England the seventeenth-century Revolution marked the victory of the industrious over the idle, whereas the French urban bourgeoisie had been defeated by the king with the help of the lawyers. Their victory was postponed until 1789. He felt that 'the prodigious changes of power and society which have taken place' thanks to the French Revolution enabled historians to understand the process of change.[39] We shall encounter some of these ideas later, imparted to Tocqueville by Guizot. They were absorbed by Saint-Simon and endured after Thierry was replaced in 1817 by Auguste Comte as Saint-Simon's 'secretary'. Thierry wrote between 1817 and 1820 for the *Censeus Européen*, working with Constant and Lafayette politically and in the *Carbonari* movement in the early 1820s.

Although a mathematician by training like Condorcet, Comte shunned this side of Condorcet's work in favour of his philosophy of history. He took scientism much more seriously than Saint-Simon and was reluctant to rush prematurely into proposing social reforms before he had laid their social scientific foundations. Comte considered that if one was to fulfil the Revolution by bringing it to an end, it was 'disorderly to invite the men of order to conquer power before the full elaboration of a theory of order'.[40] However, he wrote revealingly to a friend in 1819: 'I feel that the scientific reputation I might acquire will impart more value, more weight, more useful influence, to my political sermons.'[41] The youthful essays he composed in association with Saint-Simon laid the ground for the full-blown positivism that occupied the rest of his life, notably his 'fundamental opuscule' of 1822. A stern critic, Hayek, has called it 'One of the most pregnant tracts of the nineteenth century, infinitely more brilliant than the now better known ponderous volumes of the *Cours*'.[42] Significantly, it was the publication of this essay in 1824 that led to the break between Comte and Saint-Simon, Comte wishing to assert his independence and henceforth expound his ideas in his own name.[43] Although he repudiated his mentor, he was condemned thereafter to systematize the implications of Saint-Simon's thought in its 'scientific' and religious aspects, imparting to it a particularly strong Maistrian authoritarianism.

False solutions: the thirst for power

Before considering Saint-Simon's industrial answer to the conundrum of how to end the Revolution, we must first establish why this was not susceptible of a political solution; why constitutional attempts to organize power and militarist attempts at national aggrandizement were bound to fail because only the organization of the wealth-producing capacities of humanity could succeed in bringing domestic and international peace. Prior to Benjamin Constant (who more directly influenced Saint-Simon),

Montesquieu had stressed the role of trade in curbing warlike dynastic ambitions. His friend Jean-François Melon (in his *Essai politique sur le commerce* of 1734) had asserted: 'The spirit of conquest and the spirit of commerce are mutually exclusive in a nation.'[44] Under Montesquieu's influence, such ideas were taken further in Britain by Sir James Steuart in his *Inquiry into the Principles of Political Oeconomy* of 1767. 'When a state begins to subsist by the consequences of industry, there is less danger to be apprehended by the power of the sovereign. The mechanism of his administration becomes more complex, and. . .he finds himself so bound up by the laws of his political economy, that every transgression of them runs them into new difficulties', so that 'a modern oeconomy, therefore, is the most effective bridle ever invented against the folly of despotism.'[45]

Despite their emphasis upon agriculture or against trade and industry, the French physiocrats developed the conception of the economy as an intricate mechanism that was independent of the political will. Like Adam Smith, they agreed that it was difficult for governments to control the trader or the banker. As Quesnay and Mirabeau asserted, 'It would be useless for the authorities to force him to fulfil the duties of a subject: they are obliged in order to induce him to fit in with their plans, to treat him as a master, and to make it worth his while to contribute voluntarily to the public revenue.'[46] Adam Smith pushed the emphasis upon individual self-interest further, fusing the lust for power, vanity and acquisitive avarice into a single-minded striving which in self-seeking inadvertently served the public interest. 'Without any intervention of law, therefore, the private interests and passions of men naturally led them to divide and distribute the stock of every society, among all the different employments carried on in it, as nearly as possible in the proportions which is most agreeable to the interest of the whole society.'[47] Unlike Constant and Saint-Simon, who welcomed the decline in the aristocracy and the heroic martial spirit that resulted from the development of trade and industry, Adam Smith deplored it, while Constant, with his emphasis on political liberalism, acknowledged the conflict between individual and collective interests that Smith, Say and Saint-Simon discounted.

The implication of such ideas, not fully drawn in the eighteenth century, was that politics as the province of human folly should be superseded by work-centred production. Economics, separating itself from statecraft, should take the politics out of political economy. Say, Saint-Simon's mentor in these matters, praised Smith for beginning the separation of economics from politics and took issue with the latter-day physiocrat Dupont de Nemours who resisted their disjunction.[48] The *idéologues* generally, notably Roederer, Cabanis and Say, all argued in the late 1790s that the incentive to work, rather than state power, was the key to social organization, with the concomitant emphasis upon the need to eliminate unproductive idlers and give pride of place to those who organize productive work.[49] Saint-Simon was to take this conception of government as counter-productive much further, developing the notion of a self-administered, functionally inter-dependent industrial society. In the process, he would reject not only the popular sovereignty which, in the hands of the Jacobins and Napoleon, had retarded industrial development and promoted the aggressive nation-state instead of peaceful European federation. He also rejected the Maistrian conception of sovereignty, the only power required being diffused among the scientific and industrial meritocrats necessary to make society work harmoniously.

Praising 'the immortal Adam Smith' for stating the 'universal truths enunciated by the science of *political economy*', which Say had sharpened and made 'independent of *politics*', Saint-Simon characteristically oversimplified Smith's *Wealth of Nations*. Using the industrial enterprise as the model for the state, Smith is said to have provided 'refutations of all the actions of *governments*, and, consequently, it can perhaps be seen, as a whole, as a demonstration of how necessary it was for the people to change the *principles* and the *nature* of their *governments*, if they wanted to put an end to their poverty-stricken existence and to enjoy peace and the fruits of their labour.'[50] Why, asked Saint-Simon, had industry not acquired the political power to ensure the substitution of a regime based upon production for one based upon theft?[51] It was because the bourgeoisie that did so much to precipitate the Revolution and run it were not the industrial and scientific middle classes but the professional middle classes in association with the military.

The failure of the revolutionary experiment with liberal democracy was attributed by Saint-Simon in large measure to the 'transitional class' of philosopher–metaphysicians and (especially) extremist lawyers who had destroyed the old order but who were incapable of creating a new one. 'It is a fact that during the stormiest and most distressful years of the *Revolution*, France was governed by the *lawyers*', who had 'invented the *Reign of Terror*. . . .Bonaparte arrived and, in his turn, assumed supreme power. At once, this same body of *lawyers*, who only yesterday had professed the most die-hard *republicanism*; who had just invented the never-to-be-forgotten phrase, written in huge letters on all the walls, on all the public buildings: *Unity, indivisibility of the Republic; liberty, equality, fraternity or death*, were among the first to bow to the new *idol*.' He went on to attack 'these versatile creatures' with their 'unquenchable thirst for power' for seeking to restore Roman law despotism, source of 'the greatest despots who had ever lived', and 'the *science* practiced by the *lawyers*, as well as the *legal principles* which they undertake to apply.'[52] Just as the concentration of power had proved disastrous, so did the constitutional attempt to separate powers, by lawyers who had neither the requisite skills nor the moral authority which science alone could afford. (The shadow of Plato's distinction between 'knowledge' and 'opinion' hovers here.) Saint-Simon's cynicism on the score of democratic voting after the experience of the Revolution and Empire was great, and if there was to be a lawgiver he considered himself the only person fit for this auspicious function.

The first Restoration in 1814 seemed to Saint-Simon to afford an especially favourable opportunity to end the era of militarism and nationalism. As occurred in 1940, at another time of disastrous national defeat, a proposal was made for Franco-British unity, although in 1814 it took the form of *On the Reorganization of European Society* (written to influence the Congress of Vienna by Saint-Simon with Augustin Thierry), followed in 1815 by a letter to the minister of the interior and an appeal to all Englishmen and Frenchmen. The adoption of the English model of parliamentary government, as the best available, was undoubtedly influenced by its virtue by association with economic and military success and the need to find a compromise acceptable to French monarchists and republicans reflected in the constitutional charter adopted by Louis XVIII. More particularly, a friend of Saint-Simon's, Alexandre de Laborde, and possibly Benjamin Constant may have been the sources of inspiration. A joint Anglo-French Parliament, under English tutelage, would form the nucleus of a European federation but the proposed organization was extremely vague. Its authors seemed to rely upon a Maistrian exaggeration of medieval unity – 'Europe was formerly a confederate society united through common institutions and subject to a common government' – while not envisaging Maistre's 1819 conception of European federation which required acceptance of the Pope's temporal sovereignty, with Britain setting the example by returning to 'the *one* and *only* religion', Roman Catholicism.[53]

During the Hundred Days (March – June 1815) return of Napoleon, while Benjamin Constant was writing a new constitution, Saint-Simon was rescued from poverty by his old friend Lazare Carnot, ephemerally minister of the interior. In a characteristically euphoric letter to him, Saint-Simon asserted that 'the present era marks not only the end of the French Revolution, but also the beginning of the European Revolution without which the French Revolution would never end.'[54] However, Waterloo ended the bizarre dream that Napoleon – epitome of the militarist aberration – would be the progenitor of an Anglo-French-based European federation. The second Restoration prompted Saint-Simon's appeal 'To All Englishmen and Frenchmen who are zealous for the public good' to found an Anglo-French society to create what he had earlier called 'the community of moral and political principles, a kind of union of European nations, pending the day when they could join in a closer and more indissoluble union based on common institutions.'[55] His friend Say, while approving of Saint-Simon's sentiments, persuaded him not to publish this appeal because it would go over the heads of the public at which it was aimed. Instead, Saint-Simon now embarked upon a grandiose extrapolation from Say's liberal industrialist political economy. It was to be based upon a new spiritual and a new temporal power, as the way to end the democratic French Revolution by bringing about a European scientific and economic reorganization. He resoundingly proclaimed: 'The philosophy of the last century was revolutionary; that of the nineteenth century must be organizational.'[56]

Ending the Revolution: consensus through scientism

In *Le Politique* of 1819, one of the ephemeral periodicals through which Saint-Simon spread his ideas, he stated that the intellectual problem was to transform politics from a 'conjectural' into a 'positive' science, while the practical problem was how 'to end the liberal enterprise with which we began in 1789.'[57] He traced the prime cause of revolutions to a demand for equality which developed when those who governed lacked the capacity to rule effectively. While aristocratic privilege was no qualification to exercise political power, Saint-Simon regarded democratic election as leading first to domination by the ignorant and then to military dictatorship. To end the revolutionary process as well as to prevent its return, it was essential to organize social mobility on meritocratic lines so that the élite consisted of those most fit to govern. Authority would be reinforced because 'any governed person who merits it can enter the class of governors and the class of governors is consequently always more enlightened than the class of the governed'.[58] In an unpublished fragment of 1804 'On Social Organization', placed under the intellectual patronage of Condorcet, Saint-Simon elevated the capacity to manage into the panacea for revolutionary disorganization. 'The men who brought about the Revolution, the men who directed it, and the men who, since 1789 and up to the present day, have guided the nation, have committed a great political mistake. They have sought to improve the governmental machine, whereas they should have subordinated it and put administration in the first place. They should have begun by asking. . .who. . .are the men most fitted to manage the affairs of the nation. . . .They would have reached the conclusion that the scientists, artists and leaders of industrial enterprises are the men who should be entrusted with administrative power, i.e. with the responsibility for managing the national interest.'[59]

Frank Manuel has convincingly argued that the broad outlines of Saint-Simon's 'science of social organization' remained unchanged from 1802 until his death. 'What he chiefly vacillated about from one blueprint to another was the relative position of the proprietary industrialist and the scientist. During the course of his life's work he took every possible stand on this issue: he elevated the scientists to supremacy, he tried them as equals of the industrialists, and he raised the industrialists above the scientists. . . .He was never quite sure whether his scientists were to become a fully-fledged sacerdotal power or not.'[60] It was Auguste Comte who took this ultimate retrograde step of turning scientists into dogmatic, secular priests of positivism, even though Saint-Simon prepared the way. The latter had asserted that 'Religion is the collection of applications of general science by means of which enlightened men rule the ignorant.' He subsequently declared, ominously, that 'when politics has risen to the ranks of the sciences of observation. . .politics will be entrusted exclusively to a special class of scientists who will impose silence on all twaddle.'[61]

It is important to bear in mind that, in different forms, the need for a scientifically based spiritual power, fulfilling the macro-political function of underpinning a social unity that was threatened by political, social and economic conflict, had become an early-nineteenth-century commonplace. Since Condorcet, an ideological social science had become a rationalist alternative to Christianity, while Madame de Staël, Benjamin Constant, François Guizot and Edgar Quinet were to argue the claims of Protestantism. Yet in the early Restoration, a resurgent Roman Catholicism threatened to sweep all before it, even – in the wake of Maistre – subordinating the temporal power of the king. Not only had the charter proclaimed Roman Catholicism the state religion but in 1817 Maistre's faithful correspondent, Count Blacas, had as ambassador to the Vatican negotiated a return (with adaptations) to the 1516 concordat with the Pope. These moves contributed to the church-state struggles of the 1820s, which culminated with the expulsion of the Jesuits in 1828. Triumphant Roman Catholicism, far from acting as a politically unifying force, in fact broke up the Restoration politico-religious coalition by provoking the anticlerical aristocracy into opposition (led notably by Montlosier) and exacerbating the Gallican–Ultramontane battle (sparked notably by Lamennais).[62] Exploiting this disarray of its opponents, the liberal bourgeoisie was able to use the issue in the campaign that led to the overthrow of Charles X in 1830. Saint-Simon, seeking in science an indisputable counterweight to anticlericalism, declared in 1808 that 'The catechism is the most important of all books because it is the scientific (*sic*) bond which unites all social classes.'[63] It was Comte who gave this new-style clericalism its full expression.

In his 1826 essay 'Considerations on the spiritual power', Comte provided a 'positivist commentary on the ideas of Maistre', who had displaced Say, the advocate of industrialism, as the way of attaining consensus.[64] Comte attributed the 'great revolutionary catastrophes . . . to the spiritual disorganization of society'. The French Revolution had created a centralized 'administrative despotism' by subordinating the spiritual to the temporal power, leading to 'the most degrading of despotisms, that of force destitute of all moral authority'.[65] It had also destroyed the European balance of power. To reconstitute a modern version of medieval Europe-wide 'moral communism', Maistre was the indispensable guide; his '*Du Pape* has given the most systematic, profound and precise exposition' of it and the Catholic clergy is Comte's model for the new scientistic spiritual power.'[66] Comte flattered himself that thanks to the combined influence of his 'principal precursor, the illustrious and unfortunate Condorcet' and 'the most eminent thinker of the contemporary Catholic school, the illustrious de Maistre', whose rehabilitation of the past complemented Condorcet's futurism, 'positivism simultaneously achieves the noblest social aims of medieval Catholicism and the most important preconditions of the great programme of the Convention.'[67] It was no accident that Saint-Simon's doctrine took a less liberal turn from 1819, after Comte's absorption of Maistre's *Du Pape*, which Saint-Simon, always reluctant to read, imbibed at second hand. However, Saint-Simon had always adopted a more utilitarian attitude towards religion. His appeal for a social religion of 'New Christianity' just before his death did not lead him to subordinate his industrialist political economy to a scientistic sacerdotalism. Instead, he used the moralistic appeal of fraternity to give industrialism a more humane purpose.

Consensus through meritocratic industrialism

Of much greater long-term importance than his views on religion were the ideas that led Saint-Simon to discern the predominantly industrial character of the future. Saint-Simon's rejection of democracy and nationalism was based upon a more fundamental rejection of the classical conception of man as above all a political animal, a citizen who participated in government and patriotically defended his country. This repudiation of the civic humanist tradition, which the French Revolution had inherited via Rousseau, from Aristotle, led Saint-Simon to seek a new basis for the political community and its management. As religious beings, men would find fulfilment in social solidarity or interdependence; what a disciple of his, Pierre Leroux (in a letter to Georges Sand in 1841) was to call 'communionism'. As thinking beings, scientism would provide the means of managing those affairs that would remain the concern of the state. As acquisitive beings, men would fulfil their economic interests in productive activity through the market. Having considered Saint-Simon's communionism and scientism, it remains for us to explore his industrialism.

Far from commerce being a source of corruption, eighteenth-century political economy had tended to demonstrate, following Mandeville, that private vices were public benefits. In particular, greed, when transmuted into self-interest, became a cure for power lust. 'The belief that interest could be considered a dominant motive of human behaviour caused considerable intellectual excitement: at last a realistic basis for a viable social order had been discovered.'[68] Whereas disinterested behaviour would be unpredictable, the insatiable desire for wealth could be relied upon to operate among all people, at all times and in all places. Furthermore, by comparison with the sanguinary if heroic aristocratic pursuit of glory, the peaceful pursuit of commercial profit could be presented as innocuous. As a companion to Mandeville's dictum we may cite Dr Johnson's: 'There are few ways in which a man can be more innocently employed than in getting money.'[69] Rather than vainly expending one's energies in hazardous exercises in the fragile, formal legalism of constitutional engineering, it was better to rely upon the robust economic functionalism of the industrial constitution, based upon the division of labour and exchange. Power-seeking would be displaced by the profit incentive as the prime motive force in society. The new categorical imperative would be Guizot's call in 1841 to 'Enrich yourselves by work and saving.'[70] What was intended as a summons to acquire electoral qualification through increased wealth was interpreted by the contemporary bourgeoisie, like posterity, as merely an incitement to self-enrichment.

Among the French forerunners of Saint-Simon's 'industrialism', one may mention *pour mémoire* Joseph Barnave, a prominent Third Estate leader of first the revolutionary Jacobin Club and then the moderate Feuillants Club. As so many were to do thereafter Barnave, having prematurely asserted in 1791 that 'The Revolution is over', withdrew in disillusionment from politics in 1792. Given the turmoil of the times, what he wrote in the year before he died in 1793 appears to have exercised no immediate influence, even though 'Barnave sketched out in outline the whole theory of "industrialism" twenty-five years before it was actually discovered' according to Shirley Gruner.[71] Instead, the ground was laid by the *idéologues*, preceded by Condillac's exposition of utilitarian liberalism, *Commerce and Government Considered in Relation to Each Other*. This appeared in the same year (1776) as Smith's *Wealth of Nations*, which exercised a more decisive influence through Say upon Saint-Simon.

It seems to have been Pierre-Louis Roederer, in a 1795 article (the year when the first chair of economics was established in France, at the *Ecole Normale*), who launched the 'industrialist' economic analysis proper through a critique of the physiocratic doctrine that land was the source of all wealth. From the start, it was a deliberate challenge to the vested interests of the landowning and *rentier* classes, with their claim to exorbitant political privilege. Reversing the physiocratic distinction between productive land and unproductive industry, Roederer stressed that it was the industrial capitalists and skilled workers who alone deserved political rights because they had an interest in protecting their investments through public order.[72] 'Order, order, there is the object of all constitutions, the task of all governments, the principle of all prosperity.'[73] Because the French Revolution had made class conflicts brutally explicit, Roederer, like the other *idéologues*, was concerned to discover ways of achieving social consensus between unequal classes. Enrichment through work was the key to social order, the private vice of egotistic self-interest becoming the public virtues of productive cooperation and social harmony. Better than a police force, work would reconcile the antagonistic productive classes, developing 'esteem and reciprocal regard through the sentiment of their mutual dependence'.[74] Roederer became absorbed into Napoleon's imperial administration in the first decade of the nineteenth century and it was left to Jean-Baptiste Say and Destutt de Tracy to champion the industrialist school of political economy.

Both Say and Tracy based their political economy on a conception of the solidarity between producers, itself based upon the division of labour. Specialization, anathema to the all-round civic humanist, had – especially since Adam Smith – been accepted as the productive basis of a maximizing economic interdependence. Tracy sweepingly argued that 'commerce is the whole of society, as labour is the whole of wealth.' On the ground that man was an 'exchanging animal', Tracy extrapolated to universal solidarity. 'Commerce, exchange, being society itself, is the unique link among men, the source of all their moral sentiments, and the first and most powerful cause of the development of their mutual sensibility and reciprocal benevolence . . . it begins by reconciling all the men of the same tribe, then it links societies together, and it ends up uniting the whole world.'[75]

Rather than concerning himself with divisive political arguments about the rights of man or forms of government, Say (a descendant of Huguenot refugees in Geneva) argued in the various editions of his *Treatise on Political Economy* and in his 1815 *Catechism of Political Economy* that there was no correlation between efficient production and type of government. Economic facts, not political rights, should be the subject matter investigated.[76] This was the counter-revolutionary recipe for domestic and international peace. However, where Say parted company with Adam Smith, Ricardo, Tracy and Karl Marx was in his rejection of the labour theory of value in favour of utility. He switched the emphasis from 'objective' production to 'subjective' consumption. Utility represented exchange value, not the amount of labour needed to produce a commodity. More relevant to our purpose, he replaced Smith's identification of labour with productive activity by the more comprehensive concept of 'industry'. Instead of Roederer's four classes, Say divided the 'industrious' into three classes: scientists, entrepreneurs and workers. Say's crucial contribution to the concept of entrepreneur, previously used by Quesnay, Turgot and Smith, was to distinguish the capitalist who carried the enterprise's financial risks from the entrepreneur who organized and managed it, although in practice entrepreneurs frequently also provided part of the capital. Having escaped from Napoleon's persecution of the *idéologues* by becoming a textile spinning manufacturer from 1804–12, Say's political experience led him to develop his arguments concerning the role of the entrepreneur from the second edition of his *Treatise* in 1814. Thereafter, for Say, 'the entrepreneur is the central figure in the economy. He is the universal mediator. He mediates between the landlord and the capitalist, between the scientist and the manual labourer, between the various suppliers of productive services among one another, and between producers and consumers.'[77] This entrepreneur-centred conception of political economy was extended and popularized by Tracy and Saint-Simon.

Tracy accentuated Say's 'denigration of landed wealth, and draws out even more sharply the distinction between the "industrious" and the "idle" classes. . . .Even more vividly in Tracy's work than in Say's, the entrepreneur (from the richest manufacturer to the smallest independent farmer) emerges as the prototypically productive member of society. Tracy notes that the *savant* (scientist) and the *ouvrier* (worker) will always be in the pay of the entrepreneur, since there must first be an enterprise to which they can contribute.'[78] He distinguished between idle *rentier* capitalists and active entrepreneurial capitalists, arguing that in industrial society 'those who live on wages, those who live on rent and those who live on profits, form three essentially different classes of men.'[79] Tracy attacked the exorbitant social and political influence of the idle capitalists and landed aristocracy, by contrast with productive wage- and profit-earners. Although he was himself one of France's largest and richest absentee landlords, Tracy is closer to his fellow aristocrat Saint-Simon than to Say in his indictment of the unproductive consumers of wealth. Because every individual's happiness is equally important, Tracy argues that the largest number – the wage-earning poor – should be the beneficiaries of redistributive taxes on the *rentiers*. 'Humanity, justice, statecraft alike require that of all interests, those of the poor should be always the most constantly considered and respected; and by the poor I mean simply wage-earners, and above all those whose work is the worst paid.'[80] Despite Say's law of markets, which purported to show that because production created equivalent aggregate demand, overproduction was impossible and that there was a natural harmony of interests between all producers, both Tracy and Say recognized the danger of an increasing inequality of wealth arising from entrepreneurs exploiting their stronger bargaining power to secure an increased share of wealth at the expense of the workers.[81] Saint-Simon was to go further, both in eulogizing the industrialists and in acknowledging their limitations, formulating an ideology that became more influential than that of the *idéologues*.

In his earliest writings, Saint-Simon had distinguished three conflicting classes of scientific and artistic intellectuals, property owners and the others. Rejecting the French revolutionary principle of equality, he looked to the collaboration of the spiritual power of the intellectuals with the proprietors to ensure that the enlightened would dominate.[82] In an 1815 article in *Le Censeur*, edited by disciples of Say who were also soon to embrace the industrialist cause, Saint-Simon was still advocating the need to create an opposition party to defend the interests of the *rentier* owners of 'national property' acquired during the Revolution. However, Saint-Simon did not champion the cause of the increasing class of state *rentiers* who lived from the gilt-edged securities of the national debt because by late 1816 he had grasped Say's distinction between rentiers and industrialists. In fact, it was his collaborator Augustin Thierry who in January 1817 published the first clearly industrialist article in Saint-Simon's new review *Industry*, which in the April 1817 issue acquired its banner slogan: 'Everything by industry; everything for it.' In his pioneering article 'On nations', Thierry asserted *inter alia* that 'a nation is nothing but a large industrial enterprise' and that producers must be given priority over property owners.[83] However,

Thierry himself turned his attentions to the early history of how bourgeois liberalism emerged in France and England; Saint-Simon devoted himself to its triumph in the present and the future.

While Say and his liberal friends were politically concerned with changing the electoral law to ensure that the industrial interests would secure a parliamentary majority, Saint-Simon's aims were far more ambitious if less practical. Although it was not until 1824 that Saint-Simon coined the term 'industrialism' to distinguish his would-be 'scientific' doctrine from revolutionary liberalism and summon the industrialists to form a separate party, he had much earlier used the word *industriel* to mean not just industrial activity but the industrialists who engaged in it, those initially described as 'industrious'. 'We invite all industrialists who are dedicated to the public good and who are aware of the connections between the general interests of society and those of industry, no longer to allow themselves to be called *liberals*. We invite them to unfurl a new flag and inscribe on their banner the device: *Industrialism* . . . the only way to establish a calm and stable order of things lies in entrusting with the supreme administration of national wealth those who contribute most money to the public treasury and who take out the least. We invite them to call themselves *industrialists*.'[84] In the 'Declaration of Principles' for *Industry*, Saint-Simon made clear that by 'industry' he meant 'the most important firms' capable of a conception of the common interest. 'Industry is but one single vast body' guided by the leaders, who constituted the 'head alone which does the thinking for the body'.[85] The organicism and élitism of the *idéologues* were blatant but they were to take a form that duly led to the divorce from liberalism.

While economic determinists are inclined to see a close causal connection between the Industrial Revolution and the French Revolution, in fact France's industrial revolution – a term apparently coined by Auguste Blanqui's economist brother, Adolphe Blanqui, in 1837 – occurred well after its political revolution. Furthermore, the difficulty which 'industrialism' had in winning support was partly the consequence of French industrial backwardness and partly because of its deliberately *anti-revolutionary* character. 'Industrialism and its theoretical framework did emerge out of the politics of the French Revolution. . .but less as a means to translate the ideals of the French Revolution into reality than as a way of putting an end to social and political disorders the Revolution had caused.'[86] It was their combination of political conservatism and economic liberalism that led Saint-Simon to give the industrialists pride of place in ending domestic revolution and foreign wars. In contrast with the lawyers, the industrialists had been concerned with peaceful production, not with the seizure of power. Their three consistent aims were: '1. to avoid any political upheaval and therefore never to change the form of the established *government*, no matter what it may be; 2. to limit the action of *power* and to restrain it as much as possible; 3. to diminish the cost of *government* and all misuse of *taxation*'; from which he concluded that 'It is in the interests of *those who govern* and *those who are governed* to extend the *political importance of the industrialists*.'[87]

Having in his 1817 'Declaration of Principles' stated that government's sole task was to 'prevent the violence with which idleness threatens industry', so that producers could pursue their self-interest free from the 'throng of parasites' and 'idlers, i.e. thieves',[88] Saint-Simon went on to assert that 'industrial ideas' alone would permit 'the end of revolution'. In the sixth of his 'Letters to an American', he preached that 'the sole aim to which all our thoughts and efforts ought to be directed *is the organization most favourable to industry.* . . .Such organization calls for a government under which the activity and force of the political power are no more than is necessary to prevent useful work being hindered, a government under which everything is arranged so that the workers, whose association forms the true society, can exchange directly with each other and with complete freedom the products of their various labours;' before asserting that 'the moment has come for the general revolution. . . . Governments will no longer command men; their functions will be limited to ensuring that useful work is not hindered. They will no longer have at their disposal more than a small amount of power or money, for their aim will require no more.'[89] In considering Proudhon in Chapter 7, we shall have occasion to see the anarcho-socialist direction in which such striking but loosely formulated ideas could be taken, although this was very far from Saint-Simon's intention in 1817.

In his eighth 'Letter to an American', Saint-Simon made abundantly clear that his inspiration was Say's *Treatise on Political Economy*, which 'comprises all that political economy has yet discovered and demonstrated. It is at present the *nec plus ultra* of that science in Europe.'[90] Going further than Say, who regarded 'politics and political economy as two distinct and separate things', Saint-Simon argued that 'political economy is the true and sole foundation of politics' and would 'soon rise to its true position. At first it was dependent on politics; in future politics will depend on it, or rather it will comprise the whole of politics. . . .In short, therefore, politics is the *science of production*', Saint-Simon summarizing 'every observed fact in political science' in seven propositions. The first three state '1. The production of useful things is the only reasonable and positive aim that political societies can set themselves. Consequently, the principle *respect for production and producers* is infinitely more fruitful than *respect for property and property owners*. 2. Government always damages industry when it meddles in its affairs, even when it tries to encourage it. . .; 3. As the producers of useful things are the only useful men in society, they alone should come together to regulate its development. And as they are the only men who really pay taxes, they alone should have the right to vote taxation.'[91] Such was the 'scientific' foundation on which Saint-Simon launched his 'Producers of the World Unite' programme to unify humanity in the peaceful pursuit of commercial cooperation for mutual profit and political stability.

Saint-Simon's propaganda campaign on behalf of industrialism almost coincided with a similar campaign by the editors of *Le Censeur Européen*, Charles Comte and Charles Dunoyer, whose offices were in the same building as those of *L'Industrie*. Charles Comte (no family connection with Auguste Comte, who contributed some articles to the *Censeur Européen*) had made the acquaintance of Say in 1814 and became his son-in-law in 1818. Not only did the two journals share the same ideological paternity and physical proximity; Augustin Thierry, who had steered Saint-Simon first in the direction of political and then economic liberalism, influenced the editors of the *Censeur Européen* before leaving Saint-Simon in 1817 to join them. (He ran the journal single-handed while they were imprisoned that year for infringing the press laws, the *Censeur Européen* having been seized by the censor!)[92] The Hundred Days fiasco of 1814 had simply underlined the futility of dealing with the deep-seated socio-economic causes of the post-revolutionary crisis by political improvisation. Both Saint-Simon and Dunoyer confirmed the simultaneity of their adoption of industrialist ideas, Dunoyer (who was to become a prefect under the July Monarchy) conceding paternity of the term 'industrialism' to Saint-Simon.

Their immediate forerunners included Benjamin Constant, who in 1813 had declared that the era of war having been replaced by that of trade, 'The sole purpose of modern nations is. . .Industry'; Montlosier, who had stressed the historic role of the trading bourgeois towns in the elimination of feudalism; and above all, Say's political economy of industrial production.[93] Constant had not developed his initial argument further and in fact had strong reservations about seeking the predominance of industrialism, being allergic to the illiberal political aspects of Saint-Simon's programme. As he wrote to him: 'Your ideas are fine but I see difficulties about putting them into practice. I do not believe that the clash of systems can be terminated forever. I do not even believe that it would be good for humanity.'[94] Constant shared some of his friend Sismondi's reservations on the score of unrestrained, productivist economic liberalism, without necessarily appreciating the significance of the overproduction argument with which Sismondi attacked Say's law of markets. What particularly worried liberals like Constant was Saint-Simon's desire to go beyond 'commercial government' towards a belief that industrialism would achieve love of one's earthly neighbours, elevating positivistic social science into an authoritarian religion that endeavoured to eliminate conflict. Adding Maistre to Say was unacceptable. In other words, Constant was tactfully and by anticipation reacting to Saint-Simon as John Stuart Mill would subsequently and more vehemently react against Auguste Comte's 'frenzy for regulation' and 'systematization'.[95]

In need of financial support for *L'Industrie*, the protagonist of industry as the universal panacea naturally turned to businessmen such as Jacques Laffitte, the son of a carpenter, who had been an employee and then partner in the Perrégaux Bank (France's leading bank), which managed Saint-Simon's account when he was a rich land speculator. By 1808 Laffitte had taken over control, as one of a select group of some twenty leaders of *la haute banque*, before becoming governor of the Bank of France and (after the 1830 Revolution in which he played a leading part) an ephemeral prime minister at the start of the July Monarchy. Explaining in his *Memoirs* how he had doubled the profits of the Perrégaux Bank within three years of taking over, he wrote: 'It involved borrowing idle capital and then lending it to industry which is always in need.'[96]

After the imperial impetus petered out, the narrowness of the Restoration capital market is indicated by the fact that only seven shares were quoted on the Stock Exchange in 1816 and thirteen in 1820, rising to thirty-eight by 1830. Laffitte had managed to save the Stock Exchange from financial collapse in 1818 by loaning 5 million francs to some of those threatened with bankruptcy. He then extended his operations from public finance to investment banking. The early 1820s witnessed the first real industrial surge in France, which gave dynamic entrepreneurs a new sense of their importance at a time when France's reactionary political establishment was extremely anti-industrial. 'With the Second Restoration the *émigrés* swarmed into France resolved to resurrect prerevolutionary society. . . .But the great industrialists and bankers of France, who had acquired a consciousness of their power during the past quarter of a century, no longer were content to occupy a secondary status in the realm. Bankers like Casimir Périer (Laffitte's successor as Prime Minister in 1831), Delessert and Laffitte, industrialists like Ternaux and Richard Lenoir. . .refused to humble themselves before an *émigré* aristocracy returning to France in the train of the foreign occupation forces with all its inherited prejudices against commerce and industry intact.'[97] So the industrial lobby was pleased to have an aristocrat like Saint-Simon to act as a paid publicist and pamphleteer and subscribed to his publishing ventures while feeling more at ease with predictable liberal political economists like Say.

The first two volumes of *L'Industrie* – before the advent of Auguste Comte as Saint-Simon's secretary, coinciding with a shift away from pro-business propaganda towards sweeping expositions of historicist relativism and scientistic social reorganization – attracted the financial subscriptions of many members of the French business élite. They included seven out of fourteen regents of the Bank of France, as well as its governor Laffitte; ten out of fifteen leaders of the Paris Chamber of Commerce; the prominent woollen manufacturer Ternaux; and Lafayette, a link with Saint-Simon's youthful military service in America as well as with Restoration liberalism. Laffitte provided Saint-Simon, then and subsequently, with the most sustained and substantial financial support. After serving as Napoleon's banker, Laffitte played a crucial part in providing the loans to meet France's war debts, as well as personally lending Louis XVIII 5·7 million francs in March 1815 and 2 million to the government to pay the army in July 1815. (With acute anticipation he also lent the future Louis-Philippe 1·6 million francs in 1815.)

Laffitte personified Saint-Simon's conception of the innovative new monied meritocracy whose banking power was destined to displace political power. During the Restoration he became a liberal opposition deputy (acquiring Saint-Simon's former secretary, Augustin Thierry, as his parliamentary secretary), but the main source of his authority was his banking power. This new-style banker, it was said, 'treats the state like a private individual, a client to whom as an experienced banker he gives advice.'[98] However, he followed up his discreet support for the Orleanist cause during the Restoration by financing *Le National*, the newspaper edited by Adolphe Thiers and Armand Carrel, which played a key role in the agitation that culminated in the July 1830 Revolution. Though he stayed in bed when the revolutionary students from the *Ecole Polytechnique* called to involve him in the conflict, Louis Blanc attributes to him most influence over the Revolution's Orleanist outcome. Wealthy and popular, 'Although he was not suited to play a revolutionary role in the streets, none better than he was able to manage a palace revolution.'[99]

He deliberately chose a back seat in the first July Monarchy government as minister without portfolio but with the revolutionary process and financial crisis threatening to get out of hand, Laffitte – who with Lafayette led the Orleanist Left – was asked to form a government in November 1830, excluding the *doctrinaires* of the Orleanist Right. In the wave of bankruptcies that struck France in late 1830, Laffitte's own bank was embarrassingly forced into liquidation in December despite loans of 12 million francs from the Bank of France and 6 million from Louis-Philippe. With Lafayette tricked into resigning his key command of the National Guard and Laffitte, ridiculed as 'M. Faillite' (Mr Bankruptcy), 'torn between cultivating his popularity and seeking to preserve his creditworthiness', the reactionary and repressive wing of the bourgeoisie was installed in office by the king in March 1831 virtually for the duration of the July Monarchy.[100] Narrowly failing to become president of the Chamber of Deputies, Laffitte returned to industrial banking, in the dynamic Saint-Simonian style that was later identified with Péreire's *Crédit Mobilier*, which dominated promotional industrial banking during the Second Empire.

Another major and continuing source of financial support for Saint-Simon was provided by the avant-garde, self-made woollen textile manufacturer from Reims Louis Ternaux, who was with Laffitte the only non-deputy to serve on the Budget Consultative Committee in 1816 to deal with financing France's war debts. Made a baron by Louis XVIII, Ternaux became a *doctrinaire* liberal deputy in 1818. He beat Benjamin Constant on the third ballot, with the support of pro-government votes, concerned to keep out of parliament the more dangerous Constant. This industrialist, who prospered and was honoured during the Napoleonic Empire and Bourbon Restoration, was a leader of France's new industrial aristocracy. He has been described as 'perhaps the greatest entrepreneur in France in the earlier nineteenth century', owning more than thirty woollen textile mills and marketing outlets, employing over 20,000 workers.[101] The *Chant des Industriels* by Rouget de Lisle, the composer of France's national anthem (hence the '*Marseillaise* of Labour'), was performed in 1821 for Saint-Simon, Ternaux and his St-Ouen workers, Saint-Simon having introduced Rouget de Lisle to Ternaux and suggested the idea of a song glorifying industrialists. (The music was composed by the Saint-Simonian Félicien David.) Ternaux used his influence on the governing body of the *Conservatoire des Arts et Métiers* to secure his friend Jean-Baptiste Say's appointment to the first French chair of industrial economics. It was to his ally and patron Ternaux that Saint-Simon wrote a despairing suicide note before he tried unsuccessfully to shoot himself in 1823, convinced that he would not live to see his reforms implemented. Ternaux and Laffitte continued their financial support after he recovered and resumed his work, although like Laffitte Ternaux was forced into bankruptcy in 1830 in the general financial crisis, having in the meantime moved from manufacturing cashmere shawls into banking. However, by then Saint-Simon had been in his grave for five years, although Saint-Simonism was at last beginning to acquire notoriety.

Replacing politics by administration: the entrepreneurial élites

To understand the frustration and resentment of the thrusting entrepreneurial élites that were seeking to translate their increasing wealth into acknowledged social prestige and political power, it must be remembered that in the 1820s the aristocracy once again dominated the upper ranks of the government, the army, the administration, the judiciary and the Church. Because taxation of land was three times heavier than on trade and industry, the aristocracy predominated among those who were eligible, who themselves formed 16,000 out of a parliamentary electorate of 100,000. Of the 700 wealthiest notables in 1821, it has been calculated that three-quarters were aristocrats.[102]

Saint-Simon argued that the failures of the old aristocracy had led to the 1789 Revolution and that the revolutionary process would only end with the advent of a competent new aristocracy, marking the conclusion of a class struggle whose historical development had been comprehensively and graphically traced by Montlosier. 'We shall see arise in the midst of the old state a new state; in the midst of the old people a new people; in the midst of old customs, old institutions and old laws, new customs, new institutions, new laws. We shall see a double state, a double people, a double social order, marching side by side for a long time, finally fighting each other and fighting bitterly. Such is this great revolution which has been in itself the source of a multitude of revolutions, a revolution which, spreading through Europe, has covered it with wars and disorders. . . has everywhere left a multitude of new rights, new states, doctrines and constitutions.'[103] With this inspiration, and in the context of a Revolution in which his fellow aristocrats had been proscribed as a class and in which the return of the *émigrés* in the Restoration provoked the *parvenu* bourgeoisie into resistance against their resubordination to the idle privileged, Saint-Simon went on to formulate a class-based philosophy of history. The historical process would involve the rise of a new industrialist ruling class, which would end conflict worldwide without ending the subordination of some classes to others. But before the golden age of industrial society could come about, the idle and unproductive would first have to be eliminated from their dominant place in society.

Saint-Simon achieved his greatest notoriety in his own lifetime with his trial in 1820 on a charge of 'moral complicity' in the assassination of the Duc de Berry, heir apparent to the throne. Saint-Simon had published, in the polemical, pamphleteering style of the period, a 'Political Parable', as it was subsequently dubbed by a disciple. He had previously given deliberately provocative expression to the idea that society was divided into bees and drones, a notion originally suggested in Plato's *Republic* but more recently applied to France by d'Argenson and especially by Destutt de Tracy and Dunoyer with the suggestion that the unproductive drones should be eliminated. Saint-Simon's most direct precursor was the French revolutionary Rabout de St-Etienne, who in an influential 1788 pamphlet had declared: 'Remove by supposition the 200,000 clergy and you still have the nation. Remove by supposition all the nobles and you still have the nation. But remove the 24 million Frenchmen who constitute the third estate and what will you have left? Nobles and clergy but not the nation.'[104]

Comparing the 'national or industrial party' of those who worked with the 'anti-national party' of unproductive consumers, Saint-Simon claimed in 1819 that 'the industrials outnumber by at least fifty to one the supporters of that system in which the bees are ruled by the drones.'[105] Now he proposed as a hypothesis that France was suddenly deprived of its fifty best scientists, artists, industrialists, bankers, skilled workers and craftsmen in each socially useful activity. The result would be catastrophic because they were essential to the nation's prosperity. If instead France suddenly lost the 30,000 people reported to be the most important in the state – the royal family, ministers, generals, bishops, the rich and idle *rentiers* who lived off unearned income – 'it would not result in any political harm to the State. . . . These suppositions demonstrate the most important fact about contemporary politics. . .that men still allow themselves to be governed by violence and ruse. . .that society today is really a world upside down.' The poor were denied their essential needs so that the superfluities of the rich property owners could be needlessly increased, while 'in every kind of occupation incapable men are in charge of capable men.'[106]

With publication in November 1819, Saint-Simon was arrested in January 1820 and the affair took a much more serious turn with the murder in February of the heir apparent, named in the article, *Mikado*-like, as one of those who would 'not be missed'. Initially found guilty, Saint-Simon was acquitted on appeal, acquiring great prestige in liberal circles, as well as popularizing the idea that positions of power were only justified by social utility. His blunt, meritocratic attack on the privileges and domination of a caste recruited on the basis of birth and unearned wealth led prominent bankers (Fould and Schlumberger, as well as Laffitte), prominent scientists (Arago and Cuvier) and liberals like Lafayette and Say to rally to his support at a time of sharp ideological polarization, with the ultras in the ascendant.

Saint-Simon had already taken the firm liberal line that government was an unproductive but necessary evil and that good government was cheap government. All that would survive of the coercive state would be a modest police power, because governments should avoid economic regulation, and pacific free trade would eliminate the state's traditional function of making war. Unlike some of his posthumous socialist followers, who wanted the state to take over industry, Saint-Simon intended industry to take over the state. Saint-Simon agreed with Say, who rejected the 'entrepreneur state', but went further. The entrepreneurs should not only run industry but should assume overall responsibility for the administrative management of society, so that despite their current political indifference to being governed by others, 'in time sovereignty will be exercised exclusively by the industrialists'.[107] Sovereignty would become a collective, non-coercive, self-evident expression of scientific determinism. He asserted that 'there is no longer any room for the arbitrariness of men, or even of laws. . . .The act of governing, in the sense of commanding, then plays no or almost no part. . .decisions can only be the result of scientific demonstrations, absolutely independent of all human will, which may be discussed by all those educated enough to understand them', so that 'the three principal disadvantages of the present political system – arbitrariness, incapacity and intrigue – will be seen to disappear all at once.'[108]

Nevertheless, despite the scientism of this theoretical argument, Saint-Simon in practice believed that entrepreneurs could manage the state's activities like a bank or a textile mill, as he expounded in detail from 1820. In his important series of public 'letters' entitled 'Considerations on the measures necessary to end the Revolution', Saint-Simon declared that the leading Paris bankers were to direct the combined political action of the industrialists and be invested with political power. In particular, 'Every citizen employed in public administration must have served his apprenticeship in industrial administration.' The key Ministry of Finance and the budget should be in charge of a banker industrialist and 'The object of the budget's first article, on the expenditure side, will be to secure the existence of the proletarians by providing work for all fit men and relief for the ill.'[109]

He appealed to the king to become an industrial dictator, to destroy in a series of ordinances the old order in the name of 'true Christianity' because 'A radical change in the social system can only be effected by insurrection or dictatorship; and it is incontestable that dictatorship is a lesser evil than insurrection.'[110] Saint-Simon's formula for 'ending the revolution' was not simply to leave the liberated entrepreneurs to run society individually. The profit motive had to be supplemented by public works planning of transport, industry and agriculture, as well as of credit;

hence the important role reserved in 'industrial government' for bankers like Jacques Laffitte, who had always blamed French economic backwardness compared to Britain on inadequate credit and whose attempts to remedy this had been blocked by state control.[111] Saint-Simon's industrial constitution would establish three functionally representative assemblies. The Chamber of Invention would have the task of public works planning; hence the importance of engineers in its composition, combining as they did scientific, technological and industrial capabilities. A Review Chamber, in which scientists predominated, would consider these plans as well as preparing a general scheme for public education. Lastly, the Chamber of Deputies would be reconstituted on functionally representative lines in proportion to each industry's importance and be renamed the Chamber of Implementation, responsible for supervising the carrying out of the plans and for taxation.[112] These proposals clearly indicate the extent to which Saint-Simon had departed from political liberalism. Despite his concern for the welfare of the workers, how close had he come to socialism?

In 1820 Sismondi had, in his *New Principles of Political Economy*, separated the 'industrial class' into irreconcilably opposed capitalists and proletarians, the former seeking maximum profit, while the latter sought to raise their wages above subsistence level. Sismondi was pessimistic about ending (almost anticipating Saint-Simon's words) 'the sufferings of the most numerous and perhaps the most essential classes of society.'[113] Manuel has observed that 'In his Empire and early Restoration writings, Saint-Simon used the term *prolétaires* as synonymous with "the ignorant". . . .After 1820 Saint-Simon's sentiments towards the French proletariat underwent a complete metamorphosis and working-class humanitarianism became a dominant motif in his writings.'[114] Some workers had risen to become industrial entrepreneurs, which indicated that they had the industrial capacity to share fully in the plans to exploit the earth's resources for the collective good rather than continuing themselves to suffer exploitation. Although it was the Saint-Simonians who were to take these ideas much further, Saint-Simon was content to call for the reorganization of society 'to improve in the quickest and most complete way possible the moral and physical life of the most numerous' and 'the poorest class.'[115] Although he rejected the revolutionary principles of liberty and equality, the dialogues between a conservative and an innovator that constitute his 'New Christianity' essentially added fraternity to his social science of industrialism.

In 1820, Comte presented Saint-Simon's ideas in the form of a modernist industrial partnership between workers and managers under the leadership of capitalist entrepreneurs. 'In the old system the people were *enrolled* under their leaders; in the new they are *combined* with them. The military leaders *commanded*; the industrial leaders only *direct*. In the first case the people were *subjects*, in the second they are *partners*. . . .All the participants are in fact co-workers and partners, from the humblest workmen to the richest manufacturer and the ablest engineer.'[116] Without industrial leadership, workers would become Luddites, so they would need to be incorporated as junior partners into the new industrial society if it was to be both fully productive and durably peaceful.

Saint-Simon's counter-revolutionary legacies

Although the precise nature of Saint-Simon's influence has been much debated, its extent and diversity have seldom been questioned. Unlike Marx – with his eye particularly on Britain – who regarded industrial revolution as the prelude to political revolution, Saint-Simon – focused upon French experience – proffered an industrialist 'vision of the coming resubordination of the individual to society'.[117] E. H. Carr was well aware that far from being a socialist for which he has often been mistaken or the liberal he sometimes pretended to be, Saint-Simon was the protagonist of a modernizing tech- nocratic managerialism under the leadership of the bankers. The evidence we have presented abundantly confirms this interpretation. More generally, Carr argued that far from halting the revolutionary process, 'the study of Saint-Simon often seems to suggest that the great French Revolution, not content with the ideas which inspired and which it spread over the contemporary world, also projected into the future a fresh ferment of ideas which, working beneath the surface, were to be the social and political revolutions of a hundred years to come . . . .Saint-Simon died at the age of sixty-five in 1825, on the eve of a period of unprecedented material progress and sweeping social and political change; and his writings again and again gave an uncanny impression of one who had a hurried preview of the next hundred years history and excited, confused and only half understanding, tried to set down disjointed fragments of what he had seen.'[118]

Frank Manuel has pointed to the paradox of the prototypical finance capitalist Péreire brothers paying for the posthumous publication of Saint-Simon's complete works and for the care of his grave at Père Lachaise, while in Moscow an obelisk records that Saint-Simon was a predecessor of the Communist Revolution. The conduct of the Péreires can be explained easily. They had in their youth been active in the Saint-Simonian move- ment and were successfully to translate the master's industrial banking ideas into capitalist action. As for his purported paternity of communism, Saint-Simon undoubtedly exercised a powerful influence on Marx (initially through his father-in-law and the intellectual impact of Saint-Simonism in Germany) and more especially upon Engels, who acknowledged that Saint-Simon had been their principal precursor: 'Almost all the ideas of later socialists were contained in embryo in his theories.'[119] Despite the many historians of socialist thought who have followed in his wake and of Adolphe Blanqui who first described Saint-Simon as a socialist in 1839, the most authoritative scholars have shown that it was the posthumous transformation in his views made by the Saint-Simonian movement which gave his élitist, entrepreneurial industrialism a socialist twist. The orthodox Soviet Marxist historian Volgin, following the work notably of Gouhier, has argued that Saint-Simon cannot be described as a socialist because, far from advocating the socialization of the means of production, he accepted private property and profit; attributed a passive role to the proletariat and a dominant role to the entrepreneurial class; to which one may add that he was at his most anti-revolutionary and anti-democratic at the supposedly 'socialist' end of his life.[120] Just as Marx is said not to have been a Marxist, Saint-Simon was not really a Saint-Simonian. Manuel argued that his ideas were 'sometimes less a foundation for their beliefs than a springboard for an entirely different or at least significantly variant body of ideas' which developed both in a socialist direction and in its capitalist form, notably as expounded by Michel Chevalier. They became 'a semi-official ideology of the Second Empire', before being adopted by the managerial Right in the twentieth century both in Europe and in the industrializing authoritarian regimes of the developing countries.[121]

It was the ex-*Carbonaro* liberal conspirators like Bazard, Leroux and Buchez, in what purported to be the 1829–30 Exposition of Saint-Simonian Doctrine, who developed Saint-Simon's disenchantment with political liberalism into an all-out attack upon economic liberalism, regarded as a system based on egotistic greed and exploitation of the proletariat by the bourgeoisie. What they did was to conflate the idle class with the capitalist–industrialist entrepreneurs, separated from the rest of the producers who became the proletariat, pillorying the former as a new class of oppressors: 'rentier, capitalist, proprietor, BOURGEOIS'.[122] The Saint-Simonians used the intellectual ferment occasioned by the 1830 Revolution and the associated economic crisis to propagate their ideas, so that 'although without any influence whatsoever on the course of events at the time, the Saint-Simonists were of incomparable influence in determining how these events were later to be interpreted. . . .Thanks to Saint-Simon they knew the true meaning of the revolution; it was, in fact, the revolution of the liberal-bourgeois against the old feudalism with the aim to secure power for themselves. . .the people or *prolétaires* had made the revolution. . .but it had not been for themselves, it had been solely for the benefit of the bourgeois.'[123] This analysis was subsequently to be developed by socialists as the justification for the social revolution of the productive proletariat over (the redefined) unproductive bourgeoisie. The Saint-Simonians themselves refused to countenance *violent* class conflict, remaining faithful to the master's commitment to social peace based upon a techno-capitalist and functionally representative anticipation of neo-corporatism.

When Engels popularized the Saint-Simonian idea that 'The government of persons would be replaced by the administration of things and by the conduct of the processes of production',[124] what he anticipated in practice was the socially engineered and planned societies into which communism developed in Soviet Russia and Eastern Europe. Because of the belief that political power could simply be eliminated, the creation of industrial society has meant that political power has been acquired by 'the managers, technocrats and bureaucrats who hope to replace the "government of men" by the "administration of things" largely by the conversion of men into things.'[125]

While Durkheim attempted to reduce socialism to the functionalist management of industrial society by combining 'the positivist sociologism of Saint-Simon and Comte, respectively nineteenth century France's greatest seminal mind and most elaborate systematiser',[126] it is through the élitist technocracy of the *Ecole Polytechnique* engineers that Saint-Simon's main contribution to modern French society has come. Both Saint-Simon and Comte had close connections and a deep admiration for the *Ecole* created by Lazare Carnot to train the post-revolutionary meritocratic managers. It was therefore appropriate that Carnot's Saint-Simonian son, Hippolyte Carnot, should as minister of education after the 1848 Revolution establish an ephemeral National School of Administration, forerunner of the post-1945 *Ecole Nationale d'Administration* (ENA), on the model of the *Ecole Polytechnique*.[127] Despite the support of several ex-Saint-Simonians (and others, including Alexis de Tocqueville), it did not survive the 1849 reactionary swing to the Right although its élitist republican inspiration lived on. It laid the foundations of the state-trained élite that has, in the second half of the twentieth century, managed France's major public and private enterprises, the senior civil service and even provided many of its leading politicians. Partially depoliticized administration as a kind of applied social science became the rationale of the interlocking directorate of a modernizing industrial society in which both democracy and nationalism were relegated to a rhetorical rather than an operational role.

More generally, Saint-Simon was acknowledged by Gaetano Mosca as the main inspiration behind his theory of the ruling class. Although uneasy about acknowledging his intellectual debt to a man usually classified as a socialist, he praised Saint-Simon's exceptional originality and insight, while conceding that Comte imparted the systematic and methodological rigour that was lacking. While rejecting Saint-Simon's proposals for a technocratic industrial government, Mosca considered that 'his notion of the ruling class and of the qualities it ought to possess' had been neglected.[128] Mosca also praised Taine as another forerunner of his conception of the ruling class, whom we shall encounter as one of the architects of the *Ecole Libre des Sciences Politiques*. As a leading élite training institution, it laid the foundations during the Third Republic for the *Ecole Nationale d'Administration*, which since the Second World War has embodied the appeal to knowledge rather than popularity as the non-democratic source of public power in France.

CHAPTER FIVE

CONSTANT: PART-TIME CITIZENSHIP AND CONSTITUTIONAL FREEDOM

While Saint-Simon lived within France through the whole of the key revolutionary decade of 1789–99 and Maistre observed it at second hand from outside France, Benjamin Constant shared both the former's involvement and the latter's detachment. Until 1795 he was an external spectator, although unlike Maistre he was intensely sympathetic to all but the Terroristic phase of the Revolution. After 1795 he became an on-the-spot protagonist of the Directory, but he took a much more active part in Parisian political intrigues and polemics than did Saint-Simon, without neglecting to speculate in national property. In the modernizing optimism derived from their common mentor Condorcet, Constant was closer to Saint-Simon than to the reactionary pessimism of Maistre. Reflecting on his life's work shortly before his death, Constant declared that his response to the French Revolution was 'to properly understand the great crisis that had been in preparation for two centuries and erupted forty years ago, and to support the movement that draws the whole of mankind towards a better system of ideas and institutions . . . '[1] However, unlike both Maistre and Saint-Simon, who looked to a reconstituted spiritual unity as the basis of a counter-revolutionary social order, Constant put his trust in a comprehensive diversity. In these retrospective reflections he proudly asserted: 'I have defended for forty years the same principle: liberty in everything, in religion, in philosophy, in literature, in industry, in politics; and by liberty I mean the triumph of individuality over both authority that seems to govern it by despotism, as well as the masses that demand the right to subordinate the minority to the majority. Despotism has no rights. The majority has the right to force the minority to maintain order; but in everything that does not disturb order, everything that is internal to the person, such as opinion; everything in the expression of opinion that does not harm others either by causing or responding to violence; everything which, in industrial matters, allows a competitor to operate freely, is individual and cannot be legitimately subjected to social power.'[2]

Constant's insistence upon his consistency of political principle was partly motivated by the need to counteract his reputation for inconstancy of political behaviour and an openly scandalous lifestyle. Yet his visceral commitment to tolerance of the free expression of opinion was a link between his personality and his politics. Unlike the liberalism of a Guizot, Thiers or Laffitte, which was above all a reflection of their middle-class interests, Constant's liberalism was an expression of his individualistic private lifestyle, which made him 'the type of man most deeply distrusted by the prudent and respectable French bourgeoisie.'[3] Because of the disrepute exacerbated by the disorder of his emotional affairs, Constant never secured the undisputed standing of a leader of the emerging Liberal Party, even at the height of his popularity in the 1820s. Nevertheless, 'He gave the doctrines of his party their most complete and forceful expression, and although his colleagues might distrust him, they could not dispense with his voice and his pen. Though not their leader, he was their teacher and spokesman.'[4] By birth, education and marriage, Constant was a cosmopolitan outsider whose attempts to reconcile the absolute demands of passion and ambition made him a disturbing intrusion into a world not ready to cope with it. His personality uneasily combined 'an exaggerated individualism, a tormented egotism, a need for action, an artistic refinement, a thirst for science, a lover's feelings, a mixture of enthusiasm and acute critical sense, wild ambition, both scruples and imprudence, very genuine intentions and principles, counteracted sometimes by indecision, sometimes by the taste for adventure';[5] such was the complex character of France's foremost liberal theorist. While his turbulent private life is not our prime concern, it will unavoidably force its way into the discussion of his public fight for constitutional freedom from time to time.

Before Madame de Staël

In seeking to understand the contrast between the constancy of Constant's political values and the inconstancy of his political life, between the classical detachment of his intellect and the romantic vacillation of his will, we must start with his unstable family origins. His mother died at his birth in Lausanne in 1767. Constant's minimal family life, his father's errant existence as an army officer and his educational migrations undoubtedly contributed to his emotional volatility. Descended from the French Protestant nobility, which had emigrated to Switzerland to escape persecution and had been deprived of their title to nobility by Louis XIV, Constant belonged by upbringing to the Swiss 'aristocratic bourgeoisie'. His Protestantism left a strong imprint upon him, reflected as we shall see both directly in his conception of religion and its relation to politics, his Anglophilia and his unspoken affinity with the Natural Law Protestant tradition of resistance to state power. It is also evident in remarks about the prime need of intellectuals for independence: 'If one had to choose between persecution and protection, persecution is to be preferred in the interests of enlightenment . . . . It was far from his country, banished by tyranny, that Locke analysed man's faculties.'[6] Curiously, Locke is almost never mentioned among his forerunners by Constant, despite their ideological affinities and the role played by Locke in defending the 1688 Revolution, which many French liberals accepted as their model.

In an incomplete autobiographical sketch, Constant recalled that the happiest year of his life was spent as a student at Edinburgh University.[7] He not only amply indulged his non-intellectual tastes, developing into a lifelong debauchee and compulsive gambler, capable of squandering 20,000 francs in a single night; he also acquired an Anglophilia that outlasted the fashionable Anglomania of the 1780s. After a brief attempt to study in Oxford at the premature age of 13, Constant continued his studies in Germany before spending eighteen months from age 16 to 18 at Edinburgh, then at the height of its academic prestige, an influence perpetuated into the nineteenth century in the pages of the *Edinburgh Review*. Thomas Reid and David Hume were influential philosophic figures in the Scottish Enlightenment but Constant seems to have been especially influenced by Adam Smith and Adam Ferguson. Their emphasis upon the historical development of civil society and the foundation of political economy on the emergence of commercial life as a self-regulating and self-sustaining process, rather than the intentional result of state action, found a permanent place in his thinking. (It was in this pioneering social science milieu that Constant also acquired his lifelong preoccupation with the sociology of religion.) He was subsequently to quote frequently from Smith's *Wealth of Nations*, going further in the direction of advocating *laissez-faire* than his more circumspect mentor.[8]

Among his closest friends in the 'Speculative Society', in which he was an enthusiastic debater, was Sir James Mackintosh, who a decade later was to be made an honorary citizen of the French Republic for defending the Revolution against Burke in his *Vindiciae Gallicae*, a task which Constant himself essayed but never completed. Constant embraced in Edinburgh a radical brand of reforming Whig doctrine, which subsequently led him to eulogize Charles James Fox as 'the most cosmopolitan and therefore the

most enlightened man in England, because the prosperity of all peoples is
the best foundation for the happiness of each of them; the most generous
in his intentions, the most vehement in his love of good, the most attached
to the British constitution in its purity, i.e. with all the improvements of
which it is capable', declaring for good measure that he would prefer to be
Fox than George III.[9] Constant retained a lifelong commitment to the high
seriousness of intellectual effort in the service of a free-thinking spirit of
intellectual independence from all prejudice that he learnt in Scotland.

Like Madame de Staël, who eulogized the British constitution as 'the
finest monument of justice and moral grandeur among Europeans', an
unbounded admiration she inherited from her father, Constant wrote of
Britain: 'I feel on strong ground when I draw my examples from that dwell-
ing of freedom.'[10] Anticipating Tocqueville, he contrasted the functionless,
post-feudal French aristocracy – 'It has evaporated like a shadow because
it was only the indefinable dream of a half-destroyed system' – with the
enduring because functional English aristocracy.[11] While Constant usually
offered Britain as the model of free institutions, in the unpublished turn
of the century *Fragments d'un ouvrage abandonné sur la possibilité d'une
constitution républicaine dans un grand pays*, he once again anticipated
Tocqueville, arguing that 'America, disencumbered of nobility and royalty,
provides the aptest model for France to imitate.'[12] To appreciate the reasons
for his temporarily greater enthusiasm for this non-aristocratic offshoot
of the English stock, we must discuss the influence upon Constant of
Condorcet.

Constant probably met Condorcet in 1785 and by 1787 he acknowledged himself his disciple.[13] His main debts to Condorcet were, partly,
in his theory of human progress and in education policy, 'upon which I
doubt whether it would be possible to improve', especially in separating
the transmission of knowledge from religious, moral, philosophical and
political indoctrination.[14] Constant's historical studies in Edinburgh had
prepared him for Condorcet's liberal theory of progress. His continuing
preoccupation with the idea of human perfectibility, linked with the advance
of equality, is evident from a late 1790s sketch for an unwritten work, to
be entitled: *Du moment actuel de la destinée de l'espèce humaine ou
histoire abrégée de l'égalité*.[15] In his first major work of 1796, *De la
force du Gouvernement actuel et de la nécessité de s'y rallier*, Constant
declared that equality was the basis of all religions, although it had been
violated by 'priestly fraud . . . . The origin of society is a great enigma
but its development is simple and uniform. We see mankind emerging
out of an impenetrable cloud that obscures its birth, advancing towards
equality over the wreckage of all kinds of institutions.'[16] Like Condorcet,

to whom he explicitly refers, Constant saw the elimination of hereditary privilege and hierarchy as part of the advance of civilization, which might suffer a temporary setback but ultimately is irreversible. However, unlike Tocqueville he did not separate progress in achieving political democracy and equality from liberty, arguing implicitly against Napoleon that the right to vote was no compensation for the loss of civil liberty.[17] Constant used the desirability of gradual progress as an argument against Terrorist revolutionaries and the counter-revolutionaries, both of whom impeded reform. The past was simply a starting-point and to hark back to it like Maistre was simply to be out of date. For the relativist disciple of the Scottish Enlightenment, 'Progress is slow, uneven, endless, and, above all, inadvertent', as Stephen Holmes has put it.[18] Constant was adamant in disassociating liberal republicanism from the Terror by going back to its pre-Jacobin fathers, the Girondins. He wrote in 1797: 'It is with the names of Vergniaud and Condorcet that the foundation of the Republic should be identified.'[19]

Both at the time of the Revolution and after the publication of Madame de Staël's extended pioneering study of it, Constant shared her liberal view, although in a somewhat more striking form. They shared a very hostile conception of the pre-revolutionary regime as one of religious persecution (especially of their fellow-Protestants) and political oppression which justified the Revolution. 'The Old Regime was a mixture of corruption, arbitrariness and weakness', with arbitrariness most characteristic of Louis XIV, corruption most obvious during the Regency and weakness most evident during the reigns of Louis XV and Louis XVI.[20] Yet Constant considered, with the benefit of hindsight, that 'the real authors of the Revolution were not those who seemed to be its leaders but were its instruments . . . . I have shown in more than one book that I did not like revolutions for themselves. Usually, they miss their target by overshooting it; they hinder the progress of the ideas they seem to support. By overthrowing existing authority in the name of liberty, they provide the authority that replaces it with specious pretexts to curtail liberty. But the more one fears revolutions, the more it is necessary to be aware of what causes them.'[21]

Constant did not believe that any general rules governed the causes and effects of revolutions, although when the prevailing political forms were at odds with the spirit of the times, the latter would seek to assert itself and perhaps overshoot its mark. Premature attempts to impose improvement upon majority opinion was the cardinal revolutionary fallacy of minorities. He recalled the claim 'that we have heard repeated a thousand times during our Revolution and which all violent revolutions are inclined to repeat; despotism is necessary to establish liberty. This axiom justifies all forms of oppression and the indefinite continuation of all oppression because the duration of this despotism, to which it is claimed freedom owes its birth, is not fixed.'[22] 'Liberty is postponed until the factions are crushed. But the factions are never crushed as long as freedom is postponed.'[23]

Both Constant and Madame de Staël admired the Revolution until 1791 when in the name of 'public safety' the public ceased to be either safe or free. As Constant put it: 'There are usually two periods in revolutions, the first where unanimous feeling overthrows what is intolerable to all, the second where the artificial continuation of a movement that has ceased to be national leads to an attempt to destroy all that is opposed to the system advocated by a few. If enlightened men can halt the revolution at the first stage, the chances of success are great. Such revolutions are shortest, happiest and least bloody.'[24] Anti-Tarquin Rome, anti-Stuart England and even the American Revolution came into this category.

Unfortunately, the French Revolution fell for the temptation of 'wishing to destroy everything to rebuild anew . . . . One precedes public opinion, always hoping to drag it along behind.'[25] When, as in France, the belief predominates that 'everything must change, be reformed and recreated, revolutions never finish. Interminable divisions wrack such countries', leading to a series of despotic acts of force because 'to change everything, one must resort to tyranny.'[26] England's experience demonstrated that, following the reformist path, liberty lasted longer and ensured greater stability than absolutism. 'The reason is simple; political liberty is not only a barrier against power but a support for it. It guides power on its way; it assists its efforts, it moderates its fits of madness and encourages it when apathetic. Liberty rallies around power the interests of the various classes. Even when power struggles against it, liberty imposes certain limits which renders the failings of power less ridiculous and its excesses less odious. When political liberty is totally destroyed, power being without any limiting rules . . . begins to wander out of control. It has deprived itself of its allies in the belief that it has rid itself of its enemies.'[27] Such eloquent words are not only a trenchant analysis of French revolutionary experience but a perceptive anticipation of subsequent attempts to emulate or surpass it in speed and comprehensiveness of change.

In the early 1790s, however, Constant had not yet learnt these harsh lessons. The first sign of his active interest in the French Revolution came at a time when he was chamberlain at the Court of the liberal-minded Duke of Brunswick, nephew of Frederick the Great, whom Madam de Staël and her lover the French Minister of War Narbonne wanted to command the French forces but who instead commanded the anti-revolutionary forces at the crucial 1792 battle of Valmy.[28] As a Court functionary at the end of 1790,

Constant wrote an unpublished study of the ill-fated Brabant Revolution against Austrian rule earlier that year. He believed then that democracy was a noble ideal doomed to failure but already showed his lucid scepticism, declaring: 'At all times and in all countries, both the people's champions and its oppressors act in its name without consulting it.'[29] This scepticism was powerfully reinforced by subsequent events. Meanwhile, at the end of 1790, Constant was proposing to write a refutation of Burke's *Reflections*. Unpopular at the Brunswick Court for his ill-concealed democratic sympathies, Constant's radical views are evident from a 1790 letter: 'I don't know if universal equality is an illusion but I do know that aristocratic inequality is the most dreadful of realities', having in his unpublished study referred to democracy ending the exclusion of 'the most numerous and the most useful of classes.'[30] Despite growing disenchantment with revolutionary practice, Constant remained wedded to revolutionary democratic principles when in May 1795 he arrived in Paris with Madam de Staël as enthusiastic supporters of the Thermidorian reaction against Jacobinism.

Political activist and pamphleteer for the Directory

Constant's meeting with Madame de Staël in 1794 was the most important event in his life. With her, he successfully and overpoweringly combined sexual passion and political ambition in a way that he was unable to do with any of the many other women in his life. She not only inspired his political career and influenced his political ideas; *Adolphe*, his literary masterpiece, was in part the story of his inability to break away from her domineering hold. Constant figured in Madam de Staël's novel *Delphine*, which 'might be called the ancestor of the political novel'.[31] The feeling that they shared with a passion that she imparted to the colder Constant was love of liberty and hatred of authoritarianism. As he wrote of her shortly before his own death: 'She was impetuous against all injustice and tyranny', an intransigently combative liberal.[32]

Madame de Staël's political views largely derived from her father, Jacques Necker, on whom she doted. Necker was that unusual character, a banker who achieved enormous political popularity. The comparison with another successful banker we have encountered, Jacques Laffitte, comes to mind. Although the latter did play an important part both before, during and after the 1830 Revolution, it fell far short of Necker's role before, during and after the 1789 Revolution. Public finance offered an easy way to amass a fortune in late-eighteenth-century France and several Swiss bankers did so. 'A treasury that was chronically on the brink of bankruptcy, combined with a disarmingly corrupt administration, allowed the widest latitude to anyone who could lend capital, float loans or create credit. On the agony of the public treasury private finance grew healthy and fat.'[33] Necker's success led to his appointment as minister of finance and his popular reliance upon loans rather than raising taxes accumulated the public debt that contributed to the downfall of Louis XVI. Restored to office in 1789 to save a bankrupt Old Regime, he played a key part in the establishment of a National Assembly, while his dismissal helped precipitate the insurrection that led to the fall of the Bastille, which in turn prompted his recall to office. Although he remained in office until September 1790, he was not really in power. His inability to stem the revolutionary tide was due not merely to the failure of his financial expedients but also because a British-style constitutional monarchy did not have either Louis XVI's support or that of a majority of the Third Estate.[34] The salon of Madame de Staël, wife of the Swedish ambassador (the Swedish monarch having planned the disastrous flight to Varennes in 1791 that destroyed the hopes of the constitutional monarchists), became a focus for political intrigue as she vainly sought to mobilize the moderates like Condorcet, Lafayette and Sieyès to 'stop the Revolution'.[35] Her failure forced her into exile but she remained loyal to Necker's principles – 'To turn against the ideals of the Revolution would have meant to turn against her father' – so that through her influence upon Constant, Necker has some claim to be regarded as the grandfather of French liberalism.[36]

A revealing exchange marks Madame de Staël out as the quintessential 'committed' French intellectual. "'I detest talking about politics", Wellington told her one day. "But talking politics is my whole life!" exclaimed Germaine.'[37] In the manner of the *philosophes*, she was more of a rationalistic moralist than a romantic novelist. Her ideas were in the service of a political cause: representative government, led by a propertied élite, who could alone be relied upon to defend civil liberties. The 1688 English Revolution provided the precedent and the liberal political system it engendered was the model. Towards the end of her study of the French Revolution, she wrote of 'this England which we have ceaselessly offered as a model to French legislators, accusing them whenever they departed from it . . . . We do not believe that Providence has placed this fine monument of social order so close to France, merely to inspire the regret that it can never be equalled; and we shall scrupulously examine what should be energetically imitated.'[38] In response to the question of whether the French were capable of free and stable government, she turned to English history for a comparison and an optimistic answer. Up to 1688, the English 'had deposed, killed, overthrown more kings, princes and governments than the rest of Europe put together; and yet they have at last secured the noblest, most brilliant and most religious social order that exists in the old world. All countries, all peoples, all men, are in their different ways fit for freedom: each have or will achieve it in their own way.'[39]

In *De la Littérature* (1800) she interpreted French history as the struggle of the Third Estate for freedom. This idea inspired the liberal school of historians, initially Thierry (whom we have encountered in connection with Saint-Simon) and then Guizot (who influenced Tocqueville), Michelet and Lamartine. *'De la Littérature* was an influential book. There was scarcely an idea of the eighteenth century it did not pass on, scarcely an idea of the nineteenth century which it did not contain in germ', wrote Herold.[40] This was the remarkable woman who was to transmit to Constant a liberal legacy and a liberal programme and to collaborate in their formulation into a post-revolutionary defence of constitutional freedom reconciling civil and political liberty. She was, thanks to her influential connections, able to introduce Constant to all those who counted in Paris politics in the wake of the revolutionary upheaval, so that he might play the direct role that, as a woman, she was precluded from playing.

Until he met Germaine de Staël at the age of almost 27, Constant was a political unknown who had published nothing – although he had thought a good deal. His public liaison with her had its costs as well as its benefits: 'She had saved Benjamin from obscurity only to make him an object of notoriety.'[41] He followed in her wake as she intrigued in the salons – hers and others – that were then the focus of so much political activity; where information was acquired, opinions exchanged, tactics tried out, alliances made and unmade, careers promoted in the shifting world of Thermidorian politics. Madame de Staël quickly recognized that Constant had the intellect and wit, allied to a similarity of political views, that would make him an ideal instrument in her purpose of uniting moderates of Left and Right around an acceptance of the post-Jacobin republican status quo and thereby impart post-revolutionary stability to the new regime. It was a meeting of minds and political strategies that survived their love. Sismondi, who formed part of Madame de Staël's close circle at Coppet (a Swiss chateau, just across the French frontier) and knew them both intimately, wrote: 'He alone had the power, through an intelligence equal to hers, to bring all her intelligence into play, to enhance it by competition, to kindle an eloquence, a depth of feeling and thought that she never revealed in all their brilliance except in his presence; neither was he ever himself except at Coppet.'[42]

Constant was especially dependent upon Madame de Staël because his claim to French citizenship was very shaky – a problem that was to dog him for most of his political life. The 1791 constitution had allowed descendants of French Huguenots to retrieve their French nationality but Constant had not taken advantage of this right when the constitution was in force. Another enduring embarrassment was indebtedness, due to his gambling proclivities and to a lesser extent the cost of fighting elections. Despite (like Saint-Simon but less successfully) speculating in national property (in which he invested three-quarters of his modest fortune), he was reduced to borrowing substantial sums from both Necker and Madame de Staël, which envenomed their personal relations in later years owing to his inability to repay his debts. More important from our standpoint was their intimate community of views, which through their close collaboration – Madame de Staël initially working out her thoughts in conversation – makes it difficult to separate his ideas from hers in the formative period of the late 1790s. Edouard Herriot concluded that 'mixing in a rather curious way love and politics, these two beings had pooled all their ideas.'[43] This was especially the case in the writing of Constant's *De la Force du Gouvernement* of 1796 and Madame de Staël's *Des Circonstances Actuelles qui peuvent terminer la Révolution*, probably written in 1798 but not published until the twentieth century. Both were concerned above all else to 'end the Revolution' without returning to the Old Regime. With their daily exchange of similar views they were so much at one that isolating influences on each other becomes impossible in practice, although Constant was always less of an élitist than Madame de Staël.

Constant's brochure *De la Force du Gouvernement Actuel de la France et de la Nécessité de s'y Rallier* was written at a time of intense political and economic crisis, with threats from counter-revolutionary royalists and ultra-revolutionaries – the latter manifested in the Babeuf conspiracy as well as by Jacobin remnants – exposing the Thermidor Directory to overthrow from both extremes. It should not be dismissed as a piece of circumstantial propaganda which provoked a lively press debate because quite apart from prompting Maistre's *Considerations on France*, it has been persuasively claimed that it 'contains in embryo almost all of Constant's political thought.'[44] In the preface, Constant affirmed: 'I ardently wish to see the Revolution come to a stop because its continuation would be harmful to liberty; and that is one reason why I ardently wish to strengthen the Republic, to which all that is noble and great in human destiny is linked.'[45] He attacks the reactionaries not merely for being backward-looking but for threatening further revolutionary disruption in the name of counter-revolution. However, he carefully distinguishes absolute from constitutional monarchy – 'the one is a religion, the other a calculation'[46] – which will allow him twenty years later to accept the Restoration monarchy. Changing the political regime will not solve France's financial or economic problems because 'The form of government only influences trade through the freedom accorded to it, increasing thanks to the unlimited individual exercise of industry.'[47] Here we find the economic liberalism he learnt in Edinburgh coupled with a quietist view of modern freedom, which he developed later, that 'in all nations, the mass of the people essentially and almost exclusively want peace and quiet' and would put up with most forms of government to obtain it.[48]

Having sought to mobilize public political apathy in the service of the Republic, Constant went on to challenge the Montesquieu–Rousseau view that republics were not possible in large states because direct democracy was impracticable. Thanks to 'the sublime discovery of the representative system', Constant argued, on the contrary, that the larger the republic the easier it would be to avoid parochial concerns with sectional interests.[49] While, as we have seen, Constant championed equality in this work, acceptable natural inequality would in practice replace hereditary privilege, thanks to representation based upon a restricted suffrage. 'Leave between men the distance of intellect, talent and industry. This distance will not irritate because it always seems possible to overcome it.'[50] (Note how the principle of equality is replaced by *de facto* inequality with the help of the euphemism 'distance' and the 'seeming' ease of social mobility.) The main danger in a republic, as in other types of government, was that arbitrary power was preferred to liberty. 'As long as this attitude lasts, nothing will be stable; the Constitution will be a booklet, which each party can close at will . . . . If one is not careful, circumstances can always be invoked against principles. Factions will use the justification of one circumstance or another to bypass the law, from either good or bad motives, always demanding sweeping measures in the name of the people, liberty or country. The government must uproot this habit, which would perpetuate the revolution.'[51] However, while anticipating Constant's elaborate onslaught on arbitrary power in his later work, his stress on the need to resist opportunistic improvisation and to stick to legality was quickly to become a victim of 'circumstances'.

Despite Constant's arguments in favour of supporting the Directory, the 1797 elections showed a massive swing to the royalists and two of the five Directors (including Lazare Carnot) seemed ready to compromise with a royalist-dominated legislature. On 18 Fructidor (4 September 1797), three Directors – with the help of troops deputed by Bonaparte – staged a *coup d'état*. They purged Carnot (who managed to escape) and another Director, annulled the elections in forty departments, deported fifty-three deputies, banned forty-two Paris and provincial newspapers and arrested thirty-two journalists.[52] In his later discussion of usurpation, Constant was to write trenchantly: 'Not only do the extremes touch but they follow each other. One exaggeration always produces the contrary exaggeration.'[53] He had warned in *Des Réactions Politiques*, earlier in 1797, that the failure to secure a legitimate basis of support for its authority would perpetuate the revolutionary situation. Although, as Constant later remarked, the Directors 'were reigning in the name of a constitution they had overthrown', he meanwhile joined Madame de Staël in supporting them, even though they combined oppression and impotence.[54] They saw no alternative at a time when 'Those who spoke of freedom wanted old despotism and conspired to achieve it; those who talked of the republic wanted a new despotism.'[55] They were in the equivocal position of supporting out of expediency an arbitrary power such as they were subsequently to condemn with the utmost rigour.

Madame de Staël's *Des Circonstances Actuelles qui peuvent terminer la Révolution* was written in the turbulent interlude between the 18 Fructidor *coup* of 1797 and the 18 Brumaire coup of 1799, when the logic of relying upon the army to defend the Republic from the electorate culminated in the seizure of power by General Bonaparte. Numerous suggested modifications annotated by Constant confirm his close involvement with this work and the indefinite adjournment of its publication may well have been due not only to the changed political circumstances but also to the need to avoid harming Constant's nascent political career.[56] Madame de Staël and Constant were probably not involved in preparing the 1799 coup with Sieyès and his *idéologue* allies Cabanis, Daunou and Roederer, but some of the arguments in her book point in this direction. Sieyès was a regular visitor to her salon and she explicitly drew upon his ideas. In justifying strengthening the Directory by according it a suspensive veto on legislation and the power to dissolve the legislature as the British way of avoiding an illegal coup in the 18 Fructidor manner (but would a dissolution have solved the 1797 problem?), she adopted Sieyès' advocacy against Montesquieu of a separation of functions but a union of powers.[57] In addition she followed Sieyès not only in strengthening the executive but also in seeking to develop a judicial restraint on self-destructive democratic excesses through a modified version of his proposed *Jury Constitutionnaire* of 1795.[58]

Anticipating the argument that Constant was to render famous in his contrasting ideal types of ancient and modern freedom, Madame de Staël explained why a policy of mutual tolerance was indispensable if moderate republicans and constitutional monarchists were to secure the active support and not merely the passive acquiescence of public opinion. Unlike the classical republics which had to mobilize patriotism for frequent wars, the modern republic was based on the pacific people's 'love of tranquillity, the wish to acquire wealth and the need to keep it'. The people were not concerned to exercise power but to have their material interests constitutionally guaranteed and represented, requiring the political participation of an élite to ensure 'both the triumph of the Revolution and the end of the Revolution'.[59] When 'political science' had been established, based upon the application of Condorcet's probabilistic theory of decision-making – 'calculation will disarm force' – government might virtually be dispensed with but until then only a powerful constitutional government could be moderate.[60] She scientistically looked forward to the day when 'certainty will take hold of political science. Condorcet, Sieyès, Roederer, Godwin in the previous generation, in ours a man whose reputation will increase each year, Benjamin Constant . . . these are the statesmen for the French Revolution.'[61]

Constant has been described as an 'ally' or 'fellow-traveller' of the *idéologues*, linking the salons of Madame de Staël and Condorcet's widow, around whom were grouped the *idéologues*. During the Directory, he often dined with several leading members of this disparate group and continued to see Cabanis thereafter. However, Constant was irreconcilably opposed to Roederer even before the latter worked with Bonaparte while Constant opposed him. Specifically, Constant rejected Cabanis' justification of Bonaparte's dictatorship on the ground that nomination from above in the general interest should have priority over election from below reflecting particular interests. Defending the electoral principle against this perversion of Rousseau, Constant asked: 'What is the general interest if not the compromise between particular interests? . . . . It is always assumed that if one gains the others lose [what we now call a zero sum game] . . . . This public interest is nothing but individual interests reciprocally prevented from harming each other.'[62] More generally, despite Madame de Staël's flirtation with political scientism, Constant's admiration for Condorcet and a desire to ground his theorizing on demonstrable facts, they did not embrace the rationalist positivism and atheism of the *idéologues*, preferring an intuitionist Romanticism and Protestantism. They abandoned republicanism for constitutional monarchy, whereas the *idéologues* remained republicans in principle even when they served the Napoleonic Empire; they admired above all the English model of representative government, while the *idéologues* championed American democracy.[63]

The practical problem for the Directory liberal republicans was that while they rejected both the royalist Right and the Jacobin Left, they did not enjoy sufficient electoral support to sustain a viable Centre group. In many ways, their predicament was like that of the 'Third Force', caught

between Gaullists and Communists during the Fourth Republic. There
was no popular majority for any of the three political alternatives. What
is more, there was an attempt to conduct representative government without the acceptance of organized political parties that British experience
had shown to be necessary. The liberals could not bring themselves to
emulate the Jacobins, themselves a loose coalition. Parties were equated
with uncompromisingly divisive factions, while the liberals hoped for a
unanimity between all loyal citizens. Opposition was regarded – as it was
in practice – to be by definition disloyal, so the Directory governments
were reduced to electoral manipulation aimed at preventing the royalist
Right and Jacobin Left, both of which were capable of mass mobilization,
from securing either a majority in the legislature or the capacity to paralyse
it. The rejection in practice of democracy led to increasing electoral apathy,
voting having been devalued by government fraud. The Directory prepared
the way for Napoleon not because it was a weak government. On the
contrary, it was an arbitrary, authoritarian and manipulative government
that discredited democratic political activity and relied upon the administration and army to defend parliamentary government from the people.[64]
This intransigent, mutually excommunicating hostility of Left and Right
meant that the liberal republicans became resigned to the expedient – a
temporary expedient they hoped – of military dictatorship. Abandoning the
attempt to maintain a non-existent consensus by force, the civilian Centre
surrendered to a successful general for self-preservation.

Thermidor led to the abolition of universal suffrage by universal suffrage, the 1795 referendum restoring the practices of indirect election
and the property qualification, with electors and electoral college delegates taking an oath of hatred against royalty and anarchy, as well as
loyalty to the Republic and the constitution. The Thermidor constitution, in whose drafting the *idéologue* Daunou played a key role, had not
met with Sieyès' approval but he played a key part subsequently in both
its defence and its demise. The royalist electoral victory of 1797 cast
Sieyès in the role of revolutionary. The anti-royalist 18 Fructidor coup
was preceded by a 'providential attempt to assassinate' him by a priest,
and the wounded Sieyès was able to re-emerge into political prominence.[65]
Constant and Madame de Staël supported the coup, while having qualms
at violating the constitution in order to preserve it. This set a dangerous precedent for military intervention. Constant used at the time the
sort of spurious argument he was later to condemn. In a report to the
Cercle Constitutionnel, a political club he formed in 1797 (whose members included Sieyès, Talleyrand, Cabanis and Daunou), Constant defended
the coup: 'If a few forms have been violated, if some parts of liberty

have been bruised, we blame royalism . . . for the temporary neglect of the law.'[66]

In return for Madame de Staël having secured his appointment as foreign minister in 1797, Talleyrand tried to obtain a senior administrative appointment for Constant in the ministry but failed because of his foreign nationality. He also failed to persuade Bonaparte to appoint Constant to administer conquered Italian territory in 1797.[67] In the plots that preceded the 18 Brumaire coup which brought Bonaparte to power, Talleyrand's role was to play 'the go-between, acquainted with everybody, knowing everything, and holding in his hands the end of every string.'[68] In alliance with Sieyès, who became a Director in May 1799, Talleyrand set about destroying the tottering regime from within, before either the royalists or Jacobins could overthrow it. Mallet du Pan had wind of an earlier plot, writing at the end of 1798 of those seeking a 'constitutional monarch having Barras for Chief Minister, Bonaparte for Constable, Tallien or Talleyrand for Chancellor and Benjamin Constant for private secretary.'[69] From Sieyès' election as Director, Constant saw him almost daily until four days before the 18 Brumaire, writing to him: 'I believe in the revolution because I believe in you.'[70] Madame de Staël affected to believe in 1797 that Bonaparte was 'the best republican in France, the most freedom-loving of Frenchmen', nourishing the hope that the greatest living man and the greatest living woman would be united physically and politically as equals, a prospect which Bonaparte regarded as ludicrous and even repellant.[71] Long after the event, Madame de Staël saw the 18 Brumaire as the French nation rushing into the arms of Bonaparte to escape the ghost of a Jacobin restoration. Bonaparte despised the people whose votes he sought and Madame de Staël 'mourned not liberty, which had never existed in France, but the hope of freedom without which only shame and misfortune await this country.'[72]

She curiously blamed Sieyès for helping Bonaparte's despotic designs, when military success had ensured him mass support, by abandoning direct popular election. Constant correctly recognized that the only bulwark would be the legislature, writing to Sieyès on the day after the coup to warn against the suspension of the legislature. 'Such a measure seems to me disastrous in present circumstances by destroying the only barrier against the man you associated with yesterday's action, but who is all the more threatening to the republic for that reason; his proclamations . . . have convinced me more than ever that all he does is aimed at his own pre-eminence. Nevertheless, he has on his side the generals, the soldiers, the pro-aristocrats and all those who yield with enthusiasm to the appearance of force. The republic has for it YOU and that is certainly a great deal, and the (legislative) representatives which, bad or not, are capable of blocking the schemes of an individual and can alone issue the necessary decrees if there is an attempt at usurping power', going on to stress that 'to fight against an individual like B one must rely upon an official body.'[73] Sieyès, whom Bentham described as 'turned crazy by self-conceit', proved unequal to the basic task set him by Constant, the legislature's resistance was swept aside and a week later Constant was himself asking for Sieyès' support to sit in the *Tribunat* in the post-Brumaire legislature.[74] Like Tocqueville fifty years later, Constant was to try to collaborate politically with a Napoleon he suspected and feared, though in Constant's case he would not be an ephemeral minister but would draft an ephemeral constitution.

Against tyranny: a Rousseauist emperor?

Exhausted by a decade of revolutionary endeavour, the French people in 1799 readily accepted the advent of a populist dictatorship, amounting to misgovernment with popular consent or at least counterfeit democratic consent. The scepticism based upon experience is reflected in the well-known joke about the bookseller who, when asked for a copy of the post-Brumaire constitution drafted by Sieyès, replied that he did not sell periodical literature.[75] Constant was now no longer inclined glibly to dismiss Burke's *Reflections on the Revolution in France* with the phrase 'There are more absurdities than lines in this famous book.'[76] To understand the emergence of liberalism as a fully elaborated political doctrine in France, it must not be envisaged – as it is usually portrayed – as the celebration of a triumphant bourgeoisie but rather as the lament of a defeated intelligentsia resisting regimentation. Conscious that they lacked popular support, those *idéologues* like Destutt de Tracy, who did not rally to Bonaparte, and Constant worked out a theoretical defence of liberty in the inhospitable environment of the Consulate and the Empire. This first took the form of an attempt to institutionalize a loyal opposition in the legislature and thereafter, when it had proved intolerable to Napoleon, a systematic defence of individual liberty partly divorced from democracy.

Constant was appointed a member of the consultative *Tribunat*, which has been described as the 'last refuge of political eloquence' under Napoleon, thanks to the influence of Sieyès and Joseph Bonaparte.[77] Initially, Constant was not an all-out opponent of Napoleon, who had after all brought about a restoration of order, economic revival and enjoyed public support. An admirer of the British style of parliamentary debate and familiar with the acceptance of an opposition as a source of political system strength rather than divisiveness, Constant sought to play the parliamentary game *à l'anglaise*. Unfortunately for him, the illiberal French democratic tradition and Bonaparte's authoritarianism precluded even understanding such practices. When the government and its leader spoke in the name of the people, an opposition was bound to be subversive. Constant immediately got into trouble. On 5 January 1800, when Constant made his first speech, Roederer – his old *idéologue* opponent, now a member of the Council of State (the body that alone could propose legislation) – published an article warning the *Tribunat* not to become the focus of an 'organized opposition'. Constant's immediate reply, which marked him out as an enemy of the new regime, took the form of a speech on control of the legislative timetable. While rejecting the accusation of systematic opposition, Constant asserted the right to criticize without being blamed for the evils to which opponents drew attention. Governments were inherently intolerant of criticism, yet 'A constitution is of itself an act of distrust, since it prescribes limits to authority and it would be unnecessary to fix such limits if you thought government endowed with an infallible wisdom and an eternal moderation.'[78] He protested against the *Tribunat's* lack of control over its own agenda, leading to precipitate 'revolutionary' legislation imposed *en bloc* by a package vote. 'I thought the revolution over' but 'without an independent *Tribunat*, there would be neither harmony nor constitution, only servitude and silence.'[79] Despite Constant's courageous eloquence and prophetic perspicacity, the servile *Tribunat* inaugurated its inglorious career as a rubber-stamping body by approving the government's procedural constraints by fifty-six votes to twenty-six.

A year later, following an abortive *royalist* attempt to assassinate Bonaparte, a bill to establish joint civil–military special tribunals – used to sentence and deport large numbers of *Jacobins* – was debated in the *Tribunat*. Appealing to Article 29 of Magna Charta against special courts, which it would be unworthy for French representatives of the people to abjure twelve years after the Revolution, Constant widened his attack against the arbitrary power given to numerous subordinate government officials who, under all regimes, were avid for unlimited power. The bill was unconstitutional, championed with the usual sophism that one had to go beyond the constitution to defend it, whereas one seldom returned to a constitution that had been violated. The same was true of substituting the spirit for the letter of the law. Judicial 'Forms are a safeguard, the curtailment of forms is the reduction or loss of this safeguard . . . . If forms are unnecessary, why do you keep them in ordinary trials? If they are necessary, why do you abolish them in the most important trials? Is your need to be convinced greater when a light punishment is to be inflicted than when it is a matter of the death penalty?'[80] Constant concluded his long speech with the claim that if the bill was passed – it was by forty-nine to forty-one votes – the security of the citizen would no longer exist because the constitution would have been violated, juries eliminated and arbitrariness organized. Daunou also spoke and voted against it. A year later, in January 1802, Constant, Daunou and Say were among those who were purged from the *Tribunat* by Napoleon as 'metaphysicians' and 'vermin' in a fit of intolerant 'ideophobia'.

To understand Napoleon's vendetta against liberal intellectual critics, we must appreciate his anxiety not merely about opposition to his forthcoming concordat with the Pope and reimposition of slavery in the colonies but more generally about the illegitimate nature of his power. Condemned to survive only as long as he was successful and demanding total and unquestioning obedience, Napoleon feared those he could not intimidate or buy. He asked his brother Joseph to find out from Madame de Staël what she wanted, only to receive the reply: 'It's not a question of what I want but of what I think.'[81] Constant contrasted his attitude towards Napoleon with that of Madame de Staël: 'I cannot be silent under despotism but I do not want to be reconciled with it. She wishes to be reconciled but cannot be silent.'[82]

Constant repeatedly attacked usurpation, in works he could not publish while Napoleon was in power, showing how the regime fostered hypocrisy even more than outright tyranny. 'Despotism stifles freedom of the press, usurpation parodies it . . . . Despotism, in a word, reigns by silence and allows the individual the right to be silent; usurpation condemns him to speak, it pursues him into the intimate sanctuary of his thought and, forcing him to lie to himself, it deprives him of the ultimate consolation of the oppressed,' so that 'usurpation debases a people as well as oppressing it'; if it endures too long it renders a nation unfit for freedom.[83] In his unpublished *Principes de Politique*, written in the period immediately following his exclusion from the *Tribunat*, Constant quoted (without acknowledgement) from Madame de Staël's unpublished *Des Circonstances Actuelles* on the way in which the lack of legitimacy led to the manipulation and misrepresentation of public opinion. 'It is not enough to give power to those whom the people reject; it must be forced to choose them. It is not enough to forbid press freedom, one needs newspapers that parody it. It is not enough to silence a representative assembly; one must maintain a fake pretence of opposition, tolerated when it is futile and dispersed when it overshadows. It is not enough to dispense with the national will; the minority must offer support in the name of the majority.'[84] This anticipatory portrait of the modern totalitarian state had the disadvantage of being a critique of Napoleon's Empire that enjoyed popular support.

Tocqueville was to have the same problem with his critique of the Second Empire, which underlines why liberalism had to be disassociated from populist democracy.

While Constant was engaged between 1799 and 1802 in writing his unfinished and unpublished book *On the possibility of a republican constitution in a large country*, it was not until the subsequent years of imposed silence that he wrote his greatest work, the *Principes de Politique*. It was not published in its full version until 1980, although substantial portions appeared in fragmented form in his lifetime. This book could in one sense be regarded as his reflections on the French Revolution. Even more than his theoretical critique of the 'friends of liberty', like Rousseau, it embodies his comparison of the disparity between theories and reality. His chief purpose was to demonstrate one great liberal principle: that the refusal to limit power had destroyed liberty. Writing at a time of pervasive public disillusion with grand political theorizing, after the vogue enjoyed by Montesquieu and Rousseau, Constant was determined to teach the French how to become politically free at a time when rigorous censorship prevented his views being published.[85] Constant made a number of instructive false starts before he wrote the dismembered and posthumously reconstituted masterpiece which bridges the century gap between the liberal landmarks of Montesquieu's *Spirit of the Laws* and Tocqueville's *Democracy in America*.

The first false start was Constant's translation of William Godwin's *Enquiry Concerning Political Justice* in 1798–9 (which was not to be published until 1972). This libertarian book, which has since become a classic of anarchism, created a sensation when published in 1793 as a corrective to Montesquieu and a reply to Burke's *Reflections*. Madame de Staël particularly admired Godwin's noval *Caleb Williams* and it was she who persuaded Constant to translate *Political Justice*, which had appeared when she was in exile in England. (Godwin had been an Anglican minister and a Whig, friend of Tom Paine and Constant's old associate James Mackintosh. Godwin had read the 1797 English translation of Constant's *De la Force du Gouvernement* and was in 1815 to write a newspaper article in support of Constant's Napoleonic constitution.[86]) Godwin appealed to Constant as an ardent champion of individual liberty but he was not willing to accept that all political institutions – hereditary monarchy and aristocracy in particular – should be swept away, along with private property, as progress replaced the inequality and despotism of the past. Nevertheless, Godwin's radical critique of government and private property left its mark upon Constant, one of the formative influences upon his liberal doctrine that shared some common ground with this founding father of anarchism. Constant preserved both government and private property but in a limited form, subordinated to the supreme value of individual freedom.

However, rather than writing a critique of Godwin, Constant decided to formulate his own conception of republican government. Until then, Constant had been a successful pamphleteer but he now believed it desirable to present a defence of republican institutions as the best form of government. Before completing this study, Constant changed his mind on a fundamental point, occasioned no doubt by the demise of the Republic in France. His new, more theoretical work would be 'applicable to all forms of government' and be based on 'principles'. It incorporated parts of the earlier work, notably the ideas of a 'neutral power' (which reflected the influence of Necker and Sieyès), to which we shall return later. Whereas this 'neutral' head of state might be either a constitutional monarch or president of the republic, the earlier work rejected monarchy and all hereditary institutions as archaic, beginning with usurpation, continuing with despotism and ending with revolution. What actually provoked Constant in 1805 into beginning to write his *Principes*, was a courtier's apologia for Napoleonic despotism by Count Molé, who was rewarded with appointment as a councillor of state. (Molé, a relation of Tocqueville's, was to serve from 1837 to 1839 as prime minister under the July Monarchy.) Originally intended to be a polemical brochure, it rapidly expanded into a theoretical treatise, indifferent to forms of government and defending freedom against them all.[87]

If Molé imparted the stimulus, it was his friend Sismondi who seems to have given Constant his real inspiration, based upon the use of revolutionary experience to test political principles, in particular those popularized by Rousseau. Sismondi had fled to England after Geneva was invaded in 1792 and made a close study of British political institutions. From 1796 to 1801, he worked on his *Recherches sur les constitutions des peuples libres*; Constant read the manuscript in 1801, thinking so highly of it that he wanted it presented to the *Institut*. However, Sismondi abandoned it unfinished to publish his vulgarization of Adam Smith's economics applied to France: *De la Richesse Commerciale*, which appeared in the same year (1803) as Say's more substantial *Traité*. Constant was inspired by Sismondi to focus his attack on their fellow Swiss Rousseau, in the spirit of the remark by Lakanal: 'The Revolution explained the *Social Contract* to us.'[88] However, whereas Sismondi followed the eighteenth-century tradition of pseudo-anthropological contractualist speculation about the hypothetical origin of society in the state of nature, Constant instead followed Bentham and Godwin in rejecting notions of social contract. Rather than the traditional argument about whether the state of nature was peaceful or warlike,

Constant substituted a distinction between a traditional Hobbesian addiction to war and conquest being replaced by a modern Smithian concern with peaceful trade. He comes much closer to a political science of the contemporary world through his rejection of the nostalgia for classical collectivism, which via Rousseau's *Social Contract* became the justification for unlimited popular sovereignty.

Constant was concerned not just to personalize his argument into an attack upon Napoleon, refusing to 'transform history into a sterile study of isolated phenomena, an enumeration of facts without causes.'[89] The willing enslavement of the French people to a glorious general was due to a reaction against the Revolution, regarded as having resulted in an excess of freedom, whereas its troubles had been caused by a comprehensive denial of freedom in practice. In 1814, looking back on fifteen years of autocracy, Constant wrote: 'Montesquieu has said that despotism needed deserts as frontiers; Bonaparte could only constrain thought in France by surrounding that fine country with intellectual deserts.'[90] It was natural for liberals to turn back from a neo-Rousseauist orgy to a critical rediscovery of Montesquieu, such as was written by Destutt de Tracy in his *Commentary on the Spirit of the Laws* in 1806, which he had published anonymously in an English translation in America. Constant – who had been compared to Montesquieu by Madame de Staël in 1794, shortly after they met – seems not to have read Montesquieu's *Esprit des Lois* carefully until January 1804, when he described it as a profound and prophetic work. Later, Constant taxed Montesquieu with his conservative historical determinism and the 'partiality and indulgence inspired by his social position' for 'inequalities and privileges'.[91]

Although this last comment sounds much more like Condorcet and Sieyès than Constant, he borrowed from his fellow Anglophil a hatred of uniformity and concentration of power. 'Variety is organization; uniformity is mechanism. Variety is life; uniformity is death.'[92] This sweeping judgement is part of a defence of local self-government that looks forward to Tocqueville as well as backward to Montesquieu in seeing imposed unity as provoking resistance, a disastrous remedy to the supposed disease of diversity. Constant, as we shall see, also adopted Montesquieu's liberal prescription for the organization of government, although in a modified form, separating the powers into five instead of three. However, unlike the rigidly juristic and Continental view of Montesquieu's theory as requiring complete institutional, functional and personal separation, Constant subscribed to the view that checks and balances between partially separate powers were the workable safeguards of freedom, with competitive party politics, freedom of speech and freedom of the press as indispensable adjuncts. Where Constant parted company from Montesquieu was that he relied on the judiciary rather than aristocracy as the countervailing check upon a government dyarchy and bicameral legislature. Above all, power must not only be separated but also limited by individual rights, a view that brought Constant into conflict with Rousseau.

In the aftermath of the cult and 'pantheonization' of Rousseau – when Maistre was launching his onslaught upon him – Constant did not discuss Rousseau in his Directory writings. It was Sismondi who made him appreciate that he could organize his liberal individualism in opposition to Rousseau-inspired Jacobinism. As Hofmann (who resuscitated the 1806 *Principes de Politique*) has aptly put it, 'Constant's liberal theory only assumed its final form from the moment it became anti-Rousseauist.'[93] However, it is important to grasp that Constant did not reject Rousseau's appeal to the general will as the source of all legitimate authority. What he objected to was the claim that its authority was unlimited and Rousseau's refusal to provide a satisfactory practical expression of the general will. So, while Constant asserts that 'there are only two forms of power in the world; one – force – is illegitimate; the other – the general will – is legitimate', he goes on to denounce the fundamental error of Rousseau and his disciples: 'Everything ordained by the general will is necessarily legitimate.'[94] Montesquieu did not offer a satisfactory solution either because he had rightly challenged the idea that government necessitated unlimited authority; but by confining liberty to what was permitted by law, he did not appreciate that 'The laws could forbid so many things that there might be no liberty.'[95]

Constant calls upon the arguments against unlimited power of Condorcet, Tom Paine, Benjamin Franklin and especially Sieyès to support his views that popular sovereignty was not a guarantee of freedom but merely a way of denying any individual the right to seize authority from the whole community. Freedom existed only to the extent that sovereignty was limited. Because Rousseau (who had written good sense in his proposals for the government of Poland) ignored this in his *Social Contract*, it was used by those who wished to re-establish despotism after the Revolution. Constant wrote of the generalizing Rousseau: 'Terror-stricken at the sight of the immense social power he had created, he did not know into whose hands he should deposit this monstrous power and found no safeguard against the danger inseparable from such sovereignty except in an expedient that renders its exercise impossible. He declared that sovereignty could not be either alienated, delegated or represented. This was tantamount to stating that it could not be exercised; it was to annihilate the principle he had just proclaimed.'[96] However, Constant shows how Rousseau's abstract, unlimited power was hypocritically misappropriated and manipulated in the name of the people. 'Government can do nothing, says he, but the nation can do everything. Soon the nation – that is a few men – speaks' in the name of the people, 'acts on its behalf by imposing silence upon it, proclaiming its omnipotence while simultaneously threatening it; so that by a quick and easy subterfuge, the government seizes the real and terrible power which was initially presented as the abstract right of the whole society.'[97]

Constant is much more critical of Mably's harsh denial of individual liberty and property than the 'subtle metaphysics' of Rousseau as the source of post-revolutionary despotism, although this resulted from their shared desire to imitate the classical republics. Yet in these republics, the individual's real influence upon decision-making sovereignty was a daily reality, so that it might be assumed – as Condorcet and Sismondi had plausibly argued – that they were willing to give up their private independence. Unlike the large, modern state in which 'sovereignty could only be exercised through representation in a fictional manner', in the classical republic 'the citizen constituted himself a sort of slave of his nation; he gave himself wholly to the decisions of the sovereign and legislator, recognizing its right to supervise all his actions and constrain his will. This is because he was in his turn legislator and sovereign; he took pride in what his vote was worth in a nation whose population was small enough for each citizen to be powerful.'[98] However, the more extremist French revolutionary leaders ignored the changes in ordinary people's needs and attitudes which had occurred in 2,000 years. With humanitarian intentions, 'having adopted philosophy as a prejudice and democracy as fanaticism, they were seized with boundless admiration for Rousseau and Mably.' They had 'long before the throne's overthrow, drawn up in axioms all the maxims necessary to organize, in the name of the republic, the most absolute despotism.'[99] Without the benefit of thirty years' practical experience of the liberticidal effects of unlimited power, Rousseau could not be blamed for the misuse of his Spartan dogmas but Constant refused to show this generosity towards Restoration ministers who quoted Rousseau in support of their restraints upon freedom.[100]

The basic 'lesson' of the experience of the French Revolution and the subsequent Napoleonic Empire was the need to set constitutional limits to political power that would check power by power. 'No earthly authority is unlimited, neither that of the people, nor of those who say they are its representatives, nor beings by whatever title they reign, nor the law, which expressing the will of the people or the king, according to the type of government, should be confined within the same limits as the authority from which it derives . . . . The consent of the people cannot legitimate what is illegitimate, since the people cannot delegate to anyone an authority it does not have.'[101] To avoid the arbitrariness that comes from a lack of rules or principles, Constant insists upon the importance of formal, contractual, procedural restraints (which, of course, should not be confused with a social contract). As early as 1797 he wrote: 'Political institutions are only contracts. Contracts lay down fixed limits', adding more precisely in 1815: 'Observance of forms preserves from arbitrariness. Forms are the tutelary divinities of human associations. It is to forms alone that the oppressed can appeal. The remedy for arbitrariness is the responsibility of (government) officials.'[102] To those who wanted to deny the Babeuf conspirators a proper trial in 1796 on the ground that they would not have respected legal forms if they had been in power, Constant gave the classic liberal reply. 'It is precisely because they would not have observed [legal forms] that you should. That is what distinguishes you from them: that alone gives you the right to punish them; that is what makes them anarchists and you friends of order.'[103]

To reduce the chance of constitutions being violated, they should be as short and flexible as possible. Constant recalled in the preface to his 1815 *Principles of Politics* that in 1797 he had written that 'A Constitution being the guarantee of a people's liberty, everything concerned with liberty was constitutional but that nothing was constitutional which was not concerned with liberty: to extend a constitution to cover everything would be to convert everything into dangers for it.' It should be strictly confined to its function of setting the boundary between state and society.[104] Constant denied that the interests of the government and the governed could be identical, whatever the type of government, because those in power would always be tempted to abuse it. Against Rousseau and foreshadowing John Stuart Mill, Constant declared that popular consent could not legitimate usurpations of individual rights: 'It will be no more legitimate, even if the whole nation approves, less the citizen it oppresses.'[105] In his earlier version of the *Principes*, Constant asserted his credo of individual liberty in other words but with the same force: 'Where the individual is nothing, the people is nothing', although his target was not so much the *actuality* as the *pretext* of democracy, minorities masquerading as majorities.[106] Hence the emphasis Constant put upon free speech and a free press in the working of parliamentary government, through the impact of genuine and diverse public opinion, rather than an abstract and monolithic sovereignty.

After the disillusionments of the French Revolution, America had revived a flagging faith in constitutionally engineered checks and balances. Doubtless reflecting contrasting national experience, some like Bentham feared that a separation of powers would lead to inertia, while others such as Destutt de Tracy anticipated that it would encourage revolution. Constant proposed a more elaborate version of Montesquieu's threefold separation. Leaving the judicial power intact, Constant split the legislative power between an elected and a hereditary assembly, while the executive power was divided between a government whose ministers were individually responsible to parliament and a neutral head of state who was not accountable. He regarded this division of the executive as the fundamental principle, with the task of the head of state being to ensure that the other powers 'support, agree and act together'.[107] Whereas in 1802, when he first formulated his theory of a conservative neutral power to counterbalance the revolutionary representative power, Constant was concerned to argue the case for a republic, by 1806 he was to stress that these principles were applicable to either a monarchy or a republic. By the 1814 Restoration, Constant had accepted that constitutional monarchy on the British pattern should provide the model for the head of state. He now explicitly referred to an impartial royal arbiter who could avoid the undesirable concentration of power, either in the hands of the legislature – as in the English Long Parliament or the French Convention – or in a despotic executive, such as Cromwell or Napoleon. The six prerogative powers of the king would be: to appoint and dismiss the ministers responsible to parliament; to veto legislation; to dissolve the elected chamber; to declare war and make peace; to appoint irremovable judges; and to exercise the right of pardon. Ministers should be members of parliament but not constitute more than 1 per cent of the legislature, to avoid excessive executive influence. To enforce the principle that the king can do no wrong, ministerial countersignature of the king's acts would ensure that they accepted responsibility.[108] This is very close to the formal powers of France's contemporary republican monarch.

Appealing once again to British experience, Constant argued strongly in favour of direct election to the Chamber of Deputies because of the voters' sense of pride, participation and identification with the nation. 'Citizens can only take an interest in their institutions when they participate in them by voting and such interest is indispensable to the formation of public opinion, a power without which no liberty can endure', he maintained.[109] Constant was confident that, as in Britain and America, the voters would choose better-educated, more independent and 'enlightened property owners', while dependence upon electors would force the rich to pay attention to the needs of the poor and weak. Above all, the representative assembly's power should be limited, instructed by the consequence of the French Revolution's failure to do so. 'When the legislative power is unlimited, when the nation's representatives believe themselves possessed with a boundless sovereignty, when there is no counterweight to their decrees in either the executive or judicial powers, the tyranny of those elected by the people is as disastrous as any other, whatever it is called. The absolute, unlimited sovereignty of the people was transmitted to representative assemblies by the nation, or at least in its name, as is customary, by those who dominated it. The result was the most unheard of arbitrariness.'[110] Even with the additional safeguard of a bicameral parliament, Constant believed that France would still not be institutionally equipped for parliamentary government because it did not yet have 'a united government, a stable majority and an opposition clearly separated from that majority'.[111] Constant was to strive throughout the Restoration to instil into Frenchmen these principles derived from British experience.

Constant attached great importance to legal forms, independent courts and the jury system. The latter was imported in 1791 from Britain – a touchstone of nineteenth-century French liberalism – derived from the need to protect the individual rights solemnly proclaimed but systematically violated since 1789, despite the many lawyers sitting in the revolutionary assemblies. While admiring Bentham, Constant rejected his attack on the French Declaration of Rights for subversively divorcing rights from law on the ground that 'The doctrine of unlimited obedience to the law has been the cause of more misfortunes than all the other errors that have misled mankind.'[112] The Roman emperors through to the Committee of Public Safety had all tyrannized through an apparently impartial law. However, having rejected utilitarianism as less satisfactory than natural law, Constant conceded that 'In no country have people enjoyed full individual rights. No government has limited the exercise of social authority to what is strictly necessary. They have all extended it much further, with the full, weighty support of the philosophers throughout the ages and the writers of all parties . . . . One can always find utilitarian justifications for all commands and prohibitions . . . . It is this logic that has turned contemporary France into an immense prison.'[113]

Throughout his political life he repeated his unswerving commitment to citizen rights. 'Citizens possess individual rights independent of all social or political authority and any authority that violates these rights becomes illegitimate. The rights of all citizens are individual liberty, religious freedom, freedom of opinion, including its publicity [i.e. freedom of speech and the press], the enjoyment of property and guarantee against all arbitrary acts. Anybody who infringes these rights thereby destroys his own entitlement to exercise authority.'[114] Despite tiny circulations, freedom of the press was indispensable because it guaranteed other freedoms by attracting public attention to government violations of all other rights. In the early nineteenth century, representative government was known as *gouvernement d'opinion*, an acknowledgement that an uninterrupted official monologue put to sleep not only the governed but the governors themselves. It was the denial of press freedom which had accustomed the French people to apathy and servitude.[115] Political liberties were the means of protecting the civil liberties that were the purpose of society, so it would be absurd to sacrifice the latter to the former. 'In defending the rights of the minority, the rights of all are defended because each in turn finds himself in a minority. The whole association is divided into a mass of minorities that are oppressed in succession.'[116] He took over from Thomas Jefferson the problematic principle that individual freedom consisted in doing what did not harm others, along with the protection of minority rights and civil supremacy over the military, that formed the themes of Jefferson's inaugural presidential address in 1801.[117]

Constant reproached Montesquieu with defending private property rights more vigorously than individual liberty, and unlike Locke he treated private property as a social creation. Nevertheless, in practice, he accorded it great political significance. He welcomed the Thermidor reaction in 1795 with the judgement: 'Property and ability, those two reasonable reasons for inequality among men, will assume their rights.'[118] He was to argue in 1829 that trade rendered despotism impossible because exchange and credit made authority dependent upon property.[119] However, because of rapid social mobility, class conflict would be moderated in increasingly homogeneous modern industrial society, which had evolved towards equal rights after four historical revolutions, won successively against theocracy, slavery, the caste system and aristocracy.[120] As private ownership tended to spread spontaneously, provided laws did not restrict this process, Constant believed that property qualifications for the suffrage would not prevent the gradual democratization of the electorate.

For Constant there was a stark choice: 'Property must either reign or be abolished.'[121] Against those like Mably and Godwin who wished to abolish private property, he argued that it should be spread to all, advocating what has come to be called a property-owning democracy in preference to general nationalization. 'Only property owners can be citizens . . . . If it is claimed that because men are equal in rights, property owners should have no more rights than non-owners, one must conclude that either everyone or no one should own property because property rights establish a much greater inequality between owners and non-owners than do all political rights.'[122] Constant's first reason for imposing a property qualification for voters was that until all became property owners it would be tactically wise to placate the rich, who would otherwise reject the introduction of representative government. 'Property owners will be oppressors to avoid being oppressed.

Property will never be powerless.'[123] Secondly, Constant followed those, like Barnave, who had argued that only property owners could be relied upon to resist corruption and be independent of pressure. Thirdly, political activity required the acquisition of education and sufficient leisure. Unlike Destutt de Tracy, who rejected such property qualifications outright as favouring the idle as against the industrious classes and encouraging class conflict, Constant along with Guizot restricted citizenship rights to those possessing the necessary power and skill to form a capable political élite. They were both following Sieyès, who had argued that 'All may enjoy the advantage of society, but they alone who contribute to the public establishment are the true shareholders in the great public enterprise.'[124] To bolster up this defence of a middle-class élite of proprietorial active citizens, Constant argued that universal suffrage was in practice never universal, many being excluded on grounds of age, sex and nationality. The qualities required to die for one's country should not be confused with the political capacity to shape its political life, including the decision to go to war. However, Constant never fixed a lower limit on the property qualification and often argued that it should be lowered, which suggests that he favoured the sort of gradual extension of the suffrage which occurred in Britain in the nineteenth century.[125]

Private property not only provided the principal criterion for the exercise of political authority. It circumscribed that authority and denied it the capacity to make the all-embracing absolute demands of classical patriotism. Constant declared that 'the era of such patriotism is finished, what we love both in our country and in liberty is our private property, the security . . . of a thousand kinds of happiness. The word *patrie* reminds us of the combination of all these goods rather than a particular country.'[126] Furthermore, the development of trade and credit had made arbitrary state intervention both more vexatious and more easily evaded, if necessary by 'expatriation, which in classical city states used to be a punishment and is not merely possible but often pleasurable to modern peoples.' Napoleon's Continental System had in vain attempted to restrict trade and hunt down freedom by conquering ever more countries. He had simply shown that 'private individuals are stronger than governments in our times' and while 'the leaders might be enemies, peoples were compatriots.'[127]

However, there were limits to which Constant would not push his cosmopolitanism and calculating-cum-instrumental view of patriotism. While approving the advocacy by Adam Smith and Godwin of free trade, which had promoted Britain's prosperity, Constant refused to follow Godwin into basing his political system on the false premise that government is a necessary evil. Government was good because it prevented members of society from harming each other. Nevertheless, he praised Godwin's critique of government intervention for showing that its 'best, surest and fairest policy is to preserve peace and *laisser-faire* . . . . No writer has more clearly proved that as soon as interests are impeded on the pretext of controlling them, they are paralysed.'[128] Constant did not hesitate to proclaim side by side his commitment to economic and intellectual freedom: '*Laisser faire* is all that is necessary to give trade maximum prosperity; *laisser écrire* is all that is necessary for the human mind to attain the highest level of activity, penetration and precision.'[129]

However, while considering restrictions upon 'industrial freedom' as futile and regarding it as interdependent with civil liberties, he refused to put them on the same plane 'for fear that people who differed on the first would be inclined to challenge the important principles which are the basis of the well-being of associations and the safety of citizens . . . . Even if I were to be mistaken in my assertions about the freedom of industry and trade, this would not weaken my principles of religious, intellectual and personal freedom.'[130] This disposes of the argument that liberalism necessarily subordinates non-economic freedoms to the dictates of bourgeois acquisitiveness. While playing down the importance of self-interest, he showed that government intervention might be captured by private interests, which would use its regulatory power to promote monopolies in their sectional interests. He reminded his readers: 'To increase the strength of collective authority is always to give power to a few individuals. If the wickedness of men is an argument against liberty, it is an even stronger argument against power, for despotism is only the liberty of one or a few against all.'[131]

Relying upon evidence drawn from Adam Smith, Say and Sismondi, Constant attacked attempts to revive corporatist industrial regulation and the mercantilist provision of state subsidies, as well as the price fixing favoured by Necker. The only justification for social intervention was to prevent its members harming each other but 'If the state wanted to supervise individualism in all activities through which they might harm each other, it would restrict the freedom of almost all actions; and becoming the citizens' protector, it would soon become their tyrant.'[132] It is not clear, however, that Constant ideally wished to limit government to the minimum functions of internal order, defence and the taxation necessary to pay for them, or whether he accepted that they would not only be exceeded in practice but should be widened to cover the public provision of services such as education. His liberalism is evident in the anxiety he shows about government intervention's natural tendency to proliferate at the expense of personal freedom; more laws meant a greater likelihood of law-breaking.

He would have approved Say's rejection of Napoleon's attempt to buy off his opponents, preferring instead of try out his entrepreneurial skills by establishing a cotton mill.

1814–15: Three political gambles and three fiascos

While Constant's political principles were firm, he opportunistically adapted his political behaviour to changing political circumstances. Within the space of little over a year in 1814–15, he was in quick succession to champion the cause of ex-republican French general and Swedish Crown Prince Bernadotte, of the restored Louis XVIII and of Napoleon on his return from exile in Elba. After Napoleon's defeat at the Battle of Leipzig in 1813, Bernadotte's victorious army caught up with Constant in his German exile. Constant was persuaded to support the liberal contender for the prospectively vacant French throne in the hope (shared by Madame de Staël) that Bernadotte would establish a British-style constitutional monarchy. Constant drafted a confidential outline for a propaganda campaign to undermine Napoleon's popular support in France, rapidly followed by the publication of his most scintillating political work, *On the Spirit of Conquest and Usurpation*, directed against Napoleon's regime. Although Bernadotte hesitated and allowed his chance of the French throne to slip, Constant's work was not an ephemeral piece of political propaganda. Drawn largely from his unpublished 1806 manuscript, it argued that legitimate authority could – on the analogy of the English Parliament's invitation to William III in 1688 – be based on election, a dubious analogy as the claim of William of Orange was based, through his wife, on heredity.[133] Ironically, the Conservative British Government was most opposed to Bernadotte's claims and so Constant was compelled to switch his hopes for a British-style constitutional monarchy to the restored Bourbons.

Apart from the ultra-royalists in the Maistre tradition who wished for a return to the Old Regime, an almost universal élite Anglomania swept France at the time of the 'Restoration' of Louis XVIII in 1814. This was true not only of returned exiles like Madame de Staël, of whom it was said in 1814 that there were three European powers, Britain, Russia and Madame de Staël. The king himself accepted the English model, having spent the years 1807–14 there and having become accustomed to speaking English and reading English newspapers.[134] (And let us not forget Saint-Simon and Thierry's 1814 scheme for a Franco-British Union; see Chapter 4, p. 79–80.) Restored by foreign arms, the Bourbon monarchy had to seek an accommodation with the constitutional monarchy of 1789–91 and abandon any hope of restoring the pre-revolutionary regime. In the preface to his 1814 *Reflections on Constitutions*, Constant confessed 'I have not sought to be original: on many points, I have stayed close to the English constitution; I have explained why what existed in England was good rather than proposing something new.' More circumspectly, in a pamphlet on the freedom of the press, he wrote: 'I have recommended not the slavish imitation but the close study of the English constitution and its application here in all that suits us . . .'[135] Although France's 1814 charter had no amendment procedure and was therefore unamendable, it was like Britain's unwritten constitution in that it was capable of diametrically opposed interpretations; and much of the political battle between liberals like Constant and the ultras was over the way it was to be implemented.

Unlike intransigent republicans, such as Destutt de Tracy, who regarded monarchy and liberty as incompatible, Constant (echoing perhaps Montesquieu's description of England as 'a republic disguised as a monarchy') regarded the difference between a republic and constitutional monarchy as purely formal. The real distinction was between constitutional government and absolute monarchy.[136] This undoubtedly explains the intellectual ease with which Constant accommodated to changes in political regime, provided they did not claim absolute power as had the Old Regime monarchy and Napoleon. In his exposition of the theory of parliamentary government based on British practice, *Reflections on Constitutions*, written in a month and rushed into print ten days before the royal proclamation of the charter, Constant drew again on his 1806 manuscript for the ideas of a separation of executive powers between a neutral monarch and ministers responsible to parliament. Sir James Mackintosh compared his old friend to Montesquieu, as 'unquestionably the first political writer (of his time) on the Continent, and apparently the ablest man in France', whose discussion of ministerial responsibility 'though founded on English practice, would convey instruction to most of those who have best studied the English Constitution.'[137] Constant had adroitly adapted to circumstances but circumstances took a disconcerting turn. Constant appeared to have assured himself of the position as France's leading theorist of the constitutional monarchy, only to find that Napoleon had unexpectedly returned to power. Although during the 'Hundred Days' Constant's willing recruitment by Napoleon as constitutional draftsman was supported by his political friends Lafayette, Sismondi and Madame de Staël, the last subsequently castigated him for 'seeking to mask such a man [Napoleon] as a constitutional monarch.'[138]

Napoleon quite cynically used Constant in 1815 as he had used Sieyès in 1799. Even if he had won at Waterloo, the so-called 'Additional Act' to the imperial constitution – really a new constitution, nicknamed by Montlosier *la Benjamine* after its author – would not have been likely to survive. Napoleon told Constant, who within days produced his constitution, not to nourish any illusions; only an élite minority wanted a constitution, while most of the people simply wanted him back in power. That Constant himself had few illusions can be seen from his diary entry of 31 March 1815: 'The intentions are liberal; the practice will be despotic. Never mind.'[139] Attacked as 'councillor of state to tyranny', Constant responded by rushing into print with his *Political Principles*, yet another cannibalization of parts of his 1806 manuscript aimed at defending on grounds of principle his liberal 1815 constitution.[140] The 'June' constitution – which lasted for only twenty days – was swept away by the French defeat at Waterloo and Constant, discredited as a weathercock by his political gyrations, temporarily retreated to England to allow time to repair his severely damaged political credibility.

Against counter-revolution

From the second Restoration to his death fifteen years later Constant threw himself into an untiring battle against those who wished to turn the clock back. It has been said of him that when he was not speaking he was writing. In a letter to his electoral agent in the Sarthe, which he represented in parliament from 1819 to 1822, Constant scathingly described the ultra-royalist majority he faced in 1820: 'All the insolence of the provincial nobility, all the ignorance of the court nobility, all the fury of the counter-revolutionaries, all the greed of titled beggars, as well as the firm resolve to listen to nothing and the inability to understand anything . . . '[141] In a parliamentary speech in the same year, Constant defined counter-revolution as 'a system which will gradually attack all the rights and guarantees which the nation sought in 1789 and secured in 1814.'[142] He made over 120 speeches in his first parliament (1819–22) and some 250 throughout his parliamentary career, which like Tocqueville he spent almost exclusively in opposition. In the process, he acquired increasing popularity among the liberal-minded during the last decade of his life, culminating in the consecration of a national funeral by the newly installed July Monarchy.

Although the fashionable fascination with Britain quickly declined in France after 1815, as it became identified with anti-catholicism and the oppression of the Irish, economic crisis and widespread poverty, Constant remained the resolute champion of British parliamentary democracy, despite the absurdities of the unreformed electoral system and the fact that his Whig friends were in opposition. To him, the supreme pleasure was now to exercise his mordant wit in parliamentary debate in a style which he had learnt in Britain; a delectation shared by – among many others – Stendhal, who wrote that in his subtle and clever way 'Constant has, more than anyone else in France, taught his compatriots the meaning of *constitutional government*.'[143] Constant counter-attacked the most eloquent champion of the regime, Chateaubriand, who was later to come over to the liberal cause and describe Constant as the wittiest man since Voltaire. The leading authority on the Restoration parliamentary system has asserted that of all its champions, 'it is especially Benjamin Constant who, at the rostrum or in the press, with his speeches, articles, letters, pamphlets, books, never for an instant deserted the fight for liberal ideas. To the same and perhaps an even greater extent than Chateaubriand, he imparted a parliamentary education to liberal France; he overcame the ignorance of the unpolished bourgeoisie. His writings are more legalistic, more precise and more profound than those of Chateaubriand. Chateaubriand was a literary figure who made an excursion into politics and produced a masterpiece: the *Monarchy according to the Charter*. Benjamin Constant was a political writer who made an excursion into literature and produced a masterpiece: *Adolphe*.'[144]

In an 1817 pre-electoral manifesto, Constant set out the political standpoint of those who called themselves *Indépendants*, to distinguish themselves from the large number of government officials in parliament but also to indicate their independence of all governments since 1789. 'The independants are those who, for the last thirty years, have wanted the same things; those who have repeated the same truths to all governments . . . who, when the sovereignty of the people was proclaimed, said to the people that its sovereignty was limited by justice; who, when the stormy tyranny of that sovereignty gave way to a single person's despotism, said to him [Napoleon] that he only existed thanks to the laws; that the laws he treated as obstacles were his safeguards, that in overthrowing them he undermined his throne . . . . The independants are those who love constitutional monarchy because it is constitutional . . . detest arbitrariness under all its labels and expose the hollowness of all its pretexts.'[145] Constant narrowly failed (by eight votes) to secure election to parliament in 1818, being defeated (thanks to prefectoral intervention) by another – but less resolute and dangerous – opponent of the government, Saint-Simon's patron Ternaux. In March 1819 he was elected deputy for the Sarthe without himself having to fight a campaign, which he left to his electoral agent.

In the French parliament, there was no party system, much less a two-party system, Louis XVIII exclaiming in exasperation to his prime minister Decazes: 'Oh Tories, Oh Whigs, where are you?'[146] Three loose

parliamentary groupings sometimes met to discuss tactics but they had –
to Constant's disgust – no discipline in support of an agreed programme.
In 1819 the Right, whose leader was Villèle, had fifty-eight members;
the Right-Centre, consisting mainly of government officials, had some
sixty-seven members; the Independent or Far Left, which met at the home
of Saint-Simon's banker friend Jacques Laffitte, had about forty members;
while some fifty doctrinaire Left-Centre Liberals, who wanted to 'nationalise
royalty and royalise the nation', met at his industrial friend Ternaux's
house.[147] The Independent Left's figurehead was Lafayette, Laffitte its financier, Constant its spokesman, though it numbered Daunou and Destutt
de Tracy among its champions (Lafayette being Tracy's son-in-law).

Constant's fascinating electoral and political correspondence with his
militantly liberal election agent Goyet is very instructive of Constant's def-
ferential attitude towards his electors and of them towards him, as well as his
intransigent isolation in the Chamber of Deputies, an independant among
indépendants. 'Meetings of deputies in Paris never lead to anything I
shall act on my own in the Chamber . . . . I see no possibility other than
a complete return to the Charter . . . . I will fight anything else with all
my strength . . . '[148] He predicted that the ultra-Right, enraged by the
assassination of the Duc de Berry in 1820, would destroy the monarchy
by being more royalist than royalty, just as the Jacobins had caused the
downfall of the Republic by being more republican than the Republic. He
warned in 1822 that if the king violated the charter, he would render his
own power illegitimate, which proved prophetic of the events leading to
the 1830 Revolution. Meanwhile, Constant and Lafayette, his fellow Sarthe
liberal, were defeated at the 1822 election, Constant having been put on
trial and sentenced to a month's imprisonment just before on a trumped
up charge of involvement in conspiracy and press offences.

Constant was a tireless defender of freedom of the press from attacks
by the Restoration governments, describing such attacks as 'state crime'
against the interests of government as much as of the people. He had
argued in 1814 that 'Governments do not know the damage they do in
monopolising the privilege of speaking and writing about their own acts.
One never believes what is asserted by an authority that does not allow
others to reply; one believes everything said against an authority which
does not tolerate scrutiny by others.'[149] He did not content himself with
well-turned epigrammatic generalities. Like Voltaire's championing of
Calas, Constant defended Wilfrid Regnault, accused of murder, not merely
pillorying the official abuse of procedure and power but the threat to judicial
authority. He showed that press publicity could be a means of securing
justice as well as a political weapon for the weak. 'Publicity is the

only defence of the numberless class, the most important by its usefulness but anonymous by its multitude.'[150] So, whether it was a case of individual injustice or that of a whole class, Constant argued for the full exercise of press freedom.

If *Adolphe*, his autobiographical novel possibly named after his predecessor as Madame de Staël's lover, is Constant's claim to literary fame, his celebrity as a political thinker has been mainly due to his 1819 lecture on 'Ancient and modern liberty' which was a liberal manifesto based upon his earlier scholarly work. Anticipating Weber's formulation of ideal types, Constant developed a contrast between antiquity and modernity in which 'Modern liberty was the innovation of large-scale, caste-free, internationally open, religiously pluralistic and intensively commercial societies.'[151] Classical public liberty, focused upon leisured, *full-time citizens* participating practically in sovereignty, deciding upon war and peace, in legislation, in judicial judgements, enforcing accountability upon those in temporary authority, involved a fusion of state and society, with total subordination of the individual to society. By contrast, modern private liberty meant personal choice and secure enjoyment of opinion, property, profession, association, without having to account to others, involving the separation of a circumscribed state from society and the individual autonomy of the *part-time citizen* so busy with his own affairs that he was content to let others govern as his representatives. Constant clearly owed a debt to the Sieyès distinction between general passive citizenship and the few active citizens, which itself was based upon an analysis of modern representative government appropriate to a commercially developed society.[152]

Although the distinction was first sketched out in Madame de Staël's unpublished book on how to end the Revolution, in which Constant collaborated to such an extent that he felt entitled to transpose passages into his own work, it was in Book 16 of his unpublished 1806 *Principles of Politics* that he developed it most fully. The first difference he stressed was that 'Today the mass of citizens have only an illusory share in the exercise of sovereignty. The people can only be slave or free; it can never govern . . . . The happiness of the majority is no longer the enjoyment of power but of personal liberty.'[153] This corresponded to the Directory indifference to public affairs of the self-interested survivors of the heroic enthusiasms and exertions of the early 1790s, yearning to be left in peace and rejecting Robespierre's classical equation of public with virtue and private with corruption. Secondly, trade became a central concern, as people sought to achieve the possession of what they desired by work and calculation rather than by force and enslavement. Here, clearly, Constant was looking beyond the contemporary turmoil of the revolutionary and

Napoleonic wars to an era of peaceful commerce, such as Tocqueville was to discern as the principal preoccupation of Americans. However, to make clear that the impossibility and even undesirability of classical direct democracy did not mean a simple retreat into individualist quietism, Constant declared: 'I do not wish to renounce political liberty but to demand civil liberty with other forms of political liberty', i.e. representative institutions.[154]

What provoked his hostility towards the emerging Saint-Simonian sect in 1826 was its desire, in the wake of Maistre, to found an 'industrial papacy' to act as a new 'spiritual power'. In accents that anticipate John Stuart Mill's critique of Auguste Comte forty years later, Constant attacked the authoritarian and scientistic dogmatism that was intended to bring about a 'stationary' society. Allergic to claims to certain truths and infallible knowledge, Constant argued that industrial society was based upon and promoted liberty, whereas the Saint-Simonians wanted to organize a new and more effective tyranny.[155] Although he shared their view that the development of industrial societies would encourage the replacement of war by peaceful trade, he could not accept that the price of ending revolutionary disorder was a retrograde recourse to a superannuated corporatism, intended to provide 'police surveillance over the class of workers'.[156]

Constant's cosmopolitanism and liberalism meant that he sought to discredit nationalism by reference to both the wider need for peace and the narrower need to federalize and decentralize government within large states. Classical city-states had recruited slave labour and strengthened their cohesion by perpetual warfare, but modern states relied upon free labour and trade, which necessitated tranquillity. 'Peace has no precise purpose. Each person freely decides his own purpose, thinks about how to achieve it and makes his own calculations . . . . Some say to government: lead us to victory and to achieve it subject us to the severe law of discipline. Others say: protect us from violence and do not bother us further.'[157] Napoleon had demonstrated that war might still be enthusiastically pursued by political leaders but Constant believed that, thanks to the people's desire for pleasure achieved through the wealth created by industry and trade, they had abandoned 'the narrow and hostile spirit adorned with the name of patriotism'.[158] Willing to defend their *patrie* from attack, they were not prepared to confuse this with attacking other *patries*. While the nineteenth century lent some credence to such optimism, the twentieth century has belied it with a vengeance.

Tocqueville's advocacy of decentralization was anticipated by Constant and Madame de Staël. The violence necessary to enforce uniformity was not worth the benefit, argued Constant. 'The modest advantage of a smooth and equal surface which the arrogant eye of power can survey without any offensive hindrance is a paltry compensation for the loss of a mass of local feelings, memories and habits, which constitute the only true happiness . . . . It is by sacrificing everything to an exaggerated uniformity that large states have become a scourge for humanity.'[159] While large states were better able to protect their citizens from foreign domination and subsume sectional interests to the general good, they tended to become remote, oppressive and inert. Constant favoured a diffused pluralism, 'a new kind of federalism', by which he meant maximum decentralization. 'The patriotism that is born in the localities is, today especially, the only true patriotism', so people should be 'given in their homes, their communes, their *arrondissements*, as much political importance as possible without harming the general good.'[160]

Throughout his life Constant was preoccupied with the importance of religion. He eventually published five volumes on the subject. Against those, such as the Roman Catholic Maistre, who was concerned with monolithic religious authority as a form of social control, the Protestant Constant was above all an advocate of pluralistic religious freedom, praising both Roman polytheism and British non-conformism. Unlike Madame de Staël, who had favoured making Protestantism the pro-Republican state religion in France, adapting the Anglican pattern, Constant remained a resolute anticlerical who thought that mixing dogmatic religion and authoritarian politics combined religious indifference with political persecution. His religious pluralism accommodated state subsidies for all religions with a substantial following. 'Religions are like highways: I welcome the state maintaining them, provided each person has the right to choose his own footpath.'[161] True or false, the individual's convictions were his most sacred property. It was left to Edgar Quinet fully to place the Revolution in the historic context of a post-Reformation secular struggle of Protestant individualist democracy failing to defeat a Catholic despotism perpetuated by Louis-Napoleon's Second Empire.[162]

The Revolution resumes: a liberal apotheosis?

Constant lived just long enough to take part in the 1830 Revolution and to be disappointed at its results. Under the influence of Maistre's ideological prospectus for dynastic self-destruction, Charles X, by a combination of self-deluding arrogance and obtuse intransigence, actively prepared his own downfall through violations of the 1814 charter. In an 1827 speech in parliament, Constant warned 'We cry out to ministers: the road taken by the old regime led France into an abyss; and their reassuring reply is: do not worry, we are following the same road.'[163] Balzac, no friend of either Revolution, claimed that '1830 consummated the work of 1793'.[164] Many liberals in 1830 hoped it would consummate 1789 but it was not to be. In his last months, Constant continued to be the forlorn champion of a liberal lost cause in its apparent hour of triumph. The meanness and mediocrity of the bourgeois *politique* quickly showed itself to be far removed from the generosity and high principle of Constant's liberal *mystique*.

The liberal press campaign that preceded the king's electoral defeat and overthrow was one in which younger men like Thiers were taking over the lead from Constant. Along with Lafayette, Laffitte and Guizot, Constant belonged to the liberal electoral organization *Aide-toi, le ciel t'aidera* that helped secure an electoral victory against Charles X's absolutist pretensions by those, such as Constant, who advocated resistance to the charter violations in his March 1830 speech on the address to the king. A serious illness caused his absence from Paris in July 1830 when matters came to a head. Lafayette is said to have written to him: 'There is a dangerous game being played here in which we are risking our heads. Bring yours.'[165] Never reluctant to gamble, especially in a liberal cause, Constant played a leading role among those deputies who called on Louis-Philippe to become lieutenant-governor of the kingdom. Another prominent but querulous conspirator, Laffitte (who had probably introduced Constant to Louis-Philippe some five years earlier), had the following exchange with Constant. 'What will become of us tomorrow?' 'Tomorrow we'll be hung.'[166]

Thiers, who had helped rehabilitate 1789 with his ten-volume *History of the French Revolution* (which appeared between 1824 and 1828), worked with Laffitte and Talleyrand to prevent the republicans using Lafayette, recently appointed general commander of the National Guard, to proclaim the Republic. At a key interview with Louis-Philippe, Lafayette admitted that his American ideal could not then be applied in France, which needed 'a popular throne, surrounded by republican institutions', what he later called a 'royal republic'![167] Chateaubriand sarcastically referred to Lafayette embracing Louis-Philippe at the Paris town hall: 'The republican kiss made a king.'[168] Unable to walk, Constant was taken there on a stretcher, having, it has been claimed, criticized his friend Lafayette for refusing to assume the presidency of the Republic.[169] Be that as it may, Constant – who had already provided the description of the functions of a French constitutional monarch – was rewarded for his part by having his 200,000 francs gambling debts paid by Louis-Philippe and appointment to the chairmanship of the key section on legislative and administrative justice at the *Conseil d'Etat*.

He did not, as he hoped, become minister of education and he died a disappointed man, seeing the materialist bourgeoisie beginning to betray his brand of liberalism.

The socialist Louis Blanc has left a rather acid picture of Constant's grandiose funeral procession – liberalism's self-celebration – extending from the Madeleine to the Bastille, surrounded by National Guards and escorted by ministers, generals, deputies, delegations of workers and revolutionary combatants . . . and the students incited by Blanqui who wished to take his coffin to the Pantheon. (The government was forced to promise to inter him there but later 'forgot' to do so.) Lafayette spoke at his graveside, followed a few days later by his dismissal as head of the National Guard, the new king and his Court thinking that they could bring the 1830 Revolution to an end. With Constant was buried that pure liberalism of principle that could probably only flourish in opposition. 'From the beginning of his career as a publicist until his death, he adhered steadily to the principles of 1789. He never wavered in his advocacy of the disestablishment of privilege, jury trials, the career open to talents, popular sovereignty expressed through representative institutions (including the right to opposition), absolute freedom of speech and press, unconditional religious toleration and the laicization of politics and education.'[170] As for the Revolution, it had once again been temporarily halted and it was Tocqueville who would present the liberal view of its successor in 1848.

The July Monarchy was intellectually and politically dominated for most of its eighteen years by the conservative bourgeois liberalism of François Guizot and the *doctrinaires*. There was no love lost between them and Constant, protagonist of liberty as an absolute in theory and bohemianism in practice, whereas they were relativists who were quite ready to restrain freedom in the pompous name of the 'sovereignty of reason' and adopted a puritanical, conventionally moralistic style of life. Constant was aligned with the left-wing liberals, who became known as the party of 'movement', while the *doctrinaires* were identified with 'resistance' to much more than a change of dynasty. (One of their leaders, Royer-Collard, pushed his animosity as far as preferring a feeble nonentity to Constant for election to the *Académie Française*.) They were ideologically destined for government as much as he was for opposition, seeing the press as an instrument for guiding society rather than as a bulwark protecting society from government. However, Sismondi was right when he wrote of Constant that 'In politics, he founded more doctrines than those who have been called doctrinaires.'[171]

There was a revival of interest in Constant's ideas (and then only in part) with the liberal and non-interventionist Third Republic, when the

Orleanists and moderate republicans came together in the parliamentary group known for their pragmatism as the 'opportunists'. The way was prepared, as we shall see, by Adolphe Thiers, who played a key part, after establishing the July Monarchy, in the foundation of the Third Republic. His famous formula that 'the King reigns but does not rule' was a striking reformulation of Constant's conception of the neutral but active head of state, which was to be embodied in the presidents of the Third Republic. It was also in the Third Republic that Brissot's 1791 anticipation of Lord Acton's famous remark that 'all power even delegated power, is essentially corrupting' came into its own in a regime that institutionalized the distrust of political power.[172] Through Second Empire liberals like Laboulaye, professor of comparative legislation at the Collège de France, who republished some of Constant's writings in 1861 for use against Louis-Napoleon, the continuity of his influence, associated with that of Tocqueville, was maintained.[173] The resurgence of concern with his thought in the 1980s coincides with the resurgence of French liberalism, which has been honoured more in the breach than in the observance.

CHAPTER SIX

TOCQUEVILLE: THE DECENTRALIST ANTIDOTE TO BUREAUCRATIC DEMOCRACY

'I came into the world at the end of a long revolution which, after having destroyed the old state, had not succeeded in creating anything durable. Aristocracy was already dead when I was born and democracy had not yet come into existence; my instincts could not draw me unthinkingly towards either. I was living in a country which for forty years had tried out everything and settled permanently on nothing, so I had few political illusions.'[1] Though he could claim to his English translator Henry Reeve (*Times* leader writer and jurist who became registrar of the Privy Council) that he felt detached from his dead aristocratic past, Tocqueville's family pride gave him a particular affinity with certain aspects of the Old Regime and a repulsion for some features of the Revolution. An ancestor had fought in the invading Norman army at Hastings in 1066, while his father was imprisoned during the Terror, being saved from execution (like Saint-Simon) by Thermidor. Having a Catholic and monarchical *ultra* for a father, who became a peer and prefect during the Restoration, might not seem to have prepared Tocqueville for his role as the greatest analyst of American democracy and of the French Revolution. However, his father's prefectoral experience provided him in early 1832 with a critique of centralization as a secular trend in France, a country which was not suited to American-style federalism. An elder brother married the daughter of a governor of the Bank of France and became a member of the *grand bourgeois* '200 Families'. His relations included Chateaubriand, whose *Voyage d'Amérique* of 1827 preceded Tocqueville's own transatlantic visit and book, as well as his cousin Molé, a senior official under Napoleon, whose offer when prime minister in 1837 to help Tocqueville start his political career in parliament was spurned.[2] Although his family background undoubtedly exerted an influence upon his political behaviour, his attitude of mind was acquired from other sources, first and foremost from Montesquieu.

Predecessors

Tocqueville virtually never acknowledged his intellectual debts but in a letter written while preparing the second volume of *Democracy in America*, he declared that 'There are three authors with whom I daily commune a little: Pascal, Montesquieu and Rousseau.'[3] John Stuart Mill, in his review of *Democracy*, claimed 'The book is such as Montesquieu might have written'[4] and this is true of its pervasive liberal values and in the historical-cum-sociological comparative method of analysis he used. Fifteen years later, after a disappointing political career that convinced Tocqueville that his greatness lay as a writer rather than as a man of action, he wrote again to the same friend that he was using Montesquieu's *Considerations on the Causes of the Grandeur and Decadence of the Romans* as his 'inimitable model' for the unfinished masterpiece on *The Old Régime and the French Revolution*.[5] The closest observer of their intellectual ties, Melvin Richter, has described Tocqueville as Montesquieu's greatest and most acute disciple, while at the same time tracing their typological mode of comparative analysis back to Aristotle, Bodin and Machiavelli.[6] However, in the case of Montesquieu and Tocqueville, the focus was on types of society rather than on political regime.[7]

We saw in the previous chapter that another disciple of Montesquieu, Benjamin Constant, developed an ideal type analysis of ancient and modern liberty. It was in the generalizing second part of *Democracy* that Tocqueville used Montesquieu's ideal-type categories to select his evidence and formulate hypotheses for an implicitly comparative analysis that focused upon national culture and character, the causes and consequences of extensive equality, the interplay of associational social life and the centralization of state institutions.[8] Sharing with Montesquieu an aristocratic conception of freedom, Tocqueville observed the emergence of democratic egalitarianism with the detachment of an anthropologist visiting a primitive society. He brought together the contrasting influences of Montesquieu and Rousseau in his sociological stress upon the cultural matrix of the combination of circumstances and laws that was impelling society simultaneously towards greater liberty and equality. Nevertheless, he feared that the liberty he, with Montesquieu, valued most would be subordinated to the equality that Rousseau prized above all.[9]

Unlike Constant, who retained the imprint of Sieyès' influence, remaining preoccupied with institutional forms as of paramount importance, Tocqueville wrote to a friend in 1853: 'I attribute to institutions only a secondary influence over men's destiny.'[10] His awareness of the limitations of political structures preceded his own political experience. Learning from

Montesquieu to apply the comparative method with relativist circumspection, he wrote to his father from America in 1831: 'There is nothing absolute in the theoretical value of political institutions, and their efficiency depends almost always on the original circumstances and the social condition of the people to whom they are applied. I see institutions succeed here which would infallibly turn France upside down',[11] such as the federalism that had enabled the United States to practise demoracy in a large state. However, whereas Montesquieu and Rousseau had equated republican citizenship with classical virtue, Tocqueville's 'American' conception of modern citizenship was based upon enlightened individual self-interest in collective prosperity, not patriotic self-sacrifice. Nevertheless, he did not believe with Montesquieu and Constant that it was the entrepreneurial commercial spirit that promoted the political practices that had instilled the habit of freedom in England; rather, he reversed the argument, attributing successful capitalism to a love of civil and political liberty. Why did Tocqueville appear to fly in the face of their arguments? Evidence rather than idealism prompted his standpoint.

Writing during the materialistic July Monarchy, in which the incitement to pursue personal profit had diverted the bourgeoisie from a concern with political participation, the evidence he faced made Tocqueville refuse to subscribe to the belief that calculating acquisitiveness would foster freedom. In prophetic words, Tocqueville warned that 'There is a very dangerous phase in the life of democratic peoples. When the taste for physical pleasures has grown more rapidly than either education or experience of free institutions, the time comes when men are carried away .... Intent only on getting rich, they do not notice the close connections between private fortunes and general prosperity .... They find it a tiresome inconvenience to exercise political rights which distract them from industry .... They cannot waste their precious time in unrewarding work .... As those who work are unwilling to attend to public affairs, and as the class which might have wished thus to fill its leisure no longer exists, the role of government is left unfilled. If, at this critical moment, an able and ambitious man once gets power, he finds the way open for usurpations of every sort. So long as he sees to it for a certain time that material interests flourish, he can easily get away with everything else. He must above all guarantee good order .... A nation which asks nothing from the government beyond the maintenance of order is already a slave at the bottom of its heart. It is a slave to its prosperity, and the road is free for the man to tie the fetters.'[12] It was over such prosperous civic indifference, with the assistance of many of the disciples of Saint-Simon, that Louis-Napoleon was plutocratically to preside twelve years later. Popular acquiescence in despotism lasted for twenty years and Tocqueville did not live to see its inglorious demise or the revival of the revolutionary movement.

While Tocqueville was in agreement with Saint-Simon and Constant about the decline of militarism and the rise of pacific international commercialism, he foresaw and feared class conflict between the new industrial aristocracy and the subordinate working poor.[13] Like them, he felt the need for a religious corrective to revolutionary rationalism and capitalist cupidity. In his case this led not to Saint-Simon's liberticidal 'New Christianity' or Constant's libertarian Protestantism but to Maistrian catholicism. Maistre had blamed the secular disintegration of the organic medieval religious and political order for the political revolution and ideological fragmentation that afflicted modern society. Tocqueville followed Maistre in stressing the need to restore a religion-based social consensus but he saw this as having to be based on democracy, not upon a rejection of it. The reconciliation of catholicism and the French Revolution would offer the best form of democratic social control over what Maistre had called 'political protestantism carried to the most absolute individualism'.[14] The disruptive threat of bourgeois individualism, pilloried by Maistre and then popularized as the social disease *par excellence* by the Saint-Simonians, was contained in America by Protestant religious pluralism. However, Tocqueville believed that in France social cohesion required the undisputed authority of the universal Catholic Church. Against Protestant Constant, the advocate of modern liberty, who saw individual privacy as the sanctuary of freedom, the classical civic humanist Tocqueville regarded the selfish, isolated individual as the prey of despotism when deprived of the comprehensive shelter of traditional belief. So, turning the tables on both revolutionary secularism and anti-revolutionary dogmatism, the pragmatic and sceptical Tocqueville stressed 'the political utility of religion' for the consolidation of democracy.[15]

The conservative corrective to Tocqueville's liberalism also derived from the *doctrinaire* historical determinism he learnt particularly from Guizot in the lectures on the 'History of civilization in France' which he attended in 1829 and his reading of the *History of Civilization in Europe* that he described as 'prodigious in analysis of ideas'.[16] Whereas Constant had applied Montesquieu's ideal-type conception of social change to the explanation of political change in relation to liberty, Guizot and Tocqueville were to generalize this insight. In the process, they broke with the liberal emphasis upon individual rights and instead stressed the egalitarian social revolution that had led to the dominance of the bourgeoisie in place of the aristocracy after a prolonged period of class conflict. Whereas the pre-*doctrinaire* liberals like Sieyès and Constant had focused upon constitutional and institutional innovation in shaping the process of change, post-*doctrinaire* liberals like Tocqueville emphasized deeper-seated socio-economic structures. Not political will and legal artifice but the inexorable processes of social mobility would determine historic outcomes.

While Maistre had only offered a theory of social decay and Constant had countered with an individualist theory of human progress, Tocqueville – in the wake of Guizot – regarded the advent of nation-building democracy as part of a secular providential process, while being hostile to concurrent state-building centralization. (Tocqueville's heart was closer to Saint-Simon's former collaborator Thierry, who had linked the historic rise of the bourgeoisie with the emergence of self-governing communes, while his head compelled him to agree with Guizot, who had stressed the bourgeoisie's willingness to sacrifice local autonomy, in alliance with absolute monarchy against the feudal aristocracy.) While Guizot's pre-Tocquevillian analysis of the historic continuity between the Old Regime and the French Revolution was based upon a survey of a thousand years of pre-revolutionary European history, it was the counter-revolutionary attempt to turn the clock back to an obsolete aristocratic order which accounted for the fact that 'Guizot spoke in 1820 like Tocqueville in 1840.'[17] From 1820 to 1827, reacting to the assassination of the Duc de Berry (which as we saw led to the trial of Saint-Simon), 'In rapid succession came bills to curtail press freedom, to restrict the suffrage, to restore primogeniture and entail, to make sacrilege a crime punishable by death, to indemnify the noblesse for their losses during the Revolution . . . . The major breakthrough in sociological argument . . . resulted from the debate *under the Restoration* generated by the ultra-royalist proposals to restore the *ancien régime*.'[18] This was the formative period for Tocqueville's understanding of politics.

Despite Guizot's prominent pre-1830 role as a theoretician of a 'truly national party' representing the middle classes and his post-1830 role as its most intransigent and authoritarian political leader, it is hyperbole to describe him as 'a sort of Lenin of the bourgeoisie'.[19] He played an insignificant part in the 1830 Revolution itself but he was undoubtedly the supreme ornament and embodiment of the July Monarchy absolute bourgeoisie. In a parliamentary speech that over 200 deputies subscribed to have circulated in 30,000 copies, Guizot had proclaimed: 'I want, I seek and I bend all my efforts to secure the political preponderance of the middle classes in France, the final and complete organization of the great victory that the middle classes have won over privilege and absolute power from 1789 to 1830.'[20] While Tocqueville borrowed Guizot's interrelated themes of the bourgeois-based emergence of democracy and centralization successively as the leitmotif of his greatest books on democracy and the French Revolution (though both themes are present in each work), he could not accept Guizot's unhistoric view that the democratic tide would stop once bourgeois domination had been achieved. In an unpublished note for the second volume of *Democracy*, Tocqueville wrote: 'I do not believe in the definitive government on behalf of the middle classes and even if I believed it to be possible, I would oppose it.'[21] Like that other *doctrinaire* Royer-Collard, who was his political model as Guizot was in certain fundamentals his theoretical model, Tocqueville opposed Guizot during the July Monarchy because he believed that the social changes making for the extension of equality could not be successfully resisted by an exclusively bourgeois political regime. Guizot's ambition to stop the social and political revolutionary process was illusory, as both Tocqueville and later Marx were to argue against the historical determinist's attempt to reintroduce a foredoomed political *volontarisme*.[22] In this judgement, the vanquished aristocrat and the protagonist of proletarian ascendancy proved more perspicacious than the triumphant bourgeois. However, whereas Marx interpreted the continuing determinist process on the British liberal model of bourgeois business capitalism, in the light of French experience Tocqueville gave full weight to the statist model of bourgeois bureaucratic democracy.

If Guizot was the mentor through whom Tocqueville in the late 1820s received a conservative determinist education, Royer-Collard in the mid-1830s imparted to him a more liberal conservative legacy from Montesquieu to the post-revolutionary Restoration and July Monarchy *doctrinaires*. When they met in 1835 the former Girondin lawyer – who had served in the Directory parliament and had become a convert to constitutional monarchy and secret adviser of the future Louis XVIII in 1797, lectured on the history of philosophy under Napoleon and emerged as the foremost parliamentary protagonist of the 1814 charter – had at the age of 72 gone into opposition against Guizot's repressive July Monarchy policies. For the decisive years in which he was preparing the second volume of *Democracy*, Tocqueville came under the spell of the old revolutionary, whose mission was to free the liberal aspirations of 1789 from their revolutionary incubus. 'In both philosophy and politics' Roger-Collard was for Tocqueville 'a model and an adviser, a teacher and a confidant; he was also a friend and lastly, wrote Tocqueville, "almost a father".'[23] Royer-Collard reciprocated the 30-year-old Tocqueville's admiration, comparing the first volume of *Democracy* 'which I have read five times, to Aristotle's *Politics* and the *Esprit des Lois*.'[24]

This did not mean that they saw eye to eye on the fundamental question of democracy. Royer-Collard's indelible French revolutionary memories left him with the conviction that 'democracy in government is incapable of prudence; this is because it is naturally violent, warlike, spendthrift.'[25] By contrast, Tocqueville had seen in America a democracy that had united rather than divided the nation and was to present it as the only form of government that could stabilize a post-aristocratic society. Tocqueville did borrow from Guizot and Royer-Collard the idea that centralization was an integral part of the nation- and state-building role of monarchy and democracy. However, like Royer-Collard and against Guizot, he sought to correct democracy's centralizing propensity in the spirit of Montesquieu's aristocratic recourse to decentralization. State sovereignty had emerged to dominance through an almost imperceptible process, destroying historic intermediary bodies. It left only isolated individuals, who were dignified with the name of citizen but were reduced to the subordinate status of *administrés*. 'Centralization has not arrived with its head erect, with the authority of a principle; rather it has developed modestly, as a consequence, as a necessity . . . . That is how we have become an *administered* people, under the control of irresponsible civil servants, themselves centralized through the power of which they are agents.'[26] This view was to play an even more important part in his study of the *Old Régime and the French Revolution* than in the second volume on *Democracy*, though Tocqueville was less disposed to concentrate his fire on the bureaucratic proclivities of popular sovereignty.

Royer-Collard pushed his distrust of power further than Tocqueville, not merely refusing to belong to any political party but refusing all offers of office, identifying liberty with the capacity to resist the powers that be. The reason he did not go as far as Constant in his defence of press and religious freedom or in his insistence upon the irremovability of judges and on parliamentary financial control, was that Royer-Collard sought to limit the despotic dangers of sovereignty by an appeal to functional social interests, not to individual rights. Government was a compromise or balance between opposed interests and the 1814 charter was admirable precisely because it consecrated power sharing. It embodied a historic compromise between the claims to personal sovereignty of the king and collective sovereignty of the people in such a way 'that varying interests have combined in a result which, because limited by all, is acceptable to all.'[27] Royer-Collard had hoped that public opinion, especially middle-class opinion, reflected politically in parliament and juridically through the jury, would provide the pervasive context for a stable political authority; but Charles X's attempt to retrieve absolute power revived the revolutionary process. France was not yet ready for the type of *juste-milieu* bourgeois pluralism that the July Monarchy unsuccessfully tried to establish and the Third Republic was to found with more enduring results. The 1830s and 1850s were spent by Tocqueville in struggling intellectually with the problem Royer-Collard bequeathed to him: 'Why had the revolutionary spirit remained so active in France, long after the 1830 Revolution?'[28] From 1839 to 1849 Tocqueville plunged into a political career in which he emulated Royer-Collard's isolation from party politics, while going further in adopting an attitude of critical opposition during the latter half of the July Monarchy that lacked the oratorical sparkle but not the penetration of Constant's role during the Restoration parliaments. However, while Constant expounded an optimistic liberalism on the attack, Tocqueville expressed a pessimistic liberalism on the retreat.

Simply because Tocqueville never referred to Constant, it would be implausible to infer that he ignored his writings. Like many of his contemporaries, Tocqueville almost never cited his sources, even when – as in the case of his *Democracy in America* – we have access to his notes and drafts.[29] This general reluctance to acknowledge intellectual indebtedness was accentuated in Constant's case by Tocqueville's links with Royer-Collard, on whose animosity towards Constant we have already touched (see Chapter 5, p. ···). Isaiah Berlin exaggerates the affinity between the conception of negative liberty in Tocqueville and Constant – describing the latter as the 'most eloquent of all defenders of freedom and privacy' – neglecting Tocqueville's concern to defend the positive or classical liberty of participation in public activity which he observed in America.[30] Rather than opposing the English conception of modern liberty as the individualist right of personal autonomy against the Greek, collectivist conception of civic duty as Constant did, Tocqueville sought for France an American-style reconciliation between them.

This eclecticism got Tocqueville into difficulties when it came to reconciling popular sovereignty with its limitation. 'Benjamin Constant was able to accommodate these two principles within a much more logically consistent framework than Tocqueville' because he believed in natural individual rights, the absence of which in Tocqueville made it 'much more difficult, if not impossible, to find a logical basis for the limitation of sovereignty.'[31] So, despite the fact that they shared the desire to curb sovereign power by constitutional and judicial safeguards, Tocqueville's solution could only hold if an American-style associationist pluralism, that Constant's individualism ignored, gave his 'new kind of liberalism' social restraints upon the abuse of popular sovereignty. It is no accident that Tocqueville lacked Constant's wholehearted commitment to press freedom, writing: 'In America, as in France, it is the same extraordinary power, strange mixture of good and evil, without which freedom could not survive but with which order can hardly be maintained.'[32] While this ambivalent analysis may be nearer to the truth than Constant, in practice it opens the door to just those restraints upon press freedom that the conservative 'liberal' Guizot imposed and which Tocqueville personally opposed. Constant's intransigent liberalism, with its concern to build an illusory impenetrable protection for personal freedom, paradoxically provided a more practical bulwark than Tocqueville's more circumspect liberalism.

It was no accident that while Constant admired most of the successive stages of the first Revolution and was actively involved in the 1830 Revolution, Tocqueville was hostile to the Revolutions of both 1830 and 1848. While they both recognized that ending the revolutionary process meant completing it, Constant's radical liberalism emphasized the unfinished business of fulfilling it while Tocqueville's conservative liberalism stressed its orderly ending. Tocqueville frankly confessed in an introspective fragment of 1841: 'My mind is attracted by democratic institutions but I am instinctively aristocratic because I despise and fear mobs. At the most fundamental level, I passionately love freedom, legality, respect for rights, but not democracy. I hate demagoguery, the disordered action of the masses, their violent and unenlightened intervention in public affairs . . . . I belong neither to the revolutionary nor the conservative party. But, when all is said and done, I incline towards the latter rather than the former because I differ from the conservatives over means rather than ends, while I differ from the revolutionaries over both means and ends.'[33] Writing to Royer-Collard two months earlier, Tocqueville confessed: 'The non-revolutionary, liberal party which alone would suit me does not exist and I will not be able to create it.'[34] Writing a year later to the leader of the dynastic parliamentary opposition, Odilon Barrot, he declared: 'What has always deeply offended me is how little real liberalism one encounters in the Left, which is much more revolutionary than liberal. As long as the Opposition does not change its instinctive preferences, it will only lead to new revolutions or prepare the way for despotism.'[35] As early as 1836, he had objected to being confused with the anarchic 'democratic party' when he was 'a new kind of liberal', seeking to base a stable civic culture not upon a materialistic individualism but upon a socially integrating religion.[36] It was with this complex blend of elements reminiscent of both the Maistrian anti-revolutionary Right and Constant's cautiously revolutionary Left that Tocqueville unenthusiastically faced 'the great Democratic Revolution through which the world is passing', believing it to be 'useful and necessary' if confined within liberal bounds.[37] Such was the agenda of defensive liberalism from the 1830s: persuading reactionary royalists and revolutionary republicans that they should accept the compromise of

constitutional monarchy through a dual appeal to democratic determinism
and liberal restraint.

Understanding the democratic revolution

Guizot had already shown that Europe had for centuries been experiencing
a democratizing process by which privileges and diversity were giving way
to increasing equality and uniformity. Tocqueville argued that this gradual
process of social change was most advanced in France, which transposed it
with revolutionary brutality to the political plane of popular sovereignty.
France's claim to fame was not that it had invented the democratic social
and cultural revolution but that it gave it political direction and spread
it. So impressed were people with the apparent speed and violence with
which the process of change culminated that they exaggerated the break
with the past. Although 'A generation may well declare war on preceding
generations, it is easier to fight them than to avoid resembling them.'[38]
Tocqueville's dual conception of the revolution – a secular social and cultural revolution, as well as an abrupt political and governmental revolution
– along with his dual emphasis upon both its continuity with the past and its
innovative impetus, led to a dual conception of democracy as both a social
condition of equality and a form of government. While these concurrent
levels of argument both enrich and confuse it, their cumulation in action
accounted for the French Revolution's exceptional impact both then and
since. In contrast to Burke, who along with the revolutionaries themselves
had exaggerated the Revolution's novelty, Tocqueville stressed that it was
compelled to use 'the débris of the old order for building up the new'.[39]
However, while playing down the spectacular and experimental character of
the changes carried out, Tocqueville did not wish to devalue the Revolution
but merely to show its limitations. The most serious of these was the rapid
divergence between the initial joint commitment to liberty and equality,
with the latter taking priority over the former and – unlike American
and British experience – the sacrifice of liberalism to democracy. While
France had borrowed some liberal ideas and institutions from Britain and
subsequently Britain some democratic ideas and institutions from France,
each imitated without understanding the other. France proved unable
to reconcile a measured liberty with an undespotic order, so that while
'liberty prepared the French for the great task of overthrowing despotism,
it made them by the same token less well qualified than perhaps any other
nation to replace it by stable government and a healthy freedom under the
sovereignty of law.'[40]

To understand the enduring tendency of France's revolutionary tradition to degenerate into ideological justifications of violent class conflict, we need to touch successively upon its egalitarianism, centralism, patriotism and intellectualism. Whereas the pursuit of liberty was 'more recent and less deeply rooted', there was 'an intense, indomitable hatred of inequality' reflected in a centuries-old resentment of all past privileges and a passionate urge to sweep away all such intolerable survivals.[41] The venom with which Sieyès sought to expel the aristocrats from the nation, followed in the Terror by attempts to exclude and execute on ideological grounds a series of political opponents, marked the extreme intensification of social and political conflict. The breakdown of the old system of exclusive estates was characterized by the self-exclusion of the *émigré* aristocrats, as well as the urge of renegade aristocrats like Saint-Simon to separate the worthy non-producers from the worthless idle. In America, the unity of the nation had been preserved thanks to social mobility and an equality of esteem encouraged by Christianity. Tocqueville hoped that the abolition of primogeniture, the spread of property ownership and the revival of religion would overcome social divisiveness in France.

In his lectures on the history of European civilization which had so impressed Tocqueville, Guizot stressed that the two secular tendencies had been the growth of liberty and equality, helped notably by Protestantism, and the formation of centralized nation-states, in which monarchy played the leading role. While Thierry had praised the twelfth-century rise of the self-governing communes as the institutional spearhead of bourgeois liberation, Guizot was concerned to show that it prepared the way for the Third Estate's triumph, proclaimed by Sieyès at the Revolution, in which 'the bourgeois nation is all, the commune nothing.'[42] However, the indispensable instrument of transition was 'the silent and concealed work of centralisation' achieved by the monarchy between the fifteenth and seventeenth centuries, culminating in the administrative centralization attained by Louis XIV.[43] Tocqueville accepted Guizot's argument that centralization 'was a legacy from the Old Régime' to the Napoleonic regime, when 'The principles of the old order were revived and have been endorsed by all successive governments.'[44] However, long before the Second Empire, when the threats to liberty from administrative centralization had become systematic, Tocqueville had endorsed the liberal rather than the conservative view of centralization when he moved from historical analysis to political assessment. In a preparatory note for his *Democracy in America*, where he had observed the merits of local self-government, Tocqueville wrote: 'Administrative centralization works towards despotism and destroys *civic virtue*. People get used to living as strangers, as settlers in their own country, to saying: "That does not concern me. Let the government look after that."[45] It was to avoid such citizen alienation that Tocqueville, assisted by his American observations, returned to Montesquieu's view that local intermediary bodies were essential safeguards of freedom, which was threatened more by bureaucratic centralization than by political democracy.

Tocqueville varied in his views about how ancient civic virtue might be translated into modern patriotism. In *Democracy in America*, he contrasted the traditional, instinctive, particularist patriotism of pre-revolutionary France with the modern, self-interested and utilitarian patriotism of post-independence America. It was essential to show that public and private prosperity were interdependent and 'make the people see that individual interest is linked to that of the country, for disinterested patriotism has fled beyond recall.'[46] However by 1840, in the second volume of *Democracy*, Tocqueville acknowledged that a purely calculating enlightened self-interest was inadequate; hence the need, on utilitarian grounds, for an appeal to dogmatic religious beliefs and patriotic emotions as supports for social cohesion.[47] In the 1840s, he was advocating in parliament a belligerent foreign and colonial policy to arouse the national spirit, with France acting as the world leader of the democratic forces. He wrote in 1843 that Christianity's 'grand achievement is to have formed a human community beyond national societies. [But] the duties of men among themselves as well as in their capacity as *citizens*, the duties of citizens to their fatherlands, in brief, the public virtues, seem to me to have been inadequately defined and considerably neglected within the moral system of Christianity.'[48] By the 1850s, Tocqueville has moved even further away from a Constant-style cosmopolitanism based upon individual self-interest. Patriotism is at first sight 'a false and narrow passion. The great efforts suggested by patriotism are in reality due to humanity and not to those small fragments of the human race within particular limits called peoples or nations.' But because 'few will burn with ardent love for the entire human species', Tocqueville concludes: 'I am convinced that the interests of the human race are better served by giving every man a particular fatherland than by trying to inflame his passions for the whole of humanity.'[49] So, the universalism of the French Revolution ended up by infusing national feeling with religious fervour, uniting particular nations but exacerbating relations between them.

Indoctrination in the ideas of egalitarianism and *étatisme* – embracing centralization and patriotism – was for Tocqueville essentially the work of the intellectuals. Despite his focus upon the nefarious influence of Rousseau and Mably, their role was played down by Constant. By contrast, Tocqueville claimed that towards the mid-eighteenth century, 'men of letters, men without wealth, social eminence, responsibilities or official status, became in practice the leading politicians of the age, since despite the fact that others held the reins of government, they alone spoke with accents of authority.'[50] Owing to their influence, the French 'revolutionaries had the same fondness for broad generalizations, cut-and-dried legislative systems, and a pedantic symmetry; the same contempt for hard facts; the same taste for reshaping institutions on novel, ingenious, original lines; the same desire to reconstruct the entire constitution according to the rules of logic and a preconceived system instead of trying to rectify its faulty parts.'[51]

While a mathematician like Condorcet or a cleric like Sieyès fully reflected this spirit, the major role was played by the physiocrat economists. Saint-Simon had argued that the lawyers had made the most important impact, a pre-eminence denied them by Tocqueville although he described them as 'the natural democratic leaders' who had helped the kings transform force into authority, before they desired power for themselves.[52] In a chapter entitled 'How the desire for reforms took precedence over the desire for freedom', Tocqueville described how the physiocratic advocates of a new élite in the service of absolute monarchy prepared the way for the Revolution and its authoritarian aftermath, a 'democratic despotism' in which 'the State was a law unto itself.'[53] These heralds of centralized techno-bureaucracy were against 'secondary organizations vested with local powers, and generally speaking to all those counterpoises which have been devised by free peoples at various stages of their history to curb the domination of the central authority.'[54] Thus were imparted the egalitarian, centralist and nationalistic components of the illiberal ideology that would distort the democratic revolution. As he wrote to the English translator of *Democracy* in 1840, 'The great peril of democratic eras, assuredly, is the destruction or excessive weakening of the *parts* of the body social in favour of the *whole* . . . it facilitates despotism, centralization, contempt for private rights . . . which allows society to trample on people and makes the nation everything and the citizen nothing.'[55] Before we consider democracy in practice, we must place Tocqueville's views in the context of the successive phases of his political experience.

Three Contexts: Monarchy, Republic, Empire

Witnessing the fall of the reactionary monarchy in 1830, Tocqueville reacted with characteristic ambivalence, expressing 'a remnant of hereditary affection for Charles X (who) fell for having violated rights that were dear to me.'[56] The spread of property, thanks to the change in the inheritance laws, meant that the Bourbon attempt to restore an exclusive political aristocracy in an increasingly mobile bourgeois society was foredoomed. Tocqueville approved of the *doctrinaire* desire to canalize the threatened revolutionary flood rather than to stubbornly attempt to block it and this meant, as a minimum, replacing Charles X by Louis-Philippe. Casimir-Périer, the second prime minister of the July Monarchy, with wishful thinking sought to scale down 1830's significance. 'This country's misfortune is that many people . . . believe that there has been a revolution in France . . . . There has been no revolution, there has only been a change in the head of state.'[57] However, before the *juste milieu*, upper-middle-class regime could be firmly established against both the aristocratic legitimists and the petty-bourgeois republicans, the king called on Saint-Simon's old patron Laffitte to head an ephemeral government. 'Brought to power in an attempt to quiet the dissatisfaction of the radical Parisians, who saw themselves as robbed of the fruits of their revolution, the Laffitte cabinet had little or no support within the chamber. It remained in power on the sufferance of a disappointed parliamentary majority which feared a too abrupt transition from the days of the barricades to the status quo ante.'[58] From the start, Tocqueville saw the July Monarchy less as a reassuring imitation of the English Glorious Revolution of 1688 than as a frightening portent of another 1789. As he wrote in August 1830: 'Our present state does not seem to me to be stable. The middle classes made the Revolution. God grant that they may not soon repent of it. Already the lower classes treat them as a new aristocracy . . . . Will the middle classes be able to organize to resist the movement which is pushing them on? . . . . I hope so, but I do not dare to count too much upon it. In any case, upon the solution of that problem depends our future.'[59]

The counter-revolutionary concessions, calculated to effect enough change to ensure the hold on power of the *haute bourgeoisie*, involved a number of symbolic modifications to the constitutional charter. Louis-Philippe was not a divine right monarch of France but king of the French people, at the behest of parliament. Catholicism ceased to be the state religion. The *Tricolore* became the national flag once again. Life peers replaced the hereditary nobility in the second chamber, while the electorate was doubled by reducing the financial and age qualifications of voters and parliament acquired the right to propose legislation. Whereas 92,000 had the vote before the 1830 Revolution, the electorate rose to 175,000 in 1831 and to 248,000 in 1846, the last election of the July Monarchy. The comparative restriction of the French suffrage is evident from a comparison. While there were 32 electors per thousand population in Britain and 12 in Belgium, there were only 6 per thousand in France on average during the period of the July Monarchy. Furthermore, the vote was very unequally distributed: 1 per 50 of the Paris population, 1 per 297 in Finistère and 1 per 401 in the Basses-Pyrénées. Guizot's celebrated distinction between the extra-parliamentary *pays réel* – the mass population, who were mainly legitimist, bonapartist and republican – and the parliament-centred *pays légal* – the few, mainly rich landlords, entitled to vote and the fewer entitled to be candidates – was the regime's attempt to confine political rights to those who were judged to have the necessary political capacity as measured by wealth. Hence Guizot's famous injunction: 'Enrich yourselves by work and saving and you will become electors.'[60] In practice, the small electoral colleges – 77 seats had fewer than 300 electors in 1842 – facilitated corruption of the voters, as well as favouring constituencies that 'voted well', while the many public servants in parliament provided government with a ready means of exerting pressure. The bourgeois virtues of work and thrift often became in reality the bourgeois vices of bribery and time serving.

While Guizot's reactionary liberalism tried to dismiss, from what he hoped was the post-revolutionary scene, the class conflict that he had previously identified as the driving force of modern history, the unimaginative defence of the exiguous status quo stimulated further class conflict. Louis-Philippe's own crassly negative early version of the economic theory of democracy was: 'Democracy tends to the levelling of fortunes, and this tendency is both a check upon industry which procures wealth and a cause of disquiet to those who, having already acquired it, wish to keep it. Only a blind respect for law can attract wealth and allow it to show itself and grow without fear. I doubt whether this blind respect can endure in a democracy, where there is no force or authority capable of stopping the first impulse of the people and at least giving it time to reflect.'[61]

Tocqueville presented a fair but damning portrait of the materialist mediocrity of Louis-Philippe and his regime, as well as of the self-serving middle class which, 'when called upon to assume the government, took it up as an industrial enterprise.' 'In 1830 the triumph of the middle class had been definite and so thorough that all political power, every franchise, every prerogative, and the whole government was confined . . . within the narrow limits of this one class, to the statutory exclusion of all beneath them and the actual exclusion of all above. Not only did it thus rule society, but it may be said to have formed it. It entrenched itself in every vacant place, prodigiously augmented the number of places and accustomed itself to live almost as much upon the Treasury as upon its own industry.'[62] This sweeping indictment of unenterprising and undemocratic bourgeois omnipotence – fully accurate only of a particular time and country – has subsequently been generalized to all capitalist 'bourgeois democracy' in the wake of Marx. Tocqueville, who had seen in America a broad-based middle class that did not provoke class conflict, made a more limited inference from the July Monarchy record. 'Everything there seemed combined to produce with the machinery of liberty a preponderance of Royal power which verged upon despotism . . . and I began to believe that in 1830 I had taken for the end of the play what was nothing more than the end of an act.'[63]

Tocqueville was condemned to what he recognized to be an isolated and politically ineffective role because he could not identify with either the opposition or the government during the July Monarchy. He distrusted the opposition parliamentary groups (and notably one of its leaders, Thiers), with which he usually voted, because their political opportunism and hankering after the revolutionary past meant that they did not confine themselves to working within the existing constitutional system. On the other hand, successive Guizot governments refused to accept the need to adapt the system and adopted a repressive policy that could not preserve it. The threat to the system was more fundamental, even at the political level. Speaking on his election to the French Academy in 1841, Tocqueville complained that parliamentary party factionalism meant that 'Liberty is threatened with extinction, not because a party tyrannically abuses governmental power but because no party is in a position to govern.'[64] However, there were temperamental factors as well. Not only did he lack essential political skills. This ideological anti-individualist could not avoid putting pride in his intellectual integrity before the compromises necessary to political success. Yet he justified the fundamental ambiguity of what he called his 'very firm but non-demagogic opposition', notably on the ground that 'the only chance one has of mastering the people's wicked passions are by sharing its good ones.'[65]

While Tocqueville's observation of American democracy initially seemed to confirm Guizot's historically deterministic view that, with the advent of bourgeois dominance, revolutions would be rare, it was the experience of Guizot's own 1840s governments that made him realize that this was untrue. In France, the July Monarchy represented the domination of a small minority of the middle classes, so that a majority of the people still had an interest in revolution. In the period between the 1846 election and the 1848 Revolution, Tocqueville was working with a small informal group of 'New Left' deputies (which included Armand Dufaure, who was to play an important role in the first decade of the Third Republic) to bring about a change of government to avoid a revolutionary change of regime. In a late 1847 draft manifesto, prepared but not published for this new parliamentary group, Tocqueville showed that his reading of French socialist writers – who agreed in attacking private property – had led him to the conclusion that this was 'the final symptom of the old democratic disease of the time, whose crisis would seem to be at hand.'[66] He predicted that 'The time will come when the country will find itself once again divided between two great parties. The French Revolution which abolished all privileges and destroyed all exclusive rights, has allowed one to remain, that of property. Let not the proprietors deceive themselves as to the strength of their position, nor think that the rights of property form an insurmountable barrier because it has not as yet been surmounted.'[67]

However, while Tocqueville favoured extending the suffrage, free elementary education, the restriction of working hours and improved public assistance to the poor, these reforms were intended to render private property defensible. Tocqueville publicly communicated his forebodings in a prophetic parliamentary speech on 29 January 1848. The working classes' conviction that the distribution of private property was inequitable would bring about 'a most formidable revolution . . . we are at this moment sleeping on a volcano.' He told his audience that just as the previous, aristocratic ruling class had lost political power because they were 'unworthy to retain it', so now the propertied bourgeoisie was threatened because of the same faults. Warning his complacent and incredulous listeners that 'the earth is quaking once again in Europe', he implored them not to ignore the danger and to undertake the necessary political and social reforms while there was yet time to do so.[68]

Tocqueville stressed that the divisions within the middle classes prompted the eruption of the working classes on to the political scene in 1848, just as those of the aristocracy had prepared the way for 1789. While the working people had played a part in the 1789 and 1830 Revolutions, they did not share in its leadership. In 1848, working people were for the first time seeking to take matters into their own hands, while the middle classes did not overthrow the regime but allowed it to fall. After the event, Tocqueville declared that while he had not supported the 1848 Revolution, he had accepted it as a fact 'because I wish it to be the last one', expressing the hope that the new Republic 'should be Christian and democratic, but it should not be socialist.'[69] Having been re-elected, thanks to a universal suffrage that the revolutionaries could neither dispense with nor use to effect, he watched while they tried 'to solve this insoluble problem, namely, how to govern through the majority and yet against its inclination . . . . In establishing universal suffrage they thought they were summoning the people to the assistance of the Revolution: they were only giving them arms against it.'[70]

The scene was now set for 'a struggle of class against class, a sort of Servile War.' 'I saw society cut into two; those who possessed nothing, united in a common greed; those who possessed something, united in a common terror . . . everywhere the idea of an inevitable and immediate struggle seemed at hand', so that 'from the first it left us no alternative but to defeat it or to be destroyed ourselves.'[71] Tocqueville took an active part in General Cavaignac's emergency dictatorship to repress the June 1848 insurrection by despairing and leaderless workers, serving as a parliamentary commissioner to the National Guards as they fought in the streets. He helped to crush a revolution whose socialist and democratic character he was – with Herzen, Marx and Proudhon – one of the few to understand. Tocqueville's despair at the sanguinary outcome of the class conflict he had predicted was expressed in a letter a month after the tragic events.'I do not know if I may still hope to see established in our country a stable government which is at the same time strong and liberal . . . . One could think in 1789, in 1815, even in 1830, that French society had been stricken by one of those violent illnesses after which the health of the social body becomes more vigorous and more stable. But do we not see today that it is a chronic disease . . . and that we are destined to waver for a long time between despotism and liberty without being able permanently to sustain either the one or the other? . . . . We did not see the beginning of this great revolution in mankind, we will not see its end.'[72]

Despite his profound pessimism, Tocqueville took an active part on the committee to prepare a constitution for the Second Republic. In the preface to the twelfth edition of his *Democracy in America*, published in 1848, he stated that America was 'not only the most prosperous but also the most stable of all the peoples in the world'; that 'private property is better guaranteed there'; that 'anarchy is as unknown as despotism' – but it should not be imitated. As a circumspect comparative political scientist, he thought America's sixty years' experience should provide 'instruction rather than models'. Its main lesson was that if the 'balance of powers, true liberty and sincere and deep respect for the law' did not prevail, 'the republic will soon have ceased to exist.' The choice was 'either democratic liberty or democratic tyranny'.[73] With Barrot and Lamennais, Tocqueville sought to start by strengthening local authorities but they were defeated and Tocqueville did not join Lamennais in his protest resignation from the constitutional committee.[74] Tocqueville was also defeated in his advocacy of the vital importance of a second chamber in a democracy. 'The executive power is in a perilous situation if you place it opposite to a single chamber; there are incessant conflicts at the end of which the executive power destroys the legitimate power or else this power absorbs or engulfs the other power in some way after a short struggle.'[75]

This failure led Tocqueville to try to strengthen the executive; hence he supported direct election of the president, a popular decision whose adoption proved fatal to the Second Republic. He also regarded a strong judiciary to be a counterweight to the threat of government by assembly in the tradition of the First Republic, so he welcomed the adoption of irremovability of judges. However, Tocqueville had little influence over this ill-fated constitution, which was to fall victim to usurpation by the nephew of the man for whom Constant had drawn up his ephemeral constitution thirty-three years before. Within an electorate suddenly increased from 250,000 to 9 million voters, Louis-Napoleon was elected on a massive turnout by 5.4 million against 1.4 million for the conservative candidate General Cavaignac, who had saved the property owners in June with sanguinary savagery. Male suffrage in 1848 gave victory neither to the middle nor to the working classes but to the darling of the numerically predominant peasantry.

Tocqueville's sceptical and lukewarm attitude towards the Second Republic helps explain why it had so few resolute defenders in its hour of need. He wrote in 1850: 'I have always considered the Republic an ill-balanced form of government, which promised more but gave less liberty than Constitutional Monarchy. And yet I sincerely wished to maintain the Republic; and although there were, so to speak, no Republicans in France, I did not look upon its survival as absolutely impossible. I wished to maintain it because I saw nothing ready or fit to set in its place . . . . Louis Napoleon alone was ready to take the place of the Republic, because he already held power in his hands. But what could come of his success, except a bastard Monarchy, despised by the enlightened classes, hostile to liberty, governed by intriguers, adventurers and valets?'[76] Nevertheless, Tocqueville became Louis-Napoleon's minister of foreign affairs in the Barrot Government, which lasted from June to October 1849, having been suggested by his 'New Left' ally Armand Dufaure, minister of the interior. While he disapproved of the decision to attack the Roman Republic defended by Garibaldi, he neither refused office nor resigned over what *inter alia* was a flagrant violation of the constitution: attacking the independence of a sister republic. Ironically, France, which Tocqueville had proclaimed as the leader of European progressive forces a decade earlier, was to restore a reactionary order while he was the responsible minister.

Not only did he support the papacy abroad; he also collaborated closely with the archclerical minister of education Falloux and tried to reconcile the anticlerical Dufaure to giving Falloux a free hand. As Gargan puts it: 'The tide of reaction was flowing strongly when he assumed office, and he willingly launched his ministerial career on its flood.'[77] His five months in ministerial office were anything but a success and confirmed him in the view that he was a man of letters rather than of action. He consoled himself with the thought that Montesquieu would probably only have been another third-rate minister, while the greatest political philosophers like Aristotle, Montesquieu and Rousseau had written under absolute rulers. Yet he was even more defeatist about the impact of political thought. 'Invariably ideas play no part in unfolding events; actual practice avoids the sciences and politics ends by being only a game of chance where, moreover, the dice are often loaded.'[78]

He came to the conclusion that while liberal political institutions might delay the advent of despotism, they could not prevent it. So the rearguard action of 1850–1, culminating in the last act of Tocqueville's political career – joining with 230 deputies in a vain attempt to depose Louis-Napoleon on the day of his *coup d'état* and his brief detention – was merely the conclusion of a process that was foreseen but could not be prevented. From the class warfare of June 1848, 'The insane fear of socialism throws the bourgeois headlong into the arms of despotism.'[79] The massive December 1851 plebiscite in support of Louis-Napoleon's new constitution – 7,440,000 in favour and only 647,000 against – showed that anti-socialist panic had seized hold of more than the middle classes. That Louis-Napoleon was not a patch on his uncle, whom the newly enfranchised people had followed with servility half a century before, was unimportant. In a fatalistic anticipation of the triumph of the man whom Hugo called *Napoléon le Petit*, Tocqueville wrote in January 1851: 'The general phenomenon appears to me to be a movement of the nation away from liberty towards the concentration and permanence of power . . . we are living in a democratic age and in a democratic society where individuals, even the greatest, are of little importance . . . . At such a time, it is not the man whom one must consider but what lifts him up and carries him to power. A dwarf on the crest of a great wave can reach the height of a cliff.'[80]

Tocqueville predicted both the Second Empire's duration and demise in January 1852: 'Although this government has been established by one of the greatest crimes in history, it will nevertheless last rather a long time, unless it rushes to its ruin . . . in a manner as damaging to us as to itself, in some mad foreign adventure . . . . It will certainly die in war but its death will perhaps cost us dear.'[81] Until its comprehensive defeat at the hands of the Prussians in 1870, Louis-Napoleon's regime continued to enjoy massive popular support, winning a 'yes' vote of 68 per cent in a plebiscite on his new constitution earlier that year. By then, Tocqueville had gone to an early grave. 'Born under the autocratic rule of the first Bonaparte, he was destined to die under the second',[82] but not before he left a portrait of how the First Empire's 'bureaucratic and military despotism' had emerged and how it had prepared the way for its inglorious successor.[83]

Counter-revolutionary democracy: America, Britain and France

While the fiasco of the recourse to universal male suffrage proved disastrous not only to the Second Republic but also to political freedom, Tocqueville responded not by condemning democracy but by identifying it less with social equality or even popular sovereignty than with political freedom. Furet has argued that 'It had now become difficult to explain a set of political institutions as diverse as the July Monarchy, the Second Republic or the despotic rule of the second Napoleon in terms of a single state of society, a concept whose extreme flexibility was being demonstrated before Tocqueville's very eyes. The reversal in his approach and his new emphasis on the autonomy and primacy of purely political – more specifically of political–administrative – structures, are probably related to his experience during these years.'[84] In *Democracy in America* Tocqueville had emphasized democracy as an approximation to classlessness or social equality – not merely legal equality but limited real inequalities, a subjective sense that one was as good as anyone else, and a high rate of social mobility – rather than as majority rule by a politically sovereign people. Summarizing Tocqueville's argument, Mill wrote: 'To most purposes, in the constitution of modern society, the government of a numerous middle class is democracy ... the only democracy of which there is as yet any example; what is called universal suffrage in America arising from the fact that America is *all* middle class.'[85] Tocqueville had opposed two ideal types: unequal, aristocratic society, of which England was the prototype, and equal, democratic society, with America as the prototype. As France inevitably moved from aristocratic to democratic society, Tocqueville feared that it would achieve not American equal freedom but 'equal servitude ... a democratic state of society without democratic institutions. For in democratic institutions, M. de Tocqueville sees not an aggravation, but a corrective, of the most serious evils incident to a democratic state of society.'[86]

So as early as the 1830s, Tocqueville already regarded political democracy as the remedy to a levelling social democracy. However, he later came to understand that American 'equal freedom' had derived its freedom partly from its English liberal political culture, while France suffered the incubus of a despotic political culture. An internal exile during the Second Empire,

Tocqueville looked to England as his intellectual home and to 'English public opinion as the grand jury of humanity in matters of freedom.'[87] In his posthumously published notes for his last incomplete masterpiece, he made clear that for him democracy was synonymous with liberal democracy, combining both classical and modern conceptions of freedom. It was a form of 'government where the people more or less participate in their government. Its sense is intimately bound to the idea of political liberty. To give the democratic epithet to a government where there is no political liberty is a palpable absurdity.'[88] The experience of Napoleonic despotism was to bring him closer to Constant, that even more ardent Anglophil.

Tocqueville admired America for combining generous amounts of liberty and equality, whereas Britain had developed liberty without equality and France had given equality priority over liberty. However, unlike Lafayette, who wanted France to imitate America, Tocqueville realized that a culture characterized by a self-interested, self-reliant and self-restrained people, able to dispense with strong government, could not simply be transposed to France. What had in America been the spontaneous fruit of favourable cultural inheritance, physical circumstance and social habits would in France have to come from political action. A salient legitimizing virtue of democracy was that as the sense of social obligation weakened, cohesion could be achieved by the diffusion of rights so that all would have a share in the public interest, something to lose if it was not achieved. 'Democratic government makes the idea of political rights penetrate right down to the least of citizens, just as the division of property puts the general idea of property rights within the reach of all. That, in my view, is one of its greatest merits. I am not asserting it to be an easy matter to teach all men to make use of political rights; I only say that when that can happen, the results are important. And I would add that if ever there was a century in which such an attempt should be made, that century is ours.'[89] So Tocqueville favoured political democracy, privately asserting his belief in 1836 that 'the majority of the nation can participate in its own affairs, that political life can be spread almost universally and that the direct or indirect exercise of political rights can be very extended.'[90] Nor did he conceal this view from his exclusive electorate in 1839, calling in his election address (and partially anticipating Abraham Lincoln's Gettysburg Address) for the gradual achievement of 'a government of the people, by the people'.

Saint-Simon, in an unpublished 'Examination of the political capacity of various peoples' which Tocqueville could not have read, had reversed his earlier advocacy of the English model and instead championed that of America for reasons anticipating Tocqueville. 'The Americans who came from England to establish a colony brought along the political knowledge which the English had acquired after long labour and at the same time found themselves emancipated from the habits which were bound up with the social organization which the English had before their revolution and with the remnants of the old institutions – but this results in the fact that their political capacity is superior to that of the English.'[91] Although Tocqueville only later fully appreciated the significance of the English origins of American political culture, from the start he had a Saint-Simonian vision of a modernizing country motivated by a non-nationalistic, apolitical, orderly industrial search for profit which rendered government virtually redundant. In a letter from New York, giving his first impressions of America, he described it as 'a society without roots, memories, prejudices, routines, common ideas or national character; a society a hundred times happier than ours . . . . What serves as a link between elements so diverse and makes of all this a people? Interest? There lies the secret. Private interest crops up at every moment, and indeed it vaunts itself openly, proclaiming itself as a social theory.' In a series of sweeping generalizations, he added: America was fortunate because 'until now . . . private interest is never contrary to the general interest, which is assuredly not the case in Europe . . . . Here there is no public power, nor, to tell the truth, is there any need for it.'[92] While he later dwelt upon the significance of the separation of powers, a strong judiciary and the jury system, a decentralized administration and federalism, what most impressed him was an American culture that was too orientated towards private enrichment to disturb public order. Guizot's exhortation was not necessary and so authoritarian government was also unnecessary. Tocqueville noted in January 1832: 'The greatest merit of the government of the United States is that it is *powerless* and *passive*. In the actual state of things, in order to prosper America has no need of skilful direction, profound designs, and great efforts. But need of liberty and still more liberty. It is nobody's *interest to abuse it*. What point of comparison is there between such a state of affairs and our own?'[93]

However, this idyllic picture of a country characterized by both consensus and freedom, by self-reliance and respect for law, was disturbed by a danger drawn to his attention by Jared Sparks, one of the American interlocutors who most influenced him. It was an American dogma that the majority of an omnipotent public opinion was always right and that no countervailing power was capable of doing more than temporarily restraining it.[94] This idea of 'majority tyranny' quickly became very popular, being taken up especially by conservative politicians like Sir Robert Peel. Mill suggested that the lack of actual examples from Tocqueville implied that he was expressing anxieties about the future, which Mill shared. The fear was not so much of persecution of religious, political or social minorities as of 'unenlightened legislation for the supposed interest of the many' such as statutory minimum wages and mass conformism at the expense of independent thought.[95]

The main problem with the concept of majority tyranny is that it starts from the false premise that majorities do actually rule. Tocqueville asserted at the start of his chapter on majority omnipotence: 'The absolute sovereignty of the will of the majority is the essence of democratic government, for in democracies there is nothing outside the majority capable of resisting it.'[96] If true, this would not only render futile all the liberal and pluralistic restraints upon the popular will: free press, independent judiciary, local self-government and voluntary associations. It also ignored the fact that certain minorities were excessively powerful, although Tocqueville hinted at the future emergence of a Saint-Simonian industrial aristocracy.[97] Constant had pointed out to the Right in 1829, during a parliamentary speech in favour of liberalizing local government: 'Majority government seems tyrannical to them. I could respond that every time that there has been tyranny in France for the last forty years, it is because minorities have governed.'[98] Particularly during the Second Empire, Tocqueville also came to see that the rule of a single tyrant was the main threat. As someone who frequently proclaimed himself a critical friend of democracy,[99] it was through liberalizing it that he saw the best hope for liberty.

While Tocqueville's initial impression of America was of a liberal economist's paradise, virtual absence of government, he quickly came to appreciate that it was thanks to the federal division of power that the virtues of large and small states had been combined and America had achieved both strong and limited government. However, it would be wrong to claim that he believed that the reconciliation of local self-government with democratic equality by the federal diffusion of political power could readily be transposed to Europe. There, the concentration of power was rendered indispensable by the threat and actuality of war.[100] Unlike Saint-Simon and Constant but like Maistre, Tocqueville did not believe that international commerce would totally displace war, nor did he think with Proudhon that such conflict would be compatible with confederalism. In one of his pessimistic notes, not used in the final version of *Democracy in America*, Tocqueville wrote: 'The natural tendency of a people . . . is indefinitely to concentrate social forces until it reaches pure administrative despotism. The natural tendency of confederations is indefinitely to divide these forces until one reaches dismemberment.'[101] However, although Tocqueville did not accept the Madison–Constant argument that a large republic could avoid government oppression through a greater plurality of countervailing interests, he did endorse the Montesquieu–Hamilton view that a large federal republic could survive. Unitary France might nevertheless have to look to unitary England for a way of developing a stable and decentralist corrective to democracy's tendency to degenerate through industrialization and centralization.

We have already referred to Tocqueville's intellectual affinity with his wife's homeland, although he did not go as far as Constant or Madame de Staël, of whom it has been said that while 'she regarded America as the ideal, [she] nonetheless clung to England as the model.'[102] Writing of how Britain had withstood the might of Napoleon, Tocqueville expressed the reasons for his admiration and ideological identification. 'It is not the Channel which saves England; it is her spirit, her constitution, above all, her *liberty*. A grand spectacle: *liberty* alone capable of struggling successfully against *revolution*.'[103] However, Tocqueville believed that so hierarchical a society was doomed. As Edouard Laboulaye, liberal disciple of Constant and Tocqueville, wrote: 'Tocqueville felt that if ever France was converted to liberal ideas, this miracle would not come from the English example . . . . There is something bewildering about English society and institutions; we are more amazed than attracted. Liberty reigns supreme among our neighbours, but it derives from privilege and consequently appears archaic; justice enjoys an admirable independence but its forms are gothic; lastly, if liberty is pervasive, so is aristocracy; customs if not laws support and perpetuate social distinctions, nothing worthwhile is done except at the expense of equality. America provides quite a different picture; its customs and ideas bring it close to France.'[104]

In his notes, made during journeys in Britain in 1833 and 1835, Tocqueville nevertheless remarked that change had been gradual rather than revolutionary in Britain because élite social mobility had been promoted by an open aristocracy, based upon wealth, not a closed, caste nobility as in France. Despite his recent visit to America, he was struck by the impression that 'The whole of English society is built upon monetary privilege' and 'the real privileges of wealth [were] greater perhaps than in any other country in the world.'[105] Industrialization had exacted a high price. Following a visit to Manchester, Tocqueville's ambivalent comment was: 'From this foul drain, the greatest stream of human industry flows out to fertilise the whole world. From this filthy sewer pure gold glows. Here humanity attains its most complete and its most brutish development.'[106] Despite the polarization between a shrinking number of richer, snobbish property owners and an increasing number of acquiescent 'proletarians', Tocqueville thought that the British, thanks to a tradition of gradual, piecemeal reform, would avoid a violent revolution. He confessed to feeling close to the English radicals who, unlike their French counterparts, did not believe in compelling their compatriots but in persuading them.[107]

Because a boundless democracy was unstoppable, Restoration France should have borrowed from British and American local self-government practices as 'the only possible counterweight to democracy'.[108] Instead, they had perpetuated Napoleonic centralization. England itself appeared to be moving towards greater centralization in the early 1830s under the influence of Benthamite ideas applied to the administration of the Poor Law. This was thanks to a Royal Commission report largely written by his friend Nassau Senior, embodying an attack upon the aristocratic management of local administration. Nevertheless, the general contrast with France was marked. 'Underlying the apparent diversity, which strikes the superficial observer and so shocks him, is the true political harmony which consists in government being adapted to the needs of each locality.'[109] Tocqueville's English journey alerted him both to the democratic pressures towards centralization consequent on the 1832 extension of the suffrage, and to the desirability of combining sufficient centralization to provide the necessary authority with a general political and economic decentralization to promote both liberty and prosperity. Local self-government was thus part of his general strategy for regulating rather than resisting democracy, making it into a support for counter-revolutionary stability.

Bureaucratic centralization and its antidotes

Tocqueville's anxiety on the score of an ever-encroaching civil and military despotism developed during his preparation of *Democracy in America* and became stronger during the Second Empire. Even during the placid periods of the July Monarchy, Tocqueville was unable to share the optimistic vision – adopted by liberals like Constant and Say, as well as by Socialists like Proudhon and Marx – that the authoritarian state was scheduled for the scrapyard. Saint-Simon was much nearer the mark when he saw a new managerialism taking over but even he believed that war was a thing of the past. Modernity had a much more forbidding face for Tocqueville in the late 1830s. 'If I were permitted to raise the veil which hides the future from us, I would not dare to do it. I would be afraid to see all of society in the hands of soldiers. A *bureaucratic, military* organization, the soldier and the clerk, symbol of the future society' in which 'Not being able to be free, we at least want to be oppressed in the name of the people.'[110] However, in his published writings, Tocqueville played down the danger of militarization and instead concentrated upon the anonymous tyranny of the civil bureaucracy. This was not a new anxiety among liberals. 'Madame de Staël once said that the most popular constitution which could be devised for France would have as its first and only article that all Frenchmen are public functionaries and are paid by the state.'[111] Tocqueville, who had passed his youth in his father's successive prefectures, was to give centralized bureaucracy pride of place, alongside democracy, in a systematic understanding of the emergence of modern society and its management.

Looking back in the 1850s to the pre-revolutionary period of enlightened despotism and its predecessors, Tocqueville stressed the state-building continuity of administrative centralization from the vantage point of the 'Administrative Empire' of Louis-Napoleon. However, unlike Guizot, he stressed the contradiction between the creation of a strong state and the subsequent attempt to develop liberal democracy. 'By the time their ancient love of freedom reawakened in the hearts of the French, they had already been inoculated with a set of ideas as regards the way the country should be governed that were not merely hard to reconcile with free institutions but practically ruled them out. They had come to regard the ideal social system as one whose aristocracy consisted exclusively of government officials and in which an all-powerful bureaucracy not only took charge of affairs of State but controlled men's private lives.' After the Revolution, they combined 'a strong central administration with a paramount legislative assembly: the bureaucratic system with government by the electorate. The nation as a whole had sovereign rights, while the individual citizen was kept in strictest tutelage; the former was expected to display the sagacity and virtues of a free race, the latter to behave like an obedient servant . . . . It was this desire of combining freedom with the servile state that led during the last sixty years to so many abortive essays of a free régime followed by disastrous revolutions.'[112] Both the First and Second Republics had demonstrated the self-destructive propensities of the French conception of democracy based upon the predominance of the legislature. Tocqueville argued that 'assemblies, which are admirably suited at times to strengthen and at other times to restrain governments, are less capable than are the worst governments of directing public affairs.'[113] Would extra-parliamentary institutions work better? Unlike the Anglo-American group pluralism of voluntary associations interposed between central government and individual autonomy, French unenlightened individualism led to group parochialism which failed to mobilize private vices in the service of the public good, necessitating the intervention of coercive state power.[114] The right of voluntary association was repressively regulated in France owing to official fear of conspiracy, reinforcing the socio-cultural constraints upon the self-reliance of civil society.

In Britain and America the civic culture had been nourished by the Protestant sects but while Tocqueville was not himself a believer, he was too
closely wedded to traditional Roman Catholicism to adopt Constant's liberal
Protestant version of the alliance between religion and politics. Despite the
nineteenth-century polarization between a Catholic anti-democratic Right and
an anticlerical Left, Tocqueville pursued the forlorn task of trying to persuade
Catholics not to fear liberal democracy and the liberals that they needed the
support of religion as a counterweight to state power.[115] In fact, clerical and
political influence was so great at most times, especially under the Legitimist
Monarchy and during the Second Empire, that far from a *rapprochement*
occurring between the advocates of liberty and Catholicism, the antithesis was
total, as we shall see in discussing Proudhon in the next chapter. The union of
Church and state dogmatized politics and destabilized religion instead of providing the consensual basis of both social control and personal autonomy.

Like Constant, Tocqueville attached importance to both freedom of the
press and an independent judiciary as restraints upon oppressive government, though he was somewhat less wholehearted about the former and
more fervent about the latter. After Napoleon's persecution of the press,
Article 8 of the 1814 constitutional charter had asserted the principle of
press freedom but a repressive censorship in the 1820s helped precipitate
the 1830 Revolution. Article 7 of the revised 1830 charter reaffirmed the
right to a free press and forbade press censorship but by 1835 the July
Monarchy was using the financial pressure of stamp duties and deposits
to ensure good behaviour and fines as curbs on the press. In that year,
Tocqueville wrote: 'I admit that I do not feel towards freedom of the
press that complete and instantaneous love which one accords to things
by their nature supremely good. I love it more from considering the evils it
prevents than on account of the good it does.' Nevertheless, he was adamant
that there was no stable compromise in practice between complete press
freedom and total control. With popular sovereignty and universal suffrage,
'censorship is not only a danger but even more a great absurdity. When each
man is given a right to rule society, clearly one must recognize his capacity
to choose between different opinions debated among his contemporaries
and to appreciate the various facts which may guide his judgement.'[116]
However, Tocqueville's Second Empire thoughts on the subject place the
emphasis upon public indifference and apathy towards repression after a
revolutionary period of press excesses. 'To ascertain the real power of the
press, attention should not be paid to what it says but to the way in which
the public listens. The very vehemence of the press is sometimes a mark
of its weakness . . . . It screams only because its audience is growing deaf,
and this deafness of the public makes it safe to silence the press later.'[117]

We shall have occasion to observe the truth of this remark in discussing Proudhon's vehement journalistic activities in the next chapter.

As a lawyer and briefly a judge, Tocqueville was predisposed to favour judicial safeguards against the administrative abuse of power, as a way of protecting individual freedom and the integrity of constitutional government. The English Common Law and jury system offered a model of the one and the United States Supreme Court a model of the other. During his visit to England he noted: 'The necessity of introducing the judicial power into the administration is one of those *central* ideas to which I am led by all my investigations concerning the sources of political liberty.'[118] He unfavourably compared what at the time was a dependent system of French administrative law that separated government officials from ordinary citizens and administrative justice from ordinary justice, with independent American courts able to impose the rule of law upon both government and citizens. 'It does not seem to me that the energy of the American government has been weakened by making all officials responsible before the courts. On the contrary, I think that by so doing the Americans have increased the respect due to executive officers, since the latter are much more careful to avoid criticism.'[119] Twenty years later, under the shadow of the Second Empire's administrative arbitrariness, Tocqueville praised the English courts for their resistance to the partiality that is 'both the commonest and the most dangerous in democratic times – subserviency to the supreme power', providing indispensable 'guarantees of the individual against the State.'[120] However, in the years since these remarks were made, French administrative law has developed in the liberal direction indicated by Tocqueville, while Britain has moved in the reverse direction as the principles of crown prerogative have been imparted into the working of the ordinary courts of law.

Like his fellow liberal and Anglophil Constant, Tocqueville attached immense importance to the jury system, particularly as a political instrument of public opinion on a par with voting, rather than as a judicial procedure. 'The jury is both the most effective way of establishing the people's rule and the most efficient way of teaching them how to rule.'[121] Once again, we see the weight Tocqueville attached to not blocking the citizens' will but rather to rendering that will better able to play a judicious part in public activity.

The spectre of persisting social revolution

Like Constant but in contrast to Saint-Simon, Tocqueville did not fully appreciate the importance of industrial society. While he recoiled in horror from the satanic mills of industrial England, he was content to rely for his views on political economy upon reading Say and talking to Nassau Senior, with some corrective to their liberal views from the social catholicism of Villeneuve-Bargemont. Tocqueville's 1835 *Memoir on Poverty* expresses a dualistic view that the increasing wealth for the majority produced by manufacturing industry will be accompanied by increasing insecurity and enduring poverty for a growing minority of the population. However, his social pessimism and anti-materialism did not lead him in a socialist direction, not simply because socialism threatened private property but because it threatened liberty. In a National Assembly speech in September 1848, he castigated socialism as being characterized above all by its 'continued, varied, incessant attempts to mutilate, to curtail, to interfere with human liberty in every form; it is the idea that the State should be not only the ruler of society but should be, in fact, the master of each man . . . the State should constantly be beside him, above him, around him, to protect him, to support him, to check him', amounting in practice to 'a new form of slavery'.[122] (While Proudhon was to take a very different view of private property, he was to echo this onslaught upon state socialism.) Although Tocqueville did not conceal his contempt for the socialistic theories and programmes that leapt to prominence in 1848, he was prudent enough not to exclude their revival in a future resurgence of the revolutionary impetus.[123]

Tocqueville avoided falling into the trap of those, on the one hand, who admired democracy while underestimating its needs for liberal safeguards, as well as those, on the other hand, who feared democracy while refusing to accept its inevitability. The anti-democrat Le Play wrote of *Democracy in America*: 'Tocqueville's book has exerted the most baneful influence on our future since the publication of *Social Contract*.'[124] J. S. Mill, who Tocqueville acknowledged to be the only person fully to have understood his work, described it as 'the first philosophical book every written on Democracy, as it manifests itself in modern society; a book, the essential doctrines of which it is not likely that any future speculations will subvert, to whatever degree they may modify them; while its spirit and the general mode in which it treats its subject, constitute it the beginning of a new era in the scientific study of politics.'[125] In France, his influence was transmitted to the founders of the Third Republic by the 1860s liberals, particularly Laboulaye and Prévost-Paradol, the purgatory of the Second Empire having brought about a convergence between liberals and democrats. 'The political education of the generation which produced the constitution of 1875 was based a little on Proudhon, a great deal on the *Democracy in America*' was the verdict of a leading Third Republic constitutional lawyer.[126]

In the concluding chapter of *Democracy in America*, in his parliamentary speeches warning the July monarchy against its complacency and in the notes for the unwritten second volume of *The Old Régime and the French Revolution*, Tocqueville repeatedly returned to his obsession with the persistence of revolution in France. In an 1850 letter, he wrote: 'What is clear to me is that for sixty years we have fooled ourselves into believing that we could see the end of revolution. The revolution was thought to have finished on 18 *Brumaire*; they thought it was finished in 1814; I myself thought in 1830 that it was at last over, when democracy had destroyed all privileges except the very ancient and necessary one of property . . . . I was wrong. It is clear today . . . not only that we have not seen the end of the immense revolution which began before our time but that even a child born today will probably never see it.'[127] In his unfinished study of the 1789 Revolution, before a passage mocking those who from time to time asserted that 'the Revolution has now finally found its natural and permanent form . . . . Every government gives rise to its own sophists who, at the very time of its own mortal illness, are busily proving that it is immortal', Tocqueville placed this typically circumspect parenthesis. 'This should perhaps go at the end, when I say that when I stop it is not because the Revolution has come to an end, nor because we definitely know yet where it is going to lead.'[128] It was left to Proudhon to take this idea of a continuing revolution into that of permanent revolution.

CHAPTER SEVEN

PROUDHON AND LIBERTARIAN SOCIALISM

Of our six critics of democracy, Proudhon is the only authentic proletarian, a manual worker whose skills came in handy on 24 February 1848 when he printed the proclamation calling for the overthrow of the monarchy before uncharacteristically going off to help build barricades. He came from a worker and peasant family background based upon the rural workshop, the sort of people he always identified with 'the people'. Like most of our other critics of nationalism, he came from peripheral France, in his case the Jura hills of the east, but education was a financial struggle for him and he had to leave school to support his family without taking his *baccalauréat*. Despite a ten-hour working day, Proudhon used his trade as a printer to read voraciously, never abandoning the idea of returning to his studies. After working for a printer of mainly religious books from 1828 to 1836, rising to be first a foreman and then master printer, he became a partner in a Besançon printing firm that developed into a permanent drain on his scanty resources, his debts reducing him to semi-destitution for many years after as he struggled to make a living by his pen.

In 1838 he applied for a three-year scholarship to resume his studies, concluding with a forthright assertion of loyalty to his origins and his political purpose. 'Born and brought up in the working class, still belonging to it, today and for ever, by affection, by nature, by habits and above all else by the community of interests and wishes', Proudhon expressed his determination to work henceforth without respite 'for the complete liberation of [his] brothers and comrades'.[1] Completing his *Confessions of a Revolutionary* in prison during the Second Republic, Proudhon dated the start of his public life from this claim to his successful candidacy for a scholarship that had allowed him to begin his 'work of solitary conspiracy by study', going on roundly to declare: 'I belong to the party of Work against the party of Capital.'[2] He remained faithful to this commitment until the end of his life, although he preferred to fight his revolutionary battles with words and not with bullets, to persuade, not to coerce. However, even when seeking to reconcile, Proudhon's polemical style frequently tempted him into improvised, intemperate, impassioned but sometimes ill-substantiated pulverization of his opponents. As he admitted in April 1848 to one of the butts of his attacks, the democratic socialist Louis Blanc: 'My misfortune is that my passions are inextricably blended with my ideas; the knowledge that enlightens others scorches me.'[3]

Revolutionary reform: 1789 and 1848

Proudhon confided in 1846 to the intimacy of his diary the conviction that lay at the heart of his being, the unknown that was the starting-point of all his thinking. 'Where does this passion for justice come from that torments, irritates and makes me indignant? . . . . I do not know. It is my God, my religion, my all, and if I try to justify it by philosophic reason, I cannot.'[4] It was his commitment to the natural and rational rights of man in 1789 and his repudiation of the Jacobin dictatorship of 1793–4 that constitute the moral yardstick that made him measure the French Revolution as both a supreme manifestation of human dignity and autonomy, as well as of their abasement and violation. His ambivalence as both antagonist and protagonist of the Revolution derived from his intransigent loyalty to its initial ideal of individual emancipation and his revulsion at its subsequent despotic distortion. 'I assert with the whole Revolution, the essential morality of our nature, the liberty, dignity and perfectibility of my fellow men and their civil and political equality.'[5] However, Proudhon attempted to take the revolutionary tradition in the socialist direction of industrial equality for the workers, the 1848 Revolution having demonstrated the bankruptcy of both Jacobin and parliamentary republican variants of bourgeois politics.

Like Maistre and Constant, Proudhon regarded Rousseau as the most influential pre-revolutionary political thinker, the one who had to be refuted as the preliminary to developing a firmly based post-revolutionary politics. Not only did Proudhon take more notes from Rousseau's writings than from any other political theorist; he is the most often quoted in Proudhon's own publications.[6] Writing in 1850, Proudhon declared: 'Rousseau, whose authority has governed us for nearly a century, did not understand the social contract. He was the main cause of the great deviation of 93, since expiated by fifty-seven years of sterile convulsions, which people who are more fervent than thoughtful want us to revive as a sacred tradition.'[7] He was rejected as a reactionary, along with Sieyès,

Robespierre and Guizot, because by denying non-political rights to the people, for whom a meaningful social contract would be a multiplicity of explicit, individually willed bilateral contracts rather than a single, imaginary, generally willed, multilateral contract, 'Rousseau's social contract is the offensive and defensive alliance of the property owners against the propertyless.'[8] Under the pretence of defending freedom, Rousseau stifled it by not basing popular sovereignty upon commutative justice as the seventeenth-century French Protestant theologian Pierre Jurieu had done. In their different ways Jurieu, with his anti-authoritarian appeal to social contract, and Saint-Simon, with his conception of replacing government by industrial society, substituted an economic exchange-based anarchy for a coercive state. Trade at its most elevated was 'the act by which men, affirming that they are first and foremost producers, abdicate any pretension to government.'[9]

In warning his readers against the liberticidal consequences of following those like Louis Blanc who propagated 'politics and socialism à la Rousseau' and in championing individual rights to the point of advocating anarchism, 'there is something of an enraged Benjamin Constant in Proudhon.'[10] By reducing society to a plurality of contracting individuals linked by economic relations, Proudhon was seeking the abolition of all three elements of sovereign political power: its subordination of undifferentiated people to a supreme coercive authority. The last disguise of political absolutism, popular sovereignty, was stripped away. The Revolution meant the replacement of government by specific free contracts for specific purposes, because voluntary agreement was 'the only moral bond which free and equal beings can accept.'[11] In a note in his diary while writing his *General Idea of the Revolution* in 1851, Proudhon abruptly summed up his position: 'Contract is Liberty, Equality, Fraternity.'[12]

The experience of the 1848 Revolution and his incarceration gave Proudhon both the incentive and the leisure to think hard about the revolutionary process and about the first French Revolution. What especially annoyed him was the repetition of earlier mistakes, with the liberal conservatives seeking to revive 1789 and the red republicans 1793, while the uneducated and cowardly mass population accepted another Napoleon. He reserved a special hatred for Robespierre, lionized by historian–politicians like Louis Blanc and Buchez. Proudhon sided with Thiers, Quinet and Michelet, the last particularly, for denouncing Robespierre as a counter-revolutionary. Proudhon regarded the Jacobin leader as having converted Rousseau's ideas into alibis for exterminating opponents, political, religious and socio-economic. Proudhon's preference went to Danton, Condorcet and the decentralizing Girondins, against those who concentrated power, such as Robespierre, Sieyès and the centralizing Jacobins like Saint-Just. Anti-authoritarianism, secularism and a challenge to bourgeois property rights were what he regarded as the hallmarks of the true revolutionary. Even those he admired did not pass this test because they had relied upon political remedies to more deep-seated problems. In an ironic 'Apotheosis of the middle class' that he appended to his *Confessions of a Revolutionary*, Proudhon wrote of the first revolutionaries: 'Quickly tired of [imitating] the Greeks and Romans, we did not even bother to make a national Constitution; we borrowed one from England. Well, that was just as good as any other. Does not the sustained study of political systems teach us today that all Constitutions are equally bad and equally good.'[13]

While tempted by a regal 'moderating power' in the manner envisaged by Sieyès and Constant, Proudhon decided that the risk of it becoming an arbitrary power was to great. He tried instead to dismember government as far as possible, arguing that 'France is essentially and naturally federal and Girondin.'[14] During the first Revolution, the counter-revolutionary Thermidor bourgeoisie drove the workers to support the despotism of Napoleon. 'The country seemed to be a shareholders meeting waiting for a manager; Bonaparte appeared; he was elected with applause.'[15] This usurpation was an extreme form of the *volontariste* fallacy that society had to be authoritatively impelled rather than allowed to developed spontaneously. 'Condorcet, Turgot, Danton sought revolution from below, true democracy' but the Jacobins prepared the way for counter-revolution from above.[16] 'Liberty was replaced by Glory, the most fatal and stupid of divinities. For fifteen years, the parliamentary rostrum was silent, the bourgeoisie humiliated, the Revolution shackled.'[17]

To prevent a reversion to the errors of the past, Proudhon hoped that the 1848 Revolution would 'find a compromise that, unifying the divergent interests, identifying the private and the public good, removing natural inequality by education, resolving all the political and economic contradictions; where each individual would be both producer and consumer, citizen and prince, administrator and administered',[18] would reconcile bourgeoisie and proletariat as the only way of avoiding a common servitude. Before we see how Proudhon interpreted France's failure to avoid another Napoleonic despotism, we must first consider the influences that shaped his thinking and the pre-1848 attack upon inequality and private property which brought him as close to the Rousseau of the *Discourse on Inequality* as he was remote from the Rousseau of the *Social Contract*.

Proudhon's predecessors

In a letter to Michelet, Flaubert wrote: 'I have collected the oddest quotations from the so-called men of progress, beginning with Saint-Simon and
ending with Proudhon. They all start from religious revelation.'[19] It would
have been more accurate to have claimed that while Proudhon began with
religion, Saint-Simon ended with it. Proudhon was to become the most
formidable opponent of the post-revolutionary attempt to resacralize social
order. However, at the outset the theocratic anti-revolutionaries shaped his
initial, Catholic Church-based conception of social cohesion. Proudhon read
and reread, in 1829, 1839–40 and 1844, Maistre's *Considérations, Soirées
de St. Petersbourg* and *Du Pape* (mentioning him some forty times in his
writings), describing the latter as 'full of verve, wit and malice; perfectly
logical; veritable code of the protagonists of the principle of Authority.
De Maistre shows himself to be a man of genius', worthy to provide the
thesis to Proudhon's antithesis.[20] They are respectively the antagonist and
protagonist of the Revolution's values: divine right against the rights of
man, transcendent authority against immanent liberty.

Like Maistre, Proudhon always identified political and religious authority
as absolute, except that instead of standing together, they fell together.
Whereas Maistre rejected Rousseau's attempt to base political order on
popular sovereignty – '*I obey us*' – as the imposition of the will of others
disguised as self-government, Proudhon did so because order was plural and
collaborative, not singular and based on subordination. God and government were the antitheses of order, which would come from the abolition,
not the reinforcement of sovereignty. Both Maistre and Proudhon ridiculed
the French revolutionaries' mania for passing laws (15,479 in the six years
from July 1789 to October 1795) but they did so for diametrically opposed
reasons. The authoritarian Maistre was objecting to the view that rational
citizens could remake the world at will, while the anarchist Proudhon
rejected the attempt to impose the will of government upon each rational
citizen, who should legislate for himself.[21]

However, when it came to facts rather than values, Proudhon regarded
Maistre as the only writer to have understood war, with the possible exception of Hobbes. Although war was the driving force that prevented humanity
from stagnating, force should and could be contained by a balance of power
within as well as between states. Maistre's explanation of war as based upon
original sin was simply theocracy's fatalistic 'original prevarication' aimed
at justifying every conceivable form of inequity and iniquity.[22] War was
divine, not in the Maistrian sense that through its source in sin it fitted
into the providential pattern but because in regulating conflict it gave

birth to a primitive form of justice, the right of might. It would have to be replaced by the might of right as advocated by Grotius and Kant. As Saint-Simon had optimistically argued, after the liberal economists and Condorcet, work, trade and contract would replace idleness, combat and coercion.

There are echoes of Saint-Simon from Proudhon's earliest writings, although it appears that he did not read him at first hand until 1851 at the suggestion of Pierre Leroux. The 1840 preface to his *What is Property?* begins with a reminder to the Besançon Academy (which had awarded him a scholarship that led to his writing this explosive book) that in offering his candidature he had explicitly declared the aim of his studies. This was to seek 'the means of *improving the physical, moral and intellectual conditions of the most numerous and poorest class.'* Although he refers to Saint-Simon and the Saint-Simonians about a hundred times in his writings, as long as he relied upon second-hand accounts based upon disciples such as the 'bancocrat' Enfantin, he dismissed Saint-Simonism as a Utopian brand of authoritarianism. Even before a close reading of Saint-Simon, he had in his 1849 *Confessions of a Revolutionary* declared that 'The Revolutionary principle . . . is Liberty. In other words, no more government of man by man through the accumulation of capital . . . . *Government* is tending to become *Administration*.'[23]

Just before starting to write his *General Idea of the Revolution*, Proudhon – who had made extensive notes and comments on the works of Saint-Simon – acknowledged in his diary some affinities in their views. In particular, they both started out from the premise that 'in the natural course of events, the governmental and feudal régime will be followed by the administrative and industrial régime', so that forms of government would cease to be important, as Saint-Simon had caustically demonstrated in his notorious Parable.[24] Both his capitalist and his socialist disciples were unfaithful to him. Even his best socialist disciples, such as Pierre Leroux, had distorted Saint-Simon's views by their neglect of his major insight, instead advocating state socialism. In his late 1849 polemic with Leroux – having earlier praised his egalitarianism and later condemned his humanitarian theomania – Proudhon asserted that 'work being self-organized . . . and no longer requiring either legislator or sovereign, the workshop will replace government'.[25] These words not only anticipate late-nineteenth- and early-twentieth-century anarcho-syndicalism; they also foreshadow the vogue for *autogestion* that attracted support from the French Socialists and the CFDT trade union, especially in the late 1960s.

If Proudhon usually reserved his praise for socialism and condemnation to his fellow Socialists, he was especially critical of those Saint-Simonians who had made fortunes in industrial banking and railway promotion during the Second Empire. He had himself been involved in the attempt to secure a Besançon–Mulhouse railway concession that was won by the ex-Saint-Simonian banker Péreire (Proudhon's intention being to use his substantial consultant's fee to relaunch his ill-fated People's Bank, discussed later). Proudhon – although heavily in debt at the time – explained his refusal to accept 20,000 francs compensation in the following terms. 'Mr. Péreire is the leading representative of the Saint-Simonian principle of anti-democratic and anti-liberal industrial feudalism that is currently in control of our national economy . . . . My duty and destiny is to fight this system in all things and everywhere, so it would be strange for me to receive any money from the enemy.'[26] He went on to attack speculative capitalism, advocating ending industrial exploitation of the workers thanks to worker shareholding through producer associations. He was prepared for this to be done by state expropriation of capital to allow such worker associations to be established, but this would take a long time because 'centralization, administration and authority are still sought in business as well as in politics.'[27] While, as we shall see, Proudhon was to advocate a tactical alliance between the productive bourgeoisie and the proletariat, this was to be done in conformity with principles of social justice, not of authoritarian exploitation,

In the early 1840s, Proudhon subscribed to the scientistic view, held by Condorcet, the *idéologue* Cabanis, Saint-Simon and Comte, that social scientific principles existed and were waiting to be discovered. 'The metaphysic of *The Social Contract* and *The Spirit of the Laws* is worn out; in the place of these hollow theories arises a new science, exact, mathematical.'[28] In *What is Property?* Proudhon asserted that 'truth or political science is entirely independent of the sovereign will, of majority opinion and of popular belief', calling for 'government according to science' in which 'the sovereignty of will gives way to the sovereignty of reason and is absorbed into a scientific socialism.' However, unlike his scientistic forerunners, Proudhon is already arguing that with the destruction of monarchy and private property, 'society seeks order in anarchy. Anarchy, the absence of any master or sovereign, is the form of government that daily approaches.'[29] By 1850, in prison and disheartened by the failure of the 1848 Revolution, Proudhon stressed that Watt was a greater revolutionary than Robespierre and Saint-Simon, and Fourier than Danton and Desmoulins, calling for a switch from politics to 'positive, profound, practical, universal, inexorable social science'.[30] However, this appeal to a deterministic social scientism to bolster the flagging fortunes of social revolution itself gave way in *Justice* (1857) to a moralistic vindication of individual liberty and a repudiation of the fatalism of Saint-Simon and Comte. Proudhon's hostility was increased by the reactionary nature of Comte's latter-day 'positive politics', based upon an anti-revolutionary reconstitution of Roman Catholic theocracy.[31] The authority of science having been replaced by the far more repellent authority of the Church, might the libertarian attractions of Fourier and the liberal economists be more enduring?

While Proudhon was indebted to Adam Smith and the classical political economists, it was more for their contribution to social science through the stress on the division of labour than for their liberal policy prescriptions. His greater debt was to a Socialist critic of political economy and their oversimple self-interest psychology. He had met Charles Fourier in 1829 while supervising the printing of his *New Industrial and Social World*.[32] Although rejecting the irrationalism, immorality and inegalitarianism which characterized Fourier's brand of social romanticism, Proudhon drew more from him than a critique of commercialism. He was attracted by the idea of a spontaneous, self-regulating economy which dispensed with the need for a coercive state power. Fourier's social pluralism based upon mutualist producer associations, his advocacy of vocational education and credit cooperation, culminating in commercial federalism, not only impelled Proudhon towards anarchism. It later bore fruit in his conception of economic federalism as a means of ensuring cooperation between voluntary associations of free producers.[33] Although he frequently castigated the Fourierists, notably for their defence of private property, Proudhon wrote that 'Of all modern socialists, Fourier's disciples long seemed to me to be the most advanced and almost alone worthy of the name.'[34] Fourier was his antidote to the view current in political economy that entrepreneurs knew their own best interests or that if they did the pursuit of private profit was necessarily the best way to achieve the general interest.

While he often quoted Say, it was above all to Adam Smith's illuminating discussion of the division of labour and his labour theory of value that Proudhon acknowledged the greatest intellectual debt. However, while Smith had prepared the way for a comprehensive social science, it was left to others – Saint-Simon, Comte and Fourier – to take it further before Durkheim gave the social division of labour its full sociological extension. Adam Smith had earned esteem for classical economics by showing the economy to be based on the reciprocal services provided by a socially integrated variety of occupational functions.[35] However, Proudhon sided with the heterodox Sismondi in arguing that free market competition would lead to overproduction and underconsumption.[36] The market, unlike absolute monarchy, was an *impersonal* arbitrariness but arbitrary all the same. Economists had replaced the priests as apologists for the status quo, scarcity replacing sin as the centrepiece of the argument and striving to acquire wealth replacing a quietist resignation. This diagnosis led Proudhon to develop theories of interest-free credit that resulted in a polemical dialogue of the deaf with Frédéric Bastiat, the leading mid-nineteenth-century French exponent of liberal economics, from which neither emerged unscathed.[37] Despite criticizing the economists for justifying poverty, by combining (before Marx but after the English socialists Thompson and Bray) Adam Smith's labour theory of value with Ricardo's theory of rent, Proudhon derived the theoretical basis for his attack on private property as an unearned surplus.[38]

The onslaught on inequality and private property

Winning a scholarship in 1838, Proudhon became a mature student in Paris at 29. Although he attended lectures, he was essentially self-taught through his extensive reading. This included not only the theocrat Maistre but Montesquieu's *Esprit des Lois* and Comte's *Cours de Philosophie Positive*. Of direct interest to us in his reading of Constant's book on religion and more especially Tocqueville's *Democracy in America*, with whom he shared important affinities. However, whereas Tocqueville was resigned to the advent of equality, Proudhon rejoiced in it. 'Proudhon was a socialist with a strong liberal conscience; Tocqueville was a liberal with a social sense thrust upon him.'[39]

Not seeking academic qualifications, Proudhon within a year wrote a prize essay on the unlikely subject of Sunday observance, in which the budding socialist antitheist praised the idea of a weekly day of rest from work. However, his rejection of *rentier* property as 'the last of the false gods' prepared the way for the book with which in 1840 he first made his mark: *What is Property?* He began with a bang, borrowing Sieyès famous formula from *What is the Third Estate?* and adapting it to his purpose. To the question 'What is slavery?' he replies 'death' because to have the power of life and death over a person is to sentence him to a living death. He then asks 'What is property?' and again he replies in a word but one that was to resound then and since: 'theft'!

The idea that private property was acquired by theft was not new. The celebrated lawyer Etienne Pasquier had in 1611 put into the mouth of a convict the argument that by nature everything belonged to everyone in common, so that private appropriation amounted to the crime of theft.[40] However, private property was then regarded as a guarantee of freedom and the famous slogan 'No taxation without representation' made the further connection with parliamentary government. Nevertheless, even before the French Revolution, the critique of private property had begun with a vengeance, notably by Rousseau and Mably, followed by Babeuf and Godwin. The future Girondin leader Brissot had proclaimed in 1780 that 'Exclusive property is a *theft* in nature.'[41] However, Brissot was arguing in favour of leniency for thieves and did not advocate the abolition of private property. Proudhon had read neither Brissot, nor for that matter the Marquis de Sade's 1792 claim that property originated in usurpation: 'Theft is punished only because it attacks the right of property; but this right itself originally is only a theft.'[42] Such subversive sensationalism had disappeared from view for half a century but Proudhon was to reinvent it as an attack on unearned wealth to disturb the July Monarchy's bourgeois preoccupation with private enrichment.

Mediocrity and money-making were the hallmarks of a regime based upon the self-interested accumulation of capital. Despite the Revolution's proclamation of equality of rights, its simultaneous affirmation of the exclusive right to private property meant class conflict between the propertied few and the propertyless many. 'So in 1793 dictatorship was installed not against but for property.'[43] Proudhon mobilizes moral outrage by showing how private property infringes natural human rights and thereby is the basic source of injustice. The Saint-Simonians had rejected unearned, inherited property as illegitimate but had then supported inequality based upon the superior capacity to contribute to collective wealth, notably through the exercise of managerial skill. This also amounted to exploitation. Property could not be justified by work (as Locke had argued) because all workers are not proprietors and it is society's collective effort that multiplies the value of each person's work. Property could not come from occupation because all had an equal right to occupy property, yet private property excludes most people from enjoying this right. Nor could law alone provide a moral basis for private property because it changed to suit social conditions and the interests of those who made the law. It is the community which alone *owns* property, although its *use* is accorded to individual and associated producers linked by free contract.

Favourable testimony by Adolphe Blanqui – eminent economist and elder brother of the revolutionary Auguste Blanqui – managed to avoid Proudhon's prosecution in 1840[44] for expressing these views. However, a second and then a third memoir on property, the last entitled *Warning to Proprietors*, provoked the authorities to put him on trial at Besançon in 1842. Charged with attacking property, disturbing the peace, exciting hatred against certain classes, the government, the king and the Roman Catholic Church, Proudhon, who defended himself, was acquitted on the ground that the jury found his ideas difficult to grasp and refused to condemn what they did not understand. His incorrigible urge to shock, always seeking how far he could go too far, gave him and his views a notoriety such as Saint-Simon and Auguste Blanqui acquired in similar circumstances.

Proudhon and Marx had lengthy discussions in Paris in 1844, before Marx was expelled by the Guizot government. Marx's early published comments almost make up in their effusive praise for the dismissive denigration to which he subjected Proudhon's work from 1846, after Proudhon had in effect turned down an offer of collaboration. As they subsequently represented the two most important figures for the French labour and Socialist movements, embodying the conflict between authoritarian and libertarian socialism, their view of each other merits consideration.

In *The Holy Family*, which Marx wrote in Paris in 1844, he presented a sweeping defence of Proudhon's onslaught on property. 'All treatises on political economy take *private property* for granted,' which was dealt with only incidentally 'as Say naively admits. But Proudhon makes a critical investigation – the first resolute, pitiless, and at the same time scientific investigation – of the foundation of political economy, *private property*. This is the great scientific progress he made, a progress which revolutionizes political economy and makes a real science of political economy possible. Proudhon's treatise *Qu'est-ce que la propriété?* is as important for modern political economy as Sieyès' work *Qu'est-ce que le tiers état?* for modern politics.'[45] In view of the fact that Marx was in 1846 to assert that 'From head to foot M. Proudhon is the philosopher and economist of the petty bourgeoisie', it is ironic that two years earlier Marx acknowledged: 'Not only does Proudhon write in the interests of the proletarians, he is himself a proletarian, a worker. His work is a scientific manifesto of the proletariat.'[46] How can one explain so brutal a reversal of Marx's standpoint?

From his Brussels exile, Marx wrote to Proudhon in 1846 inviting him to become the French correspondent of a Communist Correspondence Committee (which was subsequently to become the Communist League). Proudhon's cautious reply shows that he had anticipated the anti-libertarian implications of Marx's views. While being willing to engage in intellectual debate, he went on: 'After having demolished all the a priori dogmatisms, do not let us in our turn dream of indoctrinating the people . . . let us give the world the example of an informed and far-sighted tolerance, but let us not – simply because we are at the head of a movement – make ourselves the leaders of a new intolerance, let us not pose as the apostles of a new religion.' In words that show that Proudhon misjudged the willingness of his fellow countrymen to return to the barricades (a view he was to revise shortly before the 1848 Revolution), he went on: 'We ought not to suggest *revolutionary* action as the means of social reform . . . such seem to me also to be the feelings of the French working class. Our proletarians are so thirsty for knowledge that we would be ill received by them if we gave them only blood to drink.'[47]

Marx did not take kindly to this rebuff and when Proudhon's *System of Economic Contradictions* appeared later in 1846, he responded with a celebrated reversal of its subtitle: 'The philosophy of poverty'. Proudhon's book was sufficiently popular to prompt the publication of two German translations in 1847, although it is generally agreed that it is one of his weaker books. Marx engaged in a merciless methodological and historical critique, mixing condescending and pedantic attacks on Proudhon's ignorance *and* 'plagiarism', with disquisitions on the theory of value and the necessity of class struggle to culminate in total revolution.[48] Proudhon read and carefully annotated *The Poverty of Philosophy*, possibly with a view to responding to its criticisms, but the onset of the 1848 Revolution turned his mind to more pressing concerns. Proudhon had already made clear what separated them when he wrote in the *Economic Contradictions*: 'As critic, having sought social laws through the negation of property, I belong to socialist protest . . . . In seeking to achieve practical improvements, I repudiate socialism with all my strength.'[49] We shall have occasion later to discuss the battle for control of the First International between Marxists and Proudhonians. Meanwhile we must turn to the Second Republic during which Proudhon most fully formulated his views on the subject of democracy.

1848: Class conflict or class reconciliation?

The 1848 Revolution forced Proudhon to abandon the solitary and studious life in which he elaborated his fundamental theory of economic contradictions while teaching himself philosophy by voracious reading and prolonged discussions with foreign exiles such as Bakunin and Marx. His pugnacious temperament and polemical verve predestined him for the hurly-burly of journalistic jousts and political controversy in which 'contradiction' found its daily expression. In the years preceding the Revolution, we can trace Proudhon's hesitancy between a social reformism which would be achieved within the existing political framework and a recognition with Karl Marx that political revolution was a prerequisite of serious social change. This ambivalence makes him both a milestone in pre-1848 Socialist speculation and a signpost to post-1848 Socialist thought and action.

In November 1845 Proudhon, who was already feeling his way towards his view that the credit cooperative on a national scale was the lever of peaceful yet comprehensive social reform, called upon the people not to wait for revelation or revolution but to associate themselves because 'revolution' would be the consequence rather than the cause of social reform through cooperation. Like the Fabians in Britain half a century later, he declared: 'A catastrophe is confused with a revolution and is awaited: that is all.' However, unlike Saint-Simon and Fourier, Proudhon already declares that although he will accept royal support for his scheme of social reform he 'expects nothing from the aristocracy and little from the middle class: everything must come from below.' Proudhon considered becoming a candidate at the 1846 general election, noting in his diary that political regimes should be respected until they are dislodged. However, by mid-1846, though still supporting gradualism, Proudhon was becoming impatient: 'With bourgeois prudence we shall never get anywhere', and he proclaimed prophetically that Louis-Philippe would be the last king to sit on the French throne.[50]

Even more than Tocqueville, he was aware that because the French people were unprepared for the exercise of political power, the coming of universal suffrage would pave the way for an unenlightened despotism because the democrats and Socialists lacked a practical programme of social reform. Proudhon preferred a weak and impotent constitutional monarchy to the threat of an assertive and oppressive neo-Jacobin republic or neo-Bonapartist empire. So, while he contemptuously dismissed the regime of Guizot and Louis-Philippe, the priority he attached to economic over political reform meant that he preferred Louis-Philippe to Louis Blanc. He was in no hurry for the Revolution which, like Tocqueville, he had come to regard as inevitable. He shunned the banquet campaign that preceded the Revolution. To make himself the effective spokesman of the proletariat, he wrote in his diary in May 1847 that he was planning a book entitled *Property Vanquished or the Solution of the Problem of Association* in which he reluctantly but realistically proposed to 'justify revolution, the *seizure of power*. In France, social reform is regarded as impossible unless implemented by the government. In *principle* this is false but in *fact* it is what will happen.'[51]

Therefore Proudhon the anarchist, under the heading 'What we will do immediately after the Revolution', prepared on 5 January 1848 a long list of nationalizations beginning with the Bank of France and the railway companies; the imposition of income tax; extensive government regulation of industry and trade; the five-hour working day and even electoral reform. Proudhon, like Tocqueville, sensed the coming cataclysm and with anxious perspicacity noted in his diary on 17 January 1848: 'A few men are preparing an insurrection . . . . I will be overwhelmed by events. Power belongs to the person who seizes it, just as the person who speaks loudest secures the attention of an audience. In a fight there is no room for reason.' When the anticipated, yet unforeseen, Revolution triumphed five weeks later – in which Proudhon's part consisted of helping to build barricades and printing the first proclamation of the overthrow of Louis-Philippe, as became the compositor he was by profession – Proudhon wrote of the victors in his diary on 24 February: 'They are a crowd of lawyers and writers, each more ignorant than the next, who will fight for a share of power. I will have nothing to do with them.'[52]

At the end of his 1840 book on property, which was subtitled 'Studies on the principle of law and government', Proudhon presented a dialogue in which he is asked: 'Are you a democrat?' to which he answers 'No'. 'Then what are you?' He replies: 'I am an anarchist', arguing in the name of 'political science' that all government is detestable because it subordinates some people to the sovereignty of others.'[53] At the time of his trial as a subversive in 1842, Proudhon had confessed to a friend: 'I am a man of meditation, not of revolution . . . . I exclude myself from the ranks of conspirators.'[54] His jury had agreed and Proudhon's subsequent conduct was to confirm his sincerity. Others did not share his views. In 1848, the conspiratorial Left in the unprepossessing shape of Auguste Blanqui played into the hands of the counter-revolutionary Right by trying to establish a dictatorship of proletarian Paris over bourgeois Paris and provincial peasant France.

Although Proudhon attacked most contemporary Socialist leaders as authoritarians, he had greater respect for the ruthless Blanqui as capable of actually making his nightmare a daylight reality. Reflecting in prison on the 1848 Revolution, Proudhon argued that Blanqui was a logical authoritarian in seeking to postpone elections, purge the provisional government and establish a revolutionary dictatorship. 'Among the revolutionaries at that time, one of the most intelligent, Blanqui, is obsessed with the idea that with sufficient energy and cunning, the holders of power can lead the people wherever they wish, suppress the law and destroy the revolutionary spirit' in the name of resisting counter-revolution.[55] Proudhon wrote in 1851 of this fellow-prisoner and failed Lenin *avant la lettre*: 'Blanqui is the incarnation of popular vengeance, he is, like Marat, one of the hideous but unfortunately logical and necessary aspects of Revolution! . . . Blanqui's time will come . . . . Blanqui will exterminate [the enemy] with cold calculation . . . . As for me, I shall continue to serve my contemporaries and humanity with the fruit of my studies; but I cannot conceal that I dream of standing aside, for human reason at this moment is in total eclipse, yet I do not feel within myself the strength to struggle passionately against the passions.'[56] The similarity with Tocqueville's discouragement, as reflected in his *Recollections* of 1848, is obvious, as is the choice to turn away from political action to writing. His task was to demolish the revolutionary dogmatists for whom 'Society is not alive, it is on the dissection table.'[57]

In 1848, Proudhon's failure as a parliamentary politician can be attributed partly to the fact that he did not believe in legislative or executive change from above but rather in spontaneous action by individuals and groups from below. He stood as a candidate primarily to attract attention to his ideas (receiving the journalistic support of Charles Baudelaire), but he treated his election in a Paris constituency as based upon a misunderstanding of the antipolitical attitude by his mainly working-class voters. Proudhon's contempt for political action led him to write to a friend after his first electoral discomfiture: 'The Republic is a prostitute, not worth the trouble I take over her', and even when elected two months later he asked: 'What will become of me amidst all those cretins?'[58] Unfortunately, his election to the Assembly in June 1848 was immediately followed by the civil war slaughter in Paris, at which he was a bystander.

Cooped up in Parliament, Proudhon expressed his guilt at having left the workers in the lurch in their hour of need. 'I failed out of parliamentarist stupidity in my duty as a representative. I was there to see and I saw nothing; to sound the alarm and I did not cry out! I was like the dog that did not bark in face of the enemy. As an elected representative of the plebs and journalist of the proletariat, I should not have left that mass without leadership and advice . . . . I have since done what I could to repair this irreparable mistake.' An early opportunity occurred in July 1848. At the end of a rare speech to the Assembly that overwhelmingly and vociferously rejected a bill he proposed as an attack on religion, family and property, Proudhon made clear which side he was on in the class war. 'When I say WE, I identify myself with the proletariat; when I say YOU, I identify you with the bourgeois class.'[59]

In a speech in October 1848, Proudhon declared that 'Justice did not say its last word in 1789' and 'revolutionary power . . . is no longer in the government or the National Assembly, it is in you. Only the people, acting directly, without intermediaries, can bring about the economic revolution founded in February.'[60] When the constitution of the Second Republic was adopted on 4 November 1848 by 739 votes to 30, Proudhon was in the minority. He explained that day: 'I have voted against the Constitution because it is a Constitution . . . . I am convinced that the Constitution, whose first act will be to create a presidency, with its prerogatives, its ambitions and its guilty hopes, will be a threat to liberty rather than a guarantee of liberty.'[61] Despite these prophetic words, by June 1849 – having started a three-year prison sentence just before the left-wing 'insurrection' to defend the constitution – Proudhon had rallied to the constitution, though he sought to defend it by a refusal to pay taxes. As he bluntly put it: 'I know that the 1848 Constitution is only a rag but for the moment this rag covers my nakedness.'[62] Proudhon was re-elected to the Assembly while in prison in 1849 with a substantially increased majority but he was unable to take his seat. His one-year parliamentary career was over.

Like Constant during the Restoration, Proudhon had a much more significant role during the Second Republic as a journalist than as a politician. To give himself an instrument for capturing the attention of the general public, the former printer Proudhon had been planning to publish a newspaper even before the 1848 Revolution. The day after the Revolution, four armed compositors offered their services to him so that he could start his own journal. Although, as a believer in direct popular action rather than representative government, Proudhon would have preferred simply to call the paper *Le Peuple*, he had to compromise on *Le Représentant du Peuple*. Proudhon's belief that the people should not rely on others is reflected in the fact that the four newspapers he edited during the Second Republic 'All had "people" in their title and all were eventually suppressed by the government.'[63]

Proudhon indulged his proclivity for sensational slogans in the Sieyès manner but the substance had much more in common with Saint-Simon's *Parable* of the bees and the drones. The newspaper's motto was 'What is the Producer? Nothing. What should he be? Everything!' After a month's silence, following the June class war, Proudhon added: 'What is the capitalist? Everything. What should he be? Nothing!'[64] Proudhon was now going much further than defending the industrious producer against the idle *rentier* and the unproductive lawyers, priests and nobility. He was attacking capitalism directly, the June bloodbath having swept aside his schemes of peaceful reform. As he had warned on 16 April 1848: 'Universal suffrage is the counter-revolution' because like both Tocqueville and Blanqui he recognized that an uneducated, predominantly peasant population, under the domination of priests and nobility, would vote for their masters if prematurely accorded manhood suffrage. When Louis-Napoleon was elected president of the Second Republic in December 1848, with three-quarters of the vote (55 per cent in Paris) and the Socialist candidate Raspail received only 0.5 per cent of the vote (5 per cent in Paris), Proudhon's caustic verdict was: 'The people have spoken like a drunk.'

Proudhon frequently fell foul of the press laws and as we shall see he was to spend most of the duration of the Second Republic in jail for seditious attacks on the newly elected president, accurately accused of conspiring to enslave the French people. Once Louis Blanc was forced into exile, Proudhon became the main spokesman for the leaderless and disillusioned urban working classes. *Le Représentant du Peuple* had been suppressed in August 1848 but was reborn as *Le Peuple* in October. After Proudhon was condemned in March 1849 his second paper was suppressed, having collected in its short life sixteen court cases, yielding a total of thirty-four years and two months of prison sentences and over 80,000 francs worth of fines.[65] It was while he was serving his prison sentence that he launched *La Voix du Peuple*, which survived from October 1849 to May 1850. French prisons at that time could be fairly free and easy. When Proudhon was not actually in solitary confinement (as Blanqui was for long years) he was able to write books and even edit newspapers critical of the government.

La Voix du Peuple was financed by the exiled Russian populist Herzen, who had become an ardent admirer of Proudhon's attack on the sovereign state and advocacy of decentralization, describing him as 'the only French revolutionary thinker' in 1849.[66] They formed an alliance based upon a division of labour. Proudhon was to have full responsibility for French affairs, while Herzen was to control international affairs, using the newspaper to combat Tsarist autocracy. Proudhon devoted most of his early 1850 energies to polemics with Bastiat, Blanc and Leroux, equated respectively with three aspects of absolute authority: capital, state and God. After its ninth seizure – ironically for protesting against the restriction of universal suffrage, 3 million voters being excluded by a residential and tax qualification – *La Voix du Peuple* was silenced in May 1850. Herzen was expelled from France and Proudhon was tried again for inciting the overthrow of the government in June 1850. The jury acquitted him but Proudhon returned to jail to complete his previous sentence. Although he was connected with the ephemeral *Peuple de 1850*, Proudhon's turbulent journalistic career was virtually over. Although he occasionally wrote newspaper articles, he never again edited his own journal.[67]

It is time to turn from the polemical to the constructive Proudhon as 'people's banker', his peaceful solution to the economic problem. While Proudhon had admitted in an 1841 letter that economics was not his strong point, he had from 1845 been groping his way towards the idea of 'free' credit, under the inspiration of a neo-Fourierist *Société Générale d'Echange* founded in Paris in 1829.[68] What he called in 1845 the *Association Progressive* and then the *Société Progressive* was intended to spread, thanks to his credit exchange bank, through a network of consumer and producer cooperatives. However, before the 1848 Revolution he curtly confided to his diary that 'If another 29 July [1830] is necessary to conquer the right of association, it is up to the people to win it, it is none of my business.'[69] His nostrum of reciprocal credit was based upon the replacement of the tyranny of a scarce metal, gold, by a paper currency that would have two constituent elements. Firstly, the Bank of France would become an exchange bank, supervised by the government and run by worker delegates from all the major industries, issuing notes that would be legal tender. Secondly, the bank would act as a clearing-house by endorsing bills of exchange or exchange notes based upon goods produced which would be convertible into goods and services. The precious metals, whose value had been inflated by scarcity, would be reduced to the role of small change. Full employment would become possible through the increase in purchasing power, which was automatically generated by the production of goods and the sense of security decreasing hoarding. Such were Proudhon's proposals at the end of March 1848.[70]

To understand the context in which Proudhon propounded his subsequently much ridiculed scheme is to make sense of what otherwise appears both incomprehensible and Utopian. The slump which hit France in 1847 was due to two main causes, both of which resulted in a restriction of credit consequent respectively upon an external and internal drain of gold. Firstly, bad harvest failure necessitated large imports of cereals, leading to an adverse balance of payments and an export of gold. Secondly, wild speculation in railway shares, on a smaller scale but analogous to the 'railway mania' in Britain, led to a financial panic, bankruptcies and the withdrawal of gold deposits from the banks. The 1848 Revolution accentuated the effects of financial panic and attempts to restore confidence by raising the bank rate merely increased the number of bankruptcies. The consequent restriction of credit led to a typical trade slump deflation, with falling sales and rising unemployment.

Until 1847 the Bank of France had not been allowed to issue notes of a denomination lower than 500 francs but in that year the figure was lowered to 200 francs. However, the Bank's inability to cope with the slump of 1847–9 and the run on its gold reserve after the Revolution of 1848 led the minister of finance, Garnier-Pagès, to give it a monopoly of note-issue, authorize it to issue 100 franc notes and made its notes, up to a maximum of 350 million francs, inconvertible legal tender. To sustain the money market and the wholesale and retail trade, Garnier-Pagès took further steps, reminiscent of the post-1830 crisis measures. By decrees issued in March 1848, the government firstly established discount houses, under the supervision of the Bank of France, to discount bills of exchange. Secondly, it established wholesale credit houses under the ministry of finance to provide credit on goods deposited at fourteen warehouses in Paris, which stored the goods as security in four Parisian and fifty-one provincial depositories. Though inadequate, these measures did palliate the disastrous restriction of credit that had occurred and the bank rate rapidly fell from 15 per cent to 6 per cent.[71]

These improvisations led to plans of various kinds flooding into the ministry of finance from people who thought they had the answer to the financial crisis. The scheme which Proudhon had been preparing for several years and which the scarcity of money as a medium of exchange in 1848 was to bring to the fore, was not sent to the finance ministry, Proudhon preferring to rely on voluntary association rather than state intervention. However, he did contact Louis Blanc with a view to him using his influence in the provisional government to make the exchange bank initially a state bank, but the failure of this approach led Proudhon to turn resolutely away from reliance upon government support. Briefly, his scheme, dubbed for propaganda purposes 'free credit' and the 'abolition' of money, was a utilization of the prevailing scarcity of currency to socialize credit, money being replaced by exchange banknotes.

As the prospect of state support for his scheme of an exchange bank vanished completely, Proudhon was forced to rely entirely upon voluntary association and cooperative credit literally of, by and for the people. The adventure in economic democracy began in earnest. In a series of *Le Représentant du Peuple* articles in April and May 1848, printed as a brochure entitled *Banque d'Echange* in the same year, Proudhon argued that the time for formulas such as 'property is theft' was over and it was necessary to secure increased production, equitably consumed through organized credit. On 4 May 1848, Proudhon declared that the recent elections to the Constituent Assembly had exacerbated rather than pacified class conflict and the government had shown itself impotent to deal with this as with the prevailing economic stagnation. To tackle this urgent and vital problem, Proudhon declared: 'I propose that a provisional committee be set up to organise exchange, credit and distribution amongst the workers' in Paris and throughout France, through which 'a representative proletarian body would be established in Paris, *a state within the state*, face to face with the bourgeois representatives.'[72]

Just as the *Représentant du Peuple* had been the journalistic means of propagating Proudhon's exchange bank solution to the 1848 financial crisis, so *Le Peuple* was his chosen instrument for bringing it into existence as the People's Bank, without state assistance. On 30 October 1848 he said to a meeting of his collaborators on the staff of *Le Peuple* in words that summarize his approach, his methods and his purpose: 'I warn you that I will not give you any orders either ideologically or tactically. I seek cooperators; I do not want disciples . . . . As for our economic programme, it is contained within the draft rules of the People's Bank which we have drawn up together. We will submit this scheme to the people. We will attempt to unite around this economic institution all the active elements in the socialist movement. If we succeed in this, the Revolution is three quarters achieved. Our concern therefore is to demonstrate the fruitfulness of the idea of mutual and free credit.'[73] However, although by early April 1849 the People's Bank had enrolled 49 producer cooperatives and 13,267 individual members in Paris alone, while numerous People's Bank committees were being established in the provinces, it had already received its death sentence when Proudhon was condemned on 28 March to three years' imprisonment. He refused to leave his Bank in other hands, his vice-presidential associates including the leading Fourierist Victor Considérant, the ex-Saint-Simonian Pierre Leroux, Jules Lechevalier (ex-Saint-Simonian and ex-Fourierist), while the subscribers included the state socialist Louis Blanc, the Communist Cabet and the liberal economist Bastiat! He feared that his scheme would pass under the control of those who subscribed to 'the ideas of Saint-Simon, Fourier and all the Utopians, who would run it under the title of *democratic management* and on the responsibility of citizen Proudhon! . . . . Amongst them, I did not fear their error . . . . But when I cannot any longer be present, I must be allowed not to give them a blank cheque.'[74]

In his *Confessions of a Revolutionary*, Proudhon described the months establishing his People's Bank as the best time of his life because he was not simply theorizing. He was working actively to replace capitalist statism with an anti-statist socialism in which the workers would manage their own affairs without exploitation or subordination by a 'revolution from below'.[75] Political persecution prevented Proudhon's solution from being put to the test of practical application but cooperative credit was to be revived by others, though without the preposterously grandiose consequences Proudhon had pretended it would yield: peaceful and gradual social change instead of class war between bourgeois and proletarian.

Imprisoned prophet of the Second Republic's suicide

Sentenced in March 1849 for insulting the president of the Republic in three articles at the end of January, having previously had his parliamentary immunity lifted, Proudhon went into hiding in Belgium but rashly returned to Paris. He was in despair at the People's Bank fiasco, engulfed in a pervasive feeling of personal and national failure. He also wanted to marry and become a father. (Proudhon was married on 31 December 1849 and had his honeymoon in jail.) So personal at least as much as political factors may have led to his arrest in June. His choice was somewhat surprising. He was 41 years old and she 27, a semi-illiterate working girl, a practising Catholic whose father was an ardent royalist who had served as a bodyguard to Louis XVIII when he entered Paris after Waterloo. He was imprisoned, first from 1832 to 1837 for involvement in a royalist plot and again in 1854–5 at the age of 70 on a trumped up charge of royalist plotting.[76]

During his three years in jail Proudhon not only married and fathered a child; he edited two newspapers, conducted numerous polemics and wrote four books, two of which we shall examine more closely. Just before he started his sentence we have a rather unprepossessing portrait of him by the American journalist Charles Dana. 'M. Proudhon is about 5' 8" high, and of rather clumsy person. His hair is light, his complexion fresh, his eyes blue and keen and his nose slightly *retroussé*. His face expresses quickness, intelligence and confidence. He is not an orator, though at some banquets he has been roused to real eloquence. He gesticulates considerably, and without anything like grace. His voice is harsh and unmusical, his speech distinct and monotonous.'[77] Such was the man who wrote just after beginning to serve his sentence on 5 June 1849: 'I am a prisoner but my mind is free.'[78] He indeed went on to deploy the ample resources of his mind and his pen to punishing effect.

Proudhon's two great works written at high speed while in prison – *The Confessions of a Revolutionary* and *The General Idea of the Revolution in the Nineteenth Century* – mark his transition to a liberal, even anarchic socialism. While he never abandoned his commitment to equality in favour of his passion for liberty, the stress changed from the former to the latter under the pressure of revolutionary experience. The *Confessions* were rapidly written and published a mere four months after his imprisonment. The book contains some of his most vitriolic vociferations against the French people for having allowed the repression of the Paris workers and then so readily abased themselves before another Napoleon. 'Ah! vain and servile race that we are! . . . keeping an army of 500,000 soldiers to shoot down our offspring . . . we summon the nations to independence and then abandon them to their despots [a reference to Poland, Hungary and Italy] . . . only esteem our flatterers, respect our parasites, love our prostitutes, hate our workers and the poor; once a race of heros, we are now a race of hypocrites and sycophants.'[79]

The French should have chosen a republican as president of the Republic but instead they had fallen for the Bonapartist appeal to the people against the constitution. Going further than Tocqueville's more indirect attacks on the new imperialism, Proudhon consoled himself with the belief that Louis-Napoleon, as the *reductio ad absurdum* of authority, would finally discredit state power.[80] Meanwhile, democracy had disgraced itself. 'Universal and direct suffrage, consulted on three consecutive occasions, has produced the most counter-revolutionary and anti-republican results . . . . The eruption of the masses, suddenly summoned, has made of society an incomprehensible monster' unleashing an 'anti-liberal and persecuting Church' and an unprecedentedly arbitrary state.[81] The suppression of the Roman Republic and the coming restriction of universal suffrage deprived government of its legitimacy. Proudhon wrote that only imprisonment prevented him from joining in the peaceful demonstration to defend the violated constitution on 13 June 1849 and he recommended resisting oppression by civil disobedience, non-payment of taxes and refusal to do military service.[82]

Before considering his *General Idea of the Revolution*, the culmination of his middle-period attack on God, government and property, we need to place his relationship with Louis-Napoleon in the pre-*coup d'état* political context. The National Assembly was dominated by a conservative monarchist majority, which was fatally divided between some 250 Orleanist and 200 Legitimist deputies, the Legitimist pretender Chambord's intransigence assisting the advent of the Second Empire even before he played the same role for the Third Republic. Louis-Napoleon used the 'red peril' radical republicans to frighten public opinion. He curried public favour by appealing to the Catholic vote through his restoration of the Pope and the enactment of the *Loi Falloux* which returned education to clerical control. The bourgeoisie's praetorian National Guard was weakened and the royalist head of the army was replaced by a reliable Bonapartist in January 1851.

Proudhon could see the usurper preparing his seizure of power. He sometimes called for an alliance between the Left and the bourgeoisie against Louis-Napoleon, at others with him against the bourgeoisie. Addressing the latter in the privacy of his diary, Proudhon wrote: 'The proletarian, whom you shot down, watches you die.'[83] Less than two months later (on 8 January 1851) Proudhon expressed his wholehearted abomination of Louis-Napoleon. 'No more unworthy being has perhaps ever been called by the chance of birth, popular error or party intrigue to govern a nation.' After comparing him to Caligula, Proudhon somewhat hyperbolically went on: 'It will one day be my greatest honour to have fought him almost alone, with unequalled energy, to have attacked him from the first month of his power . . . with pitiless verve, to have tirelessly pursued him, to have mocked him from the depths of my prison with a sharp and bitter irony.'[84] The truth is less simple and less flattering. Before and after the 1851 *coup d'état*, Proudhon was indirectly involved in Florentine intrigue with Louis-Napoleon, notably to block the election of Louis-Philippe's son Joinville as president of the Republic in 1852 as a preliminary to restoration of the monarchy. Proudhon was outmanoeuvred by a more subtle Machiavellian but he refused a request to solicit an early release from prison in writing, which would have been used to discredit him.[85]

In February 1850 Proudhon had launched an ironic prediction of the December 1851 coup entitled *Vive l'Empereur* and was punished by being placed in rigorous confinement that prevented him from writing. He was not tried for this new offence on condition that he gave up journalism and contented himself with writing books. He met other imprisoned Socialist leaders like Blanqui but he reacted against their dictatorial approach with horror. 'The human species wishes to be governed, it will be. I am ashamed of the human species.'[86] In his determination to 'dejacobinize' the French revolutionary movement, Proudhon broke his silence with the *General Idea of the Revolution*, dashed off in the two months from mid-April to mid-June 1851. Having in the *Confessions* explained the failure of an attempt to achieve social revolution through political revolution, Proudhon now sought to persuade republicans and Socialists to abandon authoritarian state socialism for conciliatory economic reformism. He had originally intended to entitle his book *Pratique des Révolutions* and its subtitle incorporated this idea: 'Studies on revolutionary and industrial practice'.[87]

To understand Proudhon's dithyrambic dedication to the bourgeoisie, his tactical aim was to detach all but the worst exploiters – 'the rentiers, usurers and largest landowners' – from the middle classes. They might then be brought together with the proletariat to prevent the counter-revolutionary reaction that was gathering force. The working lower-middle classes had to be split from the idle bourgeoisie if such a defensive alliance with the working classes was to be achieved. However, Proudhon had a more substantive and strategic reason for wanting such an alliance. The bourgeoisie were much more strongly committed to freedom than the proletariat. 'You have always been the most intrepid and clever revolutionaries', having from 1789 'proclaimed successively all the revolutionary ideas, religious freedom, press freedom, freedom of association, trade and industry; through your learned constitutions you have defeated the altar and the throne, established on indestructible foundations equality before the law, parliamentary accountability, publication of state accounts, the subordination of the government to the country, the sovereignty of public opinion.'[88] Had the bourgeoisie become counter-revolutionary? It had in June 1848 embraced reaction, shooting and transporting the famished and naive worker revolutionaries. Proudhon implored the middle classes to resume their revolutionary tradition. 'The people awaits you, as in 89, 93, 1830, 1848. The Revolution stretches its arms to you: save the people and yourselves, as your fathers did, through Revolution.'[89]

Proudhon had been planning a four-volume work on the history of democracy but the immediate threat by Louis-Napoleon brushed this project aside. He prophetically attacked direct election of the president as a 'prelude to Caesarism', predicting that 'the era of Caesars is dawning: an inextricable democracy will be replaced without any transition by the empire, with or without Napoleon.'[90] The will of the people was an unreliable basis for defending freedom and justice, so Proudhon declared that he would not risk a hair of his head to preserve it. The Republic – which had put him in prison – was superior to democracy but *'The Revolution is superior to the Republic'* were the words with which he ended the *General Idea of the Revolution*.[91] The general and permanent character of the revolutionary process is a crucial theme to which we shall return.

Louis-Napoleon outmanoeuvred his opponents in November 1851 into rejecting his proposed abrogation of the 1850 Act restricting universal suffrage. The Left then joined the Bonapartists in rejecting the monarchist Right's bill to give the National Assembly the power directly to requisition the armed forces to protect the Republic. The *coup d'état* followed on 2 December 1851. By chance, this coincided with Proudhon's day a week out on parole, so we have a first-hand account of his observations and reactions to what he described as a 'crime'. 'Paris looked like a woman raped by four brigands, with a knife to her throat, who, unable to move, closes her eyes and accepts her fate.'[92] He encountered Victor Hugo and tried to persuade him that resistance was futile because the people would not budge. Napoleon's purpose was to convert a republican people into an imperial populace.[93]

Proudhon returned to jail on the morning on 3 December but by the next day, after hearing of some isolated acts of resistance, he had changed his mind. 'If I were free, I would bury myself under the ruins of the republic with its loyal citizens or live far away from a country unworthy of liberty.'[94] No hope of victory, only an impassioned need to behave with dignity led him to favour resistance to a parricidal and cowardly army, just as the deputy Baudin perished heroically at the barricades to show the anti-parliamentary French public 'how one dies for twenty-five francs a day'. Significantly, for a few days in December 1851, Tocqueville, Proudhon and Blanqui simultaneously languished in jail.

A week later, Proudhon was already adopting a more reflective viewpoint. Democracy would need a long process of education before it became worthy of emancipation. Yet, as the population was about to plebiscite Louis-Napoleon on the first anniversary of the coup by 7,824,189 votes against 253,145, Proudhon exclaimed: 'On Second December the last of the Gods died, the People . . . . I have never adored the People, I have tutored it. Not cult but culture. Eternal culture, so an eternal incapacity . . . . We woke up citizens and we shall go to bed as subjects.'[95] The great realist painter Gustave Courbet, Proudhon's friend and admirer, remembered this period on hearing of his death in 1865. 'The nineteenth century has lost its pilot . . . . We have no compass and humanity and the Revolution are adrift . . . . I am in a state of moral prostration and discouragement such as I have only felt once before in my life (on 2 December, when I went to bed and vomited for three whole days). Like Proudhon, I cannot accept that the Revolution should be led astray by throwing a bone to the people.'[96] Proudhon's own reaction was described in a letter at the time: 'I spent a fortnight after the 2 December like a man sentenced to death . . . the crime's horror crushed my consciousness . . . so many outrages, so much shame . . . and so much stupidity', meant that the greedy bourgeois and peasantry, the ignorant workers, would have to expiate putting power and money before justice and good faith.[97]

In letters Proudhon wrote early in 1852, he reiterated that the 'vile multitude' had proved its unfitness for democracy, whose prerequisite was 'demopedia', education of the people, a task in which Proudhon accurately predicted he would work himself to death.[98] Until the people had been educated in the exercise of its political rights one could not count on them. 'It is an inert and passive mass . . . . The Republic made a mistake in 48 . . . in taking this mass as its sovereign inspiration, instead of considering it as a collection of children, unable to exercise their rights or even to understand them. What we mean by the *People* is always and necessarily the least *advanced* part of society, consequently the most ignorant and cowardly', the most susceptible to Bonapartist demagoguery.[99] Proudhon declared that if he was to take the People as he found it, the only rational regime would be a dictatorship in either the Blanquist or Bonapartist fashion.[100]

His diaries of 1850–1 contain several comments on Blanqui whom he got to know in jail. Of all the 1848 revolutionaries, 'Blanqui alone seems to merit an honourable mention' but despite his intelligence and organizational skill, this embittered throwback to Robespierre would merely reverse the oppression of workers by the bourgeoisie, installing a repellent dictatorship.[101] The measure of the chasm between Proudhon and Blanqui will become fully evident only when we explore the latter's activity in the next chapter. Whatever his reservations about democracy Proudhon accepted, as Blanqui did not, that 'The right to insurrection disappears with the implementation of universal suffrage.'[102]

It would not be objective to remain silent about Proudhon's singular sacrifice of political principle to political expediency: his attempt to do a political deal with Louis-Napoleon, which recalls Constant's expediential rallying to Napoleon in 1815. Proudhon did it openly, for what he conceived as the public good rather than his personal benefit and with immense mental reservations. Louis-Napoleon had asked to meet Proudhon shortly after the 1848 Revolution allowed him to return to France. They were elected to the same National Assembly, both 'outsiders' in their different ways. Proudhon had voted against allowing the pretender to take his seat. From the first Proudhon suspected his intentions but he was entrusted by the people with power when 'he ought to have been shot'.[103] Proudhon was serving his sentence for 'insulting' Louis-Napoleon in December 1849 when he was approached on behalf of the president with a proposal that his People's Bank be relaunched.[104] Louis-Napoleon was doubtless engaging in a political manoeuvre but he had always been inclined towards 'socialist' schemes, though during the Second Empire these took the ultra-capitalist form of the ex-Saint-Simonian Péreire's *Crédit Mobilier*, not Proudhon's People's Bank!

As Proudhon wrote in 1853 to Prince Jérôme Napoléon (nicknamed *Plonplon*), Louis-Napoleon's cousin: 'M. Péreire is the representative and leader of the Saint-Simonian principle of industrial feudalism which at present rules our national economy, a principle I consider to be anti-democratic and anti-liberal . . . fatal to the people's emancipation.'[105] From 1853 to 1856 Proudhon cultivated the pro-republican and anticlerical *Plonplon*, visiting him about a dozen times. Proudhon hoped he would as heir presumptive succeed Louis-Napoleon (until the latter belatedly acquired a son in 1856) and further the 'Revolutionary' cause. Meanwhile, Proudhon sought *Plonplon*'s help on behalf of victimized friends and to use his presidency of the 1855 Paris World Exhibition Committee to promote the People's Bank idea against the super-capitalist enemy Péreire.[106] Proudhon's vain recourse to *Plonplon* was the consequence of his failure to convert Louis-Napoleon to the quixotic view that he could become the agent of the nineteenth-century socio-economic revolutionary process.

That this was not a totally absurd proposition is evident from the fact that Louis-Napoleon was educated by a Saint-Simonian tutor and had published a monograph in 1844 on *The Extinction of Poverty*. However, as Proudhon prepared to leave prison in 1852, he had few illusions about the dangers in

trying to make the best of the perjured president's crime. He confided
to his diary: 'Engaging in politics is to wash one's hands in dirt' and
'Seeking a solution from a cutthroat, an explanation for an ambush!
a meaning for perjury! . . . a principle and a cause for tyranny! is
to prostitute's one's reason.'[107] Yet, with open eyes, that was what
Proudhon proceeded to do. It was no justification in terms of his
own philosophy to declare that 'The most numerous and poorest
class (note the Saint-Simonian terminology, calculated to appeal to
Louis-Napoleon), that grand army (Napoleonic allusion) of universal
suffrage, that we tried to emancipate through its own initiative, has
given its reply twice, on 10 December 1848 and 20 December 1851' by
voting overwhelmingly for Louis-Napoleon.[108]

Although publication of *La Révolution sociale* was first banned, it was
allowed to appear shortly after Proudhon left prison in June 1852 – to the
dismay of the Left, who regarded it as a betrayal. Yet Proudhon presented
himself to the emperor as an adversary, who had tried to teach the people
to embrace decentralization – even *'anarchy, which like all principles
indicates an ideal rather than a reality'* – rather than the centralized
dictatorship of a Caesarist Second Empire.[109] Proudhon's forlorn hope of
steering Louis-Napoleon to the Left was quickly dissipated and by October
1852 he was writing in his diary: 'L-N (*sic*) is leaning towards the bourgeoisie, the jesuits and counter-revolution.'[110] The tactic of dissuading the
new regime from its capitalist and clericalist penchants was a misguided
if not dishonourable failure but Marx's *The Eighteenth Brumaire of Louis
Bonaparte* is a much more perceptive and penetrating analysis of the
Bonapartist phenomenon in mid-nineteenth-century France. Proudhon's
despair in late 1852 is evident from his unpublished *Testament ou Société
des Vengeurs*, in which he considers the possibility of tyrannicide but rules
it out except as the judicial sentence of a people. Louis-Napoleon was
basking in popular approval.[111]

Towards industrial democracy: a universal working middle class?

In the early, more exclusively critical phase of his work, Proudhon had rather
scorned the piecemeal and gradualist voluntary associationist methods of
reforming society. After the Second Republic, during which his combative
inclinations culminated in paroxysms of polemical hyperbole, Proudhon's
emphasis altered to practical small-scale pluralist ways of achieving his
libertarian purpose. He wrote in his diary a week after the 1851 *coup d'état*

that he defined 'the word *democracy* no longer through government of the people, but through the progressive *emancipation of the people* . . . . The people are beasts of burden, whose whole business is to drink, eat, sleep and make love: they care little for anything else. For my part, I have never been democracy's dupe . . . my socialism has justice for its point of departure, not the sovereignty of the mass, the competance of the people.'[112] The great works of this final period of Proudhon's life were *On Justice in the Revolution and the Church* (1858), *The Federal Principle* (1863) and the posthumous *On the Political Capacity of the Working Classes* (1865). As he wrote in *Justice*: 'Now the period of demolition is over.'[113]

He took up again his earlier idea of winning over the working middle classes to an alliance with the proletariat because despite their conflicting interests they had complementary virtues. While the bourgeoisie were not as stupid as the working people, they were much more cowardly and corrupt in their acquisitive pursuit of wealth. However, their saving grace was their passion for freedom, which the masses did not share. In an essay on 'Bourgeoisie and plebeians', appended to *Justice*, Proudhon observed: 'The people have no conception of municipal, departmental and corporative freedoms, of guarantees of the freedom of the individual, of the home, much less of procedure. They are in favour of large organizations: centralization, the indivisible republic, the unitary empire. For the same reason, they are prone to communism.' In the *Confessions*, he had envisaged a future society based upon the 'universalisation of the middle class' in which the Saint-Simonian principle of each being remunerated according to his work would prevail.[114]

In the 1840s, Proudhon had periodically lapsed from his commitment to voluntary contract into a scientism that recalled the positivism of Saint-Simon and Comte. In 1840, at the end of *What is Property?*, Proudhon argued that 'Politics is a science, not just sharp practice; the legislator's function in the last analysis is lifted to the methodical search for the truth.'[115] Decisions by ministers, magistrates and mass opinion were dismissed as scientifically worthless expressions of will, not reason. A decade later, in *The General Idea of the Revolution in the Nineteenth Century*, Proudhon was still claiming that 'The day when SOCIAL SCIENCE has replaced social *conventions*, the legislator, government, courts, police, jailers, all the repressive and coercive apparatus becomes superfluous.'[116] However, by 1851 he was less optimistic about predicting the imminent advent of the reign of a libertarian social scientism.

Given the castigations that Proudhon had repeatedly inflicted upon the political incapacity of the people and its protagonists, it comes almost as a surprise that all extra-contractual collective action was to be decided by voting. Haubtmann rightly points to the paradox that 'The social thinker who most energetically criticised universal suffrage is also the one who tried to build his whole anarchist community on the unlimited multiplication of voting.'[117] Using an undated and unpublished fragment from 1863 contrasting mass democracy – a mob of atomized and irrational individuals – and pluralist democracy – groups sharing informed interests – which subsumed his critique of democracy in the *Confessions* and *General Idea*, Haubtmann shows how the paradox is resolved in Proudhon's mature works. Rational collective decisions would emerge from the free clash of opinions in a pluralist democracy represented by 'the working, teaching group; the industrial, intellectual, artistic enterprise; the university, school, local authority; the national assembly, the club, the jury.'[118] Government was reduced to a modest component in this pluralistic political universe and would itself be pluralized by functional representation. All else would be the societal sphere of free and reciprocal contracts between groups. Decisions would be built upwards from the bottom and from the periphery to the centre. This in practice was how Proudhon hoped to approximate to the state of anarchy or non-government.

In the voluminous and inchoate outpourings of Proudhon's prison writings, one can detect the outlines of the anarcho-pluralist republic which he was seeking to delineate. The economy would be run on almost free credit ($1/4$ to $1/2$ per cent interest on loans) and the private farming of land owned by the communes, with large-scale enterprises being run by industrial democracy (of which more later). General and vocational education would be combined and run by the commune, with the teachers subject to parental control. Parishioners would elect the priests, who in turn would elect bishops. Judges would be elected by universal suffrage and in turn elect appellate judges. Police and public finance would be controlled by the communes, while there would be no need for ministries of agriculture or public works. In the army, the rank and file would elect the NCOs, who would elect the junior officers, who formed the electorate of the highest-ranking officers. Foreign affairs as such cease to exist because 'there is no nationality, no country in the political sense of the word; there are only birthplaces. Whatever a man's race or colour, he is really a native of the universe; he has a citizen's rights everywhere.'[119]

The social division of labour through a decentralized industrial democracy harmoniously achieves what a merely political separation of powers fails to attain: social solidarity based upon freedom. The social constitution being based upon free contract, the division of labour and reciprocity would replace the political constitution founded upon authoritarianism, class distinction and centralization. Whereas political democracy had led to dictatorship, industrial democracy would disperse power among 'a mass of free citizens, making compromises between their interests, sometimes individually, sometimes collectively in councils, undertaking without intermediaries all economic and social tasks.'[120] Proudhon asserted in the *General Idea* that whereas hitherto 'The history of governments is the martyrology of the proletariat', the future prospects were better. He added in October 1851, as a postscript to the *Confessions*: 'The proletariat, gradually dejacobinised, seeks its share not only of direct suffrage in the affairs of society but of direct action.'[121] The intellectual inspiration of the anarcho-syndicalist movement half a century later is adumbrated even before the apotheosis of *The Political Capacity of the Working Classes*.

In the mid-1840s Proudhon had come into contact with the Lyons-organized working-class movement, and its associationist practices were to influence him in the post-1848 period. As previously mentioned, Proudhon had opportunistically approached Louis Blanc as a member of the 1848 provisional government with a view to securing pump-priming state support for his idea of a People's Bank, on condition that the state would subsequently withdraw in favour of associate enterprise. In *The Federal Principle*, fifteen years later, Proudhon explained: 'I understand, I accept, I even demand where necessary, state intervention in all large scale initiation of public utilities but I do not see the need to perpetuate state provision . . . . I called in 1848 for state intervention in the establishment of national banks, credit institutions, insurance as well as railways; but it never entered my mind that once the state had created these institutions, it should forever remain banker, insurer, transporter and so forth.'[122] The repudiation of state socialism as a form of permanent organization is clear, even if it might be a useful adjunct to the workers' attempts through their voluntary associations to institutionalize social justice.

Ironically, it was in an 1854 potboiler called *Manual of a Stock Exchange Speculator*, most of which Proudhon did not write, published as a means of earning money, that he coined in passing the term 'industrial democracy'. Joint-stock companies would be replaced by associated workers cooperatively sharing not only in the profits but in the management, mutualizing industrial property and industrial power. 'Worker companies' would deal with the problem of large-scale production, consumer cooperatives would handle the retail trade, and friendly societies would cover old age pensions and social insurance – Proudhon later adding building societies to provide housing for rent and sale.[123] As Proudhon wrote in 1856, while the means of production should be publicly owned, production itself should be organized by worker companies because workers were no more incompetent than shareholders if they were properly advised.[124] Of course, shareholders do not manage firms, so Proudhon was not facing up to the fatal problem that 'workers control' ventures have confronted in the nineteenth and twentieth centuries. However, while Proudhon's idea of industrial democracy was not calculated to commend itself to the Stock Exchange speculators, it was to have an admiring audience in the anarcho-syndicalist movement that developed at the end of the century, after premonitory rumblings in the 1860s. Proudhon's posthumous *Political Capacity of the Working Classes* was specifically prompted by these early signals from the industrial wing of the French labour movement. When he declared that 'By democratising us, revolution has impelled us towards industrial democracy', Proudhon was arguing that this should be the superior, socio-economic counterpart of political democracy, based upon a federation of voluntary associations, to avoid the latter's dictatorial propensities.[125]

In his *Social Revolution* of 1852, Proudhon had presented a threefold classification of the French people. First, there was the 'bourgeoisie', the propertied *rentiers*, idle capitalists and governing class living from unearned income. Second, there was the working 'middle class' of entrepreneurs who personally put their capital to work to secure higher earned incomes. Last, there was the 'working class and proletariat', those without capital and earning the lowest incomes.[126] The peasantry were an ambiguous group because while they put their land and capital to work (and in that sense were middle class), their low incomes and precarious livelihood brought them closer to the proletarians. Because they identified the confirmation of the revolutionary land reform with Napoleon, the peasantry were predominantly Bonapartist. Proudhon saw that the existing inferior status of the working classes also made most of them deferential and manipulable. They had acquired class consciousness in 1848 but did not know how to use it to good effect politically. By instilling in the workers a sense of their dignity and capacity to manage their own affairs once they had been educated, Proudhon sought to fulfil his life's work as set out in his candidature for the scholarship he won in 1838.

While Proudhon often referred to class conflict, he never regarded the classes as irreconcilable. However, by 1857 he had come to the conclusion that although the classes would gradually merge into a single working middle class, the cynical exploitation of the workers meant that for the present no compromise was possible between the classes. The workers must achieve their own emancipation. In 1857, Proudhon turned down several offers to stand for election in various constituencies but by 1863 he was advocating electoral abstention by spoiling votes to reject both the Second Empire and the mainstream political opposition. Making a virtue of refusing to take the oath of allegiance to the Second Empire – the precondition of contesting the election – which he had earlier accepted for tactical reasons, Proudhon argued that the liberalized Empire still offered insufficient freedom of speech, press and association, coupled with sustained prefectoral pressure and gerrymandered constituencies, to allow proper democratic activity. Proudhon's attempt to mobilize a principled abstention fell flat, partly because the printers were too afraid of prosecution to publish the manifesto of the Abstentionist Committee. While in exile Proudhon had in any case lost touch with the Paris working class; there were only a few hundred blank ballots in 1863 and the republican Left swept all nine Paris seats, eight in the first ballot. His main concern, however, was to distinguish his own 'federalist' standpoint from that of all other opponents of the Second Empire.[127]

The idea of worker candidates was not new, having been advocated in 1832 by the Saint-Simonian Jean Reynaud in an article entitled: 'On the need for special representation of the proletarians.'[128] Nominations of working-class candidates had been discussed in 1863 but had been rejected by the republican journalists who constituted the leadership of the opposition, notably the ex-Saint-Simonian Hippolyte Carnot. Nevertheless, the 1864 by-elections allowed the issue to re-emerge and this time, according to Maxime Leroy, it gave rise to one of the great socialist manifestos, worthy of ranking alongside the better-known 1796 Babeuf–Maréchal *Manifesto of the Equals* and the 1848 Marx–Engels *Communist Manifesto*.[129] It was the key exposition, along with the book by Proudhon that it inspired, of the dominant reformist wing of the working-class movement of the 1860s. The 1864 *Manifesto of the Sixty* – so-called because it was signed by sixty skilled workers, some of whom were to play a leading part in the First International, also launched in 1864, and most of whom were associated with the cooperative movement – aimed at stirring the employed classes into achieving through their own associated efforts the social and economic equivalent of the manhood suffrage which they had achieved in politics. It advocated a separate working-class party, concentrating on social and economic problems, in contrast with those that supported priority for the political issue of republicanism.

The electoral *Manifesto of the Sixty* was inspired by an engraver in bronze, Henri-Louis Tolain, but was drawn up on behalf of the workers by the left-wing politicians Henri Lefort (future member of the First International) and Léon Gambetta (future founder of the Third Republic and like Lefort a great admirer and voracious reader of Proudhon's writings).[130] It was published on 17 February 1864 in *L'Opinion Nationale*, edited by Guéroult, another ex-Saint-Simonian. Only the workers signed the manifesto. Many of them, including their leader Tolain, had attended the 1864 London World Exhibition as worker delegates and were active in the First International. One of them – Camélinat – became ephemeral Director of the Mint during the 1871 Commune and lived to be displayed as a heroic relic by the Communist Party in the 1940s.[131] It was Tolain, author of an 1863 brochure on the Paris elections (who was to have a political career first as a radical deputy and then as an opportunist senator in the Third Republic, in the wake of the opportunist Gambetta, after holding aloof from the 1871 Paris Commune), who personified the resurgent skilled working-class movement of the 1860s. Maxime Leroy observed in words that are still true: 'Tolain is almost forgotten today, with the greatest injustice, because he is the first great name of a working class seeking self-emancipation through its own efforts.' The rapporteur of the 1884 Act legalizing French trade unions 'had rendered signal services to the working class but he has been rejected from its history because he was too moderate.'[132] Now that it has learnt moderation, is it not time for the French labour movement to repair that injustice?

The 1864 Act that initiated the process of legalizing trade unions was a major issue on which Proudhon did not see eye to eye with his successors in the French labour movement, both labourist like Tolain and anarcho-syndicalist like Pelloutier. Whereas Tolain argued in 1863 that 'The trade union will be, in the economic and industrial order, the mother institution of all future progress',[133] Proudhon was never in this sense a syndicalist. However, unlike the Bonapartist press and the opposition republicans (who counter-attacked with a *Manifesto of the Eighty*), Proudhon immediately wrote to Chaudey, to whom nearly a year later he dictated on his deathbed the conclusion to *Political Capacity of the Working Classes*: 'The principles advocated by the workers are ours.' He fixed as the purpose of his book 'carrying their thought even further'.[134] Asked by groups of workers in Rouen and Paris on how to react to the *Manifesto of the Sixty*, Proudhon replied that while he supported their *ouvrierisme*, he went further in acknowledging class conflict and its resolution not by electoral or strike action but by worker self-management.[135]

Proudhon's version of the Manifesto's libertarian and legalistic socialism was taken up by the French participants in the First International. Tolain – who had not until then read Proudhon – acquired from Proudhon's *Political Capacity of the Working Classes* a sense of the wider significance of the skilled workers' struggle. This book – prompted by the class-conscious avant-garde of the workers – was described by Proudhon as his socio-political 'testament', asserting his faith in 'the working people, who for the first time would speak in their own name.'[136] Proudhon spent his last energies in the struggle to complete the work which he hoped would be 'an important contribution to the *federalist party*'.[137] It is to this federalist pluralism, characteristically couched in the polemical slogans of antitheism and anarchism, that we now turn.

Against absolute authority:
antitheism and federalist pluralism

Proudhon's anarchism was partly based upon a childhood sense of injustice and oppression, exacerbated by his three years' imprisonment. While he toned down this hypersensitive reaction to authoritarian arbitrariness into the affirmation of a libertarian order, based on voluntary contract between people of equal dignity, he regarded it as an ideal to which one might increasingly approximate without ever attaining it fully. Although it was a decentralized, pluralist ideal of family and group autonomy within their own spheres, Proudhon's authentic voice is to be heard in his heartfelt assertion of personal freedom. As he wrote in 1851: 'I want order, as much and even more than those who disturb it with their so-called government but I want it as the result of my will, a condition of my work and a law of my reason. I will never submit to it coming from a foreign will, imposing servitude and sacrifice as preconditions.'[138] Proudhon was, with the publication of *Justice* in 1858, to regard justice as the means of reconciling freedom and order, allowing him to place justice before individual freedom, freedom before democracy and democracy before tranquility. But to his dying day Proudhon asserted his independence: 'My conscience is mine, my justice is mine and my liberty is sovereign. Even if I die for eternity, at least let me be a man for one revolution of the sun.'[139] It was just such an individualism that had attracted Constant to Godwin.

Proudhon is entitled to claim paternity rights over anarchism because before his self-description as an anarchist in *What is Property?* it was only used as a term of abuse. He went on in the mid-1840s, under the influence of the German Young Hegelians – especially Feuerbach and Moses Hess rather than Marx – to a generalized rejection of authoritarian alienation, identified particularly with God, government and property. A decade before Henry Maine formulated his evolutionary law of the development from status to contract, Proudhon was arguing that contract was the means by which economic and political authority could be replaced by reciprocal exchange.[140] In the preface to his *Confessions*, entitled 'What is government?', Proudhon recalled Aristotle's scepticism about identifying the best form of government. 'We, who in sixty years have worn out seven or eight forms of government; who hardly having become a Republic are already tired of our Constitution; we, for whom the exercise of power has only been . . . the practice of oppression and arbitrariness . . . do we have more faith than Aristotle?' Dismissing both God and the state as 'fictions' – 'the first duty of a free mind is to send them to museums and libraries' - Proudhon asserted: 'We no more accept the government of man by man than the exploitation of man by man.'[141] Fifteen years later, Proudhon more modestly wrote: 'Anarchy in the full sense has not been established anywhere; it doubtless can never completely exist; but if federation and mutualism guarantee freedoms, we shall have a state that could be called anarchic.'[142]

Pierre Haubtmann, sometime almoner of *Action Catholique Ouvrière* and rector of the Paris *Institut Catholique*, judged that 'Proudhon was in the nineteenth century the most determined, the most implacable, the most original enemy of the Catholic Church. His masterpiece, *De la Justice dans la Révolution et dans l'Eglise*, still remains the most substantial compendium of intelligent anticlericalism.'[143] After losing his faith in his late teens, Proudhon subsequently recalled that 'At 21, the idea there was no God made me feel faint.'[144] However, unlike others in this predicament, Proudhon did not embrace materialism or replace God with Humanity. He embraced the ideal of justice. In the name of justice, he became an uncompromising opponent of Roman Christianity, dedicated to its extirpation. Received as a Freemason in January 1847, Proudhon answered the ritual question: 'What does man owe to God?' with an unorthodox but characteristic reply: 'War'.[145] This was to be expected from a man who had recently published the *Economic Contradictions*, which start and finish with antideistic diatribes against the supreme personification of absolute authority. 'God is stupidity and cowardice; God is hypocrisy and falsehood; God is tyranny and poverty; God is evil. For as long as men bow before altars, mankind will remain damned, the slave of kings and priests.'[146] While Proudhon acknowledged his debt to the *philosophes* and the *idéologues* as his predecessors, he stood their scepticism on its head. For Voltaire God did not exist but was socially useful; for Proudhon God did exist but was socially harmful, as the embodiment of oppressive absolutism.

Proudhon's work had already been placed on the Pope's *Index* in 1852 but the uproar caused by the appearance in 1858 of *Justice* surpassed all others he had provoked. The Second Empire *Ordre Moral* context was anything but propitious. In 1857 Flaubert had been prosecuted and *Madame Bovary's* publication suspended for 'outraging public and religious morality' and in January 1858 Orsini's attempt on the emperor's life led to intensified repression of subversive opinion. Proudhon rejected attempts to dissuade him from publishing *Justice* and prepared for the inevitable prosecution. Two thousand advance subscriptions prompted the police to make intimidatory 'inquiries' of publisher and printer. The publisher expected to sell 30,000 copies by the year's end. In anticipation of it being banned, 6,000 copies were sold within six days. It was then seized and Proudhon was charged with, *inter alia*, 'outraging public and religious morality', 'provoking hatred of citizens against each other' and 'undermining the respect due to the laws'. Warned by his lawyers that he could expect a five-year prison sentence, Proudhon initially chose to counter-attack rather than flee. During his interrogation, he switched from the role of accused to accuser. He vainly petitioned the Senate, denouncing the Concordat with the Roman Catholic Church as unconstitutional. When this petition was published and seized, it led to further charges. Sentenced to three years' imprisonment and a 4,000 franc fine, Proudhon took refuge in Brussels to carry on the fight in freedom.[147] He was not to return until 1862.

Justice is an immensely long and discursive confrontation between transcendental 'divine right' and immanent 'human right' in all spheres of activity. Proudhon's denunciations of ecclesiastical dogmatism in the name of revolutionary moralism are expressed with all the fury of some latter-day reincarnation of an Old Testament prophet. The alliance between spiritual and temporal tyrannies was too tempting if perilous a target to be resisted. He was conscious that such was religion's appeal to the masses that mystical sects rather than immanent justice were more likely to fill the vacuum left by the Church. Still, despite a Catholic wife, he personally refused to be married in Church or have his daughters baptized, declaring: 'When the Pope becomes a *social democrat* I will allow him to bless my marriage.'[148] This did not prevent Proudhon having a very traditional conception of marriage and indulging in the most uninhibited anti-feminist theory and practice.[149] From the triumph of revolution over revelation, he was concerned to protect the family as an enclave of male domination. The anti-chauvinist was a male chauvinist.

Proudhon could have returned from exile at the end of 1860 because he had been pardoned in the wake of the decree liberalizing the Second Empire. He did not in fact return until September 1862 because he did not wish to avail himself of an imperial favour, and he wanted to finish his *War and Peace*. The uproar that followed its publication in 1861 led him to wonder whether he could publish freely in France. Knowing that his letters were read by the police, he wrote in 1861: 'I become anxious as the moment approaches when I will have again to submerge myself in this dead sea, this sunken lake in which people no longer seem to understand what the words *law* and *liberty* mean.'[150] When he finally returned to France in 1862, he had less than two and a half years to live but in that time he produced not only his posthumous masterpiece on *The Political Capacity of the Working Classes*; he also published in 1863 his *Principle of Federation*. While it was rapidly written, prompted by attacks on his polemic *La Fédération et l'Unite en Italie*, parts of it have been recognized as a classic exposition of the case for federalist pluralism. While this meant a conscious return to the liberal tradition of Montesquieu and Tocqueville, there were important continuities with Proudhon's earlier writings.

Georges Sorel, whose own thought was suffused with Proudhonian influences, declared: 'I think *Democracy in America* had a considerable and perhaps decisive influence on Proudhon's earlier works.'[151] While this has some truth, both in the idea of the inexorable advance of equality and in the anxiety about its democratic concomitant, it is only at the end of his life that Proudhon domesticated anarchism into federalism and in the process enthusiastically embraced Tocquevillian pluralism. In an 1862 letter, Proudhon stressed the consistency of his thought when he wrote: 'If in 1840 I started out from anarchy, the result of my critique of the governmental idea, this was because I had to finish with *federation*, the necessary foundation of the law of European peoples and eventually of the organization of all states.'[152] While anarchy was an unattainable ideal, the freest countries were those – such as the United States and Switzerland – whose government was weakest. In 1849 Proudhon had acknowledged that effective government required centralization but if it was unitary it would lead to absolutism, to which the separation of powers was a desirable but partial palliative. While he then hoped that authoritarianism was condemned to disappear, he had decided by 1851 that the French Revolution 'had fulfilled none of its promises. By proclaiming freedom of opinion, equality before the law, popular sovereignty, the subordination of government to the people, the Revolution had made of society and government two incompatible things. This incompatibility has been the cause and pretext of the liberticidal, all-absorbing concentration of power which parliamentary democracy admires and loves because it naturally tends towards despotism: CENTRALIZATION.'[153] In support, Proudhon quoted an 1822 speech by Tocqueville's mentor Royer-Collard in which he had referred to the French having become 'an administered people' owing to centralization (see Chapter 6, p. 120).

The *General Idea of the Revolution* prepared the way for his future federalism by an all-out attack on centralized administration. In this 'anarchic' phase, he called for the abolition of all courts of law and of all ministries, notably the 'Finance Ministry [which] is to the State what the feeding trough is to the donkey', providing the resources for activities government should not perform.[154] In a characteristic tirade, he castigated the prefects who ruled the French provinces. 'Entrusted with the affairs of the *département* and the State, responsible for the judicial police, intermediary, plenipotentiary, instructor, director, supervisor, assessor, controller, reformer, corrector, tutor, commander, manager, municipal officer, judge: such is the prefect, such is government!'[155] Not content to give vent to the exasperation of the administered, Proudhon went on to attack the élitist educational system which then as now underpinned this bourgeois bureaucratic nobility. 'Our schools . . . are aristocratic seminaries. The Polytechnique, Normale, Saint-Cyr and Law Schools have not been founded for the people but to maintain, strengthen and widen class distinctions, to consummate and make irrevocable the split between the bourgeoisie and the proletariat.'[156] The same attacks have been levied against the *Ecole Nationale d'Administration* since its establishment in 1945, intended in part to counteract these criticisms but in practice pushing a Parisian bourgeois-dominated meritocracy to its limits.

Proudhon mocked those latter-day Jacobins like Louis Blanc who attacked the decentralizers by reviving the guilt by association of 'federalism' with royalist provincial separatism. Once state centralization had been made redundant, because society would organize itself in a federally integrated plurality of strictly limited, piecemeal, reciprocal contracts, in Pascal's description of infinity the 'centre is everywhere and the periphery nowhere'.[157] There was no need for government because 'CONTRACT resolves all problems . . . . To claim that the country, i.e. each locality in what concerns it, does not have the right to manage, administer, judge and govern itself; to deprive the people of control over its resources on the pretext of a one and indivisible Republic; after having overthrown despotism by insurrection to reestablish it by metaphysics; brand as *federalists* . . . those who champion freedom and local sovereignty, is to be false to the true spirit of the French Revolution, to its most authentic tendencies and to reject progress.'[158] Proudhon subscribed in other words to what Lamennais, a fellow neo-Girondin, who had in 1848 vainly tried with Tocqueville to incorporate decentralization into the constitution, asserted: 'With centralisation, you have apoplexy at the centre and paralysis at the periphery.'[159] How could one avoid centralization, which Proudhon equated with all forms of absolutism, including communism?[160]

By the 1860s, Proudhon could no longer subscribe to his simplistic anarchist credo of 1849, which derived from a combination of Rousseau and Adam Smith. 'All men are equal and free: society is naturally autonomous and in effect ungovernable. Each citizen's sphere of activity being fixed by the natural division of labour . . . order results from the free action of all; there is no government. Whoever lays a hand on me to govern me is a usurper and a tyrant. I declare him my enemy.'[161] Politics, which had been banished in favour of a pluralistic socio-economic autonomy, made its re-entry in the 1860s with the federal constitutional contract. Just as contract had replaced coercion in economic affairs, it could be used to curb coercive political power, not used to reinforce it as had been done in the wake of Rousseau's *Social Contract*. In the aborted *History of Modern Democracy* that Proudhon had planned in 1851, he had intended to show that humanity was developing towards increasing autonomy of the individual, commune and province. With *Justice* in 1858, he devoted a whole section of the book to the 'necessary evil' of the state and declared that 'the true obstacle to despotism is in federal union.'[162]

In a letter of 1863, Proudhon expressed his determination to 'stop democracy sliding down the fatal slope of centralization' and in the *Federal Principle* he resumed his attack on bureaucratic proliferation. 'The state is not an entrepreneur providing public services, which would identify it with public works industrialists. Whether it decrees, acts or supervises, it is the initiator and the supreme director of change; if it sometimes becomes directly involved, it is to pioneer, to make a start and set an example. Once the venture has been launched, the state withdraws, leaving the local authorities and citizens to provide the new service.'[163] If government became permanently involved in providing public services, its empire-building public servants would dispossess and oppress, yielding to their tendency to be self-serving, self-absorbed and self-multiplying. Like Tocqueville, Proudhon was worried that the people would resign themselves to a benevolent paternalism in which 'Government is no longer made for the people but the people are made for government . . . . The citizen is only left to perform his little task in his little corner, receiving his little wage, raising his little family, relying for the rest on government provision.'[164] This anxiety that individual self-reliance will be sapped has become fashionable with the late-twentieth-century reaction against the comprehensive welfare state.

It is in *The Federal Principle* that Proudhon gives the fullest statement of his belief that while human progress is from authority towards liberty, this must be based on a balance between them. This dualistic balance he called the federal contract, 'whose essence is always to reserve more to the citizens than to the State, to municipal and provincial authorities than to central authority', more to the smaller than to the larger organizations.[165] Proudhon's micro-federalism is not that of the macro-federalist United

States of Europe advocated by the Saint-Simonians so much as that of the 36,000 communes and the 22 regions of France. It is an internal federalism, restraining the centralizing impetus of the French state by dispersing its authority. Proudhon accepted a European Community only on condition that it was not a federation of unitary states but a modest and peaceful 'confederation of confederations'.[166] Despite the affinities with Tocqueville, Richard Vernon persuasively argues that Proudhon returned to Montesquieu's (and one could add Rousseau's) idea of reconciling large states with liberty through confederation to achieve three objectives. First, small-scale political structures facilitate self-determination through increased opportunities for direct political participation. (France's communes in 1989 elected 503,000 councillors.) Second, arbitrary rule would be hindered by territorial checks and balances. Third, confederation would provide an 'institutional shell for local cultures' and historic identities.[167] The separation of powers is now described by Proudhon as 'one of the greatest ideas of political science',[168] experience of the illiberal-democratic despotism of Louis-Napoleon having reinvigorated the liberal views that Proudhon had previously treated with reserve.

As a socialist, Proudhon went further than both Montesquieu and Tocqueville in giving prior emphasis to economic decentralization, developing an anticipatory market socialism in which equal and contractual exchange relationships would replace both state socialism and the unregulated market. With his customary exaggeration, Proudhon declared in *The Federal Principle* that 'All my economic ideas, developed over the last twenty-five years, can be defined in three words: *agro-industrial federation*; all my political views may be reduced to a parallel formula: *political federation* or *decentralization*.'[169] In the *Political Capacity of the Working Classes*, Proudhon sketched out more fully his economic federalism, even exaggerating his conviction that local self-government had to be uninhibited. Assertions such as 'There is no middle way: the commune will either be sovereign or subsidiary, all or nothing' suggest a relapse from pluralism to anarchism.[170] Sovereignty is by definition incompatible with federalism but Proudhon's enthusiasms were inclined to run away with him in a rush of verbal incontinence. His concern to champion the federalist cause led him vainly to seek permission to found a weekly called *La Fédération*, reaffirming the true, decentralist principles of 1789. He had to be content to predict in his book that 'The twentieth century will open the age of federations, or else humanity will undergo another purgatory of a thousand years.'[171]

If Proudhon's micro-federalism is regarded as Utopian, his hostility to nationalism was clearly against the tide of public feeling. In 1851 he dismissed fashionable claims that France was 'the chosen people, specially charged with propagating, heralding and supervising revolutions' and in a letter to Michelet in 1856 he declared: 'Where justice is, there is my country.'[172] In recommending abolition of the central administration, Proudhon explicitly included the foreign and defence ministries. Anticipating the Leninist and Trotskyite argument, Proudhon asserted: 'Revolution will be ineffective if it does not spread; it will perish, even in France, if it does not become universal.'[173]

For Proudhon, workers and capitalists were not really fellow citizens but there was a more deep-seated basis for his anti-nationalism. His conception of citizenship was rooted in a Grecian localist preference for his *polis* and not in the expansionist Roman and revolutionary universalist conception of patriotism. Proudhon repudiated the nationalistic vainglory inspired by the Crimean War. 'I detest these rivalries between races and states; these competitions between bellicose vanities; above all I detest this *chauvinist fanaticism*, which goes to the length of asserting the patriotic prerogative against the eternal law and the freedom of nations.'[174] Justice was morally superior to the patriotic myth, yet the latter had a much greater hold upon the mass imagination. After the French victory at Sebastopol, he anticipated 'a redoubling of Caesarist insolence, clericalist hypocrisy, judicial arrogance, military brutality, plebeian oppression and bourgeois rapacity.'[175] In the 1859 Franco-Austrian War over Italy, which allowed France to annex Nice and Savoy as the price for uniting Italy, the two protagonists shared 100,000 casualties, prompting Proudhon to condemn the Left for being swept along by nationalism. This conflict inspired his 1861 book on *War and Peace* and then his *Federal Principle*, federation being Proudhon's alternative to the creation of nation-states – as the solution not only to the Italian problem but for all countries.[176]

It was during his Belgian exile of 1858–62 that Proudhon particularly devoted his attention to international affairs, especially the linked issues of war and nationalism. War – along with economic acquisitiveness – promoted nationalism. In his discussion of universal war, Proudhon drew not upon Darwin's *Origin of Species*, published two years before, but upon Hobbes, Vico, Hegel and Maistre, as well as the Old Testament. For Hobbes war was a fact; for Maistre it was a providential fact; for Vico it was a historic and providential fact; for Hegel it was a historical, providential and just fact.[177] Proudhon presented war as a synonym for the pervasive phenomenon of the use of force in human conflict. In 1846 he had already written: 'The state of war is the primordial state of mankind. Before being devoted to each other, men begin by devouring each other. Sacrifice of your neighbour always precedes sacrifice for your neighbour.'[178] War was the basis both of stability, through its use in support of law and government, and of change. Though his aim was explicitly to show how civilization progressed from war to peace, his extended initial praise of war – carried away by his taste for provocative paradox – made his subsequent glorification of peace seem an anticlimax. His argument that right not backed by force would be impotent was misinterpreted to mean that Proudhon equated might and right.

To avoid French censorship, *War and Peace* was published in Brussels and enjoyed a *succès de scandale*. Despite the reprobation of the democratic advocates of nationalism, Proudhon declared that 'nationalities will increasingly disappear under the impact of economic organization, the decentralization of States, intermarriage between races and intercontinental communication.'[179] Conflict would be sublimated into economic competition and free trade would help to preserve international peace, provided steps were taken to ensure that exchange was conducted on an equitable basis.[180] The balance of trade would replace the balance of power as the best way to guarantee peace. But even more important was the priority of justice over patriotism because Proudhon was a moralist rather than an economist. 'Where man finds justice, there is his fatherland. Poor French nation, apostate on 18 Brumaire, apostate on 2 December, insolent towards its constitutional monarchs, grovelling towards its despots, without principle, dignity or conscience! I would be capable of sacrificing my fatherland to justice if I had to choose between them.'[181]

On Herzen's recommendation, Tolstoy visited Proudhon in April 1861, as the latter was finishing *War and Peace*. How much he influenced Tolstoy's much more famous book is disputed. The Russian novelist greatly admired and was probably much influenced by both Proudhon and Maistre. He wrote in his diary, three months after hearing of Proudhon's death and while he was hard at work on his own *War and Peace*: 'Property is theft is a much greater truth than what lies at the base of the English Constitution. It will survive as long as humanity. It is an absolute truth.'[182] However, Proudhon's hostility to aristocratic–clerical–reactionary Polish nationalism led to conflict with Herzen and was especially unpopular in 1863 when the Polish revolt against Russia was being brutally repressed. Proudhon's call for 'the application to international affairs of the Declaration of the Rights of Man'[183] proved too advanced for his times but resurfaced in the late 1980s.

Permanent revolution from below: the rhetoric of unending reform

The term 'permanent revolution' is a piece of pugnacious rhetoric that has become associated with Trotskyism in the twentieth century but which had different connotations when it was used in the nineteenth century. It first seems to have surfaced in 1815 at the start of the Restoration, during one of the many attempts to 'end the Revolution'. It appeared in that remarkable periodical *Le Censeur*, which we discussed in connection with Saint-Simon (see above, Chapter 4, p. 89). In an article entitled 'Of revolutions in general and the current revolutionaries', Charles Dunoyer stated: 'There is only one way for peoples to prevent major revolutions; it is to adapt themselves to a state of wisely regulated permanent revolutions.' Shortly afterwards, his fellow editor Charles Comte wrote in the same sense in an article on legislation. An intelligently led nation 'shelters itself from revolution, or better still it installs itself in a gentle and gradual permanent revolution, to accompany smoothly the progress of reason.'[184] It is clear that the term was first used to advocate a programme of gradualist reform as part of a strategy of dynamic conservatism. The way to prevent revolution from disrupting and destabilizing society was to routinize it as incremental change. Piecemeal and calm reform would be substituted for comprehensive and catastrophic upheaval.

It was in his speech at a socialist banquet in October 1848, published in *La Peuple* as 'Toast to the Revolution', that Proudhon used the phrase to explain his conception of social change. 'Revolutions are the successive manifestations of JUSTICE in human activity. That is why the starting point of each revolution is an earlier revolution . . . . So it follows that revolution is permanent and that strictly speaking there are not several revolutions but only one and the same perpetual revolution.'[185] While he appears not to have repeated the phrase, Proudhon reiterates that revolutions accelerate and precipitate change but there is a Tocquevillian emphasis upon *continuity* in the underlying direction of change. Proudhon distinguishes four great revolutions in the secular movement towards justice. First came the Christian religious revolution of fraternal equality before God. Second came the Renaissance and Reformation philosophical assertion of the freedom of the mind. Third, there was the eighteenth-century political revolution proclaiming equality before the law and the constitutional limitation of power. Last, the 1848 social Revolution had signalled the triumph of labour over capital but this would occur only if not state socialism but the associationist, market socialism he advocated was adopted. (Otherwise one would be open to the late-twentieth-century jibe: 'What is capitalism? The exploitation of man by man. What is communism? The opposite.') There was an 'immanent and perpetual' process of evolutionary social change, whereas 'government is naturally immobile, conservative, hostile to initiative, even counter-revolutionary . . . '[186] While Proudhon's 'permanent revolution' hyperbole masks his moderation, his libertarian message that there is an unending struggle with *raison d'état* and *exploitation* to achieve justice is no obsequious recipe for lukewarm quietism.

Six months after Proudhon had championed evolutionary reform under the appellation 'permanent revolution', Marx and Engels adopted the slogan but gave it a more menacing twist in their March 1850 London Address of the Communist League Central Committee. 'While the democratic petty bourgeois wish to bring the revolution to a conclusion as quickly as possible . . . it is our interest and our task to make the revolution permanent, until all more or less possessing classes have been forced out of their position of dominance, until the proletariat has conquered state power' with the 'battle cry . . . . The Revolution in Permanence.'[187] In his *Class Struggles in France* published in the same year, Marx makes clear that he is identifying the phrase with dictatorial communism as envisaged by Blanqui, not with Proudhon's anarcho-socialism. Expressing his wishes as predictions, Marx claims that among the contending socialist schools 'the *proletariat* rallies more and more around *revolutionary socialism*, round *communism*, for which the bourgeoisie has itself invented the name of Blanqui. This socialism is the *declaration of the permanence of the revolution*, the *class dictatorship* of the proletariat.'[188] We shall consider this Marxist affinity with Blanqui in the next chapter but we must here touch on the clash with the Proudhonians during the First International and the 1871 Paris Commune, when the actions of the disciples of Proudhon and Blanqui demonstrated the chasm that separated these two enemies of capitalism.

The French delegation to the 1864 foundation meeting of the First International in London was led by Tolain and was supported especially by his fellow Proudhonian bronzeworkers who played a leading part in the agitation for a ten-hour working day. The French Proudhonians, who were genuine workers and not middle-class revolutionaries, dominated the early congresses of the International in Geneva (1866) and Lausanne (1867), partly because they had the largest delegation. However, at the 1868 and 1869 congresses they were defeated by the effects of the dissolution and police persecution of the French section of the International in 1868 and an alliance between the Marxists, the Bakuninists and the Blanquists.[189] The Proudhonian 'Internationalists' were also to fight a losing battle within the 1871 Paris Commune, although this time they succumbed to a centralist–dictatorial alliance of Blanquists and old-style Jacobins, protagonists of a Committee of Public Safety caricature of 1793–4. Although the National Guards who made up the bulk of the Commune's forces were known as the Federals, the Proudhonians undoubtedly suffered from the fact that the 'federalist' revolt had taken place in the capital and its provincial emulators were quickly repressed. After all, Proudhon had written to Chaudey in 1862: 'To save the nation and liberty, free the plebs, establish peace and develop Revolutionary principles in Europe, I see only one means, the division of France into twelve independent states and the abolition of Paris.'[190]

Many Proudhonians played a prominent part in the Commune, notably the journalist and novelist Jules Vallès, who was largely responsible for its federalist and social reformist programme, and Gustave Courbet, the naturalist painter (a personal friend; he painted Proudhon *en famille*) who paid with exile his part in the symbolic demolition of the Napoleonic Vendôme Column. They were split between moderates and radicals. The moderate Tolain, elected to the Versailles Assembly, vainly tried to mediate but ultimately sided against the Commune. Malon and Lefrançais favoured a Bakuninist brand of Proudhonism. Eugène Varlin became a leading Communard, was captured, tortured and shot. In the struggle for power within the doomed Commune, the Blanquist extremist advocates of violence increasingly took control, personified above all in police chief Raoul Rigault. He was responsible for the vindictive execution of Gustave Chaudey, Proudhonian moderate and his literary executor, responsible for the posthumous publication of the *Political Capacity of the Working Classes* (see Chapter 8, p. 257).

While a fuller discussion of the Commune's paradoxical attempts to assert the autonomy of the capital will be postponed until the next chapter, it is significant that thereafter the Proudhonian legacy has its moderate and radical offshoots in both the political and industrial wings of the labour movement. Ex-anarchists played a leading role in the socialist parties from the 1880s, with Paul Brousse leading the ultra-gradualist and reformist 'municipalist' wing of the 'Possibilist' Party and ex-Communard Jean Allemane leading its radical wing into schism in 1890.[191] Revolutionary anarcho-syndicalism, associated initially with the Allemanist Workers Socialist Revolutionary Party, was to develop under the inspiration of Pelloutier into the predominant philosophy of the French trade union movement until the First World War.

In the early post-Commune trade union congresses of 1876 and 1878 the dominant role was played by the moderate Proudhonian Joseph Barberet, but his opposition to strike action and reliance upon worker education, cooperatives and labour exchanges was rejected at the 1879 congress by a new Guesdist majority.[192] The radicalization of Proudhonian *ouvrierisme* began modestly enough with the institution of labour exchanges, which quickly became local trades councils. Started in Paris in 1887 at the instigation of the Possibilists, by 1892 they had spread and ten of them established the *Fédération des Bourses au Travail* (FBT).[193] Trade unions had been legalized in 1884 but the small Trade Union Federation was under the control of the Marxists led by Jules Guesde, who subordinated industrial to party activity. It initially looked as though Marx's prediction at the outbreak of the Franco-Prussian War in 1870 would come true: 'The French need a sound thrashing. If the Prussians win . . . the weight of the German power will transfer the centre of gravity of the labour movement in Western Europe from France to Germany . . . . The German working class is superior to the French from the standpoint of theory and of organization. Its preponderance over the French on the world scene would at the same time be the preponderance of our theory over Proudhon's.'[194] After Proudhonian concern with the formation of producer cooperatives in the 1870s, the French trade unions came under the political influence of the Guesdists until the anarcho-syndicalist counter-attack led by the ex-Guesdist journalist Fernand Pelloutier in the 1890s.

Revolutionary syndicalism went back to the split in the First International between the anarcho-federalists led by Bakunin and the Marxists. The outlaw mentality which developed in the clandestine years and the ineffectiveness of democratic political action fostered the idea of the revolutionary general strike as the means of achieving working-class self-emancipation. Although Aristide Briand and Pelloutier secured the unanimous adoption of the general strike tactic in 1892 by the Guesdist trade union federation, it was the more Proudhonian Workers Socialist Revolutionary Party and the Blanquists that made it the centrepiece of their strategy in its rival, the FBT. Blanquist involvement underlines their revisionism because the general strike was intended as a substitute for Blanqui-style insurrectionary tactics. Helped on its way by municipal and non-Marxist socialists, the FBT became the instrument of worker autonomy from any form of political control, as preached by Proudhon. While Briand launched into a political career that took him twenty years later to the role, as prime minister, of strike-breaker in 1910, Pelloutier became the general secretary of the trades council FBT in 1895, the year in which the trade union movement escaped from Guesdist control to become the CGT.

Jacques Julliard has admirably described the role of Pelloutier, who before his early death in 1901 had not only established himself as the leading French theoretician of trade unionism. He also created the intellectual basis for a single CGT trade union movement (thanks to the 1902 fusion with the FBT) united around the pansyndicalist Amiens Charter of 1906. Pelloutier was the most Proudhonian of all the pre-First World War trade union leaders, sharing his anti-authoritarian and federalist political philosophy. He referred to Proudhon frequently, drawing from him a class analysis based upon the moralistic critique of private property, the primacy of the worker as a producer and his view that the working classes must emancipate themselves by direct industrial action. Yet, where Proudhon would have rejected the idea of a revolutionary general strike, Pelloutier regarded this as the only way in which the workers would liberate themselves from the alliance of coercive state and capitalist employers.[195]

Proudhon may not have been read by many workers but they received his ideas at second hand from those who did. In the twenty years from 1895 to 1914, thirty-two books and seven doctoral theses were devoted to him. Many of the leading trade unionists had been anarchists, although the first general secretary of the unified CGT was an ex-Blanquist, Victor Griffuelhes. However, the salient point was that Proudhon – whom Trotsky dismissed as 'the Robinson Crusoe of Socialism' – appealed to working-class instincts much more than did Marx, partly because his ideas sprang from such instincts. When the Marxist revisionism of Edouard Bernstein was attacked at the turn of the century as a revival of Proudhonism, he replied: 'It is not me but reality that has regenerated the author of *The Political Capacity of the Working Classes*.'[196]

Georges Sorel was an even more enthusiastic admirer of Proudhon than Pelloutier, whose posthumous *Histoire des Bourses du Travail* he prefaced. Sorel's brand of revolutionary syndicalism was based upon an attempt to reconcile Proudhon and Marx, in which the Proudhonian influence was predominant at the beginning and end. He is remembered today essentially as the author of *Reflections on Violence*, whose inspiration is (along with Bergson and Nietzsche) self-confessedly derived from Proudhon's *War and Peace*. Sorel bases himself on the permanence and pervasiveness of war, going back to the Green city-state identification of citizenship and military service. Like Proudhon, Sorel wanted to transform warrior communities into worker communities, focused not upon fighters but producers.[197] However, he is most explicit about his intellectual debt to Proudhon – 'the only great French nineteenth century philosopher' – in *Materials for a Theory of the Proletariat* (1919), describing it in his dedication as written by 'an old man determined to remain, like Proudhon, a disinterested servant of the proletariat.'[198] Against the socialists, Sorel argued Proudhon's superiority to Marx in showing how class struggle led to the development of new legal rights. Against the bizarre attempts by *Action Française* nationalists and monarchists to annex Proudhon in the early twentieth century, Sorel quoted copiously to demonstrate Proudhon's repudiation of chauvinism as a 'national *idiocy*'.[199] However, Sorel himself distorted both Proudhon and Pelloutier by treating federalism and the revolutionary general strike as myths. Just before his death in 1922 he was taken in by the Bolshevik Soviets, writing that 'The Russian Revolution has given life to institutions which approximated Proudhon rather than the teachings of those who made such poor use of the inheritance of Marx.'[200] Sorel did not live long enough to see that the Bolshevik Revolution represented not the working producers' triumph but that of a dictatorial political party.

Paul-Boncour, socialist lawyer, deputy minister and briefly prime minister (1932–3), was a theoretician of reformist syndicalism. His very influential book *Economic Federalism* of 1900 advocated a decentralized, integral federation, professional as well as regional, implementing economic as well as political democracy based upon a plurality of groups (particularly trade unions) that spontaneously created their own rules. He was particularly struck by Proudhon's thought, as formulated in *Justice* and *Political Capacity of the Working Classes*, proclaiming at the end of the introduction to his major work: 'Freedom to work and associate through contractual relations tend to become relations of sovereignty and gradually constitute a sort of economic federalism.'[201] He not only reiterated Proudhon's central tenet but in the process confused sovereignty and autonomy. Paul-Boncour gave his services as a lawyer to the Paris *Bourse du Travail* and defended the CGT in parliament and in court in 1920 when it was formally outlawed after calling a general strike, having in the interim been minister of labour in 1911.

Sorel and Paul-Boncour were simply two among many French socialist intellectuals, more or less associated with the labour movement, who revived and popularized Proudhon's ideas in the early twentieth century. At the turn of the century Eugène Fournière, as editor of the *Revue Socialiste*, spread a contractarian version of liberal socialism that owed much to Proudhon. The *Amis de Proudhon* was founded in 1912 at the suggestion of the historian Maxime Leroy (who was involved in drafting the 1906 Amiens Charter of the CGT) following discussion of a book on Proudhon by the sociologist Célestin Bouglé, director of the *Ecole Normale*. Leroy sought to synthesize Proudhon with Saint-Simon just as Sorel tried to reconcile him with Marx. This galaxy of Proudhonian scholars was responsible for the remarkable Rivière edition of his works following their 1920 collective book *Proudhon and Our Time*.[202] In the mid-twentieth century, the leading French Proudhonian writer was the sociologist Georges Gurvitch, being succeeded by the cleric Pierre Haubtmann among others. So Proudhon's alternative to the Marxist brand of socialism never disappeared from view and remained an important inspiration in the inter-war CGT under the leadership of the former anarcho-syndicalist Léon Jouhaux.

In Britain, Cole's guild socialist movement and the popularity of pluralism were also evidence of Proudhon's influence. Harold Laski wrote to Oliver Wendel Holmes in 1917, as he was preparing *Authority in the Modern State*: 'I have discovered Proudhon . . . . Really he is immense and he has all the virtues. He is clear-headed, far-sighted, anti-religious and his theory of the state satisfies all my anarchist prejudices . . . . He seems to me to have anticipated most of Karl Marx and to have said it better. He realises the necessity of safeguarding the rights of personality and at the same time he is not afraid of collective action.'[203] In the 1930s Laski was to abandon pluralism for a liberalized Marxism and reinstall the state as the supreme coercive power. The envenomed class conflict of the depression years made the libertarian search for social justice seem to be the pursuit of an unattainable ideal and revived in Spain the violent brand of anarchism that owed more to Bakunin than to Proudhon.

Proudhon's anarchist legacy was strongest in Russia where, apart from Tolstoy, exiles like Herzen, Bakunin and Kropotkin absorbed and spread his ideas. In his autobiography, the greatest Russian populist Herzen asserted that 'a man who has not *lived through* Hegel's phenomenology and Proudhon's contradictions of political economy, who has not passed through that furnace and been tempered by it, is not complete, not modern'. In a subsequent *rapprochment* between these two seminal minds, Herzen claimed that 'Reading Proudhon, like reading Hegel, cultivates a special faculty, sharpens the weapons and furnishes not results but methods. Proudhon is pre-eminently the dialectician, the controversialist of social questions . . . . He is as much the poet of dialectics as Hegel is, with the difference that the one rests on the calm heights of the philosophic movement, while the other is thrust into the turmoil of popular passions and the hand to hand struggle of parties.'[204] Herzen and Bakunin significantly had in some ways more in common with Blanqui than Proudhon. Like Lenin, the Russian context led them to doubt the possibility of peaceful change, hence a willingness to accept dictatorial change from above.[205] Bakunin defined his carnivorous brand of anarchism as 'Proudhonism fully developed and pushed to the limit', by which he meant violence. The more herbivorous Kropotkin, when accused at an 1883 anarchist trial in Lyons of having fathered anarchism, denied this as 'doing him too much honour. The father of Anarchy is the immortal Proudhon.'[206] Kropotkin (who had edited a newspaper in the 1870s with the fellow exile and future French 'Possibilist' leader Paul Brousse) published in 1902 *Mutual Aid*, the last great exposition of anarchist doctrine. Anarchism reappeared in 1968 on the streets of Paris, more as an act of student defiance than syndicalist affirmation, although the comprehensive challenge to centralized authority showed that Proudhon's message of permanent revolution was still attractive in the latter half of the twentieth century.

Proudhon died in 1865 aged 56. Thousands – including many workers – attended his non-religious funeral. His books continued to be widely read, while a much more diffuse influence survived in the French labour movement, even after the conquest of the CGT by the Communist Party following the Second World War. 'Proudhon was never forgotten, and the desire to incorporate some part of his heritage has been *the* distinguishing trait of French Socialism (as distinct from Communism) down to the present day.'[207] His most pessimistic predictions seem not to have been fulfilled. In the *Confessions* he wrote: 'It is clear to whoever has reflected on the combined action of the banks, mortgages, industrial firms, to which must be added the political centralisation that is their coercive and penal sanction, that the French people has by law been handed over defenceless to exploitation by an oligarchy which has emerged spontaneously from the mismanaged play of economic forces and was not envisaged by the '89 revolutionaries. If this unreliable régime lasts for another fifty years and small-scale industry and property are abolished, there will only be an enormous mass of mercenaries serving the lords of the land, vine, rail, coal, iron, cotton and so forth. Society will be divided into two castes, the exploiters and the exploited: the whole middle class will have disappeared.'[208] The Paris Commune of 1871 seemed to confirm the class polarization that the sombre pamphleteer anticipated but in retrospect we can see that it dramatized the death throes of violent class confrontation in France.

A hundred and fifty years later, Proudhon's hope that society would consist of an enormous working middle class has to some extent come about in advanced industrial societies. There is still an underclass and an élite of plutocrats, bureaucrats and managers but between them there is an increasingly educated middle class and skilled worker public that shape the prevailing reformist consensus. They are less independent-minded than he would have wished them to be, more devoted to material wealth than to the ideal of liberty, as Tocqueville had acknowledged with regret. Yet however submissive to government they may appear to be, no French authority is immune from the threat of insubordination. Proudhon not only shared this proud trait of national character; he was the intransigent and impassioned exponent of individual civic courage.

CHAPTER EIGHT

CONSPIRATORIAL COMMUNISM, REVOLUTIONARY DICTATORSHIP AND BLANQUI

Looking back on the 1848 Revolution in 1870, Bakunin – who owed so much to Proudhon for his anarcho-socialist ideas and to Blanqui for his activist methods – declared that there were only 'two real men: Proudhon and Blanqui.'[1] Despite or perhaps because of their enormous differences, these two 'outsiders' of mid-nineteenth-century French socialism had a genuine esteem for each other. Hearing that Blanqui was back in Paris, Proudhon wrote in 1860 that he supposed that Blanqui was plotting against Louis-Napoleon. 'Frankly, I give him absolution in advance; but I tremble to see him end as he started . . . this *friend* does not seem to me to have a real chance of success. It is enough for his name to be associated with a venture for it to fail if ever it takes off . . . . Blanqui cannot accept that he is as unable as I am to take part in a revolutionary coup: he is identified with the guillotine and I with pillage.'[2] Learning a year later that Blanqui had been rearrested, Proudhon could not conceal his exasperation: 'I have little sympathy for this martyr of conspiracy . . . '[3]

Whereas Proudhon's life was constituted primarily of his published works, like Babeuf Blanqui's works were insignificant by comparison with his life. Although Blanqui spent far longer in prison than Proudhon, he did not use his enforced inactivity to write books, despite his omnivorous reading. An activist above all, he was unable to make combative use of his confinement. It was as the personification of implacable opposition to the status quo that Blanqui became the French bourgeoisie's bloodthirsty Red bogy and the French proletariat's selfless Red martyr, a dual role in which he took a grim pleasure.

Jacobin communism: Babeuf's legacy through Buonarroti to Blanqui

After the 1880s, Blanqui was quickly forgotten until the Bolshevik Revolution led to his rediscovery as 'the connecting link between Babeuf and Bolshevism' in asserting the need for a post-revolutionary transitional dictatorship.[4] It has been argued that against a bourgeois dictatorship from above through the Committee of Public Safety, Babeuf advocated a 'conception of that popular dictatorship of which Marat and the *Hébertistes* had spoken without defining it; through Buonarroti, he bequeathed it to Blanqui and then to Lenin, who turned it into reality.'[5] During the power struggles of 1792–4 the model of Roman republican dictatorship, as a crisis assumption of extensive power by an individual, was transmuted to fit the new circumstances of mass politics. Although it had later led to imperial despotism, republican dictatorship in Rome was for three centuries accepted as constitutional. It was limited to abrogating existing laws, without the power to make new laws, and temporary (lasting a maximum of six months). Brissot's attack on the dictatorship of the *Hébertiste*-led Paris Commune indicates that what the Girondins feared was a plebeian dictatorship. It was to be a salient argument of Babeuf and his left-wing Jacobin supporters that Robespierre's failure was due to the fact that, having swept aside the Girondins and the *Hébertistes*, he had not become a dictator in the name of democracy.[6]

It has been claimed that 'If the "revolutionary extremist" exists at all as an identifiable type, he exists in purest incarnation as Gracchus Babeuf.'[7] It was one thing to portray Babeuf as the 'First revolutionary Communist' in the late eighteenth century; it is quite another to personify in him twentieth-century 'totalitarian democracy' as did Jacob Talmon.[8] By profession a *feudiste*, engaged in tracing feudal claims, he lost his occupation with the abolition of feudalism, so 'the Revolution turned Babeuf into a *déclassé*.'[9] (We shall return to the significance of this social status in discussing Blanqui). His pre-revolutionary profession had given him first-hand experience of the iniquities of private property that Rousseau – whom he ardently admired – had denounced. He was quickly imprisoned in 1790 for his activist part in a tax strike agitation but was extricated with the help of Marat, who took up his cause. He quickly concluded that popular sovereignty would be betrayed by its representatives, so he advocated direct democracy, including recourse to the referendum, popular initiative and recall. However, he declared that 'Sooner or later, but always and unavoidably, the majority is subordinated to the arbitrary use of power of the one or of those who must rule.'[10] Nevertheless, one should not assimilate too readily the strictly limited insurrectionary dictatorship envisaged by Babeuf with the open-ended dictatorship advocated by Blanqui, still less that of Lenin and the Bolsheviks. It was to last a matter of weeks, with a maximum 'three months duration, during which the Republic would be purged of royalist influence and its public opinion enlightened, in preparation for the handing of power back to the people through the application of the Constitution of 1793.'[11] Babeuf's backward-looking aim was to resume Robespierre's unfinished Jacobin Revolution; it was not an anticipation of permanent totalitarian rule in the Soviet manner. It was his fellow conspirator Buonarroti, who argued in his 1828 account of the Babeuf conspiracy that the revolutionary dictatorship would have to last until the common happiness had been established, that anticipated Lenin through Blanqui.

It was not merely in his conception of democratic dictatorship that Babeuf shared the late-eighteenth-century obsession with Rome. In 1793 he adopted the forename Gracchus to show his identification with the Roman protagonist of the redistributivist agrarian law, embodying the egalitarian urge to champion the virtuous plebeians against the immoral patricians. It was also reflected in the title of his newspaper *Tribun du peuple*, which sought in vain to rouse the dwindling ranks of the diehard Jacobins with a Marat-style journalism. His crude collectivist system, aimed at eliminating competition and establishing equality in fact and not merely of rights, was improvised out of a combination of the agrarian Utopianism of Morelly and Mably, with his own practical experience in the Jacobin food administration in Paris. Consumer communism was to be achieved by 'the total bureaucratic control of the distribution of commodities.'[12]

The four-man Insurrectionary Directory set up in March 1796 included the poet Sylvain Maréchal, who drafted The Manifesto of the Equals. Starting with a quotation from Condorcet, it went on in apocalyptic, millennial fashion. 'The French Revolution is but the forerunner of another revolution, far more grand, far more solemn, and which will be the last . . . . Away for ever with the revolting distinctions of rich and poor, of great and little, of masters and servants, of *governors* and *governed* . . . . The moment for great measures has arrived . . . . Chaos, under the name of politics, has too long reigned . . . . The moment is come to found the REPUBLIC OF EQUALS.'[13] The conspiracy was betrayed by one of the conspirators and Babeuf – self-proclaimed as the 'last of the energetic republicans' – was sentenced to death after a fair, three-month jury trial, which made legal history by being the first at which a verbatim report was kept by stenographers. Babeuf owes his place in history to a fellow leader of the Insurrectionary Directory, Buonarroti, who lived to tell the tale. He gave it a twist that converted a provisional dictatorship to restore Jacobin democracy and impose a primitive communism into long-term rule by a Parisian élite of professional revolutionaries to establish a Robespierrist reign of virtue.

Bakunin, who could compete with Buonarroti and Blanqui as the prototypical professional revolutionary, described Buonarroti as 'the greatest conspirator of the century.'[14] They refused 'to accept the verdict of Thermidor as a final one. These men regarded the fall of Robespierre, the death of Babeuf and the triumph of the counter-revolution as temporary setbacks in a continuing struggle to achieve a perfect society – as battles lost in a war that could still be won .... Buonarroti was, perhaps, the first man to shape his life in accordance with the requirements of this "permanent revolution".'[15] A patrician descended from Michaelangelo's brother, he studied law in Pisa before becoming a disciple of Rousseau. He accepted at an early age the primacy of politics. His enthusiasm for popular sovereignty led to him obtaining naturalization as a French citizen in 1793 and membership of the Jacobin Club, before serving as an administrator in conquered Italian territory on the Côte-d'Azur in 1794–5. Recalled and imprisoned in 1795, he met Babeuf and others involved in the 1796 plot, setting the pattern of prison as the school for professional revolutionaries. Although he was to spread Babeuf's fame through his account of the plot thirty years later, Buonarroti never regarded himself as a Babouvist spokesman of the underdog but always as a leader in the Robespierrist Jacobin manner.[16]

While serious historians have rightly ridiculed the Abbé Barruel's conspiracy theory of the French Revolution, which he attributed to the machinations of the Freemasons and other secret societies, Buonarroti revelled in the myth of conspiracy and was adept at infiltrating Masonic lodges as camouflaged front organizations for his conspiratorial activities. He maintained that 'The secret society ... is a democratic institution in its principles and in its end; but its forms and its organization cannot be those of a Democracy .... This society is nothing else but a secret army' in which the leaders controlled both doctrine and action from above.[17] The conspiratorial organization he established after being released from prison in 1806, and over which he exercised close personal control, set the pattern for the Italian *Carbonari* and French *Charbonnerie* during the Restoration. 'Like the secret societies formed later by Blanqui and Bakunin, it might be described as the private army of the professional revolutionist who created it, who wielded it, whose life span set a term to its existence.'[18] Buonarroti was the prototype – almost the caricature – of the compleat conspirator such as Blanqui was to become. 'The odd somber attire, the piercing glance, the air of mystery were eventually so carefully cultivated'[19] that they set a pattern of stage-managed personal magnetism which we shall encounter again in Blanqui.

Buonarroti's history of Babeuf's *Conspiracy for Equality* proved to be far more influential than his tireless revolutionary activities. In it he rehabilitated Robespierre and prepared the way for Blanqui by explaining the need for an insurrectionary dictatorship. 'The experience of the French Revolution . . . sufficiently demonstrated that a people whose opinions have been formed under a regime of inequality and of despotism, is little calculated, at the commencement of a regenerating Revolution, to distinguish wisely [by its suffrages] the men most capable to direct and consummate it with success. This difficult task can belong only to certain wise and courageous citizens, who, strongly impregnated with the love of country and of humanity, have long before fathomed the sources of public calamity – have disenthralled themselves from the common prejudices and vices of their age – have shot in advance of contemporary intellects, and who, despising money and vulgar greatness, have placed their happiness in rendering themselves immortal by ensuring the triumph of Equality. Perhaps, therefore, in the beginning of a Revolution, it is of less consequence, even as regards [and for the sake of] the real popular sovereignty itself, to busy ourselves in collecting the suffrages of a nation, than to make the supreme authority fall by the least arbitrary means possible, into hands that are wisely and vigorously revolutionary.'[20]

Despite this clear assertion of the need for rule by an élite revolutionary vanguard, Buonarroti declared that the Babeuf conspiracy was committed to direct democracy and accountability. It was intended that 'Immediately after the destruction of tyranny, the people of Paris was to meet in general assembly in the Place de la Révolution. There the Secret Directory would have rendered it an account of its conduct . . . and would have invited it to approve the Act of Insurrection. Afterwards it would have been proposed to the insurgent people to create on the spot a Provisional Authority charged to terminate the Revolution, and to govern the country up to the moment of putting the popular institutions in activity.'[21] At least an appearance of democracy was to be preserved but in an unpublished manuscript Buonarroti made it clear that the people were confined to supporting the heroic revolutionary activists. The Parisian revolutionaries were the chosen people but 'the people are incapable of either regenerating themselves or of designating the people who must direct the regeneration.'[22] The shape of 'popular democracy' to come had begun to cast its shadow.

Buonarroti was allowed back into France thanks to the 1830 Revolution and his book was republished there, but it had already been reviewed in 1829 in *Le Globe*,[23] a newspaper for which Blanqui served as parliamentary correspondent. Although the evidence of direct contact between Blanqui and Buonarroti is slim (membership of *Amis du Peuple* in 1832, of the defence committee for the Lyon insurrectionaries in 1834 and a letter from Buonarroti mentioning Blanqui in 1835), there is a close resemblance in their egalitarian objectives and above all in their revolutionary methods. It should be no surprise that the secretive Blanqui never mentioned either Babeuf or Buonarroti in his writings. As an acute scholar has remarked: 'When in 1796 the *Babouvists* attempted to seize political power in order to force a fundamental change in economic institutions, they established the historic precedent for Blanquism. The combination of communism and conspiracy distinguish both groups from their fellows in the French socialist movement up to 1871.'[24] To explore this claim let us turn to Blanqui, who imparted to the timid early-nineteenth-century socialist movement a revolutionary boldness derived from the radical republicanism of the secret societies of the 1820s and early 1830s, which were rooted in the Left Jacobinism of the French Revolution. In the process, he tried ideologically and practically to subordinate industrial revolution to political revolution.[25]

The making of a prototypical professional revolutionary

Neither right-wing conspiracy theorists like the Abbé Barruel nor left-wing conspirators like Blanqui grasped the vital fact that the revolutionaries were the creation, not the creators, of the French Revolution. As a result, Blanqui spent most of his life trying to start a revolution. He had a hand in every French Revolution during the nineteenth century but this led to his incarceration in prison for thirty-three and a half years out of the seventy-six years of his life. To this should be added two death sentences and ten and a half years' exile or house arrest, the end product of fifteen trials.[26] 'Blanqui brought a lifetime of unrivalled experience to the perfection of the role of defendant at a political trial. He usually began by denying the competence of the court and accusing it of political or class bias; then he would verbally indict and convict the institutions of capitalist society and go on to outline some of his own prescriptions for social justice. He almost invariably received a harsh sentence, but had, at least, the satisfaction of reading his most inflammatory utterances in the official journals.'[27] He has had the posthumous vindication that he set the behaviour pattern of revolutionary Leftists in a mode of heroic futility into the late twentieth century.

The place (Nice) and time (1805) of Blanqui's birth marked him for life. Garibaldi was also born in Nice, (until the French Revolution, part of the Kingdom of Sardinia, of which as we saw Maistre was also a subject). However, whereas Garibaldi became both an Italian superpatriot and internationalist, Blanqui dismissed the 'Risorgimento as superstitious, priest-ridden, incurably bourgeois and worst of all implacably anti-French.'[28] His father, a teacher of philosophy and astronomy who welcomed the French 'liberators' in 1792 and went to Paris in 1793 to request Nice's annexation to France, quickly became a Girondin deputy. He was imprisoned during the Terror, freed by Thermidor, and became a legislator on the Council of Five Hundred during the Directory, serving as a sub-prefect after Brumaire.[29] Blanqui's hyperpatriotism was fostered by the coincidence of his family's humiliation with the fall of Napoleon and the return of Nice to Sardinian control when he was 9 years old. His lifelong nationalism and hatred of the reactionary Right was firmly rooted in his adolescent experience.

Although Blanqui never committed himself to a precise view on the French Revolution, unlike Buonarroti he had a profound antipathy for the dictatorial deism of Robespierre and preferred the anticlerical Girondins (especially Condorcet) and the populist *Hébertistes*. Blanqui was influenced by reading Lamartine's *Histoire des Girondins*, the book responsible for making them into a legend. He denounced Robespierre as a power-hungry fanatical reactionary, who had after all imprisoned his father. 'Robespierre was a premature Napoleon' who had 'destroyed the Revolution'.[30] However, Blanqui was closest to the *Hébertistes*, who were not only atheists but who also embodied mass agitation within the popular movement that controlled the Paris Revolutionary Commune in 1793. 'If any men before the *Babouvistes* can be considered the progenitors of Blanquism, they are the zealots who poured into the Paris streets behind Hébert.'[31] They were the insurrectionary avant-garde, heroically striving to keep up the revolutionary momentum. As the *Hébertiste* Collot d'Herbois, a member of the Committee of Public Safety, declared at the height of the Terror: 'Some wish to moderate the revolutionary movement. What! Can a tempest be steered? The Revolution is one. We cannot and we must not check its motion.'[32] What above all commended the *Hébertistes* to Blanqui and the Blanquists was their willingness to stop at nothing to 'Complete the unfinished agenda of the French Revolution.'[33] It was this will by a dedicated minority to mobilize the violent means to transform the political system that was the legacy of the Jacobin Left to Carbonarism and to Blanquism.

Family poverty meant that Auguste Blanqui was not as well educated as his elder brother Adolphe, who was to go on to become a distinguished liberal economist, the leading disciple and successor of Say as professor of economics at the *Conservatoire des Arts et Métiers*. Adolphe paid for his brother's education and maintenance, proudly writing to his father: 'This child will astonish the world.'[34] He would . . . but not quite in the way his brother imagined. Auguste Blanqui taught to earn his living while studying law. He certainly acquired no love for the law in the process, earning the deserved reputation as 'the most unrelenting insurrectionist' and 'political outlaw'.[35] He came to know the courts of law not as an advocate but as a defendant. A champion of the jury system, he pilloried the partisanship of the judiciary. As he wrote in prison in 1849: 'I would rather collect dung on the road than be an examining magistrate; it is a cleaner job.'[36]

Blanqui was quickly drawn into the conspiratorial world of the secret societies that flourished in the 1820s, in revulsion against what Croce has called the Restoration's 'mingled odour of sacristy and police station'.[37] The French wing of the *Carbonari* movement, the *Charbonnerie*, was started in 1821 by Bazard, Buchez and Flotard. (The first two were later to become leading Saint-Simonians and Buchez was president of the National Assembly when Blanqui 'invaded' it in 1848.) Blanqui joined as soon as he left school in 1824, generating the first of many police reports in that year. The movement was by then already in decline, torn by ideological disputes that had been initially avoided to maximize resistance to the Bourbon Restoration. 'The organization survived as long as it defined itself by action alone; as soon as its members began to concern themselves with theory, internal fissures were revealed which probably contributed as much as political failure to the destruction of this movement.' From this experience, Blanqui learnt 'his dislike of theories which neglected practical action.'[38] The whole of Blanqui's subsequent existence could be regarded as his attempt to revive and perfect Carbonarism. The salient formative event in his life occurred in 1822 when, at 17, he witnessed the execution of the 'Four Sergents of La Rochelle' for *Carbonari* anti-monarchist conspiracy.[39] He swore to avenge them and this traced his path as a professional revolutionary thereafter. He became single-mindedly dedicated to the destruction of the established disorder.

The *Carbonari* movement's political spread had ranged from Bonapartists and moderate republicans like Lafayette to future Socialists like the printer Pierre Leroux (via Saint-Simonism) and Communists like Cabet. At the height of its activity, the movement had about 8,000 members equally divided between Paris and the provinces. Blanqui took part in student demonstrations in 1827. He was wounded twice by sabre cuts and once by a bullet. He was also a member of the liberal activist society *Aide-toi, le ciel t'aidera*, a sort of middle-class proto-political party, led by Guizot, that helped organize the opposition's electoral success in 1827. Blanqui worked for Leroux's newspaper *Le Globe* as a parliamentary reporter in the months preceding the 1830 Revolution. Whereas the more moderate members of the editorial staff were defeatist about the possibility of successfully resisting Charles X's ordinances, Blanqui predicted a violent outcome and did his best to bring this about. He stirred up the students and journalists to insurrection, writing a call to arms that was probably never printed. At his trial in 1832 for membership of the *Société des Amis du Peuple*, Blanqui – during his defence statement – nostalgically recalled the atmosphere of the July Revolution: 'those intoxicating days, when we wandered, rifle on shoulder, through unpaved streets and barricades, bewildered by our triumph, chests puffed out with happiness, dreaming of the fear of kings and the joy of peoples when they heard the distant roar of our *Marseillaise*.'[40] This passage powerfully evokes Delacroix's 1831 painting of *Liberty Guiding the People* in the storming of a barricade – the supreme artistic representation of nineteenth-century revolution in Paris.

The 1830 Revolution was the only one in which Blanqui personally participated on the winning side. Disillusion quickly followed. It was republicans and Bonapartists that carried out the Revolution but it was the Orleanists who reaped the rewards. The constitutional changes were limited to amending the Restoration charter. The 1814 preamble, implying divine right monarchy, was replaced by national sovereignty as the legitimizing principle. The contractual basis of the July Monarchy was emphasized, the king ceasing to enjoy a monopoly of legislative initiative. Catholicism was no longer the state religion. What the Orleanists regarded as the vindication of 1789, establishing constitutional monarchy in France on the model of the 1688 English Revolution, Blanqui and the republicans regarded as usurpation by a bourgeoisie that was as hostile to the working people as they were to the aristocracy. On an English interpretation, 'The essential point is that on July 30, 1830, the revolutionary settlement becomes henceforth the unquestioned basis of modern France. Here, if anywhere, the history of the Revolution ends . . . the revolutionary idea becomes permanently *conservative*. Only a negligible element in it, the republican tradition, survives as an aggressive and revolutionary force', but Lord Elton regards it as negligible because 'the Republic means no more than a change of forms.'[41] For François Furet, in 1830 'To stop the Revolution is also an English strategy . . . . The aim is to avoid a repeat of 1793 at all costs by stopping the Revolution in its initial phase by turning to Louis-Philippe, to repeat 89 in an improved form, on the model of the English 1688 . . . base the monarchy on the Revolution.' However, in France 'there is some '93 in every '89' and 'The ninety-threeism of those defeated in July is the inventory of an aborted promise and a society to be remade.'⁴² For Blanqui, the revolutionary process was anything but over.

Ironically, it was the death in 1830 of the great protagonist of the 'English solution', Benjamin Constant, that provided Blanqui with a pretext to launch out on his role as a revolutionary leader for the next fifty years. Initially, Blanqui tried to rouse the Paris medical and law students. Constant had been concerned to keep in touch with the young intellectual élite. In an 1827 'Letter to the law students of the Paris Faculty' he had proclaimed his belief that 'as long as there are representative forms and a forum in a country, liberty may be bruised but it will not die . . . . We are a transitional generation, born under arbitrariness. Let us sow the seeds of freedom. You will harvest it and the harvest will not be long delayed.'⁴³ On the news of Constant's death on 10 December 1830, Blanqui published a tract calling upon the students to come with arms to the funeral of a great champion of freedom, who had fought for 'our revolution'. Lafayette, who was to give the funeral oration, had approved but the riot Blanqui had hoped would follow the attempt to take Constant's coffin from the cemetery to the Pantheon failed to materialize.⁴⁴

The students had played a significant part in the 1830 Revolution but this attempt to inject a new momentum through student Leftism failed. (It does show, however, that Blanqui anticipated not only Lenin but also the 1968 *gauchistes*.) He organized an *Association patriotique et scientifique des Ecoles* and a *Comité des Ecoles* after the Constant demonstration, seeking to mobilize the students against the new regime by a liberal campaign against state-controlled education. 'We demand the destruction of the University; we demand the end of the most odious and harmful monopoly, which dries up civilization at its source and is an outrage to human intelligence . . . .The University fashioned by Napoleon, a despotic instrument so fully utilised by the Restoration, should not survive these two tyrannies . . . .Only Liberty is entitled to our love and our venera-tion.'⁴⁵ Blanqui was treated as the ringleader of the student disturbances, suspended from the university and briefly imprisoned. All this radicalized him further and Blanqui's liberal language – whether tactical or from conviction – was to take a Socialist turn in 1832.

What was distinctive about Blanqui among French nineteenth-century Socialists was his indifference to theory and his devotion to revolution-ary action. He never bothered to write any substantial work of socialist theory, considering that there was already too much divisive theorizing. He confined himself to scattered remarks in articles which reflect a simplistic, eclectic and pragmatic conception of socialism, treated as self-evident truth. In an 1879 *Times* interview, Blanqui bluntly declared: 'I have no theory. I am not a professor of politics or socialism. What exists is bad. Something else must take its place.'[46] His impatience with hairsplitting theorizing and programmes was partly intrinsic and partly tactical. Such 'revolutionary scholasticism' neglected the socialist agreement on fundamentals; rejection of capitalism. He was sceptical of the programmes used by politicians to delude the people into providing them with support. 'Programmes are futuristic fictions intended to make people forget past history.'[47] His practical socialism was deliberately eclectic, to avoid excluding any who would be willing to take part in anti-capitalist action. Blanqui was always content to sacrifice ideological precision to political pragmatism.

He wrote off as madmen the Utopian Socialists who had in their pockets a detailed plan of the future Socialist society. 'We must get on with today. Tomorrow is beyond our reach and is not our concern. Our sole duty is to prepare good material for its organization. All else is not within our competence.'[48] The positive side of his scepticism was Blanqui's faith in the practical creativity of the revolutionary process itself. He wrote from prison in 1852: '1830, a mere change of dynasty, brought forth socialism, which until then had only existed in an embryonic state.' Despite the failures after the 1848 Revolution, socialism had developed further and Blanqui predicted: 'The next cataclysm will finally establish it on the wreckage of the old world that has been overthrown. A revolution improvises in a day more ideas than thirty years of midnight toil can wrench from the brains of a thousand thinkers.'[49] He backed this up in another letter, sent at almost the same time, with the pluralist argument that truth emerges from free discussion, so that theoretical debate was a source of strength. 'Proudhonians and Communists are equally ridiculous in their reciprocal diatribes, showing a lack of understanding of the immense utility of doctrinal diversity.'[50] This assertion is not consistent with his pragmatic desire to minimize conflict in the service of united revolutionary action but such inconsistency is precisely the contradiction into which eclecticism tends to land those who seek to sidestep choosing in matters of theoretical dispute. Blanqui ended the same letter by blandly declaring: 'Practical socialism does not belong to any particular sect . . . .It takes what suits it from each system . . .to build the future on the new foundations provided by socialism enlightened, developed and determined by events.'[51] A belief in the inevitability of human progress provided Blanqui with his escape route, allowing him to flee forwards from his contradictions.

Blanqui's self-assurance about the validity of socialism can be considered by reference to the Saint-Simonians and Proudhon. He had come into direct contact with Saint-Simonism through his brother, who had written for *Le Producteur* (its first periodical, from 1825 to 1826), and his work with Leroux on the *Globe*, even though it did not become an organ of the movement until 1831. However, repetition of the Saint-Simonian condemnation of 'the exploitation of man by man', in particular the idle owners of the means of production, was asserted simultaneously with an egalitarianism which was profoundly repugnant to both Saint-Simon and his disciples, though not Leroux. Nevertheless, the radical thrust of the 'Parable' (see Chapter 4, pp. 93–4) is there in an 1834 draft article. 'Axiom: the nation becomes poorer with the loss of a worker; it becomes richer with that of an idler. The death of a rich person is a blessing.'[52] Blanqui's collectivism was learnt from the Saint-Simonians but he was repelled by their religiosity and their appetite for capitalist industrial enterprise. In the name of 'the French Revolution which has carried forward the code of Equality', Blanqui castigated the Saint-Simonian 'restoration of the middle ages with its monied papacy and the sanctification of Capital.'[53]

Prolonged periods of imprisonment cut Blanqui off from the post-1840 development of the French economy and working-class movement, so he remained attached to a simplistic, moralistic equation of capitalism and the levying of interest with stolen labour, the result of usury and unequal exchange. He had read Say, Smith and Ricardo (to whom he preferred Malthus), as well as his brother. However, his attacks on the liberal economists, when they were not empty rhetoric, were derivative from his reading of Proudhon, although he borrowed the notion of saving as leading to underconsumption from Sismondi. So 'The principles upon which Blanqui's economic criticism are based are Proudhon's, expressed in a hard, incisive, coldly violent language, with an imperious, almost dictatorial brevity.'[54] Blanqui's ritual attack upon the pseudo-science of economics that serves as a lightning conductor protecting capitalism from public indignation is also applied to journalism. 'A newspaper is capital. Whoever has money publishes at will.' Or again: 'Behind every daily newspaper, there is a capitalist faction, open or concealed enemy, acting by violence or jesuitism.'[55] Such arguments have become the stock-in-trade of the Left, offering a picture of capitalist conspiracy to which revolutionary Socialist conspiracy is the symmetrical riposte.

Blanqui described Proudhon in an unpublished manuscript as 'A writer of immense talent, the prince of economists, a philosopher who does not shoot.'[56] Blanqui asks 'Are capitalist abuses inherent in the system of exchange or can they be abolished by the methods envisaged by the Proudhonian school? Will the future lie with mutualism or . . . communism?'[57] This theoretical uncertainty, combined with tactical pragmatism, led Blanqui uncharacteristically to write to Proudhon from prison in November 1848 that they should work together for a peaceful victory through ideas![58] An 1850 note declared in his eclectic vein: 'Proudhonism and communism are fife and drum. The two instruments are not alike but they can combine well and make society dance pleasantly to their tune.'[59] In his more pragmatic vein, Blanqui wrote: 'Communism and Proudhonism argue vigorously on the bank of a stream over whether there is a field of corn or wheat on the other side. Let us cross first, we shall see when we get there.'[60]

Such willingness to leap into the dark was in the long run untenable and came to grief in the 1860s over the moderate reformism of Proudhon's disciples in the First International and the cooperative movement. Blanqui could not accept the Proudhonian primacy of liberty as the means to equality and the need for the workers to emancipate themselves by economic action rather than relying upon the insurrectionary conquest of state power to abolish capitalism.[61] Whereas in 1848 Proudhon and Blanqui were fraternal enemies of a state controlled by reactionaries in the service of capitalism, by the 1860s Blanqui decided one could not be opposed both to the state and to capitalism and chose the former to destroy the latter. Despite their common anticlericalism, Proudhon for his part could never accept communism, much less naive Blanqui claims such as 'Communism . . . resolves by commonsense all economic problems.'[62]

Subversion as a way of life

Since the French Revolution, there had been a sense of the fragile character of political order and a fear that mass violence could easily destabilize the political system. During the Restoration, Barante expressed his anxiety that 'The least change in the narrow upper level of political power, a success won by surprise, an intrigue which displaces a few men, a riot which causes terror, would change everything at the centre and then find a people incapable of any regular resistance, a servile flock which awaits its fate without knowing how to influence it and which knows only servility or revolt.'[63] Such fears of a continuing revolutionary process were revived in 1830, Chateaubriand portentously declaring in 1831 that 'A great revolution is accomplished, an even greater revolution is being prepared.'[64] To conjure this menace, the banker–prime minister Casimir Périer declared in the debate on the king's speech on 9 August 1831: 'The July Revolution has come not to resume but to end our first revolution.'[65] Such reassurances, along with Guizot's attempts to exorcise threats to the new regime by calling the attempts at insurrection anachronistic convulsions of a Revolution historically sentenced to death, were backed by a repressive government policy. Against this resolute attempt to halt the revolutionary process was arrayed the puny republican opposition.

The nucleus of the conspiratorial revolutionary opposition in the early 1830s was constituted by three men, but Buonarroti enjoyed the ascendancy. A biographer has claimed that 'much of the propaganda of the left-wing of the republican opposition during the early years of the July Monarchy was directed and controlled by the trio Teste-d'Argenson-Buonarroti and that the three men worked so closely together that at times they formed an indivisible unit.'[66] Teste had been close to the Saint-Simonians in the 1820s but he became Buonarroti's secret agent in the 1830s. In his *Projet de Constitution Républicaine et Déclaration des Principes Fondamentaux de la Société* (1833) he advocated a temporary revolutionary dictatorship, including the right to suspend elections, as well as free speech and a free press. This was to allow time for the preparation of the people to run the new, egalitarian institutions.[67]

Voyer d'Argenson was descended from the family that had in the eighteenth century produced the pre-revolutionary Marquis d'Argenson (See Chapter 1, pp. 8–9). He had been Lafayette's aide-de-camp from 1789 to 1792 and later sat as a member of the liberal opposition in the Restoration Parliament alongside Constant and Lafayette. He combined this with a conspiratorial role, financing the *Charbonnerie*. After the 1830 Revolution, Voyer d'Argenson broke with Lafayette and joined Buonarroti's group, financially supporting him in his last years in Paris. He was tried for publishing a pamphlet entitled *Boutade of a Rich Man with a Popular Bent* but his main efforts, along with Teste and Buonarroti, were devoted successively to the *Société des Amis du Peuple* and the *Société des Droits de l'Homme* until they were crushed by government repression. (D'Argenson was included by Blanqui in the provisional government that would have been formed had his 1839 insurrection succeeded.) The agitation and propaganda methods, pioneered by these organizations in which Blanqui participated, developed 'The extreme verbal violence, the forcing of issues and the courting of censorship and repression, the exploitation of political trials for public purposes' of which Blanqui would become the exponent *par excellence*.[68]

Blanqui was arrested in July 1831 as a vice-president of the *Société des Amis du Peuple* (which had some 500 members) and founder with François Raspail of its journal *Au Peuple*. He was charged with violation of the press laws and with treason. Thanks to an influential friend he was released on bail but he confessed to her: 'In politics I have the most violent passion. I have suffered for a cause. The enemies of that cause are my enemies, enemies that I hate.'[69] At the January 1832 trial, the charge of treason was dropped and had Blanqui not deliberately provoked the Court by his defence statement, he would have been acquitted and left a free man. Instead, he was sentenced to a fine and one year's imprisonment for 'trying to disturb the peace by exciting contempt and hatred of citizens against . . . those described as "rich", "privileged" and "bourgeois".'[70] The declaration Blanqui made to the jury that prompted the judges to sentence him to jail was a calculated declaration of class war. Because it is a seminal statement of the simplistic stereotypes of revolutionary socialism, we must give it extended consideration.

At the outset, when asked for his profession, Blanqui replied: 'Proletarian'. Told that this was not a profession, he protested: 'It is the profession of thirty million French people who live from their work and are denied their political rights.'[71] Postponing for the present Blanqui's dubious claim to being a proletarian, let us consider the stark picture of France as a class-divided society that he presents. The dichotomizing rhetoric, in which Blanqui pitted the mass of the industrious and poor people against the 100,000 bourgeois, idle and privileged rich, suffuses his defence statement. It began: 'I am accused of having told thirty million French proletarians like myself that they have the right to live.'[72] He immediately turned the tables by shifting from the status of accused to unrepentant accuser, using the publicity to acquire a notoriety that he never subsequently lost. He told the Court that he had entered it on 29 July 1830, when 'We thought that we had cleaned out the temple of justice. . . .In this as in all else, our revolution was betrayed but the memory of those days should teach you a lesson.'[73]

Apart from threatening his judges with revolutionary justice, Blanqui hastened to confirm their fear of class war, 'the war between the rich and the poor, willed by the rich because they are the aggressors'. Why was reform impossible? 'The laws are made by 100,000 electors, applied by 100,000 jurymen, enforced by 100,000 urban national guardsmen. . .the same people . . . so that the same man in the morning, makes a deputy, i.e. the law, applies that law in the afternoon as a juryman and enforces it in the street that evening in the national guardsman's uniform.' The advocates of representative government had justified it in terms of the separation of power but 'it is precisely the representative system, as applied by its apologists, that concentrates all three powers in the hands of a small, privileged number, united by the same interests', leading to 'the most monstrous of tyrannies.'[74] To prevent the mass of the French people being treated as outsiders, it was essential to base elections upon universal suffrage. This would ensure that taxes would be switched from the poor to the rich.

In a bloodcurdling speech before an audience of some 1,500 people organized by the *Société des Amis du Peuple* shortly after sentence had been pronounced but before he began to serve it, Blanqui accentuated his attack upon the status quo, grounding it upon a class analysis of the Restoration period. 'There is no point in denying that there is a war to the death between the classes that constitute the nation' and that 'the truly national party, to which patriots should rally, is the party of the masses.'[75] He divided the French people into three classes: the upper, the middle or bourgeois class and the people. Whereas Louis XVIII had secured an alliance of the upper and middle classes on the basis of the charter, the reactionary Charles X declared war on the majority of the middle class which rallied to the minority (like Constant) that had always been anti-Bourbon since 1815. The bourgeoisie, however, only fought from 1825 to 1830 to defend the charter, which 'guaranteed their power' and 'gave them supremacy in the state. Legality was invented to represent this interest of the bourgeoisie and be its flag.'[76]

However, at the end of July 1830, when the bourgeoisie was relying upon a tax strike to resist Charles X's attempt to restore absolute monarchy, France witnessed the reawakening of the people after its long sleep. During the revolutionary days 'the bourgeois were torn between two fears, first of Charles X and then of the workers' but they were quick to profit from the workers' efforts once the fighting was over. Blanqui then asked: 'Why did fate decree that this revolution carried out by the people alone, which should have ended the exclusive domination of the bourgeoisie and inaugurated the triumph of the people's power and interests, only establish middle class despotism, increase the misery of the workers and peasants, plunging France deeper in the mire?' His answer was that 'its natural leaders . . . did not have enough time to emerge from the crowd', so that the 'masses [who] had not formally expressed a precise political will' supported the bourgeois-led parliamentary opposition. The result was that the middle class, adding cunning after the victory to prudence before it, ensured that 'the people, who had done everything, remained nothing.' Blanqui warned that there would now be a bitter war between the middle class and the people.[77]

Given the confusion over the conception of the class system in the re-emergence of the notion of class conflict, as an embryonic socialism developed in the 1820s and 1830s, it is not surprising that Blanqui's own perception of classes was vigorous but rather imprecise. As early as 1825 his brother Adolphe – during his flirtation with Saint-Simonism – divided the people into two classes: those who lived from their work, the plebeians, and those who lived from the work of others, the patricians. This was refined in 1832 by the Saint-Simonian Jean Reynaud into a conflict between wage-earning proletarians and an exploitative bourgeoisie living off unearned income.[78] This influential distinction raised many unresolved questions. What about the working bourgeoisie? What about the peasantry? The confusing word 'people' continued to be used, by Blanqui among others, sometimes in a broad and sometimes in a narrow sense, as political tactics changed with circumstances. The sleight of mind in which a sympathetic interpreter like Dommanget becomes embroiled is revealed in his description of Blanqui: 'Defender of the poor, he had resolutely become one of the poor and this break with his original social class made him part of the working class.'[79] Spitzer is closer to the truth when he describes Blanqui as a 'self-styled proletarian revolutionary'.[80] What is clear is that Blanqui was never a professional revolutionary in the bureaucratic, twentieth-century sense of the modestly but securely paid full-time party official. When he was not in prison, fed and accommodated by the state, he was an insecure pauper, living from hand to mouth, 'kept' by his family and friends.

Given that the mass of 'unenlightened' and unrevolutionary people were not willing to support, much less engage in insurrection, who could be relied upon to inject the necessary impetus? It was during the Second Empire that Blanqui formulated the idea, based upon his own experience, that the true insurrectionary force was an advance guard of enlightened, Parisian, middle-class revolutionaries, together with select skilled artisans and workers. Against Proudhon's reliance upon the working class, Blanqui was convinced that without leadership by a revolutionary élite the mass population would be incapable of resolute action. In 1832, Blanqui had distinguished between the business bourgeoisie and the intellectual bourgeoisie, the latter being a minority that was more inclined to side with the revolutionary assertion of popular sovereignty.[81] By the end of the Second Empire, Blanqui concluded that revolutionary leadership must come from 'the *déclassés*. . .pariahs of the intelligence. . . .They horrify and frighten Capital. . . .These *déclassés*, the invisible weapon of progress, are today the secret ferment that silently leavens the mass of the people and prevents it from subsiding into inertia. Tomorrow, they will be the reserve army of the revolution.'[82] These concluding remarks from his essay 'Communism, the future of society' summarize the lessons of his personal efforts to bring about a Socialist revolution.

Seventeen years earlier, in 1852, Blanqui had explained the class basis of his revolutionary strategy in his *Letter to Maillard*. To those who declared that they were neither bourgeois nor proletarian but democrats, Blanqui answered that whereas the first two alternatives had a precise meaning, the word democrat was all things to all people. Returning to his class war terminology of twenty years before, Blanqui asserted that using such terms did not encourage civil war but simply recognized that one had been waged for many years. He numbered the bourgeoisie at a maximum of 4 million people who owned property, were educated and lived either from unearned income or from exploiting others. The rest, some 32 million, made up the proletariat, propertyless and living precariously from their manual wage labour. Without yet using the term *déclassé*, Blanqui admitted that although by his origins and education he was bourgeois, he had joined the 'proletarian camp' and had been rewarded with imprisonment. It was bourgeois like him who constituted the proletariat's 'most persistent' force. 'They bring it an enlightenment that the people unfortunately still cannot provide. It is bourgeois who first raised the flag of the proletariat, who formulated egalitarian doctrines, spread them and support them, revive them after their downfall. Everywhere, it is bourgeois who lead the people in its battles against the bourgeoisie.'[83] The true revolutionary socialist élite consisted of the self-selected and dedicated social outcasts who had chosen to achieve 'real equality' by ending economic exploitation and political oppression.

By 1834, Blanqui had allied his 1793-style revolutionary zeal with a Socialist indifference to forms of government except as a means to social change. Blanqui was struggling with the same problem that Lenin and the Bolsheviks were to succeed in solving in 1917: how to bring about a Communist and proletarian victory in a country with few Communists and proletarians. Spitzer had explained Blanqui's solution of relying upon leadership by a *déclassé* bourgeois minority organized for conspiratorial action. 'This revolutionary elite would have to make up what it lacked in numbers by determination, organization and a shrewd reading of the historical conditions necessary for revolutionary enterprise. Its ability to elicit mass support before the revolution would be limited by the legal and political structure it was committed to overthrow. Therefore, its eventual purpose of instructing the masses could only be effected by cutting itself off from them in order safely to fashion a clandestine force which could strike off the chains forged by capitalism and its allies.'[84] This meant exercising a dictatorship not *by* but *on behalf of* the proletariat. However, while Blanqui claimed that 'the day the gag comes out of the mouth of labour it will enter the mouth of capital',[85] this programme of Leninism before Lenin would undoubtedly have led to gagging *both* capital *and* labour.

To his combination of Saint-Simonian élitism and *Carbonari* conspiratorial methods, Blanqui added a Jacobin and Babouvist dictatorship of revolutionary Paris as the embodiment of the French nation's general will. He wrote in November 1848: 'Paris is the brain ... 89, 1830, 48 are the results of its dictatorship, enthusiastically applauded by the country.'[86] However, Blanqui did not learn the lesson of 1848, when revolutionary

Paris was defeated by a provincial alliance of bourgeoisie and peasantry. The same mistake was repeated in 1871, when the Paris Commune attempted to usurp dictatorial power from the representative Assembly of the whole of the French nation. He claimed much later: 'One year of Parisian dictatorship would have spared France and History the quarter of a century that is coming to an end. If it requires ten years this time, we must not hesitate. After all, Paris government is government of the country by the country, the only legitimate one.'[87] Even the circumstances of foreign invasion in 1871 – not present in 1830 and 1848 – could not mobilize patriotic fervour, as in 1792–3, for the purposes of waging a class war. But this is to anticipate the sanguinary repeat in May 1871 of the massacre of June 1848. Blanqui's conception of communism was 'the application of the doctrine that gives the State omnipotence and omnidirection',[88] the very antithesis of Proudhon's conception of political authority in its centralized authoritarianism. It would not only be necessary to purge the state's political and administrative personnel; freedom of the press would be denied to the enemies of socialism. 'Persecutors and executioners are only entitled to reprisals and the axe.'[89]

Before turning to a description of Blanqui's theory and practice of the organization of a revolutionary movement, it is necessary to comment briefly on his authoritarian, domineering personality. He assiduously cultivated his image as a persecuted, imperious, indomitable hero, entitled to demand total commitment and discipline from his associates. He could argue that a conspiratorial leader required unquestioning subordination in the service of subversion. A description of Buonarroti is apposite to his insurrectionist heir: 'He was impervious to criticism from those who had made lesser sacrifices, he was incapable of criticising himself. He could demand from others blind obedience because he was never acting in his own interest. He hated egoists yet he was himself both proud and wilful, incapable of trusting any leadership save his own.'[90] It was indispensable to control everything personally from the top. Such was the austere, taciturn, calculating, meticulous conspirator who set out to control his own secret society.

In 1834 the leaders of the Society of the Rights of Man who operated in the open were easily arrested by an increasingly repressive government. Blanqui was in the unusual position of organizing a committee for the defence of the accused at their trial in 1835. However, whereas some republican Socialists like Raspail considered that 'One would be mad to engage in Carbonarism when one can engage openly in propaganda', while others like Fieschi resorted to attempts (there were six between 1832 and 1840) at assassinating the king, Blanqui set about systematically preparing his insurrectionary instrument.[91] This involved a Buonarrotist-cum-*Carbonaro*-style combination of semi-Masonic initiation rites and semi-military organization and discipline. In mid-1834 the *Société des Familles* was founded and by the end of the year Blanqui had assumed control. It was organized on 'democratic centralist', clandestine cell lines, with the head of each 'family' of six members known only to the other heads. Five or six 'families' made up a section and two or three sections made up a quarter. The heads of these 'quarters' were responsible to the 'revolutionary agent', himself responsible to a mysterious committee. Preparations for insurrection were disrupted by the discovery in Paris (where most of its thousand or so members – students, artisans and workers – were concentrated) in 1836 of the place where gunpowder was being manufactured and stockpiled. The leaders were arrested and tried, Blanqui being sentenced to two years' imprisonment.[92]

Amnestied less than a year later in May 1837 and placed under surveillance at an assigned residence north of Paris, Blanqui immediately resumed his conspiratorial activities. The structure of the new *Société des Saisons* started at the bottom with a Week of seven members, Sunday being its head. Four weeks composed a Month of twenty-eight headed by a twenty-ninth, the leader. Each Season was composed of three Months, plus its own head, making eighty-eight members. Four Seasons made up a Year of 353 men, headed by a revolutionary agent. One of the three revolutionary agents was Blanqui, who was also commander-in-chief. In fact, the aim of achieving over a thousand members was not attained, reaching about 900 shortly before the insurrection. Associated with the Society of the Seasons was a group of German political refugees, the Federation of the Just, headed by Wilhelm Weitling, some of whom took part in the insurrection.[93]

It is claimed in criticism of Blanqui that his conspiratorial methods necessarily meant that he was cut off from the working class. While this is broadly true, there was an attempt at revolutionary propaganda by the Seasons. Between November 1837 and September 1838 two newspapers, *Le Moniteur Républicain* and *L'Homme Libre*, successively published twelve issues that were deposited in shops and doorways or sent through the post. However, Blanquist propagandist publications were always ephemeral because surreptitious preparation for insurrection was given priority over winning mass support. Successful revolutions in 1789, 1830 and 1848 were possible because such mass support had been secured by extended preliminary propaganda. Without this, Blanqui's insurrectionists could not form the advance guard of a successful revolutionary movement. They lacked the support of public opinion and so were easily isolated and liquidated once the public authorities recovered from the initial surprise attack. *Putschism* by an activist minority had lost its effectiveness in a modern mass polity where

popular support had, through the process of democratization, become decisive.[94] So, despite Blanqui's unusually successful avoidance of the penetration
of his movement by police informers, on the day he struck he startled not
merely the government but his potential supporters among the Parisians.

In one of his manuscripts, Blanqui described himself as 'a person who
believes that the world can be regenerated from one day to the next.'[95]
This disarming *naïveté* was combined with an impatience to precipitate
the regenerative process, an attitude that was encouraged by his nucleus
of activists. Furthermore, such psychological propensities, characteristic
of most people attracted to insurrectionary movements, were fortified by
the fear that delay would increase the likelihood of being unmasked by
the police. Blanqui was pushed into attempting an insurrection by his
temperament and strategy, as well as by the need to prevent his impetuous
followers from disbanding out of disillusion unless they were motivated by
the imminent prospect of action.

The economic and political circumstances also appeared to be highly
favourable in the spring of 1839. Lamennais (whom Blanqui appointed
without his consent a member of his post-revolutionary provisional government) wrote to a friend in April 1839: 'Bankruptcies multiply. Anxiety
suspends all commercial transactions. Workshops are ceasing production
and the workers are dying of hunger.'[96] The defeat of the Molé government in the March 1839 general election led to a prolonged political
crisis, envenomed by personal rivalries and issues of principle. The sixth
attempt by Louis-Philippe to form a government failed just before the 12
May insurrection. The political establishment was split and power was in
the listless hands of a caretaker government. Reports of violent Chartist
demonstrations in England provided further encouragement for the view
that the hour of insurrection had struck.

The trio of revolutionary agents who led the insurrection were Blanqui,
Armand Barbès and Martin Bernard. Barbès and Bernard had belonged
(along with d'Argenson, Lamennais and Raspail) to the defence committee
for those members of the Society of the Rights of Man tried in 1835,
which met at Blanqui's home. Barbès was the Creole son of a wealthy
family. 'Everything about him was big – physique, height, brawn and
beard, courage, loyalty and generosity' – all of which he brought to his
association with Blanqui from 1834 and in the previous Society of the
Families.[97] Bernard was a former Saint-Simonian printer, who had also
been involved in the 1836 Families 'gun powder plot' and was the one with
the best links with working men. Blanqui and Bernard reviewed 'sections'
of their members each Sunday throughout April 1839 and the decision
was taken by the leaders to call the insurrection for 12 May, without

those summoned for action being aware that this was not just another rehearsal.

Despite the audacity of the assault by about 500 members of the Seasons – they captured the *Hôtel de Ville* but not their main objective, the *Préfecture de Police* – the insurrection failed to rouse either the students or workers and the carefully planned barricades did not withstand the troops, who regained control of Paris the same day. Barbès was wounded and about a hundred people died, of whom thirty were soldiers. A mini 'popular' rising occurred *the day after*, when it was too late.[98] Blanqui went into hiding for four months but was arrested when trying to escape to Switzerland. He refused to testify at his trial and forbade his lawyer to defend him. Like Barbès, he was sentenced to death but both sentences were commuted to life imprisonment. Louis-Philippe was reluctant to carry out the death sentence for political offences, his father having been guillotined during the French Revolution. The ironic immediate result of the 1839 insurrection was to allow the king to form a government (nominally under Soult but effectively under Guizot) that was to stay in power – with one short break in 1840 – until the 1848 Revolution.[99]

The fiasco was not only more complete than in 1836 because the 1839 insurrection went according to plan; it also left a legacy that was to resurface with a vengeance in 1848. Blanqui's revolutionary standing depended above all upon his reputation for intransigence. So, when in 1848 the *Revue Rétrospective* published what purported to be a confession given to the minister of the interior in October 1839 by Blanqui after the attempted insurrection, it proved devastatingly discreditable to him. As Spitzer, who judiciously writes that the authenticity of 'the accusation has never been decisively proved or disproved' has put it: 'For Blanqui ever to have cooperated with the reactionary police under any circumstances was the very negation of his political being. Even an unproved allegation did him considerable damage' because he was 'a prisoner of his own reputation'.[100] Because Blanqui's conduct in 1839 is symbolically so important for the assessment of a revolutionary, whose test was deeds rather than words, let us consider briefly the rival arguments before following Proudhon in his sympathetic but damning judgement.

The case for the defence is stated fully by Dommanget, who has written most extensively upon the life and ideas of Blanqui. In 1924, Dommanget's first view of what has come to be known as the 'Taschereau Document' (after the person who published it) was an open verdict but by 1948 he came down in favour of Blanqui's innocence. Dommanget now argued that the 'confession' was fabricated by a former associate turned police spy, to be used against Blanqui at his 1840 trial. However, it was not so utilized but was drawn from police archives in 1848 to smear him, which it successfully did, despite the vigour and partial success of his reply, 100,000 copies of which were distributed.[101]

The view that Blanqui did confess in 1839 is developed especially by Decaux and Paz. They focus upon Blanqui's failure to call for evidence from the interior minister to whom he was claimed to have confessed. Duchâtel was a leading light of the *Globe* at the end of Charles X's reign when Blanqui was its parliamentary correspondent, so they had been colleagues. Was it a coincidence that when Blanqui was freed from prison in 1844, Duchâtel was once again interior minister? At the 1848 trial for defamation brought by Taschereau against Blanqui, who claimed that he had been victim of a forgery, damning evidence of Blanqui's confession was produced from four senior ministers who confirmed that the cabinet had authorized the interior minister to receive Blanqui's testimony. Duchâtel's successor in 1840, Rémusat, also confirmed that he had heard from his predecessor of Blanqui's confession. Duchâtel was not called to testify in 1848 because he had taken refuge in England following the overthrow of Guizot's government, in which he had been minister of the interior. Blanqui never denied meeting Duchâtel in 1839 and although Duchâtel lived until 1867, having returned to France in 1849, Blanqui never sought exoneration from him. Decaux and Paz conclude that the evidence points to Blanqui having dishonourably confessed, so that his death sentence might be commuted.[102]

Proudhon was asked to report on the evidence for and against Blanqui heard by a *jury d'honneur* set up by the left-wing clubs in 1848 under the pressure of Barbès, estranged revolutionary associate of Blanqui, convinced that he had confessed. Blanqui refused to testify before a tribunal established by his enemies. Proudhon vainly favoured reconciliation and blamed the squabbling revolutionary leaders for the grave disservice they were doing to the common cause. His private opinion is to be found in a January 1851 letter: 'These men actually aspire to govern the world!. . .I wanted to remain neutral but I had been made the arbitrator.' He was convinced that in a moment of weakness Blanqui had confessed in 1839 but 'In my eyes this does not reduce his claim to be a revolutionary and a democrat.' However, Blanqui could not afford openly to admit his human failing because of 'the false and mean-minded revolutionist outlook. . . .To merit esteem in their world one has to be ferocious. As Blanqui, rightly or wrongly enjoys in the highest degree the reputation of a ferocious beast, he believes himself lost if he allows it to appear before the Court of his Peers that he had weakened. It is to such detestable scruples that the republican religion has descended, more worthy of brigands than of citizens.'[103] No trace of Proudhon's report has survived. He did not publish it, probably to avoid fuelling old resentments. The slur upon Blanqui's reputation as a revolutionary above reproach not only dogged him for the rest of his life; it has survived his death.

1848: The culmination of class war

Blanqui spent 1840–4 in harsh conditions of solitary confinement. An attempt to escape from his Mont-Saint-Michel prison failed. His wife died in 1841. A serious illness in 1844, when Blanqui was thought to be near death, led to his removal to milder forms of detention and then a formal pardon by minister of the interior Duchâtel. Blanqui rejected this 'odious pardon' and remained for health reasons in the prison hospital. He later told the historian Michelet that he had spent so much time in jail that he 'felt more secure and self-confident in prison.'[104] Yet, within hours of hearing the news of the February 1848 Revolution, Blanqui was back in Paris. His first symbolic act was to issue a manifesto deploring the decision to retain the *tricolore* as the national flag instead of replacing it with the Red Flag.

A new demonstration of armed citizens wearing red cockades approached the *Hôtel de Ville* on 25 February, along streets resplendent with red flags. Would the Provisional Government give way to the Socialist demand that the 'Orleanist' *tricolore* be replaced? Initially, the Red Flag was identified as a symbol of law and order rather than revolution. The Red Flag was flown from the Paris town hall to signal the proclamation of martial law to deal with food riots in 1789, while in July 1791 it was used at the massacre of anti-royalist demonstrators. This provoked Babeuf into demanding an end to flying the Red Flag, in Jaurès' words 'the sanguinary symbol of bourgeois repression'. (In 1792 the republican revolutionaries turned it into a symbol of defiance by inscribing on their red flags: 'Martial law of the sovereign people against the rebellion of the executive power.')[105] Thereafter, the Red Flag went into eclipse. The *tricolore* carried all before it for the rest of the Revolution and under Napoleon, being readopted at the 1830 Revolution as the emblem of the July Monarchy. The Left sought an alternative and at first it was the Black Flag symbolizing a fight to the death that appeared in the 1831 Lyons riots, with its slogan: 'Work or Death'.

In February 1848 the Red Flag appeared during the insurrection for the first time as a workers' banner on a large scale, alongside the *tricolore*. It symbolized their wish for a break with the Orleanist past but the patriotic, poetic eloquence of Lamartine, on behalf of a majority of the Provisional Government, persuaded the February 25 demonstration that the *tricolore* represented France's national glory. Since 1848 was the high tide of national revolutions in Europe, the call by Proudhon to internationalism raised few echoes. He predicted in March 1848 the internationalization of the Red Flag, writing: 'Keep if you wish the *tricolore*, symbol of our nationality. But remember that the red flag represents the final revolution. . . .The red flag is the federal standard of humanity!'[106] Julian Harney adopted the Red Flag as a Chartist symbol on 31 December 1849, and on 10 November 1850 European Socialist exiles in London adopted it in place of their national flags, a prelude to it becoming the emblem of the First International in 1866. However, whereas for Proudhon the Red Flag and the *tricolore* were not incompatible, Blanqui insisted that the former must replace the latter, as occurred in March 1871 during the Paris Commune. On the day after Lamartine's *tricolore* triumph, Blanqui published a tract 'For the Red Flag' in which he denounced the *tricolore* as having been washed in worker blood in 1832, 1834 and 1839, as well as 1848. He warned: 'Workers! your flag has fallen. The Republic will quickly follow it.'[107] Four months later, the 23–26 June Days were to see the decisive defeat of the social democratic Republic. The antisocial and undemocratic Republic was to go down before Louis-Napoleon nearly four years later.

As soon as he returned to Paris, which he had left as a prisoner eight years before, Blanqui warned the Provisional Government against making timorous concessions. He went to see Caussidière, a former secret society activist, now installed as secretary general in the very Prefecture of Police that Blanqui had tried to capture in 1839. 'If you press forward, you will have my full support; on the other hand, if you retreat . . . you will find me barring the path back to the past.'[108] On the same day (25 February 1848) Blanqui spoke with great lucidity at the foundation of his club, the Central Republican Society. He warned against false hopes and premature action that would frighten the provinces. 'France is not republican, the revolution that has just occurred is no more than a welcome surprise.' He advised abandoning the Provisional Government to its 'ephemeral power. We have the people and the clubs, where we shall organize ourselves in a revolutionary way, like the Jacobins did. Wait a few more days and the revolution will be ours! If we seize power through an audacious coup, like thieves in the night, who will guarantee the survival of our power? . . . . We need the mass of the people, the insurgent suburbs' to provide the necessary support for an enduring revolution.[109] It is clear that the *putschism* of 1839 had been abandoned for more sophisticated tactics based upon mass agitation and propaganda that the Bolsheviks later made familiar.

The problem is whether a revolutionary opportunity was missed during the interregnum between the overthrow of the July Monarchy and the establishment of an elected republican government when no serious resistance was to be anticipated. Blanqui's judgement was that a revolutionary dictatorship could not last without sufficient mass support and so he set about building up such support. Yet he did not adopt the reformist strategy followed by Louis Blanc, who allowed himself to be sidetracked into the theoretical discussions of the Government Commission for the Workers where, as he himself put it, he was forced to 'lecture on hunger to the hungry people'.[110] Instead of exhortation to make the sacrifice of three months' more poverty to help the Republic, Blanqui encouraged both the workers and the unemployed to arm themselves.

At a time when many others (notably Proudhon) took advantage of press freedom, Blanqui did not establish his own newspaper, relying upon his skill as a public speaker. There are several descriptions of the cold yet incisive eloquence, demonstrating inflexibility and intransigence, self-control and single-minded determination, of the diminutive, prematurely aged Blanqui. Even an enemy like Lamartine described his oratory as 'penetrating, clever and considered . . . . One sensed a plan, a line, a means, a purpose. His club was not a futile echo of tumultuous passions, like the other anti-social clubs. It was a revolutionary instrument, which he manipulated to rouse and direct mass passions.'[111] Many clubs were set up in the spring of 1848. There were about 145 by the end of March and 300 by the end of June but Blanqui's was the only one feared by the government because it had a nucleus of seasoned and armed professional revolutionaries under a resolute leader. Club propaganda provoked more fear than support, arraying much of Paris and almost all of provincial France against the continuation of the revolutionary process. Yet Blanqui was confident that, with time, he would succeed in winning over public opinion, so that in the short run he had nothing to gain from violence. He later wrote: 'After the February Revolution, many years of intellectual preparation would be necessary to precede and prepare a general election. It is through ideas, never by force, that one should conquer a nation.'[112]

Whereas in 1832 Blanqui advocated manhood suffrage without reservation, by the late 1830s Seasons conspiracy he thought its implementation would have to be postponed until the majority of the people had been educated to use the vote to sustain and not reverse the revolutionary process. In the interim, a dictatorial 'revolutionary power' would be necessary. The matter became urgent in 1848. After some hesitation over the right of revolutionary Paris to proclaim the Republic without first consulting France, the Provisional Government went ahead, subsequently securing overwhelming approval by the Assembly elected by manhood suffrage.

Blanqui's club started the agitation to postpone the election indefinitely because he was convinced that it would legitimize the authority of those concerned to halt and then reverse the Revolution. He protested at his subsequent trial that he sought to delay the election because of his respect for the will of the sovereign people. 'It is precisely because the National Assembly was for me a power invested with an unlimited, sacred and inviolable authority, that I made despairing efforts to delay its meeting. I knew that once it existed, its authority would be unchallengeable, it would have to be borne without murmuring or resisting.'[113]

The elections were first scheduled for 9 April 1848 and Blanqui's club launched two petitions in favour of postponement on the ground that an apparently free vote would allow the reactionaries to win by cunning what they had lost by force. Particularly in the second petition, Blanqui argued that fewer workers than bourgeois would be registered to vote. In the towns, many of the workers 'would abstain or be led by their masters like blind cattle. In the countryside, all influence was in the hands of the clergy and the aristocrats', so the peasantry would have their inexperience exploited to perpetuate their slavery. Blanqui called for a year's delay to overcome the effects of decades of domination; otherwise there would be 'civil war because Paris, the heart and brain of France, would not retreat in the face of an offensive return to the past.'[114]

While it was Cabet's Central Fraternal Society that initiated the call for a mass demonstration on 17 March to postpone the elections, it was Blanqui's club that organized it. Over 150,000 people marched to the town hall. A delegation headed by Cabet asked the Provisional Government to delay the Assembly elections until the end of May, while Blanqui kept in the background. The demonstrators were intimidated by a show of force by the National Guards, shouting 'Death to the Communists', 'Down with Blanc', 'Down with Blanqui', 'Down with Cabet'. With his hand strengthened, Lamartine replied that the Provisional Government's duty was 'to restore to the nation itself the powers that we had seized for the common salvation, and not to prolong for a minute longer the sort of dictatorship that we adopted under the pressure of circumstances.'[115] The Assembly election was merely postponed two weeks and as Blanqui had predicted the revolutionary Left was resoundingly defeated. Not a single candidate of his Central Republican Club was elected and Blanqui himself, who did not campaign, won a negligible vote.[116] The minority of revolutionary activists was drowned in the sea of mass democracy. As Blanqui later lamented: universal suffrage, while 'admirable for the future, is fatal at present.'[117] One could not harvest a republic until a field long planted with monarchy had been ploughed and furrowed several times.

Ironically, it was the miscarriage of a venture in street politics on 15 May 1848, to which he was opposed – along with Proudhon and most of the Socialist leaders – that led to Blanqui's arrest even before class conflict came to blows in June. Pressure by the rank and file proved irresistible, prompted by the provocative activities of a police spy. (As one such spy put it 'The tail led the head, as was customary.')[118] While Raspail probably initiated the idea of a demonstration and petition to the National Assembly in favour of an independent Poland, this was a pretext for the extreme Left to destabilize the newly elected reactionary Assembly. The key man behind the demonstration was probably interior minister Ledru-Rollin, seeking to increase his popularity, but it got out of hand (there was no *service d'ordre* in 1848), leading to an invasion of the Assembly. Blanqui's cool-headed advice against involvement was rejected (he feared it would fail because of lack of popular support) and the 'revolutionary opportunist' allowed himself to be fatally compromised in what he regarded as inopportune circumstances. Blanqui was carried to the rostrum and spoke in a frail but clear voice. He advocated a revolutionary war to secure Polish independence, coupled with the need to provide work and food for the French people. Not to be outdone, Barbès threatened the deputies with being declared traitors and the police secret agent Huber created pandemonium by declaring the Assembly dissolved. The leaderless demonstration moved on to the town hall where Barbès tried to proclaim a revolutionary government. He was arrested, Blanqui's club was dissolved and he himself was arrested on 26 May.

After his trial, in anticipation of Ledru-Rollin's June 1849 declaration in similar circumstances – 'As I was their leader, I had to follow them' – Blanqui explained why he had followed where he should have led. 'One is not the master of mass movements. One is often led to play a role which is anything but political and serious. Well, such was my position. I declare that it was almost ridiculous; one is not a politician when one allows oneself to be tossed about like a child and carried like a dummy . . . . People think that it is politicians that lead the masses. It is not true, it is the masses that often lead us where we do not wish to go.'[119] The masses were in fact manipulated but by the *agent provocateur* Huber, not by the revolutionary agent Blanqui.

The May fiasco was only the dress rehearsal for the full-scale class warfare of June, from which the imprisoned Blanqui was absent, as he was to be from the Paris Commune of 1871 – the two moments in his life when he would have had the opportunity to practise what he had preached. The June confrontation was deliberately precipitated by the government decision, in conditions of mass unemployment, to stop taking on more workers in the outdoor relief national workshops, seen as a preliminary step to their abolition. The insurrection that occurred was more a collective act of defensive despair than the mythical 'fight for the preservation or annihilation of the *bourgeois* order' that Marx sought to make of it, still less a call for the *'Dictatorship of the working class.'*[120]

Tocqueville, who was an unsympathetic eyewitness, wrote that for four days a hundred thousand 'insurgents fought without a war-cry, without leaders and without flags. . .a struggle of class against class, a sort of Servile War. . . .This formidable insurrection was not the enterprise of a certain number of conspirators, but the result of one whole section of the population against another.'[121] This leaderless, *ouvrieriste* character impressed Tocqueville. 'In general, insurrections. . .begin without a leader; but they always end by securing one. This insurrection finished without having found one' and being confined to the Paris proletariat, it was crushed once the government's provincial reinforcements arrived: 'The insurgents received no reinforcements, whereas we had all France for reserves.'[122] Although Tocqueville's prosaic view of those four bitter June days is more accurate, culminating in the shooting of insurgent prisoners out of hand or their mass transportation to Algeria without trial, Marx's rhetoric conveys their subsequent symbolic significance when martyrdom made their rising into a revolutionary myth. 'Only after being dipped in the blood of the *June insurgents* did the tricolour become the flag of the European revolution – the *red flag!*'[123] In particular, it was Marx's theoretical gloss upon these events in French history that generalized their influence, through the impact of Marxism.

Interpreting the failure of 1848

It is estimated that during the June Days 12,000 insurgents were killed and 25,000 were taken prisoner. Second-rank Blanquists played an active role and some of them escaped to exile, notably in London. Blanqui himself was sentenced to ten years' imprisonment at his trial in March–April 1849 on the accusation that in May 1848 he had attempted to start a civil war aimed at overthrowing the new democratic government. Although he had no direct part in the Paris class war, he was identified with it by those who saw June 1848 not as an anachronistic throwback to an old-style revolution but the first attempt at a new kind of revolution.

Before discussing Blanqui's influence upon Marx and later on Lenin within the Communist movement, let us briefly consider the repulsion he provoked in political enemies like the anti-revolutionary Tocqueville and

Hugo and political friends like the pro-revolutionary Herzen and Bakunin. Tocqueville's nightmarish description of Blanqui during the invasion of the Assembly on 15 May 1848 reflects a liberal aristocrat's revulsion at this creature emerging from the social depths. 'It was then that I saw appear, in his turn, in the tribune a man whom I have never seen since, but the recollection of whom has always filled me with horror and disgust. He had wan, emaciated cheeks, white lips, a sickly, wicked and repulsive expression, a dirty pallor, the appearance of a mouldy corpse; he wore no visible linen; an old black frock-coat tightly covered his lean, withered limbs; he seemed to have passed his life in a sewer and to have just left it. I was told it was Blanqui.'[124] Later the same year, Victor Hugo saw Blanqui in his Vincennes prison. His portrait combines hostility with a grudging respect. 'Harsh, hard, grave, never laughing, repaying respect with irony, love with disdain, inspiring extraordinary devotion . . . . He was a sort of lugubrious apparition in which all the hatreds born of all the miseries had become incarnated. Strange countenance of a cold blooded fanatic that has its savage grandeur.'[125]

When we turn to Herzen and Bakunin, repulsion from the denizen of prisons past, present and future gives way to admiration for the resolute opponent of parliamentary democracy and the proponent of revolution without half measures. Herzen wrote: 'Blanqui is the revolutionary of our time. He has understood that nothing can be merely readjusted, but that the primary task is to pull down the existing structure. Gifted with remarkable eloquence, he roused the masses; all his words were an indictment of the old world.'[126] For a while the populist Herzen and the anarchist Bakunin looked to a revolutionary dictatorship to overcome resistance to change but they quickly reverted to an affinity with Proudhon in their common rejection of communism.

While Blanqui and Marx had very different theoretical and practical conceptions of communism, they shared a common revolutionary intransigence. On Marx's brief stay in France during the 1848 Revolution, his links were with the radical republican Ledru-Rollin. He did not visit Blanqui's club and neither then nor at any other time did they meet. In London, Marx did collaborate with Blanquist exiles in the shortlived World League of Revolutionary Communists in 1850, but when this organization broke up the Blanquists sided against Marx. Rejecting Proudhon's 'doctrinaire socialism', Marx claimed with more wishful thinking than accuracy that 'the *proletariat* rallies more and more round *revolutionary socialism*, round communism, for which the bourgeoisie has itself invented the name of *Blanqui*. This socialism is the *declaration of the permanence of the revolution*, the *class dictatorship* of the proletariat as the necessary transit point to the *abolition of class distinctions generally.*'[127] These phrases have led many to argue that Marx derived the notion of proletarian dictatorship from Blanqui, which is not the case.

In the most thorough analysis of the matter, Draper has shown that while Blanqui never used the phrase, Marx did use it on eleven occasions. In 1850–2 and in 1872–5, in the wake of the 1848 Revolution and the Paris Commune, 'Marx used the term particularly *in connection with* the Blanquists . . . combined complete rejection of the Blanquist putsch, to be made by a conspiratorial group, with great admiration for Blanqui as a devoted and honest revolutionist.'[128] Marx and especially Engels distinguish between a Blanquist dictatorship by an active Parisian revolutionary minority and a 'class dictatorship' based upon majority mass support. Engels wrote in 1874: 'Blanqui is essentially a political revolutionist. He is a socialist only through sentiment, through his sympathy with the sufferings of the people, but he has neither a socialist theory nor any practical suggestions for social remedies. In his political activity he was mainly a "man of action", believing that a small and well-organized minority, who would attempt a political stroke of force at the opportune moment, could carry the mass of people with them by a few successes at the start and thus make a victorious revolution . . . . From Blanqui's assumption, that any revolution may be made by the outbreak of a small revolutionary minority, follows of itself the necessity of a dictatorship after the success of the venture. This is, of course, a dictatorship, not of the entire revolutionary class, the proletariat, but of a small minority that has made the revolution, and who are themselves organized under the dictatorship of one or several individuals. We see, then, that Blanqui is a revolutionary of the preceding generation.'[129] We have quoted at length because, as we shall see later, although Blanqui was harking back to the Paris secret societies of the 1830s, he was also anticipating the Leninist tactics of 1917, which in practice owed more to Blanqui than to Marx. Blanqui's emphasis upon political will contrasts with Marx's economic determinism (apart from Marx's flirtation with Blanquism in the 1847–50 period) and this explains why Lenin found him more suited to his revolutionary purpose.

How did the jailbird revolutionary employ himself in the two decades that separated the 1848 Revolution and the Paris Commune? During the Second Republic, while he recognized the scope for propaganda, he reiterated his old message condemning 'the exclusive infatuation with theorising, neglecting the only guaranteed practical factor: force. Weapons and organization are the decisive means of achieving progress, the serious way of ending poverty. He who has iron has bread. . . .When France is bristling with armed workers, then socialism will come.'[130] This message delivered from prison on the third anniversary of the 1848 Revolution was not well received in London where it split his exiled disciples, so Blanqui followed it up with a diatribe anticipating that of his fellow prisoner Proudhon a few months later (see Chapter 7, p. 169). 'Away with you, race of slaves, who dare not raise either your eyes or your hands against your tyrants! Rebels one day, penitent and prostrate the day after, continue to cower in your poverty and servitude! Do not attempt to break your chains! You would have to weld them together again with your own hands. Make no more revolutions, to avoid the shame of having to ask for pardon on your knees.'[131]

Blanqui's exasperation at the supine attitude of his fellow countrymen did not endure. His will to see the overthrow of the bourgeois state and social order kept his hopes alive during the Second Empire. He encouraged a fellow prisoner in 1857 to be patient with the words: 'The Empire will collapse and disintegrate one day in its putrefaction, that is inevitable. My whole consolation is that we shall bury it but it will not happen tomorrow. . . .We must obstinately go on living, despite persecutions and vexations. . .survive, so that at last we can overthrow the enemies of the people and of liberty.'[132]

The heroic activist condemned to inactivity devoted his enforced leisure to unsophisticated speculation. He argued that the three forces dominating society were 'Ideas, Capital and Arms' and of these the most important was the first. 'The material causes of poverty such as capitalism and all the other forms of exploitation only exist because of the ignorance of the masses.'[133] Education became the panacea through which the ideological transformation necessary to communism could be achieved. Against Montalembert, who had argued in 1850 that two armies were struggling for supremacy, the 40,000 priests who made up the 'army of the good' and the 40,000 schoolteachers who constituted the 'army of the bad', Blanqui replied: 'Liberty is education! Equality is education! Fraternity is education! Teachers and books. . .they are the real revolutionary agents.'[134] Communism and education were mutually indispensable. Government could be dispensed with when all were equally educated and occupational differences would entail no inequality of respect, remuneration or power. However, for this work of enlightenment to occur, secular education – free of charge, compulsory and vocational – would have to dispel Church-sustained obscurantism.[135]

Blanqui follows in the wake of Proudhon in seeing God as the personification of oppressive authority and the Church as the champion of privilege and despotism, teaching submission. Against the permanent conspiracy of capitalism and clericalism, Blanqui – who had before 1848 been a deist admirer of primitive Christianity à la Lamennais – became increasingly anticlerical during the Second Empire, culminating in the Third Republic, symbolized by the slogan-title of his last newspaper *Ni Dieu, Ni Maître*. He favoured the confiscation of Church property and the 'expulsion of the whole black army, male and female.'[136] His militant atheism was expressed in crudely aggressive language that became widespread in late-nineteenth-century anticlerical circles. 'The triad of sword – money – holy water sprinkler can only sustain its sovereignty by violence and stupidity. Universal suffrage, its miserable slave, walks to the polls, held by the scruff of its neck by the policeman and the priest, escorted by Capital, kicking it in the behind.'[137] Such sentiments helped Blanqui recruit supporters in the 1860s among the clientele of law and medical students he had acquired thirty years earlier but the most promising, such as Clemenceau, were unwilling to accept the total personal subordination on which Blanqui insisted.[138]

If Blanqui was close to Proudhon in his anticlericalism, he was remote from him in his suspicious attitude towards the trade union and cooperative movements, although he recognized that strikes might be 'pregnant with civil war'.[139] This divergence became clear after Proudhon's death, with the foundation of the First International. Blanqui strongly challenged the standpoint of the more reformist Proudhonians that there was a peaceful, economic road to socialism. Those Blanquists who attended the International's 1866 Geneva Congress despite the master's boycott instructions were expelled. The 'Internationalists' were accused of dressing up Malthusian economics in Proudhonian clothes by denying the need for state intervention. Blanqui argued that 'The State will not remain for ever what it has been up to now, the policeman of the rich against the poor.'[140] When the government denied the French section of the International the right to exist in 1868, Blanqui indulged in the pleasure of 'I told you so' recrimination. Political action could not be replaced by economic action. 'An attempt was made to submerge the citizen in the worker, to make him ignore general matters by getting him absorbed in the sole pursuit of his private interest . . . . Only fools can believe that a people can free itself without bothering with the government, as if the State was not the people in action and as if it could achieve its purpose without involving State action.'[141] Blanqui's attitude was motivated in part by his 'leftist chauvinism'. As Spitzer puts it, 'Blanqui never really belonged to that supranational community of leftist exiles which was such an important element in the radical movements of the nineteenth century.'[142]

As became a man for whom Machiavelli's *Prince* was his bedside book but uncharacteristic among Socialists, Blanqui gave plenty of attention to military matters. He may even be said to have tried in a rudimentary way to advance street fighting techniques in 1868. Blanqui bluntly declared: 'A

Parisian insurrection . . . has no chance of succeeding nowadays.'[143] The last time it had worked was in 1830, because in 1848 the July Monarchy had not seriously defended itself. Governments had now learnt how to win a street fight and had over the insurgents the advantages of weapons and organization. While Blanqui wanted the abolition of a professional army and military training for children from the age of 8, he argued that it would require exceptional organizational skill to make an effective insurrection. This was not to deter him from attempting it after the collapse of the Second Empire.

1871: The Paris Commune and Blanqui's legacy

The Franco-Prussian War seemed to offer Blanqui yet another opportunity for an insurrectionist seizure of power but events again proved his methods ineffective. When, under pressure from his subordinates, he attempted a premature rising on 14 August 1870, in the La Villette working-class area of Paris, he was exposed once again as a general without either an army or popular support. (As he confessed in an article a week later: 'The people seemed dumbfounded.')[144] Blanquist involvement in the 4 September 1870 overthrow of the Second Empire and proclamation of the Republic was marginal and the brief seizure of the town hall and arrest of members of the government on 31 October 1870 was another premature fiasco. Blanqui and several of his disciples had been elected commanders of National Guard battalions, but he quickly lost his command after new elections organized by the government of National Defence to eliminate those who campaigned against its willingness to capitulate to the Prussians. Blanqui was an active member of a revolutionary provisional government for about ten hours before the authorities regained the upper hand and he had to go into hiding. While he had argued that the time was not ripe for a revolution, both in August and October 1870, he reluctantly allowed himself to be thrust into the forefront of an unpropitious fight.[145] The price he paid was that when, on an even larger scale than in June 1848, a worker army in Paris looked for leadership the general was in gaol, arrested the day before the Paris Commune for his part in the October coup.

Blanqui campaigned in his newspaper *La Patrie en Danger*, as he had done in 1848, against elections that would give democratic legitimacy to the bourgeois republican peacemakers. At first he concentrated upon the unifying theme of nationalism. 'Do not forget that tomorrow we are going to fight, not for a government, not for interests of caste or party, not even for honour, principles or ideas, but for what is the life and breath of all, for what constitutes humanity in its most noble form, for country.'[146] However, his appeal to revolutionary patriotism was quickly followed by a rejection of representative assemblies. His attacks upon parliamentary democracy are important because they were subsequently to be influential on the Socialist and labour movements. 'The Estates General signalled a resurrection. The Parliamentary system profited from this glorious ancestry and nearly a century of disappointments have now disillusioned us.'[147] The cowardly and corrupt character of the Second Empire parliaments had not sufficed to dispel the prestige of representative democracy. Blanqui warned: 'France is lost if it falls into the hands of an assembly at this moment. She would survive any disaster but that one.' A parliamentary assembly 'is a bunch of ciphers and egoisms, in which a few verbal artists and the mischievously clever take charge and soon become the shepherds of the flock and masters of everyone.' Blanqui was prepared to concede that in peaceful times 'The people might suffer but would not die as a result. But in stormy and disastrous times, when the country rocks on its foundations, the egoism of all these mediocrities leads to catastrophes. The instinct that dominates is first fear, then interest.'[148]

These views did not prevent Blanqui from standing for the 8 February 1871 election to the National Assembly and campaigning against an armistice. However, he received only 53,839 votes and the minimum to win a seat was 68,200 votes. Despite the promise that he would not be prosecuted for his part in the October 1870 coup, Blanqui was sentenced to death *in absentia* by a military tribunal on 9 March 1871 and arrested in the provinces on 17 March. A day later, the insurrectionary Paris Commune was launched but Blanqui remained throughout totally unaware of the momentous events in Paris and the attempt to exchange him for the Archbishop of Paris and other hostages.[149]

The Paris Commune, both in terms of its leadership and its ideology, was an improvised combination of neo-Jacobinism, Blanquism and Proudhonism. Its protagonists were divided among themselves, with the neo-Jacobins being the least organized and clear in their purpose. The Blanquists were most determined to secure control over the military and police activities of the Commune, while the Proudhonists and Internationalist trade unionists were more influential in the embryonic development of the Commune's politically federalist and associationist economic and social programme. An initial attempt by the Blanquists to suspend democracy and place power in the hands of a committee of public safety was abandoned because of opposition by the Commune assembly. However, once the early optimism dissipated, and once faced with the imminent defeat of a heroic Paris by the weight of provincial France and the bulk of the professional army, the Blanquist tendency to revert to the First Revolution's terrorist methods gained the upper hand. Violence by extremists against the moderates regarded as the treasonable 'enemy within' became the order of the day. The arch-subversive Blanquists became ideologically and practically obsessed with subversion. The execution of political hostages by Raoul Rigault, the dictatorial and fanatical sadist who disgraced the Commune as its prefect of police, was its worst manifestation.

The 'Bloody Week' atrocities as the Commune was in its own death throes at the end of May 1871 were marked by ritual murders, the most symbolic of which was the execution of Proudhon's literary executor Gustave Chaudey, with Rigault in personal command of the firing squad. As assistant to Jules Ferry, mayor of Paris, Chaudey was accused of ordering the troops to fire on a pre-Commune demonstration. Although 'Chaudey appeared to many Communards a committed republican, a man of courage and integrity, who had accepted heavy responsibilities during the siege and given clear evidence of loyalty to the Commune', for Rigault Chaudey 'personified his fears and hatreds of Girondin treachery.'[150] This obsessive, repressive and sanguinary end of the Commune was followed by a much more massive and bloody counter-revolutionary slaughter of neo-Jacobins, Proudhonians, Blanquists and many wholly innocent people caught up in the indiscriminate repression. As far as Blanqui is concerned, Spitzer has rightly stressed that 'the Commune represented the actual consummation of his political ideas – that is, the seizure of Paris by a militarized organization of the armed workers led by the left-wing of the radical movement – and that this "success" was, in fact, the occasion of a decisive and bloody defeat of French radicalism.'[151] Despite its many subsequent vicissitudes (to which we shall return in the final chapter) and the 'events' of May 1968, parliamentary democracy was never again seriously threatened by revolutionary Communist insurrection in France.

Tried in February 1872, Blanqui was at 67 sentenced to another term of life imprisonment. In 1861 he had written with dignified pathos at the start of a four-year sentence: 'I do not wish to return to the night without speaking my mind. I have fought all my life for justice and right against iniquity and privilege, for oppressed majorities against an oppressive minority. I have lived poor and captive, I shall die poor and captive.'[152] Just as the Marxists had retrospectively, in an act of grave-robbing, taken over the Commune – Engels declared 'the Commune was the grave of the Proudhon school of socialism' – so his leading French disciple Jules Guesde used the campaign to amnesty the Communards in general and its incarcerated symbol, Blanqui, to promote Marxist dominance of the Socialist and labour movements in France. The Guesdist kind of historical determinism 'rendered the revolutionary tradition and Blanqui innocuous.'[153] Although ineligible, Blanqui's candidacy was presented at several by-elections where he lost, then in Bordeaux in 1879 when he was elected on the second ballot. He had received the support of old opponents like Louis Blanc and young sympathizers like Georges Clemenceau. Although invalidated, he was pardoned. Ironically, despite his distrust of the mass electorate, Blanqui owed his freedom to a popular vote. Perhaps this was an indication that the Revolution was at last ending! However, the voters were more interested in his emancipation than being represented by him. He narrowly lost the new Bordeaux by-election and lost again when he stood in Lyons in 1880.[154] The old insurrectionist died on 1 January 1881, at age 76. The number attending his funeral has been variously estimated as 20,000 to 200,000. Absent during his life, the masses were present at his death. He is symbolically buried in the *Père-Lachaise* cemetery, by the wall against which the last Communards were shot *en masse*.

Blanqui's legacy was surprisingly diverse, appealing not only to the politically activist Communist Left but also to revolutionary syndicalism, giving Proudhonian *ouvrierisme* a violent emphasis among its extremist adherents. Through its involvement with Boulangism in the late 1880s, it contributed to the emergence of a populist–nationalist anticipation of Fascism, Mussolini using Blanqui's slogan 'He who has iron has bread' on the masthead of *Il Popolo d'Italia* in 1915. However, its main influence was upon Bolshevism. The Blanquist movement as such spent its declining energies in 'sustaining revolutionary fervour in the absence of revolutionary situations.'[155] This took the form of a cult of the Commune as the nostalgic celebration of a revolutionary tradition devoted to looking for revolutionary situations to exploit at a time when the Third Republic was offering peaceful ways of advancing the Socialist cause through both political and industrial action. Instead of subversive activities that doomed its proponents to impotent opposition, the new radicalism was represented by a Clemenceau, so it is interesting to touch upon Blanqui's attempt to make this future war prime minister of France his revolutionary successor as the heroic leader of the parliamentary Left.

After his early 1860s links with Blanqui and his role as mayor of Montmartre in securing Blanqui command of the Montmartre battalion of the National Guard in 1870, Clemenceau displeased both the Right and the Left because of his middle-of-the-road stance during the Commune. While refusing to challenge the authority of the elected parliament and government, he sought to mediate between them and the Commune, because he supported continuing the war against Prussia. He paid a high price for this stand. The opportunist republicans regarded him as 'unsound' and kept him out of office for decades, while he was not forgiven for 'deserting' the Commune and so failed to rally sufficient Paris working-class voters to his radical republicanism. Just before his release from prison in 1879, Blanqui wrote to Clemenceau saying that they must keep their friendship quiet for fear of the political harm it would do his career. He looked to him as the only heroic leader of the extreme Left. 'You alone can deliver blows, you alone are formidable. That is all I have taken notice of for the whole of my life. . . .Become leader of the Left. . . .Become in parliament the man of the future, the leader of the Revolution. It has not been able to find one in 1830 or since.'[156] This pathetic appeal from the old revolutionary, with its characteristic recall of 1830, was too backward-looking to perpetuate Blanquism. Its future lay as a component of the Socialist Party in 1905 and the Communist Party of 1920. If not Clemenceau, was the residuary legatee Vaillant, as many have claimed?

Edouard Vaillant had been a Proudhonian 'Internationalist' before and during the Commune. He never gave up his commitment to workers demonstrating their political and economic capacity through the trade union and cooperative movements. Vaillant flirted with Blanquism and Marxism in the 1870s and 1880s but he was above all the champion of an eclectic socialism that sought to combine the analytical insights of Marxism, the self-managing *ouvrierisme* of Proudhon and the revolutionary activism of Blanqui. The 1874 Blanquist manifesto of the Revolutionary Commune, written by Vaillant, was committed to atheism, communism and the revolutionary dictatorship of the proletariat 'because the Commune is the revolutionary proletariat armed by dictatorship to abolish privileges and crush the bourgeoisie.'[157] However, in the 1880s, old-style Blanquism reacted to the advent of mass politics by embracing the anti-parliamentary authoritarianism of General Boulanger, before degenerating under Henri Rochefort in the 1890s into a nationalist socialism and anti-Semitic racism that heralded Fascism.

Vaillant rejected the Blanquist label, declaring the movement in 1890 to be dead and buried. Vaillant's Revolutionary Socialist Party climbed to a membership of 35,000 in 1895, electing four candidates to the Chamber of Deputies in 1893 and seven in 1898.[158] The old guard deplored socialism having taken the parliamentary road. Da Costa declared: 'brought up in Blanqui's school, having struggled for years with his friends, we continue – with him and them – to think that a thousand revolutionaries well organized for action will always be necessary to triumph over the indecision of hundreds of thousands of demonstrators and lead them.'[159] Vaillant rejected in advance this refrain of Leftist revolutionaries in France up to and including the *Action Directe* terrorists of the 1980s. Having got rid of those who deserted to Boulangism, 'we have never adopted the label "Blanquists" applied to us. However great our respect for the memory of Blanqui and all the heroes of thought and Revolution, we do not intend to wear their moral or intellectual livery, nor submit to their example, because our task is to continue their work and not repeat it.'[160] Vaillant pursued Socialist unity of the trade union and party movements – achieved in the first decade of the twentieth century – by an eclectic appeal for *both* electoral *and* industrial action. He referred imprecisely from 1892 to the 'impersonal dictatorship . . . of the socialist proletariat',[161] words that were used at the 1920 Tours congress split of the Socialist Party he had helped to unite by Léon Blum in resisting the Leninist line championed by the founders of the French Communist Party.

We mentioned earlier that Marx had a non-determinist, Blanquist phase, stressing revolutionary will and activism, that culminated with the publication of his 'Letter to the Central Committee of the Communist League'. Bertram Wolfe has argued that because the call for revolutionary dictatorship was never repudiated, 'The *Circular* of March 1850 lay like an undetonated bomb on the Marxian road, an explosive manual of Leninist strategy and tactics, to be joyously dug up by Lenin in the following century.'[162] Thereafter, the Social Democratic Marxist view – reflected notably in the 'revisionist' work of Edouard Bernstein, whom Engels appointed the executor of his will – was that as against Blanquism, which regarded democracy as a repressive force on the model of the Jacobin Terror, 'Democracy is in principle the suppression of class government, though it is not yet the actual suppression of classes.' Against the revolutionary dictatorship envisaged by the mid-century *Communist Manifesto*, Bernstein argued that by the end of the nineteenth century dictatorship of the proletariat was an 'antiquated' idea, 'to be looked upon as a reversion, as political atavism.'[163] While such reformist gradualism might seem appropriate from 1889 to the Second International in the advanced industrial societies of Western Europe, through a reconciliation of Marx and Proudhon in industrial democracy from below, elsewhere the insurrectionary road to communism was still available. As Engels wrote presciently if prematurely to the Russian Socialist Vera Zasulich in 1885: 'The Russians are approaching their 1789. The revolution *must* break out there in a given time; it *may* break out there any day . . . . This is one of the exceptional cases where it is possible for a handful of people to *make* a revolution . . . . Well now, if ever Blanquism – the phantasy of overturning an entire society through the action of a small conspiracy – had a certain justification for its existence, that is certainly in Petersburg.'[164] In anticipation of the October Revolution succeeding the

February Revolution in 1917 Russia, Engels added: 'When 1789 has once been launched, 1793 will not be long in following.'[165]

The link between Blanqui and Lenin is provided by Peter Tkachev, a leading ideologist of Russian Jacobinism who joined the Blanquist movement as an exile and was prevented only by ill health from delivering a funeral oration at Blanqui's burial, although it was subsequently published. Tkachev followed the classic Blanquist path of student conspiracy, leading to a clandestine lifetime with its catalogue of prison and exile in the 1860s and 1870s. Preoccupied with the organizational techniques of conspiracy, he envisaged a peasant revolution led by a committed minority of disciplined intellectuals. Rejecting the federalist anarchism of Proudhon and Bakunin, Tkachev stressed that 'any organization is always authoritarian', so that revolution must 'turn once again to the old centralized organization.'[166] Although Lenin was to repudiate the attempt to link Bolshevism with Blanquism, their affinity has been pointed out by critics from both the Left and the Right.

In the key Bolshevik text *What is to be Done?* (1902), Lenin rejected the type of historicist fatalism which was represented by Bernstein's *Evolutionary Socialism*. In words that recall Blanquist theory and practice, Lenin declared: 'We must have a committee of professional *revolutionaries*', with students pushing the workers forward from 'outside'. 'We can never give a mass organization that degree of secrecy without which there can be no question of persistent and continuous struggle against the government.' He denied that this undemocratic concentration of power in the hands of 'as small a number of professional revolutionaries as possible', as well trained as their secret police opponents, meant rejecting mass involvement. 'Centralization of the most secret functions in an organization of revolutionaries will not diminish, but rather increase the extent and enhance the quality of the activity of a large number of other organizations that are intended for a broad public and therefore are loose and as nonsecret as possible, such as workers' trade unions.'[167] So, while going beyond Blanquism in not confining the revolutionary struggle to conspiracy, Lenin was certainly committed to the conspiratorial leadership of revolutionary activity and extremely scornful of 'infantile playing at "democratic" forms' in Russian conditions.[168] Lenin also went beyond Blanquism by his development of a centralized and dictatorial new-style *party* that was to be led by a new category of *déclassé* revolutionary intellectuals, masquerading as the dictatorship of the proletariat. As Wolfe has put it: 'The vanguard's doctrine was the doctrine of the proletariat by definition. And its organization was the "highest form" of the working class by definition. By definition, too, it was the officers' corps and general staff of the future revolutionary armies of the working class and all other classes.'[169]

Lenin developed a spurious fusion of Marxism and Blanquism by the reductionist redefinition of the people identified with the proletariat, the proletariat with the Communist Party, the Communist Party with its apparatus and the party apparatus with its leadership. The dangers implicit in this were quickly perceived by Trotsky, who argued against Lenin's standpoint in 1904. 'In the internal politics of the party, these methods lead, as we shall yet see, to this: the party organization is substituted for the party, the Central Committee is substituted for the party organization, and finally a "dictator" is substituted for the Central Committee', adding that 'a proletariat capable of dictatorship over society will not tolerate dictatorship over itself.'[170] Wolfe argues that Lenin's fascination with the techniques and organization of insurrection reflected 'his natural extremism, his obsessive concentration on power, his Jacobinism, his greater kinship with such Russians as Tkachev, Nechaev, Bakunin. . .than with West European socialists, his Blanquism, his inclination to vanguardism, terror and dictatorship.'[171] Neither Lenin nor his successors were ever able to explain how the proletariat could exercise dictatorship, yet this was precisely what was supposed to distinguish a Marxist–Leninist class dictatorship from an élitist Jacobin–Blanquist dictatorship. They could not explain the distinction because in practice there was little difference. In this sense, 'Blanqui stands midway between Babeuf and Lenin',[172] which accounts for the revival of interest in Blanqui after the Bolshevik Revolution.

In her 1904 essay 'Leninism or Marxism', Rosa Luxemburg produced the most devastating analysis of the 'conspiratorial centralism' and 'military ultra-centralism' that identified Lenin with Blanqui. She argued that 'The two principles on which Lenin's centralism rests are precisely these: 1. The blind subordination, in the smallest detail, of all party organs to the party center, which alone thinks, guides, and decides for all. 2. The rigorous separation of the organized nucleus of revolutionaries from its social-revolutionary surroundings. Such centralism is a mechanical transposition of the organizational principles of Blanquism into the mass movement of the socialist working class.'[173] Political liberty was essential for the workers to develop the capacity to take over and Lenin proposed to dispense with this precondition of social democracy. 'We practice self-deception when we apply the same term – discipline – to such dissimilar notions . . . . What is there in common between the regulated docility of an oppressed class and the self-discipline and organization of a class struggling for its emancipation? . . . It is a mistake to believe that it is possible to substitute "provisionally" the absolute power of a Central Committee (acting somehow by "tacit delegation") for the yet unrealizable rule of the majority of conscious workers in the party, and in this way replace the open control of the working masses over the party organs with the reverse control by the Central Committee over the revolutionary proletariat.'[174] She explained Lenin's approach by the Blanquist conditions prevailing in early-twentieth-century Russia, in which the 'rigorous despotic centralism that is preferred by opportunist intellectuals' seeks to make up by force exercised by a *déclassé* élite – the 'omniscient and omnicompetent Central Committee' – for the immaturity of the proletariat.[175]

In 1917, what had been a theoretical debate became an urgent matter of practical revolutionary tactics. In his essays 'On dual power' and 'Marxism and insurrection', Lenin sought to distance himself from the accusation of Blanquism. 'In order to become a power the class-conscious workers must win the majority to their side. *As long as* no violence is used against the workers [that came later] there is no other road to power. We are not Blanquists, we do not stand for the seizure of power by a minority.'[176] Writing on 'The Russian Revolution' in her German prison, Rosa Luxemburg in 1918 attacked the abandonment of representative democracy because mass participation was the indispensable counterpart of genuine proletarian dictatorship. 'The tacit assumption underlying the Lenin–Trotsky theory of the dictatorship is this: the socialist transformation is something for which a ready-made formula lies completed in the pocket of the revolutionary party, which needs only to be carried out energetically in practice. . . .Socialism by its very nature cannot be decreed or introduced by *ukase*. . . .The negative, the tearing down, can be decreed; the building up, the positive, cannot.'[177] Without democracy, dictatorship would lead to 'the rule of the Jacobins', so what was required was not the abandonment of democracy but socialist democracy: 'a dictatorship of the *class*, not of a party or a clique – dictatorship of the class, that means in the broadest public form on the basis of the most active, unlimited participation of the mass of the people, of unlimited democracy.'[178] Luxemburg's attempt to correct Lenin's Blanquist distortion of Marxism, by arguing that proletarian 'dictatorship consists in the *manner of applying democracy*, not in its *elimination*',[179] was to be adopted in 1920 by Léon Blum in his resistance to the Leninization of the French Socialist Party.

In his youth, Blum had belonged to Vaillant's Revolutionary Socialist Party, so he was well aware of Blanquist ideas. When the Socialists were confronted at the Tours congress with the Twenty One Conditions for membership of the Comintern, Blum stigmatized the replacement of a mass party controlled from below by 'disciplined homogeneous advance guards, subject to a rigorous command structure' amounting to 'a sort of secret society, a grand Carbonarism' of a hundred years ago.[180] He traced Lenin's Bolshevism to 'the old Blanquist doctrine because the link is certain. . . .This tactic of the unconscious masses, led unawares by advance guards, the conquest of power by a surprise *coup de force*, my friends and I cannot and never will accept.'[181] Mussolini had already demonstrated that the masses could be mobilized in support of Fascism as well as communism.

Blum went on to explain how Socialist and Communist conceptions of party dictatorship differed decisively. 'We have always considered in France that, after the revolutionary crisis, the dictatorship of the proletariat would be exercised by groups of the Socialist Party itself, becoming thanks to a *fiction which we all accept*, the representative of the whole proletariat. The divergence as I have said lies in our differences on the conception of revolution and its organization. Party dictatorship, yes but a party organized like ours, not like yours. Dictatorship exercised by a party based upon popular will and liberty, consequently the *impersonal dictatorship of the proletariat*. Not dictatorship exercised by a centralized party, where all authority rises hierarchically to be concentrated in the hands of an open or occult Committee. Party dictatorship, yes, class dictatorship, yes, but no to the dictatorship of a few known or unknown individuals.'[182] Blum concluded that far from being temporary, Bolshevik dictatorship would have to be permanent because it was not the product of a mature capitalist society. It would persist indefinitely, so that unlike Blanquism, 'you conceive terrorism not as a last resort, not as an extreme measure imposed upon bourgeois resistance, not because it is vital to the Revolution, but as a regular means of government.'[183] Blum lost the vote, although historically in the light of the subsequent Communist record of the Soviet Union and Eastern Europe, he clearly won the argument.

In a chapter on 'The art of insurrection' in his *History of the Russian Revolution*, Trotsky lends credence to Blum's analysis. He presents a favourable view of Blanqui, arguing that he was a revolutionary realist in regarding conspiracy by an élite minority as the necessary preparation for mass insurrection. 'An active minority of the proletariat, no matter how well organized, cannot seize power regardless of the general conditions of the country. In this point history has condemned Blanquism. But only in this. His affirmative theorem retains all its force. In order to conquer power, the proletariat needs more than spontaneous insurrection. It needs a suitable organization, it needs a plan; it needs a conspiracy. Such is the Leninist view of this question.'[184]

Even if, as Trotsky suggests, Blanquism is the 'revolutionary essence of Marxism'[185] as conceived by Lenin, revolutionaries seldom if ever bring about revolutions, although they may take advantage of revolutionary situations created by forces beyond their control. The time for insurrection has long since passed in France. The French Communist Party, despite its revolutionary posturing, seems incapable of breaking out of the dead-end in which its Leninism has confined it. The Soviet Union's prolonged pretence has itself disintegrated. Instead of dismantling the repressive Russian state, the Bolshevik Party reinforced it. Lenin's historic role, in retrospect, would seem to have been to 'stall' Communist societies in a pre-capitalist stage of development. The power of the party bureaucracy postponed for decades the advent of liberal democracy and of nationalism, though it has proved incapable of indefinitely forestalling them. In France, liberal democracy and nationalism were too well entrenched for the Communist Party to dislodge them.

CHAPTER NINE

IS THE REVOLUTION OVER?

Until the shaky advent of the Third Republic in the 1870s, authors and protagonists of a succession of ephemeral constitutions and governments triumphantly proclaimed that they had arrested the Revolution, only to see their ambitious claims and institutional artefacts collapse in ruins. As France lurched from one improvised stability formula to another, its more lucid observers ceased to engage in such speculation. Prévost-Paradol, a link between Constant, Tocqueville and the architects of the constitutional compromises of the Third Republic, accurately reflected this scepticism. He observed in 1861 that it was illusory to believe the revolutionary process to have 'ended every time it comes to a stop . . . . Where it is going, what it seeks, what effect it will have on the world which it first stirs into violent agitation and then allows to subside, no one knows. Only false prophets predict the answers with confidence.'[1] So, a century later, when asked for his views on the French Revolution, Chou En-Lai was to reply circumspectly that it was too early to judge.

Those in search of a way to stabilize and liberalize the democratic impetus looked to Britain as a model. However, in his anonymous 'Letters on the French *Coup d'Etat* of 1851' Bagehot offered an analysis, based upon national character and culture, of why France was not yet fit for parliamentary government. Lacking the English disposition to humdrum consensus based upon stolidity – what he chose provocatively to dub 'stupidity' – the French addiction to novelty required a strong 'anti-barricade executive' to repress revolutionary upsurges. Despite 'the uncompact, unpractical, over-volatile, over-logical, indecisive, ineffective rule of Gallican Parliaments', Bagehot expressed 'the hope that it may in the end be found possible to admit into a "French" political system a representative and sufficiently democratic Assembly, without that Assembly assuming and arrogating to itself those nearly omnipotent powers, which in our country it properly and rightfully possesses, but which in the history of the last sixty years, we have, as it seems to me, so many and cogent illustrations that a French Chamber is, by genius and constitution, radically incapable to hold and exercise.'[2] It was to take over a century before France was able to overcome this handicap of seeking to convert a formal parliamentary sovereignty into an actual government by assembly.

In the introduction to an 1872 edition of *The English Constitution*, Bagehot returned to his pessimistic assessment of French parliamentarianism. 'Since 1789 France has always been trying political experiments from which others may profit much, though as yet she herself has profited little. She is now trying one singularly illustrative of the English Constitution.' Describing the 1872 Assembly, which Thiers was attempting to manage as head of the executive, as an 'unstable, capricious, and unruly' sovereign, Bagehot went on: 'The experiment of a strictly Parliamentary Republic – of a Republic where the Parliament appoints the Executive – is being tried in France at an extreme disadvantage, because in France a Parliament is unusually likely to be bad, and unusually likely also to be free to show its badness.' Without popular support for the parliamentary system and subdivided into uncompromisingly hostile parties, Thiers alone was able to hold the government together and Bagehot predicted: 'He is the exception of a moment; he is not the example of a lasting condition.'[3] (At the dawn of the Fifth Republic, similar statements were often made about de Gaulle.) Returning to the attack in 1874, Bagehot declared that France was 'not yet fit for a representative Government', being torn between 'two simultaneous, but contrary excitements; one of the revolutionist, who wants to revive the *Commune*; the other of the peasant or the shopkeeper, who fears the Commune .... There is no soil so unsuitable to Parliamentary Government.'[4] Without going into Bagehot's idiosyncratic and dated cultural stereotypes, it will be our task to show how these sweeping judgements by an acute observer contained much immediate truth and ultimate error. They nevertheless help to explain why it took another century before France was able to reconstitute a stable democratic system, based upon a strong president directly elected by the people.

It is instructive to turn from Bagehot's psychology-based stress on political culture to Hoffmann's history-based emphasis on a socio-cultural explanation of the working of the French political community. A hundred years after Bagehot, when France was establishing the enduring democratic system of the Fifth Republic, Hoffmann focused attention upon Third Republic France as a stalemate society. Resting upon a backward economy and guided by a peculiar style of authority combining an aspiration after and fear of strong government, the Third Republic epitomized the problems France had to surmount to become an effective modern democracy. This took the form of purchasing post-revolutionary stability at the cost of stagnation by limiting state intervention to preservation of the existing socio-economic equilibrium. Rather than Bagehot's picture of turmoil, Hoffmann dwelt upon the protection of the status quo. The fear of executive domination meant confiding government to a non-interventionist bureaucracy, not of the modernizing Saint-Simonian variety but nearer to that envisaged by the liberal Tocqueville. Parliament's function was close to Constant's conception – protecting the citizen's liberty from arbitrary interference by government. 'Parliament was supreme but immobile . . . the risks for the social and political stability of France which many had seen in universal suffrage and in the representation of all opinions were minimized' because a sovereign parliament was protected from populist pressures.[5] We shall return to Hoffmann's analysis when we examine the twentieth-century disintegration of the 'republican synthesis'. First, we must consider the way in which threats from both hyper-revolutionaries and counter-revolutionaries were repelled and an anti-populist, parliamentary regime that excluded its extremist enemies to the Left and Right was built and justified. This achievement necessitated immense political skill as well as reliance upon the early-nineteenth-century liberal critique of democracy.

While it is habitual to refer to 'Two Frances', such as the Right and Left, monarchist and republican, clerical and anticlerical, bourgeois and proletarian, in 1871 the protagonists of the 'republican synthesis' had initially to fight on two fronts. Symbolically, only after the *tricolore* had defeated the Red Flag could it see off the claims of the White Flag. It was only by crushing the revolutionary *Commune* that the parliamentary republicans were able to round on the counter-revolutionary advocates of monarchy and clericalism. 'The moderate republicans became *all* the Republic, because the other [Republic] was imprisoned or in a cemetary.'[6] The apparent elimination of the revolutionaries allowed the reformist republicans to take over and defend the revolutionary legacy from its reactionary enemies. This has led historians in Britain and France to dismiss the Commune as 'The Last Revolution' or to claim that with its defeat 'the French Revolution bids farewell to history' and 'the workers' movements went into exile within French democracy.'[7] Such assertions are much too simple, as is the companion view that France handed the revolutionary torch to Lenin, the Bolsheviks and the Soviet Union, which in any case has discarded its claims in this respect. The provisional triumph of a new republican synthesis, which seems in some senses to spell the exhaustion of the revolutionary impetus in France, had to await the marginalization of the Communist Party first by Gaullism and then by socialism, culminating in the constitutional consensus of the 1980s. Even the *Front National* re-emergence of the extreme Right challenges some of the 1789 humanistic values but not (formally) its democratic institution. To explain why France appears to have retrieved and adapted the centrist republicanism of its heroic, late-nineteenth-century expression (helped by the extrusion of communism and the absorption of institutional Gaullism) we must reconsider that foundation period of French republicanism.

Thiers and the taming of the French Revolution

In his seventies, Thiers ended his active political life as a constitutional monarchist by establishing a conservative republic. He hoped thereby to halt the revolutionary process to whose history he had contributed a widely read liberal interpretation in ten volumes by the age of 30. Furet has written of Thiers: 'His life was engaged in every twist of the nineteenth century French political crisis; it was involved in every turn and tried to direct several of them . . . . Starting out in favour of the Revolution, he followed and betrayed the cause according to circumstances, to preserve the possibility of a free and conservative, a parliamentary and bourgeois government.' Because, 'in a century during which the French Revolution continued to wear everyone out, [he] finished by wearing out the Revolution', Thiers was in Furet's opinion 'the greatest French statesman of the nineteenth century'; he had 'tamed the French Revolution.'[8] This is a doubly provocative claim. It presupposes, as Furet has sometimes asserted, that the Revolution was completed by the end of the 1870s. It also selects one of the most despised and hated of French politicians for this encomium. He was described by Cavaignac (the republican presidential candidate in 1848) as a 'Talleyrand bourgeois' (Talleyrand had been Thiers' mentor), while Bagehot called him 'an adroit and dexterous intriguer'.[9] Although politically close to Thiers during the July Monarchy, Tocqueville wrote to a friend that 'M. Thiers will always symbolise and personify for the country insincerity and intrigue in political matters.'[10] On the Left, he was particularly execrated for his ruthless repression in 1834 of the Lyons and Paris worker uprisings and even more sanguinary summary mass executions at the end of the Paris Commune.[11] So how did such a detested politician earn in retrospect the title of consummate statesman?

Part of the answer is that his anti-worker repression of 1834 was preceded by anti-royalist repression in 1832, inaugurating the fight on two fronts that he was to resume in 1871. A leading representative of the self-made men of the middle classes that would dominate the Third Republic, Thiers disdained both his social inferiors and social superiors, proudly describing himself as a *petit bourgeois*. This is reflected in his remark that 'to show that he could make something still more stupid than democrats, God had created aristocrats and then rested, realizing that he could go no further.'[12] Having worked against and sometimes for almost every political party, Thiers is remembered above all for a partially quoted phrase that he first used at the time of the Second Republic, though it was to become really apposite in helping the gestation of the Third Republic. (He did so in a parliamentary speech on the 1850 Falloux Law promoting Church schools, personally inspired by Thiers' perception of the need to utilize the priests to quell social unrest at source. This is ironic, as his republican allies in the 1870s were ardent secularists, who would reverse the clericalism of the 1850s.) Thiers declared: 'Rest assured that, although I neither sought nor helped bring about the Republic, I am not its enemy today. In my eyes it has a virtue: *of all forms of government it is the one that divides us least.*'[13] Talleyrand had said to the receptive Thiers in 1829 that he had brought the Bourbons back in 1814 to secure European peace but he now believed that they should be expelled in the interests of France's domestic peace. Thiers played a key role in replacing Charles X by Louis-Philippe in 1830 and assisted Louis-Napoleon to become president of the Second Republic in 1848 in the belief that he could easily be manipulated, recalling Sieyès' illusion about his uncle in 1799. However, he had come to realize that the Republic was the best constitutional shelter for a conservative regime in which the successful bourgeoisie could rule the roost. He bluntly told its left-wing protagonists in 1850 that the Republic would survive only if the republicans did not govern.[14] This was precisely what would happen in the 1870s, when the Third Republic's institutions were designed by constitutional monarchists. In then blocking the return of the Bourbons, Thiers was continuing to play the part of a latter-day Talleyrand.[15]

In 1871 Thiers was enormously assisted by the suicidal intransigence of both the ultra-monarchist Comte de Chambord and the ultra-republican Communards, as well as the astute moderation of the law-and-order republicans led by Gambetta. Thiers had to resolve a problem which he posed in similar terms to those we have already encountered in Bagehot. Writing in mid-1850, Thiers argued that 'in France kings cannot make concessions and the people cannot be patient. Consequently, the régime that suits England so well appears in France only to demonstrate its impossibility.'[16] His 1830s failure to persuade Louis-Philippe that 'the king reigns but does not rule' and his 1850 belief that 'real Republicans fear the mob, the vile mob that has . . . delivered over to every tyrant the liberty of every Republic'[17] meant that it was necessary to try to achieve the impossible: establish a republican hybrid variant of British-style parliamentary government in France. This could not be achieved by a doctrinaire resistance against democracy in the Guizot manner but by grasping that parliamentary democracy would provide, under proper presidential guidance, the best antidote to both authoritarianism and anarchism. Circumstances in the shape of France's military defeat by Prussia and the collapse of the Second Empire were to give Thiers his opportunity.

The National Defence government of 1870 has been described by a constitutional historian as the most 'abnormal' of all French political regimes. Installed in the Paris town hall and essentially made up of Paris deputies – including Gambetta and Ferry but not Thiers, who refused to join – it was an 'improvised dictatorship' which was transformed by the February 1871 election of the National Assembly into a single-chamber 'parliamentary dictatorship'.[18] Elected simultaneously by a virtual plebiscite in the twenty-six constituencies (multiple candidacies were then allowed), Thiers was chosen as chief executive by an overwhelmingly monarchist Assembly majority in the mistaken belief that he would restore monarchy. The interim regime was 'semi-parliamentary' only in that dictatorial power was divided between the Assembly and its chief executive. Thiers' victory over the Commune and indispensability in organizing the payment of indemnities to the Prussian occupant to secure its evacuation ensured his initial dominance. He persuaded the monarchist Assembly to designate him president of the Republic on 31 August 1871 by 533 votes to 68 and mocked Chambord (who on 5 July 1871 had declared that the White Flag of the Old Regime would fly over his tomb) as 'the true founder of the Republic'.[19]

Thiers mobilized the moderate republicans and some of the constitutional monarchists around a centrist, stalemate society programme that temporarily split the Orleanist Right-Centre, reassuringly proclaiming in the Assembly on 13 November 1872: 'The Republic will either be conservative or it will cease to exist.' However, the Centre itself split in May 1873 and in his last-ditch speech as chief executive Thiers prophesied that 'The Republic, natural government of democracy, will be, in time, the final form of government in our country.'[20] Thiers died in the midst of the 1877 constitutional crisis that was to fix the stalemate republican synthesis in place until the Second World War. Unlike de Gaulle, who was also unable to use ephemeral post-war unanimity to establish the institutions of the second republican synthesis at his first Fourth Republic attempt in 1945, Thiers did not have a second chance to amalgamate the revolutionary and Napoleonic styles of authority. His successors failed to create the strong and stable executive that would have to await de Gaulle's second advent.

In fact, Thiers and the constitution makers of the 1870s were more concerned to return to the early-nineteenth-century parliamentary regime, particularly in its 1830 version as embodied in the constitutional charter of the July Monarchy, than as to whether they were creating a monarchy or a republic. In this they were close in spirit to Constant and Madame de Staël, who had argued in 1800 that when forced to choose between a moderate republic and an absolute monarchy, the former was clearly to be preferred.[21] Their aristocratic grandson, Duke Albert de Broglie, was much more conservative than liberal because unlike them he was a liberal Catholic in the Montalembert tradition, not a liberal Protestant. A disciple of Tocqueville, Broglie did not so much reject republicanism as regard it, on the basis of past experience, as inappropriate to French conditions.[22] Even more did he reject Thiers' attempt in 1873 to establish a republic with a strong president, responsible to Parliament, although ironically he was by 1877 to champion Thiers' successor, MacMahon, in his struggle with a Chamber of Deputies now controlled by the republicans. However, while Broglie and the Orleanist Right-Centre were able to replace Thiers by MacMahon in 1873, they were unable to restore the monarchy because Chambord refused their constitutional conditions. By supporting MacMahon in 1877 against the Chamber of Deputies, they provoked a reaction which converted their would-be parliamentary regime into a government by Assembly, curbed only by the Senate.[23]

Broglie did bequeath one long-lived institutional legacy to the future Republic: the seven-year presidency. Against the extreme Left who wanted to abolish the office, and Thiers who wished to make the president responsible to parliament, Broglie did not simply establish a transitional arrangement pending a problematic monarchical restoration. He created what Chateaubriand had called a republican monarch who could play the role of arbiter head of state as envisaged by Broglie's grandfather, Benjamin Constant. Although a ten-year term was considered, in November 1873 a seven-year presidency was deliberately adopted to exceed the five-year term of the deputies. There followed over a year's hesitation before the monarchist Assembly, under increasing public pressure thanks particularly to Gambetta's tireless campaign of speeches throughout the country, unenthusiastically accepted that a historic compromise was inevitable.

Matters came to a head at the end of January 1875. Laboulaye, despite an eloquent invocation of Constant in support of the affinity between constitutional monarchy and a liberal republic, failed to secure acceptance for the Republic on 19 January by 359 votes to 336. It was a low-key proposal on the following day by Wallon (a friend of Broglie from the Right-Centre) to end the provisional political system by formally declaring that 'The President of the Republic is elected for seven years' that was carried by a single vote margin of 353 to 352. His argument that the Republic was already France's *de facto* regime and that no better alternative was available won enough votes from the Right-Centre to tip the scales.[24]

Of the remaining 'constitutional laws' (without any declaration of rights preamble) that settled the institutions of the Third Republic, the most important was the creation in February 1875 of a Senate, intended as a conservative bulwark against the radical propensities of the Chamber of Deputies. Having reluctantly accepted a president, the Left had now to swallow a Senate. Broglie, who hoped that the Senate would be a Grand Council of Notables, had to settle for what Gambetta called the 'Grand Council of French Communes', though he was consoled that the Senate would still act as a check on universal suffrage. The Assembly overwhelmingly (by 476 votes to 30) refused to adopt the principle of popular sovereignty and on 25 February 1875, anniversary of the euphoric proclamation of the Second Republic, the Third Republic's constitutional laws were unenthusiastically enacted. Thanks to Gambetta's tactical adroitness and vision, the republican Left was willing, as Chambord was not, to abandon 'the convictions of a lifetime' as the price of securing a favourable constitutional settlement.[25] They were rewarded in 1876 by a sweeping electoral victory, the republicans exceeding the monarchists and Bonapartists combined by more than two to one in the new Chamber.

The appearance of constitutional consensus, which the moderate premier Jules Simon sought to preserve, vanished in the unrelenting conflict between President-Marshal MacMahon and the new republican majority that followed the dissolution of the Chamber of Deputies on 17 May 1877. Prompted by what Daniel Halévy has called a 'senile conspiracy' in which Bishop Dupanloup played a leading role,[26] MacMahon selected Broglie to head a government (in which almost all the ministers were senators) to stem the anti-monarchist and anticlerical tide. The attempt to assert presidential authority was in fact to emasculate it and destroy the delicate balance of power between executive and legislature. The arbitrament of universal suffrage, following an especially vitriolic campaign (in which Thiers played a prominent part, although his death prevented him becoming president), produced a reduced but clear majority of 317 republicans against 199 for MacMahon's paper *coup d'état*.[27] When Grévy replaced MacMahon in January 1879, following the republican conquest of a Senate majority, what Ferry feared and predicted during the electoral campaign came about. He warned that by making the issue a 'popular, plebiscitary, impassioned and revolutionary one' the Right were gambling with the fate not merely of the presidency but of constitutional liberty and the country. 'After new elections, there will only be a single power in the Republic: the one which has received the most recent, precise, disputed and consequently powerful investiture by the national will. Thereafter, the balanced and constitutional Republic will give way, whatever one says or does, to the Convention Republic' or as we would say government by assembly.[28]

The new head of state had in 1848 proposed not having a president of the Republic at all. 'For Jules Grévy, to govern was to abstain and he was not alone in thinking this . . . being supported by a whole generation of republicans, fashioned during the Empire and in reaction against its excesses, who sincerely believed that to be a liberal meant governing as little as possible.'[29] To avoid the abuse of presidential power meant having a restrained president who would be chosen by parliament and not challenge its claim to be the sole legitimate authority to speak in the name of the people.

There quickly followed a series of symbolic acts. First, Parliament returned from Versailles to Paris, by decision of both Chambers, reuniting it with the capital, followed in 1880 by an amnesty of the Communards. Thereafter, it was accepted as a convention that constitutional revision would require the agreement of the Senate as well as the Chamber of Deputies.[30] Second, the *Marseillaise* was formally made the French national anthem; and third, Bastille Day, 14 July, was chosen from among eleven alternatives to commemorate the Revolution as an annual national holiday.[31] The symbolic culmination of what some then and since have seen as the triumphant end of the Revolution was the 14 July 1880 celebration in Paris of the fall of the Bastille by French troops, with the public applauding the sight of the *tricolore* and the sound of the *Marseillaise*. That this anthem was composed by an army officer in 1792, who was only liberated from a Jacobin prison by Thermidor,[32] makes its revival all the more appropriate to symbolize the triumph of the conservative Republic.

Yet we shall not endorse François Furet's claim that these symbolic acts of 1879–80 establish that 'The French Revolution has entered port.'[33] Even at the symbolic level, the revolutionary Socialist Left re-emerged in the 1880s and quickly matched the *Marseillaise* with the *Internationale* (France's other great contribution to political music), the *tricolore* with the Red Flag and 14 July with 1 May. While the counter-revolutionary Right may have been finally defeated in the Second World War, it took longer to tame the revolutionary Left.

Republican élitism: its political, scientistic and educational constituents

As early as 1791, leaders like Barnave and Duport had been converting their hopes into beliefs by prematurely claiming that the Revolution was over, an aspiration shared during and after the Restoration by Guizot among others.[34] The search continued, resurfacing at the end of the Second Empire. In a speech to Freemasons (accused by the Right of having started the French Revolution), the republican conservative Jules Simon bluntly declared in 1869: 'It is repeated that the revolution is not over. We wish it to be.'[35] By the 1870s, the realization came that only a democracy born of revolution would provide that mass support for representative institutions of which an exclusive élitism was incapable; that it would allow the revolutionary process to be halted because it had been fulfilled, because power and the benefits of power were more widely shared. This was, after all, an implication of Tocqueville's analysis of American democracy.

Part of the credit for the momentous change must go to Gambetta, who sought to complete the work of Thiers. The latter had written the history of the Revolution before attempting to bring it to completion. At the height of the 1877 battle for the soul of the Third Republic, Gambetta tried to dissuade the Right from supporting MacMahon's anti-democratic standpoint. 'Can you not see that if you allow universal suffrage to function freely, if when it pronounces, the independence and authority of its decisions are respected . . . you have a way of peacefully ending all conflicts, resolving all crises and that if a fully sovereign universal suffrage operates, *no revolution is possible*, because no revolution is to be attempted, no *coup d'état* is to be feared, when France has spoken.'[36] Gambetta, Ferry and their late-nineteenth-century successors, as we shall see, sought ideologically to bolster their liberal conservatism, in the Constant–Tocqueville manner, with a scientism derived from Saint-Simon and Comte.

The chief exponents of an Anglophil liberal conservatism, who vulgarized in the 1860s the ideas of Constant and Tocqueville and prepared the way for the constitution of the Third Republic, were Edouard de Laboulaye and Anatole Prévost-Paradol. Laboulaye, a disciple and editor of the works of Constant, was for thirty years professor of comparative legislation at the *Collège de France*. As a deputy from 1871 to 1875 and thereafter senator until his death in 1883, Laboulaye was an architect of the 1875 constitutional settlement. Although he side-stepped choosing how the President of the Republic should be elected, his 1872 *Sketch of a Republican Constitution*, in its attempt to institutionalize a strong president like Thiers and avoid government by Assembly, is a remarkable anticipation of the Fifth Republic. His liberal individualism led him to place a particular emphasis upon rights in the tradition of Locke and 1789. He did not resign himself to democracy but accepted it enthusiastically: 'Nothing seems finer to me than a society where everyone is master of his rights and shares in government.'[37] Laboulaye's lectures and Prévost-Paradol's articles in the 1860s shaped the liberal values of those like Boutmy, who were to play a leading part in creating the institution *par excellence* for training the élitist republicans in the 1870s.

While Paradol's family link was with Saint-Simon (he was the illegitimate son of a *Comédie Française* actress and the poet Léon Halévy, who succeeded Comte as Saint-Simon's secretary and championed a rationalist rather than religious Saint-Simonism), he repudiated this intellectual legacy in favour of liberalism. 'I reproach the Saint-Simonian school with its exclusive concern for the material fate of peoples and a culpable indifference for their liberty and political dignity. In a word, they apply the principle of the sovereignty of ends to the development of industry and well being. They are not concerned with whether peoples govern themselves or are governed by a master.'[38] In the 1860s, at a time of rigorous and repressive press regulation, such as Constant had successfully circumvented in the 1820s, Paradol emerged as the leading political journalist of his generation. Writing in a chastened, classic style, his langourous, exquisitely crafted sentences in the *Journal des Débats* made of him 'a prince of liberal youth, a new Benjamin Constant'.[39] His support for the liberal Empire in its death-throes led to less flattering analogies with Constant's role in 1815. Despite presenting his act as the Empire becoming liberal rather than a liberal embracing the Empire, Paradol was less capable of shrugging off accusations that he had betrayed his principles than Constant had been; he committed suicide in 1870, shortly after taking up the post of ambassador in Washington.[40]

Paradol wrote approvingly of Constant's stillborn 1815 constitution that 'It is the 1814 Charter, with the difference that it gives more influence to parliament and leans more towards parliamentary government.'[41] Like Constant, Paradol was really a French Whig who thought England had provided a model of how to master the 1648 execution of a monarch, a Cromwellian dictatorship and a Restoration with a conservative 1688 Revolution. His unbounded admiration for England, amounting to Anglomania, was based upon the view that it had successfully combined liberty and prosperity, aristocracy and democracy, through a gradual extension of the suffrage. Judicial protection of the rights of the accused, a cheap press to expose abuses of power, decentralization and an unwritten constitution were all examples of Britain's superiority over a France which since the Revolution was prone to 'democratic despotism'.[42] One of the ways in which he influenced the 1875 constitution makers was his inductive, British-style rejection of abstract declarations of rights. In an essay on the French Revolution, Paradol mocked the 'constitutional preambles which are one of our national weaknesses and have contributed more than a little to compromise our reputation in the world . . . . Have we not had enough of so many ridiculous contrasts between the principles with which we have headed most of our constitutions and the laws which have purported to apply them? . . . What is the use of such vain declamations? If you do not apply them or do so in a way that denies in practice the rights you proclaim in theory, how embarrassing, what a public scandal, how shameful for the country! Make laws from which your principles can be deduced and avoid establishing principles that risk making you blush for your laws.'[43]

While he had a characteristically Orleanist preference for constitutional monarchy over a republic because he thought, with Constant, that a king would be better able to wield powers like dissolution in a neutral way, like his patron Thiers Paradol was willing to advocate a republican form of parliamentary government. His main concern was to use the democratic mass to intimidate the revolutionary minority, 'reducing the enemies of order to their natural impotence by isolating them from the rest of the nation'.[44] To avoid the dangers of anti-parliamentarism that had destroyed the July Monarchy, representative government must be broad-based. 'Expressly constituted to avoid any serious discontent surviving in the various social classes, provided with regular means of permanently consulting opinion and preventing any misunderstanding between the people and the authorities, parliamentary government . . . is both the strongest and the gentlest safeguard against anarchy, depriving it of the means of action and the only allies which can constrain' a representative government.[45] As one would expect from an admirer of Constant, Paradol asserted that 'Free elections, a respected Parliament, responsible ministers, such are our first and only needs, because everything else comes in addition';[46] in this way the unfinished French Revolution would achieve political completion.

Other champions of post-revolutionary élitism looked beyond parliamentary liberalism as the foundation of order to a dynamic conservatism, which in Comte's slogan would combine 'order and progress'. In his 1852 collection of articles *Conservation, Révolution, Positivisme*, Littré – renowned in France for his dictionary – had argued that the only way of reconciling conservative order and revolutionary progress was a Comtian positivism. But in his 1855 *Appel aux Conservateurs*, dated 'sixty seventh year of the great crisis', Comte declared that the revolutionary process had still not been stabilized. Littré's achievement was to strip Comte's scientism of its authoritarian religiosity, which was replaced by a commitment to secularism and an élitist republicanism, not unlike that envisaged earlier by Condorcet and the *idéologues*. In this form, it would influence Gambetta and more especially Ferry, with class struggle being replaced by a cultural struggle that reconciled the idealist and positivist traditions, appealing respectively to revolutionary rights and scientific facts.

In a pragmatic way, Littré extended Thiers' argument that the Republic least divided France into the assertion that 'Monarchy is what divides us most.'[47] Exploiting the divisions between divine right monarchists, constitutional monarchists and Bonapartist imperialists, Littré argued in the 1870s that only through accepting the Republic as a determinist, historical fact would France avoid both revolution and counter-revolution. This would allow it to adopt reforms that commended themselves to opportunists on the Right and possibilists (reformists) on the Left, thanks to free debate and parliamentary approval. Although Comte had claimed that the British parliamentary system would not work on the Continent, Littré praised it and argued that it was spreading successfully. The French cycle of monarchy – Republic – Empire, twice repeated since the Revolution, with restoration of the monarchy only narrowly avoided in the 1870s by the establishment of a Republic (that was to face a Bonapartist-style attack by Boulangism in the 1880s), had to be broken by a period of prudent 'republican apprenticeship'.[48] Only then would the doubly disastrous legacy of revolution and reaction be transcended in a republican synthesis of democracy and science.

This democratic apprenticeship would have to learn from past errors in an inductive fashion which Littré borrowed from J. S. Mill, also adopting the reliance upon education to prepare both élites and masses for their new responsibilities. Littré believed that 'In the republic, the only neutral and impersonal form of government, the unity of the superior classes is possible. It alone also allows them to play . . . a preponderant part in the management of public affairs' and act as 'the counterweight to universal suffrage.'[49] This secularist and scientific élitism, distrustful of the dangers of mass democracy, was to be powerfully advocated by the anti-revolutionary historian Taine in the *Origines de la France Contemporaine* and by Renan in his *Avenir de la Science* and *Le Réforme intellectuelle et morale*. Taine helped Boutmy to found the *Ecole Libre des Sciences Politiques* to train the new élite, while Renan gave a new interpretation of the idea of the nation that was to provide the mass support for underpinning élite rule.

Despite its proclamation of equality of rights, the Revolution was committed to inequality both in principle and in practice. Article 6 of the

Declaration of the Rights of Man had given rise in 1789 to an important amendment of Talleyrand's formulation that 'Since all citizens are equal before [the law], all are equally admissible to all dignities, offices and public employment.' Significant restrictive precision was added, at the instance of the moderates Mounier and Lally-Tollendal, with the phrase 'according to their capacities and without any other distinction than those of their virtues and abilities.'[50] This principle of selection by merit for public service was to play a crucial part in the replacement of the old aristocratic élite not by egalitarianism but by a formal equality of opportunity that produced a bourgeois bureaucracy recruited by selection and training rather than heredity. No longer able to rely upon the acquisition of the traditional ruling skills within the nobility, numerous attempts were made after the Revolution to devise an administrative replica of the *Ecole Polytechnique*. Among others, the *idéologue* Destutt de Tracy in 1800 and Laboulaye in 1845 made elaborate proposals. However, it was not until the ex-Saint-Simonian Hippolyte Carnot became Minister of Education in 1848 that an ephemeral School of Administration was actually established (see Chapter 4, p. 99).

Although Emile Boutmy declared that his *Ecole Libre des Sciences Politiques* (which Laboulaye helped him to found, together with participants in the ill-fated 1848 venture such as Le Play) was a continuation of the *Ecole d'Administration*, there was a difference of inspiration and intention.[51] He had a fundamentally liberal conception of higher education, as against the Saint-Simonian stress upon specialist training. However, while he successfully defended his school's autonomy against Hippolyte Carnot's attempt between 1876 and 1881 to revive its 1848 forerunner, he was increasingly forced to professionalize it, a feature that has persisted since the creation of a separate *Ecole Nationale d'Administration* in 1945.[52] In retrospect, Boutmy's *Ecole Libre* can be seen as a private, Third Republic transition between the Second Republic failure and the Fourth Republic success in establishing a meritocratic élite, a state-trained administrative civil service which became the source of most élite positions in French society.

It was in the wake of France's demoralizing defeat in 1870 by what was presented as a better organized, educated and trained Prussia that Boutmy proposed in February 1871 to found what became later that year the *Ecole Libre des Sciences Politiques* or, as it came to be known, *Sciences Po*. His former teacher and friend, Taine, had inculcated a positivist faith in science as an antidote to democracy. Boutmy combined this with a commitment to liberal idealism in shaping the training of a new republican élite or 'government by the best'. As he wrote in setting out his proposal, the hitherto dominant political classes 'are threatened. Privilege has gone, democracy cannot be halted. Compelled to submit to the right of the majority, those who describe themselves as the upper classes can only preserve their political dominance by invoking the right of the most capable. Behind the crumbling ramparts of their prerogatives and of tradition, the tide of democracy encounters a second bulwark, built of manifest and useful abilities, the most unquestionable prestige of superior qualities, which it would be madness to forgo.'[53] The inability to reform French university education meant that Boutmy was reluctantly compelled to create another specialized *grande école* to meet an urgent and specific national need, as had occurred in the eighteenth century and would continue to recur throughout the twentieth century.[54] The network of Anglophil and Protestant élite connections that had helped Boutmy create *Sciences Po* preserved it from being nationalized in 1881 thanks to the support of Jules Ferry, then both education minister and prime minister.[55] This exploit was repeated after the Second World War, when *Sciences Po* was formally incorporated into the state higher education system but in practice remained distinct from it.

The consolidators: in search of an elusive consensus

François Furet has asserted that the 1870s republicans successfully concluded the Revolution by reconciling liberalism and democracy.[56] That this was their aspiration is not in doubt. His supporting claim that in the process they synthesized the individual rights liberalism of a Constant with the democratized scientism of Saint-Simon and Comte seems to fit Jules Ferry, as does Nicolet's view that Condorcet and the *idéologues* provided a First Republic anticipation of the élitist republicanism of the early Third Republic.[57] Quite apart from whether such an ideological synthesis is possible or was achieved, the governmental and regime instability of the Third Republic inspired in its protagonists a paralysing fear of its unreconciled enemies to Right and Left. The price of anticlerical, antiradical and antisocialist 'republican defence' was to maximize support from the socially, economically and politically conservative forces in France by fostering social inertia, economic protectionism and weak government. This was because Gambetta, who looked particularly to the aspiring urban lower middle classes and Ferry, who relied principally upon the peasantry, sought support from those whose opportunities for advancement had improved thanks to the Revolution but feared its further extension as a threat to their treasured if modest acquired rights. The 'moderation' of the 'opportunists' was inspired by a centrist concern to consolidate a shaky parliamentary regime. This would be achieved by relying upon a majority lower middle class and clientelized peasantry to hold at bay the pretensions of the upper-middle-class old élites from above and the nascent proletariat from below. Prudent, piecemeal adaptation of a 'dynamic conservative' kind, just enough change to avoid destabilizing change, was combined with an unbounded faith in universal suffrage provided it was in safe hands. In 1881 Gambetta tried to reassure the 'new men' who had emerged thanks to the Revolution and the Republic that democratic processes would allow them to achieve all their objectives: 'Thanks to this form [of government] all the complicated problems of the modern social world will be resolved'.[58] It would take another century before this naive claim acquired a semblance of plausibility.

By contrast with Gambetta, the ardently eloquent, lower-middle-class southerner, adept at swaying mass meetings, Ferry was a cold, high-handed *haut bourgeois* from Lorraine, a formidable parliamentary debater. And unlike Gambetta, he lived long enough to carry out his political programme. He was one of many future lawyer-leaders who refused to go into the public service during the Second Empire and reflected the shift from revolutionary to legalistic republicanism. They concentrated not merely on acquiring power but institutionalizing it in an enduring way. Reacting against the ineffectual romanticism of 1848, Ferry sought an orderly scientific foundation for progressive political action. He found it from 1857 in Comtian positivism, with education as the main instrument for replacing religion by science. He also explictly harked back to Comte's precursor Condorcet. He shared the latter's antipathy to catholicism and advocacy of both a free, secular and scientific mass education and an élite university education, the basis of the new spiritual power alongside parliamentary political power. Ferry's positivism was adopted in the form republicanized by Littré, given an additional twist by liberal Protestantism and an admiration for John Stuart Mill's version of Adam Smith's economic liberalism. Applied science was now undermining the hold of the Church in rural as well as urban areas, the people seeking scientific solutions to their practical problems rather than appealing to the parish priest. Ferry was able to rely upon this groundswell of public opinion that promoted the spread of secularism, in which the Masonic lodges played an important part. His secularist educational legislation of the early 1880s was heralded in 1875, when together with his fellow positivist Littré, Ferry was received into Freemasonry.[59]

Like so many of his generation of republican leaders, Ferry combined a humanitarian positivism with a fervently anti-Jacobin conception of the Revolution. Following Constant and Quinet, Ferry argued that despotic

Jacobinism, utilizing the sinister concepts of revolutionary necessity and the public good, had destroyed liberty and prepared the way for Bonapartism. Developed in 1866, this argument was to acquire its full practical significance in 1870–1 when, as mayor of Paris, he first overcame the Blanquist insurrection of 1870 and then fled from the Commune. As he wrote in 1879 in another connection: 'Between the Blanquist Republic and the one I have always defended, there are irreductible incompatibilities.'[60]

In the Second Empire context, Ferry was an ardent champion of decentralization, seeking in 1865 the abolition of the prefects who imposed central authority. 'If you want a hardworking, peaceful and free people, you must avoid a strong government. Fragment it to weaken it . . . . France needs a weak government . . . . Break up prefectoral authority, abolish the very name of this institution derived by direct descent from the Caesars of the decadence';[61] such was the 1860s liberal programme in the Tocqueville tradition. This minimalist state standpoint was reversed after the defeat and civil war of 1870–1, Ferry becoming the advocate of a strong central government, albeit with – apart from Paris – democratically elected mayors.

The people's vote as the only legitimate and firm basis of political authority was the faith ecstatically proclaimed by Ferry in his 1863 *Manuel électoral* for the guidance of anti-government candidates. 'Universal Suffrage is not only a sacred and sovereign institution, it is a whole politics and almost a symbol. It is not merely based on fact, law and justice, it is also the Inevitable. It is the whole of the present and the future. Universal Suffrage is dignity for the multitude of ordinary people, the guarantee of those who inherit no property, class reconciliation and rule of law for all. It is our sole life, hope and belief. We must love it, even when it is hostile.'[62] Although Ferry never abandoned his democratic faith, he subsequently subordinated it to a republican constitutionalism. This provided a conservative check on the people's plebiscitarian propensities, thanks to an institutional breakwater against the engulfing waves of populism.

Only within stable constitutional limits would French political life bring the revolutionary turbulence to an end by establishing a definitive form of government. This led Ferry in 1875 to accept a Second Chamber that would provide the rural protection against anti-parliamentary radicalism. The 'mob' or 'crowd' had deserted Bonapartism for Boulangism in the 1880s but was thereafter available for exploitation by extremists of Left and Right. Ferry was inspired to proclaim his faith in the rural Republic after intensively visiting his constituency in 1875. 'We shall emerge from the revolutionary state, we shall no longer live perched upon a branch: *la République sera paysanne ou ne sera pas* . . . . Now is the time to become conservative.'[63] In 1889, a century after the Revolution, he repeated his view that the mass of peasant voters were the Republic's reliable supporters and expressed his pleasure at how slowly life was changing in France's villages.[64] His fellow opportunist and Vosges deputy Jules Méline began in 1885 as minister of agriculture, in Ferry's government, the policy of agricultural protectionism that was generalized in 1892 to preserve the rural Republic by tariff protection. While the rural population shrank from three-quarters of the total in mid-nineteenth century to 60 per cent at the end of the century, the price of preventing an acceleration in its decline was the economically backward stalemate society that France would only overcome in the second half of the twentieth century. The great leap forward, economic and political, only came after a long period of marking time.

In 1879 Ferry became education minister in the first post-MacMahon government, headed by a Protestant (Waddington) and in which five out of nine ministers were Protestant *grands bourgeois*. This was due to the fact that most of the old political élite were monarchists and Catholics, so the new republican government had to look elsewhere for its leaders. (Its finance minister Léon Say was the *idéologue* Jean-Baptiste Say's grandson.) From February 1879 until Ferry's fall from power in March 1885, a period in which he was almost always in office as education minister and half the time as prime minister, an ambitious liberal conservative programme was enacted. Ferry, who had initially made his name with a series of articles on *Les Comptes Fantastiques d'Haussman* in *Le Temps*, attacking the speculative urban Caesarism of the prefect of Paris, promoted the 1881 law freeing the press.[65] The subsequent newspaper expansion was to popularize and spread the demogoguery of General Boulanger that threatened to engulf the Third Republic, at the height of which (in 1889) Ferry lost his seat in parliament.

Above all, Ferry relied upon his centralized and secularist education programme to create a more enlightened, united and democratic France, resuming the task that Condorcet had started, the Directory had continued but the First Republic had not been able to carry through. Unlike Thiers (who had inspired the Falloux Education Act of 1850), Ferry refused to mobilize the Black International against the Red International because he had confidence that with an army of teachers to spread scientism, patriotism and republicanism, it would no longer be necessary to rely upon the priesthood to exercise social control.[66] Littré having included the word 'anticlerical' in his *Dictionary of the French Language* in 1877, Ferry proceeded to put it into practice, helped by a Protestant-led team at the education ministry. It has been claimed in rosy retrospect by Furet that by 1885, when Ferry left office, 'the French Revolution is at last in power.'[67] However, its institutional structure, Ferry's peasant-supported parliamentary republic, immediately came under threat. The Boulanger crisis inaugurated an era in which, far from representing a comprehensive consensus, the protagonists of parliamentary democracy were frequently on the defensive. Only well after the advent of the Fifth Republic did France's political institutions no longer have to be apprehensively 'defended'.

It was Ferry's former secretary and close political friend Paul Cambon who wrote in 1885: 'The general impression is that the Republic is played out.' After speculating about the possibility of a reaction to 'revolutionary excesses' leading to 'some sort of dictatorship', he asserted: 'There is no government in France.'[68] While Ferry continued to champion conservative government against Clemenceau's radicalism and so was prevented from becoming president of the Republic in 1887, it was the latter's protégé, General Boulanger, who was to emerge as the champion of strong, anti-parliamentary government based upon popular sovereignty. Rallying point of those, both on the Right and Left, who felt excluded from the Parliament-centred Republic, the jackbooted Jacobin conducted a calculated populist campaign. He used patriotism as a means of arousing mass hopes of retrieving Alsace–Lorraine, along with attacks on scandals in high places. He declared that the people had been betrayed. Parliamentarism, which the Third Republic had reintroduced after its July Monarchy failure, 'by its intrigues, errors and hatred of universal suffrage', was a regime of impotence and shame. To those who feared a revival of Bonapartist dictatorship, Boulanger promised that he would not 'return to 1851 but to 1789.'[69] Although Boulanger's mass appeal to the people against their elected representatives was to end ignominiously in suicide, the support that he aroused was a warning that too many Frenchmen felt alienated from a democracy reduced to what de Gaulle later called the 'pleasures and poisons of the [parliamentary] system' for the threat of insurrection to be ignored.

While the divisive ferments of nationalism and socialism were beginning to make themselves felt, attempts to promote a sense of national and social solidarity were being made through educational, political and philosophical channels. Although it had its heterogeneous advocates in the early and mid-nineteenth century, it was not until the late nineteenth century that 'solidarism' became for a while the official philosophy of the Third Republic.[70] The need to replace reactionary Catholic values by a patriotic civic secularism that united the nation was persuasively conveyed in a modest school textbook published in 1877, *Le Tour de la France par deux enfants*. The author's pseudonym, G. Bruno, was believed to conceal the identity of Alfred Fouillée, though in fact the real author was his companion and

future wife (once divorce became legal in 1884). The three million copies of
this book were sold in the first ten years, an annual average of a further
200,000 copies until the end of the century bringing the total to six
million, which by 1976 had risen to eight and a half million copies, with its
readership a multiple of that figure. Just as Fouillée in his numerous works
of political philosophy for adults propagated the need to reconcile the liberal
idealism of individual rights with the socialist scientism of collective needs,
so Madame Fouillée wrote an 'ecumenical book' intended to consolidate
support for the Republic by discreetly indoctrinating children.[71]

It was Léon Bourgeois, former prefect, radical politician, minister and
prime minister (from November 1895 to April 1896), elected deputy in
February 1888 against Boulanger, who gave solidarism its fullest extension
as an eclectic ideology. It was intended to allow the radicals to replace
opportunism as the inspiration of the Centre that needed to be held against
challenges from counter-revolutionary Right and ultra-revolutionary Left.
His attempt to transcend nationalism by advocating an organized 'Society
of Nations' only half-succeeded after the First World War, which witnessed
an efflorescence of new nation-states.[72]

National integration and socio-economic change

While Ernest Gellner is right to stress that historically nationalism is not
simply an arbitrary avoidable aberration but a decisive new departure, he
is rather cavalier in dismissing its ideological statements as 'hardly worth
analysing' because if one writer did not formulate them another would have
done so.[73] His emphasis upon the transition from agrarian to industrial
society as the way in which a centralized, unitary polity is formed out
of subcultures, bringing about 'that fusion of culture and polity which
is the essence of nationalism', postdates the advent of nationalism as
an ideology; so that it is true, but not in the sense in which Gellner
intended, that 'It is nationalism which engenders nations, and not the
other way round.'[74] Again, while he rightly emphasizes the importance
of nationwide education – imposition of the French language being a
priority task of the Jacobins, who stressed that 'speech must be one, like
the Republic' – Gellner overreaches himself with his provocative reversal
of Maistre's notorious elevation of the executioner into the mainstay of
society (see Chapter 3, p. 56). He claims that 'At the base of the modern social order stands not the executioner but the professor . . . . The
monopoly of legitimate education is now more important, more central
than is the monopoly of legitimate violence.'[75] Despite Napoleon's efforts

to achieve such a state monopoly of education and the major secularist effort of the Third Republic to overcome the duality of French education and socialize everyone into a united nation, such an objective has still not been achieved.

The modern conception of nationalism came into existence with the French Revolution as the cohesive community that could accept democracy to take its collective decisions. The term itself was probably coined by one of the Revolution's vitriolic opponents, the Abbé Barruel, in 1798. 'The Christian religion became incredible, even ridiculous, but the God which the Enlightenment offered in place of the Christian God was emotionally inert.' To supplement reason, the nation filled for many the 'yawning emotional void left by the discredited notions of God and King.'[76] As we saw earlier, Rousseau and Sieyès among others utilized the nation to displace the old regime conception of the state in favour of popular sovereignty. However, the French revolutionary determination to spread its liberating message through forces replacing aristocratic internationalism by democratic internationalism provoked counter-revolutionary national-isms,[77] of which the Prussian–German version was to amputate France of its culturally Germanic Alsace–Lorraine provinces. The defeat of 1870 and Commune of 1871 marked the start of a shift in the protagonists of patriotism and nationalism from Left to Right. Although for some, like Clemenceau, patriotism remained inseparable from the Revolution, the increasing importance of socialist internationalism and pacifism allowed the Right to champion national unity against divisive class conflict. Whereas in 1817 Saint-Simon identified them, Blanqui in 1870 opposed the concepts 'society' and 'nation', arguing 'French society is not the French nation. Let us not confuse two distinct and hostile entities. Society is Capital and Master – the Nation is Work and Slave.'[78] Significantly, some of Blanqui's disciples shifted their loyalties to the Right in answering the Boulangist *revanchard* call in the late 1880s, heralding the ethnic nationalism of Barrès and Maurras.

The loss of Alsace–Lorraine to Germany prompted an early repudiation of the racist basis of nationality from the Breton historian Ernest Renan. In 1871 he wrote to a German: 'The individuality of each nation is doubtless constituted by race, language, history, religion but also by something much more tangible, by present consent, by the will of a state's various provinces to live together . . . . Too sharp a division of humanity into races, besides being based upon scientific error, few nations having a really pure race, can only lead to wars of extermination' and the fatal replacement of liberal politics by 'ethnographic and archaeological politics'.[79] A decade later, in a celebrated Sorbonne lecture, Renan elaborated his argument that popular consent and national self-determination were the supreme criteria of state boundaries. 'Human history is essentially different from zoology.'[80] Neither race, language, religion nor geography could provide a reliable basis for nationality, which was based upon forgetting past wrongs and brutalities as well as remembering common achievements and aspiring to new ones. 'A nation is thus a great solidarity, based upon feelings of the sacrifices made and which one is still willing to make. It presupposes a past but it is summed up in the present by a tangible fact: consent, the clearly expressed wish to continue the common life. A nation's existence is, forgive the metaphor, a daily plebiscite',[81] not the stage-managed plebiscite of would-be populist dictators. His prophetic anticipation of exterminating horrors in store from a race-inspired nationalism was supplemented by a happier prophecy. 'Nations are not eternal. They begin and end. European confederation will probably replace them. But such is not the edict of the century in which we live. For the present, the existence of nations . . . guarantees freedom', each dissonance contributing to the universal harmony.[82] We are a long way from the exclusive nationalism of Maurras' cry: 'France for the French' that survives into the 1990s in the mouth of Le Pen; much closer to Mitterrand's call for European Confederation.

At the end of his study of the modernization of rural France in the early decades of the Third Republic, Eugen Weber declared that by 1870 France 'was neither morally nor materially integrated; what unity it had was less cultural than administrative.' Weber earlier argued that 'The Republic under which Renan formulated his idea had inherited a territorial unit but a cultural jigsaw. It was up to the Republic to turn the legal formulas into actual practice . . . . The fact is, the French fuss so much about the nation because it is a living problem, became one when they set the nation up as an ideal, remained one because they found they could not realize the ideal.'[83] The revolutionary assertion of national unity was an integrating ideal, not the description of reality that all too many have taken it to be, failing to observe the discrepancy between rhetorical principle and actual practice. It was compounded by identifying a would-be indivisible unitary state with an all too divided plural society, in which diversity rather than uniformity was prevalent. Weber's considered assessment is that 'The national ideology was still diffuse and amorphous around the middle of the nineteenth century. French culture became truly national only in the last years of the century.'[84] Weber is wise enough not to insist upon any particular period – even 1880–1919 which he favours – as having made France modern. Just as there is no agreement on when the Revolution ended (if it has), the process of national integration, whether linguistic and educational, in urbanization and transport, was an extended and uneven one. Weber rightly treats the

French 'nation not as a given reality but as a work-in-progress, a model of something at once to be built and to be treated for political reasons as already in existence.'[85]

While Stanley Hoffmann stressed the importance of the three decades 'from the early 1930s to the early 1960s, when a combination of deliberate policies and external shocks produced almost revolutionary changes in French society',[86] others writing later have dated the break in the social, economic and political stalemate in the two decades from 1965. Admittedly Hoffmann was circumspect enough to pronounce the 'revolutionary' changes taking place to be 'both recent and incomplete'.[87] Clearly the process is a continuous one, so it lends a spurious precision to a complex and dynamic phenomenon to claim 1965 as the 'turning point' as the sociologist Henri Mendras has done. Though the weight given to the heterogeneous contributory factors and statistical indicators changed between 1979 and 1988, Mendras has asserted that a 'Second French Revolution' occurred in the period 1965–84, picking out the first direct presidential election and the expansion of supermarkets and mass higher education as key factors in 1965.[88] While we need not attach undue importance to his dates and should discount his propensity to see the bright side of things, Mendras shows that the elimination of most of the peasantry and *rentiers* in favour of what Proudhon called the 'working middle classes'; the end of sharp urban–rural conflict; the decline of the Catholic Church and collapse of communism; a new bourgeois consensus focused on sustained economic growth and competitive business profitability; and a culturally united nation, linguistically, educationally and through the mass media, have created a generally prosperous and integrated society. Rather than amounting to a 'Second Revolution', this may be regarded as a fulfilment of the First Revolution. Before we examine this more closely, we must consider those who, for a century, have felt excluded from the process of reformist permanent revolution.

The excluded: anti-revolutionaries and ultra-revolutionaries

If the Third Republic consolidated itself on the basis of a parliamentary liberalism that owed much to the critique of the Revolution by Constant and Tocqueville, while Saint-Simonian technocratic modernization came to the fore during Vichy and the Fourth and Fifth Republics, our remaining post-revolutionary protagonists appealed to the extremists of Right and

Left who did so much to prevent the completion of the Revolutionary process. The emerging republican synthesis was forced on to the defensive, with Boulangism's populist appeal to the extremes of Blanquist Left and Barrèsian Right preparing the way for the nationalism of the extreme Right, while the extreme Left turned towards internationalism at the end of the 1880s.

The anti-revolutionary Right was divided between an intolerantly reactionary clericalism and an intransigently reactionary monarchism that Maurras' *Action Française* wedded to Comtian positivism. While in some respects they could both look back for inspiration to Maistre, the great precursor's ultimate appeal to a global papal authority meant that Maurras' new style authoritarian racism and nationalism, if not an anticipation of Fascism, at least prepared the way for the Vichyite collaborators with Fascism. When Maurras was sentenced after the Second World War, he declared it to be 'Dreyfus' revenge'. During the 'Affair', which gave birth to *Action Française*, French nationalism was anti-Semitically defined by exclusion, whereas the French Revolution, with its inclusive conception of nationality, had recognized Jews as full citizens. Despite Le Pen's National Front revival of such ideas, they have not yet been accompanied by an overt challenge to parliamentary democracy. More relevant than Maurras to the future regime of the Fifth Republic was the conservative politician André Tardieu (three times prime minister between 1930 and 1932), who revived the Boulangist appeal to a 'captive' popular sovereignty against a parliamentary sovereignty which had usurped power in French democracy.[89] It was only after the failure of the Fourth Republic's resurrection of a parliament-centred political system that de Gaulle was to give the 'real country' the feeling that the 'legal country' was not managing affairs in isolation from them.

On the anti-parliamentary Left, there were also sharp divisions. Various political movements, led notably by Guesde, Vaillant and Jaurès, in theory sought to capture state power by political revolution but devoted most energy to their rivalries until their 1905 unification in the SFIO (French Section of the Workers' International). However, despite their revolutionary rhetoric, by the 1890s they were spending much of their time fighting parliamentary and local elections, imperceptibly being absorbed into the workings of the abhorred liberal democratic system. The other, more working-class wing of the labour movement was constituted by the anarcho-syndicalists. Whereas the Socialist political parties tended to be Marxist or Blanquist in inspiration, the trade unionists were inclined towards Proudhon's anti-statist economic federalism. Legalized in 1884, their more radical conception of class warfare, reflected in the (General

Confederation of Labour) CGT's Amiens Charter of 1906, encouraged them
to rely upon the general strike as the way of achieving their revolutionary objectives. This led in the first decade of the twentieth century to
bloody confrontations with the governments of Clemenceau and Briand
in particular. Thereafter, the failure to mobilize the international labour
movement against the First World War and the Bolshevik Revolution led
to post-war splits in both the SFIO and CGT.[90] While the Socialists and the
CGT majority moved in practice to an increasingly reformist position that
accepted parliamentary institutions and a regulated-cum-planned market
economy, the Communists sustained their supporters with expectations
of the imminence of insurrection. Even a cursory consideration of a succession of revolutionary mirages would allow us to detect the hollowness
of revolutionary pretence. Protestations notwithstanding, Communist acceptance of incremental amelioration of the status quo rather than its
comprehensive transformation is what is evident from the behaviour of
the party and its trade union auxiliary. A pseudo-religion could no longer
masquerade convincingly as the science of salvation.

In retrospect it can be seen that what are presented as profound crises and dramatic confrontations are more a matter of the melodramatic
re-enactment of a revolutionary past than a portent of the changes that
have usually come as a result of impending or actual military or economic
disaster. The collapse of the Third and Fourth Republics were examples of
the former and the 1982 Socialist reorientation an example of the latter.
As Hoffmann persuasively argued, protest is a pervasive norm in France.
Paraphrasing Alain's model of French political behaviour, the citizen 'aban-
dons decisions to elites he distrusts and leaves the task of supervising
those elites to representatives he also distrusts.' Hoffmann went on to
claim that the French frequently revolt 'against a central authority that
is expected to have the final say, rebellion within an established pattern,
not revolution against it.'[91] In his related socio-cultural explanation of
the need to present change in France as comprehensive and cataclysmic,
Michel Crozier maintained in 1963 that 'To obtain a limited reform in
France, one is always obliged to attack the whole "system", which is thus
constantly called into question .... Reform can be brought about only
by sweeping revolution. Reformers, in any case, cannot succeed without
counting on the pressure generated by revolutionary or quasi-revolutionary
movements.'[92] By the 1980s, Crozier's pleas that one could not govern
effectively by decree and that policy objectives should be modest became
widely accepted. This suggests that France has become capable of piecemeal
change. It is no longer the case, as de Gaulle claimed, that 'France only
undertakes reforms in the wake of revolutions.'[93] The 1969 resignation

of the heroic leader after his failure to master by plebiscite the 1968 surge of mass protest did not presage further turbulence. What some presented as a cultural revolution, but which is more prosaically referred to as 'events', obscured the emergence of a humdrum consensus about fundamentals.[94]

Republican reconciliation

The long sought for constitutional unanimity developed in the 1960s and 1970s, as the Fifth Republic demonstrated that it was not just another ephemeral episode. Public support for the semi-presidential system, misleadingly presented in 1958 by its main author, Michel Debré as a genuine form of parliamentary government eventually compelled acceptance by its most vociferous opponents on the Left, such as François Mitterrand. Those, such as Mendès France, who refused to accept the new institutional arrangements, were condemned to political impotence by self-exclusion. De Gaulle's achievement was to adapt and implement solutions adumbrated in the 1930s and 1940s. Whereas Clemenceau, France's First World War heroic leader, had remained faithful to the revolutionary Left's view that one could simply dispense with a president of the Republic, de Gaulle relied upon a powerful president to reinforce state authority. This would overcome economic backwardness and military weakness, thereby allowing a modernized France to retrieve her lost status as a major world power. While Jean Monnet was able to launch a Saint-Simonian style economic modernization through the planning process, without reforming French political institutions, it was only with de Gaulle's return in 1958 that the Revolution's unfinished institutional business was at last settled. It was based upon a combination of the modernizing Right's Saint-Simonian stress upon industrial development with a Constantian constitutionalism, whose liberal logic only became clear after de Gaulle himself had left the political scene.

The possibility that the Resistance urge to make a new institutional start in 1945 would take a presidential form was severely inhibited by Marshal Pétain's practice, even though the Vichy regime never proceeded beyond draft constitutions centred upon a ten-year presidency. Instead the Resistance constitution makers looked to British-style parliamentary government based upon a small number of disciplined political parties as their model. With the president confined to a formal, monarchical role, executive power would be concentrated in the hands of the prime minister who, it was hoped, would have a parliamentary majority for the duration of the legislature, until the next election. It was to this model that Mendès France remained loyal, as can be seen in his *A Modern French Republic* of 1962.[95]

Hybrid versions of parliamentary and presidential government were promoted by Michel Debré, directly and through his influence on the draft constitution proposed by the Resistance *Comité Général d'Etudes*. 'In so far as the legislature retained the right to overturn a ministry, it was still a parliamentary system. However, the power of the President was large, that of the Prime Minister largely unspecified, and there was at least the possibility that executive power would pass wholly to the President who was not accountable to parliament.'[96] The ambiguity of Debré's abortive wartime proposals foreshadow his successful 1958 constitutional draft in combining both parliamentary and presidential ways of strengthening executive power. In 1945, the issue of presidential power became identified with a revulsion from de Gaulle's personal role. The Constituent Assembly, in which the Communist and Socialist Left predominated, was more concerned to prevent him acquiring too much power and to abolish the Senate, leaving control in the hands of a party-dominated National Assembly.[97]

Confronted by what was to emerge as more like a resurrection of the latter-day Third Republic than the modern Republic envisaged by reformers like Mendès France, de Gaulle went into ostentatious opposition. While the Fourth Republic's constitution was in gestation, de Gaulle delivered a speech at Bayeux in June 1946, setting out in ringing phrases his view of the democratic nation-state that was to be enshrined in the constitution of the Fifth Republic. Although national resurrection would not have been possible without 'an elite which sprang spontaneously from the depths of the nation', and 'would not have succeeded without the assent of the great mass of the people', de Gaulle asserted the pre-eminence of state authority but based it firmly on popular support. New political institutions were indispensable because only the state was 'capable of rebuilding the unity of the nation', being 'legitimate because it rested on the interest and the feelings of the nation.'[98] The political weakness of the Fourth Republic, when confronted by a coalition of insurgent Algerian colonists and an insubordinate colonial army, gave de Gaulle his opportunity to build the strong state that he had been unable to build at the end of the Second World War.

In 1958 Michel Debré, who had been de Gaulle's unofficial constitutional adviser since 1945, was charged as minister of justice with preparing the Fifth Republic's constitution, prior to playing a major role as prime minister from 1959 to 1962 in applying it. One month before the French people approved the new constitution by a majority of four to one, with only

15 per cent abstaining in the September referendum, Debré explained its ambitious purpose. 'It is, first and foremost, to try to reconstruct governmental authority without which there is neither State nor democracy . . . neither France nor Republic.'[99] While in 1958 Debré still presented the Fifth Republic as an attempt to establish a stable form of parliamentary government, by 1962 the shift to the direct election of the president by the people marked the decisive change, although a semi-presidential system was already implicit in Debré's 1943–5 constitutional schemes. He now openly asserted that 'The keystone of the constitutional structure is no longer parliament but the president.' The General had personified the 'general will' to retrieve national independence but the general will could not permanently be equated with the will of the General. His successors would need to rely upon an institutionalized democratic legitimacy. To prevent the National Assembly, as the only institution legitimized by direct popular election, from retrieving its lost omnipotence in the service of impotence, it was essential to reinforce the president. 'Facing the assembly elected by universal suffrage there must be another authority, also elected by universal suffrage, and having in consequence the same legitimacy but capable of taking decisions . . . . Henceforth . . . legitimacy is shared. The Assembly no longer has a monopoly of universal suffrage', the president having the upper hand because of his popular standing and longer term of office.[100] However, before these new institutions could be said to have finally achieved a republican resolution of the Revolutionary predicament, it was indispensable that they attract the allegiance of their opponents.

No one personified, it seemed, a more intransigent rejection of the Fifth Republic than Mitterrand, yet appearances were deceptive. From the start, he made it clear that his objection was more to the coercive, insurrectionary context than the substantive, institutional text. 'If General de Gaulle is the founder of a new form of democracy . . . if he restores national unity, if he also provides France with the necessary continuity and authority, I will give support.'[101] Unlike the Communist Party, which defended the Fourth Republic as having provided 'the most progressive institutions which our country has had since the Revolution',[102] although it only offered support at its birth and at its death, the majority of the Socialist Party led by Guy Mollet actively helped to found the Fifth Republic on the assumption that it would be a parenthesis to a Sixth (parliamentary) Republic. 'Bonapartism' could be parliamentarized by exploiting the constitution's flexibility, thanks to 'a constitutional text and a clearly presidential practice, whose relative strength would be determined by a power struggle.'[103] However, the 1962 censure of the Pompidou government, followed by dissolution of the National Assembly and the election of a Gaullist majority supporting direct election of the president, meant that the power struggle had gone against a revival of French-style 'parliamentarism'.

Since the Fifth Republic had neither fulfilled their pessimistic prognostication of becoming a dictatorship nor their optimistic anticipation that it could rapidly be replaced, the Left had to reach an accommodation with it. Despite the lucidity of a Léon Blum, who had during the Third and Fourth Republics recognized the need to strengthen the executive and even envisaged the direct election of the president only to reject it as impracticable, the Left had hitherto failed to find an institutional formula capable of preserving the Republic from the fate it had already suffered on four occasions. The prospect of standing in the first direct presidential election of the Fifth Republic in 1965 prompted Mitterrand to the realization that he could achieve his prime objective, modernizing the non-Communist Left and dominating its Communist ally, only by using de Gaulle's institutional innovation for this purpose. 'By supporting him, *the Left accepted the substance of the Constitution, the principle of majority backed government, the mechanism of a political presidential election and almost the political supremacy of the President*.'[104]

For the 1974 presidential election, the Left in the person of Mitterrand went further in accepting presidential supremacy. The 1974 Common Programme of the Communists, Socialists and Left radicals had already allowed them to disguise the constitutional concessions that they had made in accepting the key principles of the Fifth Republic by focusing attention upon their mutual compromises and concessions.[105] France's political institutions ceased to be a matter of dispute, even though the way they were operated by the Right was still challenged. Meanwhile, the Communists had gradually, implicitly and pragmatically been abandoning the Blanquist conception of revolutionary dictatorship in favour of the unreserved acceptance of universal suffrage, with the Communist Party formally repudiating the dictatorship of the proletariat doctrine in 1976. The election of Mitterrand as president in 1981, at the third attempt, completed the process of accepting the duality of being a head of state who was both a unanimist constitutional monarch and the republican leader of one of the bipolarized political forces in France. 'The institutions were not designed with me in mind. But they suit me', as Mitterrand ironically put it shortly after taking office.[106] De Gaulle's conception of constitutional law as 'first a constraint that one hates, then a habit that one accepts and finally a tradition one reveres' was a process that occurred with great rapidity in the 1960s and 1970s.[107] De Gaulle and Mitterrand completed the unfinished institutional business of the 1870s when, as we can see in retrospect, 'the Revolution had been "suspended" rather than "ended".'[108]

However, if Mitterrand – who had castigated the Fifth Republic at its origins as constituting a *Coup d'Etat permanent* – deserves some credit for completing the work of republican reconciliation, de Gaulle must be acknowledged as its progenitor. Using the May 1958 crisis to settle a 169-year vicious circle of 'discontinuity, agitation and improvisation', he was able to fuse liberal Catholic and democratic republican values in a 'national ecumenism', personified by what Blum and Debré (after Chateaubriand) had called a 'Republican Monarch'.[109] In this way universal suffrage, first through the constitutional referendum, then through the direct election of the president, separated democracy from its association solely with parliament. By his conduct as a powerful, popularly elected President, de Gaulle freed the office from its guilt by association with democratic dictatorship since Napoleon III, resigning on his defeat at the 1969 referendum. Unlike Thiers, whose resignation a century before was not the prelude to a republic equipped with a strong executive authority, de Gaulle could rest assured that he had established just such an institution, firmly based upon mass public support whose legitimacy is accepted by the whole political class. The 1969 presidential election settled the institutional issue raised in 1789. In the 1970s and 1980s, de Gaulle's successors extended his reconciliation between authority and democracy within France into a reconciliation of nationalism and internationalism within the European Community.

The Revolution is not entirely over

In the avalanche of books published in 1989 to commemorate the bicentenary of the French Revolution, it was refreshing to encounter one by a non-Marxist historian based upon twenty in-depth interviews with French politicians ranging across the Left–Right spectrum that could choose as its title *La Révolution française n'est pas terminée*. After all, the leading exponent of the dominant revisionist school, François Furet, had repeatedly and categorically asserted that the Revolution was over . . . though not always at the same time. The coincidence of the bicentenary with the spectacular collapse of communism in Eastern Europe seemed unmistakably to signal the 'abandonment of revolutionary political culture' and its universal replacement by liberal democracy and the principles but not the practice of 1789. Tocqueville had long since demonstrated the conservative (and illiberal) propensities of democracy but 1989 appeared to be 'celebrating democracy to forget revolution'.[110] However, Furet seems to concede that although acceptance of the legitimizing principle of democracy has imparted to political institutions an impressive integrative and stabilizing capacity, its subversive propensities have not been entirely dissipated. Having earlier declared that 1789 had become 'a foundation rather than a promise', his concluding sentence reads: 'Abandoning the belief that they have mastered, still less exhausted the meaning of 1789, our societies have started to reconsider the implications of the rights of man.'[111] The open-ended nature of liberal democratic values precisely precludes the possibility of halting the impetus of the revolution, still less of the historical process. While in liberal democratic polities the methods used may have become reformist, the emancipatory purposes they serve continue to be capable of causing disruption. Elsewhere, the aspiration to achieve liberal democracy will continue to be revolutionary in means as well as ends.

A hundred years ago Clemenceau, a neo-Jacobin of the Left, proclaimed the indivisibility of the Revolution. Even though a neo-Jacobin of the Right like Debré has acknowledged that the myth of unity imperfectly concealed a diverse reality, we must consider why the myth has been both powerful and enduring.[112] This is because the Revolution both divided and united Left and Right. Although the Terror, violence, authoritarianism and anticlericalism proved repellant, they have come to be seen as undesirable means to desirable ends. In retrospect, the results are regarded as more enduring than the methods used to achieve them. So in 1893 the *Ralliement* of French Catholicism, more to the Republic than the Revolution (two years after Clemenceau's speech), was only the start of a lengthy integrative process that has taken almost another century. Meanwhile, between 1945 and 1980 French communism first emerged as the other subculture opposed to the democratic mainstream and then declined into marginality as did traditionalist catholicism. So the religious and ideological cleavages, the class and political divisions that polarized France have been bridged by a slow process of secularization and a more rapid process of *embourgeoisement*. As Furet has expressed it, 'Over this last half-century, the economy and institutions have contributed to moving the French from revolutionary democracy to democracy pure and simple. On the Right de Gaulle has put an end to Catholic exile, while Mitterrand has ended Communist exile on the Left.'[113] Healing the ideological wounds of the past by personifying a national ecumenism, the 1980s as the first enduring period of government by the Socialist Left has made it possible for the French Revolution to symbolize not rupture with the past but its irreversibility, the Right using it to exorcise the reproach of conservatism and the Left the link with collectivism.[114]

French society has seen a decline of class conflict despite enfeebled attempts by the Communist Party and the CGT to fan any flames that appear. However, the decline of trade union membership and activism has meant that the potential support is episodic and usually sparked by specific material grievances. Although social movements of an ethnic or environmentalist kind have presented unconventional challenges to the established political parties, they have not – despite anxieties on the score of the National Front – disturbed the fundamental trend towards socio-political consensus. While bipolarization has had something of a setback on the Right, the need to create an effective alternative to Socialist domination of the Left will exercise strong pressure towards greater unity within the enduring multi-party system. On most of the traditional issues of political controversy, the French public does not perceive significant differences between Right and Left. Agreement is seen to predominate on education, European policy, social welfare, human rights and unemployment. While 'socialism' is regarded favourably by 54 per cent and negatively by 30 per cent as a result of experience in the 1980s, support for 'liberalism' and especially profit has also increased.[115] The shift towards a tolerant democratic consensus in public attitudes is a salient feature of the quiet revolution that has been blurring old isms and reducing the explosive potential of erstwhile disputes to matters of piecemeal reformism.

An opinion poll in 1987 showed that the French Revolution had a favourable public image, with 77 per cent saying it was 'a good thing', a view particularly held by men, the young and on the Left. Almost the same number were against establishing 'a British-style constitutional monarchy' (74 per cent to 11 per cent). When asked which event best symbolized the French Revolution, the Declaration of the Rights of Man was well ahead with 74 per cent, while the salient features of its legacy were equality before the law (69 per cent), public education (47 per cent) and a constitution (25 per cent). The symbols of 'Liberty, Equality, Fraternity' (47 per cent), and the *Marseillaise* and *tricolore* (21 per cent) also figured prominently. The Revolution's significance was regarded as mainly worldwide (35 per cent), national (31 per cent) or European (20 per cent). Asked which Revolution had exercised the most positive and most negative effects, the French Revolution was rated by 52 per cent most positive and 4 per cent most negative; the American Revolution 16 per cent and 7 per cent; and the Soviet Revolution 7 per cent and 46 per cent respectively.[116] When a sample of the French public was asked in November 1989 which of the three revolutions had been in the end most beneficial, 71 per cent said the French Revolution, 10 per cent the American Revolution and only 5 per cent the Bolshevik Revolution. By autumn 1989, the views of the people of Eastern Europe and the Soviet Union were not out of line with those of their French counterparts, 87 per cent considering that the ideas of the French Revolution had beneficial effects on contemporary society.[117]

It is only with the emergence within France of a liberal democratic consensus, on values as well as institutions and the public service role of the state, that the 1789 Declaration of Rights could secure a prominence that it did not enjoy for most of the two centuries since it was drawn up. A powerful contributory factor has been the international role of human rights – at the United Nations and European level – in the promotion of which France took the lead as part of its universalist vocation. Having uprooted the traditional values upon which Old Regime legitimacy had been built, it was essential to root the new democratic institutions and governmental functions in the liberal legitimacy of individual rights. So the unfinished 1789 Declaration (significantly incomplete because incapable of satisfactory finality in an open society) became the touchstone of political authority's new legitimacy. However, because the French quickly became less preoccupied with curbing political power than with reconstituting a powerful political authority, Declarations of Rights became less important than constitutions, and these of less practical importance than necessities imposed by circumstances. Nevertheless, on subsequent occasions, notably in 1848 and 1946, associated with a change of regime, it became important to extend the individualist rights of 1789 in a more social direction. This was particularly marked in the preamble to the constitution of the Fourth Republic.[118] The Third Republic had avoided promulgating a Declaration of Rights, partly out of a commitment to unrestricted parliamentary sovereignty but also because of a pragmatic suspicion of asserting pretentious principles that it might be inconvenient to practise in all cases.[119] However, constitutional lawyers during the Third Republic (Acollas, Jèze, Duguit, Hauriou) laid the doctrinal basis for the subsequent 'constitutionalization' of the Declaration of Rights.[120] While the Fifth Republic contented itself with reaffirming the earlier Declarations of 1789 and 1946, it took a decisive step forward by making what were previously symbolic assertions of pious hopes into enforceable rights through the powers required by the constitutional council to interpret law. Henceforth, all laws passed by a democratically elected parliament were not *ipso facto* good.

A major achievement of the Fifth Republic has been to attain a large measure of consensus on formerly highly controversial constitutional principles and practices. In the first post-revolutionary monarchical constitution, France had already moved away from the British model of representative government by making the function of minister and member of parliament incompatible, rejecting bicameralism and denying the executive the power to dissolve parliament. These principles were extended by republican constitutions in the direction of government by Assembly, inspired by the Jacobin dictum that the government is the prime enemy of the people. However, as Lockean optimism was replaced by Hobbesian pessimism, bicameralism was adopted and the power of the executive was strengthened (including the power to dissolve parliament). Under the Fifth Republic, the president fully emerged as an elected 'republican monarch' of a highly active kind and acts of parliament became subordinate to the judgements of the constitutional council. The multiplicity of parties became bipolarized by the direct election of the president. Rials concludes his analysis of two centuries of constitutional evolution and revolution by declaring 'The Revolution is over. Dead are the fears, as well as the hopes'.[121] The French no longer quarrel ardently over the legitimacy of their political regime and have settled for a lukewarm, liberal democratic constitutional relativism. Arguments over the length of the president of the Republic's term of office – five rather than seven years – do not amount to challenging the constitutional rules of the political game. Popular discontent is reflected in increased electoral abstention rather than in street riots. Their civic alienation is passive rather than active.

Accompanying the processes of ideological and institutional disarmament has been the development of the welfare state in France, which in turn is increasingly preoccupied with practical policy considerations rather than issues of principle. Starting out from an uneasy combination of revolutionary emphasis upon individual rights, private property and personal responsibility with a Catholic stress on social duties, Church charity and family responsibility, France groped its way towards a compromise acknowledging social rights based upon social solidarity. Initially, this took the Proudhonian form of collective self-help through 'mutualist' voluntary associations or friendly societies, but public assistance from the state proved to be a necessary corrective to the particularist privileges of special schemes. Justified in terms of the need for social insurance against the risks and insecurities of all derived from social interdependence, the political pressure of a democratic society in which citizens could use their votes to secure such protection led to legislation first to increasing equality of opportunity in education and then to protection for the young, the old, the ill and the unemployed. Although the long-predominant rural society slowed down the development of the secularist 'solidarist' corrective to both individualist neglect and Catholic paternalism, the impact of two World Wars speeded up the acceptance of public guarantees of social and economic rights, as reflected in the preamble to the constitution of the Fourth Republic. Paradoxically, it was notably as a result of twentieth-century mass involvement in war that the warfare state was supplemented by the welfare state, although

Saint-Simon's vision of the latter *replacing* the former remains an aspiration, particularly in the Third World.

The Revolution: retrospect and prospect

The requiem of the French Revolution has been so frequently sung that it is surprising that the question is seldom asked: why is it necessary to repeatedly reinter what is dead? William Doyle in his bicentenary history actually dates the death from the solemn mass celebrated in *Notre Dame* on Easter Day, April 1802. He could point to Napoleon having reconciled the Roman Church and the French state with a concordat, turning the bishops of a 'self-governing and self-taxing' Gallican Church into 'clerical prefects'.[122] However, Napoleon failed to create a liberal political regime, relying instead upon cynical authoritarianism. 'A constitution should be drafted so as not to obstruct government action and not compel the government to violate it.'[123] It was after the achievement of a less successful general but a better politician, Charles de Gaulle, that one could make a more plausible claim on his behalf to having ended the Revolution. Endorsing Furet's boast in the light of public opinion poll evidence, Olivier Duhamel asserted that 'The Revolution is over because it no longer divides the French.'[124] Identified with liberal democracy and human rights, attitudes towards the Revolution no longer fundamentally distinguish Left from Right. However, it is worth noting that while 3 : 1 think that the French Revolution was a necessary stage in national development, the proportions are 5 : 1 in the case of the Socialist and Communist voters but only 9 : 4 among the right-wing voters (UDF and RPR), falling almost to 1 : 1 in the case of the extreme Right *Front National*.[125] There are still significant ideological residues, indicating that past wounds have by no means fully healed. That the French now seem less concerned about ancestral hostilities may be due to the belated achievement of Mignet's July Monarchy hope that France was 'a great nation that now only wishes to be a prosperous nation.'[126]

This gives us an important indicator of why the Revolution still represents an unfulfilled ambition and unsatisfied promise. The abandonment of participationist and public 'ancient liberty' for abstentionist and private 'modern liberty' which Constant had detected has meant that the extension of democracy has been accompanied by increasing political indifference. It is no accident that conformity with minimal democratic expectations, such as the modest demand that the citizen vote at infrequent intervals, much less be active in a political party, seems to have withered most in the oldest democracies of the United States and Switzerland.[127] This suggests that democracy's practical success – which continues to expand in the Second and Third Worlds that were widely regarded as destined to replace liberal democracy or demonstrate its unsuitability – has been followed by its failure to mobilize the enthusiasm of the mass population in its homelands. The pursuit of private pleasures seems to have crowded out even the modest demands of Constant's part-time citizenship, while élites have become more concerned with personal enrichment than with public service.

Sieyès and Constant had advocated representative democracy in preference to direct democracy not merely because the latter was impracticable in large states or out of élitism, but precisely because they anticipated that it would make unrealistic demands. Universal suffrage by depersonalizing the voters, reduced from a select public to an anonymous mass, at first increased the importance of the candidate. This was especially true of plebiscitarian Bonapartism – which was destroyed only by military defeat in 1815 and 1870 – but survived at the parliamentary level in the shape of local notables before being revived in the Fifth Republic with the directly elected president. This was imposed by de Gaulle upon the political parties, which had largely reduced parliamentary representatives as well as the voters to the passive status of supporters. Turnout depended upon exciting the voters ephemerally with mendacious propaganda and the lionization of leaders. This was intended to permit those who purport to speak for the majority to exert compulsion that minorities can accept without losing face.[128]

The reason why so many democratic politicians persist in claiming that a majority of the people voted for them when they only have at best a parliamentary majority is that otherwise the legitimacy of their power would appear questionable. De Gaulle organized the presidential electoral system so as to make the legitimizing myth a democratic reality. De Gaulle's triumph in the role of Rousseauist legislator was due to the fact that during the Second World War, from 1940, as well as after the threat of civil war in 1958, he was for a while able to personify both national and democratic legitimacy in France. The Fifth Republic's attempt permanently to institutionalize them is necessarily imperfect and cannot in any case foreclose further progress in both the political process and the objectives it seeks to attain. Despite France's efforts to replace the hated privileges of birth and wealth by merit and election, the exclusive character of the political–administrative élites means that the Revolution's emancipatory ambitions remain unfulfilled. There is still the pending agenda of extending democracy from the political process proper into the way individual enterprises and a pluralist society are organized.[129] Unless these ambitions are dismissed as Utopian aspirations, the Revolution will remain permanently subversive, unfinished and probably interminable.

Our six critics took very different approaches to the democratic revolution and its future. Tocqueville argued that the French Revolution had never happend because there was no gulf between the old and the new. For Maistre, it had been a divine punishment and could be repeated at God's will. Proudhon maintained that the Revolution was an unending, permanent process. Our three remaining protagonists considered that the Revolution would become redundant. In Saint-Simon's case, the coming of an organized industrial society, for Blanqui the abolition of capitalism, for Constant the emergence of a market society and representative system of government, would deprive the Revolution of its indispensable dynamic. Let us leave the final word to a latter-day protagonist of a Proudhonian 'continuous revolution', the self-designated Caliban as spokesman of the working people of France. Jean Guéhenno explained in 1939, for the 150th anniversary of the Revolution, why it could not be immured in a museum. 'It is the perpetual dissatisfaction, the continuous refusal to submit to what has been given to us' that constituted 'the Revolution on the march . . . the building will never be finished because the demands of reason and justice will never be satisfied.'[130] Political perfection not being something we shall ever attain, it can safely be assumed that the liberal democratic Revolution's unfinished business will be indefinitely with us as a summons to effort in pursuit of lofty ideals.

NOTES

Chapter 1

1. Hannah Arendt, *On Revolution*, London, 1963, p. 36; cf. 13, 41, 205–6.
2. Alexis de Tocqueville, *'The European Revolution' and Correspondence with Gobineau*, New York, 1959, p. 58.
3. Tocqueville, p. 103; cf. 155; cf. Arendt, pp. 188, 201–3, 247.
4. Tocqueville, p. 86 and François Furet, 'The French Revolution revisited', *Government and Opposition*, XVI/2, Spring 1981, p. 209; cf. 208–10.
5. Hannah Arendt, 'History and immobility', *Partisan Review*, XXIV/1, Winter 1957, p. 27; cf. 14. Britain, having been 'spared' the Revolution, struggled two hundred years later with the introduction of decimal coinage and the metric system. On the significance of the republican calendar, see Isser Woloch, 'Republican institutions' in Colin Lucas (ed.), *The Political Culture of the French Revolution*, Oxford, 1988, pp. 373–84.
6. Charles Tilly, 'Revolutions and collective violence' in Fred I. Greenstein and Nelson W. Polsby (eds.), *Handbook of Political Science*, III, Reading, MA, 1975, Ch. 5, p. 519. See also Charles Tilly et al, *The Rebellious Century, 1830–1930*, London, 1975, Ch. 3 on France and Leon Trotsky, *The History of the Russian Revolution*, London, 1929, 1967, Eastman translation, I, pp. 202–7.
7. Tilly, *Revolutions*, p. 521; cf. 522–3.
8. Tilly, *Revolutions*, p. 547; cf. 533–41.
9. François Guizot, *Essai sur l'Histoire de France*, 1823, quoted in Georges Gusdorf, *La Conscience Révolutionnaire: Les idéologues*, Paris, 1978, p. 65.
10. Krishan Kumar, *Revolution: The theory and practice of a European idea*, London, 1971, pp. 41–3.
11. Kumar, p. 19; cf. 15–16, 20, 42, 48, 79, 84.
12. Arendt, *On Revolution*, p. 154. On how the Revolution created the concept of an Old Regime see Diego Venturino, 'La naissance de l'Ancien Régime' in Colin Lucas (ed.), *The Political Culture of the French Revolution*, Oxford, 1988, Ch. 1.

13. Alfred Cobban, 'The decline of divine-right monarchy in France' in J. O. Lindsay (ed.), *The New Cambridge Modern History*, VII, Cambridge, 1957, pp. 214–5.
14. Nannerl O. Keohane, *Philosophy and the State in France: The Renaissance to the Enlightenment*, Princeton, 1980, p. 16; cf. 5–27.
15. Keohane, p. 70; cf. 67–77.
16. Keohane, p. 169; cf. 154–7, 171–5, 220–3 and more generally W. F. Church, *Richelieu and Reason of State*, Princeton, 1972.
17. Cobban, p. 220.
18. Germaine de Staël, *Considérations sur les principaux événemens de la Révolution Française depuis son origine jusques et compris le 8 juillet 1815*, Paris, 1818, I, p. 142; cf. 129, 143.
19. Tocqueville, *'The European Revolution'*, pp. 34, 40.
20. Merle L. Perkins, *The Moral and Political Philosophy of the Abbé de St. Pierre*, Geneva, 1959, p. 130; cf. 49, 99–119, 141 and Keohane, pp. 365–6, 371–2.
21. Keohane, p. 390; cf. 376–80.
22. Keohane, p. 384 note; cf. 383–91 and Nannerl O. Keohane, 'Democratic monarchy: the political theory of the Marquis d'Argenson', Ph.D. dissertation, Yale, 1967.
23. Lord Acton, *Essays on Freedom and Power*, Boston, MA, 1948, pp. 232–3, from the first of Acton's *Lectures on the French Revolution* entitled 'The background of the French Revolution'.
24. Lord Acton, p. 231; cf. Keohane, pp. 31–2, 304–6, 349–50, 407; Robert Shackleton, *Montesquieu: A critical biography*, Oxford, 1961, pp. 12–13, 247–8.
25. Melvin Richter, *The Political Theory of Montesquieu*, Cambridge, 1977, p. 85; cf. 9–12; Shackleton, pp. 284–7, 298–301; Keohane, *Philosophy and the State in France*, p. 394. See also Elie Carcassonne, *Montesquieu et le problème de la constitution française au dix-huitième siècle*, Paris, 1927.
26. W. B. Gwyn, *The Meaning of the Separation of Powers*, New Orleans, 1965, pp. 33–4, 37–51.
27. Tocqueville, *'The European Revolution'*, p. 70.
28. Norman Hampson, *Will and Circumstance: Montesquieu, Rousseau and the French Revolution*, London, 1983, p. viii; cf. 24, 58–9, 153 and Chs. 1–3 passim; and N. Hampson, 'From regeneration to terror: the ideology of the French Revolution' in N. O'Sullivan (ed.), *Terrorism, Ideology and Revolution*, Brighton, 1986, p. 51.
29. Marginal note by Rousseau to Helvétius, *De l'Esprit*, quoted by Robert Derathé, *Jean-Jacques Rousseau et la Science Politique de son Temps*, Paris, 1950, 2nd edn 1970, p. 357. On democracy as fit only for gods, see *Social Contract*, 1762, Book III, Ch. 4.
30. Keohane, p. 388.
31. Derathé, pp. 61, 273–6. See Rousseau's *Social Contract*, Book III, Chs. 12 and 15; and the C. E. Vaughan edition of the *Political Writings of Jean-Jacques Rousseau*, Cambridge, 1915, I, pp. 95–102, 318–9, 356.

32. *Social Contract*, Book II, Ch. 2.

33. Rousseau, *Lettre à M. de Beaumont*, III, p. 87, quoted by Derathé, p. 69; cf. 68.

34. This is quoted from the seventh of Rousseau's *Lettres écrites de la Montagne* in Vaughan edn of *Political Writings*, II, p. 217. See also *Social Contract*, Book III, Chs. 16 and 18. On Rousseau's debt to Althusius, who in refuting Bodin anticipated Rousseau's own critique of Hobbes, see Derathé's comments, pp. 93–9, following in the wake of Gierke.

35. *Social Contract*, Book III, Ch. 10; cf. Chs. 4 and 16.

36. Jacques Julliard, *La faute à Rousseau*, Paris, 1985, p. 19; cf. 32–7. For the more extreme modern view of Rousseau, see J. L. Talmon, *The Origins of Totalitarian Democracy*, London, 1952, Part 1, Ch. 3 on 'Totalitarian democracy'. For the opposing standpoint see Alfred Cobban, *Rousseau and the Modern State*, London, 1934, 2nd edn 1964.

37. Rousseau discussed this mainly in his 1772 *Considération sur le Gouvernement de la Pologne*. See Derathé, pp. 277–9. The clearest exposition of Rousseauist direct democracy during the French Revolution came from Pétion. See the contributions by Ran Halévi and Patrice Guenifey in Lucas 1988, pp. 79–81, 243–4.

38. *Social Contract*, Book III, Ch. 18.

39. These quotations from *Considérations sur le Gouvernement de la Pologne* are drawn from Keohane, p. 441 and Herbert Lüthy, *From Calvin to Rousseau: Tradition and modernity in socio-political thought from the Reformation to the French Revolution*, New York, 1965, English edn 1970, p. 261; cf. 264–5. More generally, on the post-Rousseau substitution of republican patriotism for monarchic and aristocratic honour, see Norman Hampson, 'The French Revolution and the nationalisation of honour' in M. R. D. Foot (ed.), *War and Society*, London, 1973, Ch. 12.

40. Cobban, *Rousseau and the Modern State*, p. 116 and more generally Ch. 4 on 'Rousseau and the nation-state'. For a contemporary but unreliable review of Rousseau's influence on the French Revolution, see Sebastian Mercier, *De Jean-Jacques Rousseau considéré comme un des premiers auteurs de la Révolution*, Paris, 1791, 2 vols.

41. Shirley M. Gruner, *Economic Materialism and Social Moralism*, The Hague, 1973, p. 31; cf. 28–33. On the life of Condorcet, see Elisabeth and Robert Badinter, *Condorcet. Un intellectuel en politique*, Paris, 1988.

42. Keith M. Baker, *Condorcet: From natural philosophy to social mathematics*, Chicago, 1975, p. 384; cf. 55–6, 81–2, 260–2. On a more limited continuing twentieth-century attempt in this sense, see Duncan Black, *The Theory of Committees and Elections*, Cambridge, 1958.

43. *Essai sur la constitution et les fonctions des assemblées provinciales*, 1788 in *Oeuvres de Condorcet*, 1847–9, viii, pp. 188–9, quoted in Baker, p. 260. The *Observations* appeared as an appendix to Destutt de Tracy's 1819 commentary on the *Esprit de Lois*. The earlier quotation is from an unpublished manuscript cited in Baker, p. 445 note.

44. Condorcet, *Essai sur la constitution*, p. 656, quoted in Baker, p. 264.

45. 'Fragment de justification', July 1793 in Condorcet, *Oeuvres*, i, 1877, pp. 574–5.
46. Gusdorf, 1978, pp. 200–1.
47. Baker, p. 334; cf. 225, 228–30. For the Montesquieu and d'Argenson reference, see Condorcet's *Essai sur la constitution*, p. 186.
48. Baker, p. 230; cf. 228–31, 236. The Rousseau reference is to the *Social Contract*, Book II, Ch. 3, which quotes d'Argenson in support.
49. Baker, p. 256.
50. *Essai sur la constitution*, pp. 132, 134–5, quoted in Baker, p. 253; cf. 209. Condorcet did not, however, follow Turgot in allocating votes in proportion to ownership of property.
51. Baker, p. 263.
52. Gusdorf, pp. 209–13. Condorcet's essay is reprinted in his *Oeuvres*, viii, pp. 1–113.
53. Baker, p. 330, quoting *Oeuvres de Condorcet*, xii, p. 612. See also Baker, pp. 267–334.
54. Peter Campbell, 'Sieyès and *What is the Third Estate?*' introduction to E. J. Sieyès, *What is the Third Estate?*, London, 1789, 1963 edn, pp. 3, 10, 24.
55. Quoted by C.-A. Sainte-Beuve, *Causeries du Lundi*, Paris, 1852, p. 193; cf. 196; from an unpublished fragment on 'Political economy'. See also Paul Bastid, *Sieyès et sa Pensée*, Paris, 1939, 2nd edn 1970, pp. 293–4.
56. Etienne Dumont, *Souvenirs sur Mirabeau et sur les deux premières assemblées législatives*, Paris, 1832, p. 66; cf. 65.
57. Letter and comment quoted by Bastid 1939, pp. 183, 193. See also Burke's *Reflections on the Revolution in France*, 1790, in the 1888 edn of his *Select Works*, Oxford, pp. 71–2.
58. J. H. Clapham, *The Abbé Sieyès*, Westminster, 1912, p. 199. As Baker puts it in Keith M. Baker (ed.) *The Political Culture of the Old Regime*, Oxford, 1988, p. 487, 'Thus the privileged orders were defined out of the nation according to a political logic of citizenship, according to which they cannot be equal, just as they have been excluded from it according to a social logic of productive activity, according to which they cannot be useful.' More generally, see Patrice Higonnet, *Class, Ideology and the Rights of Nobles during the French Revolution*, Oxford, 1981.
59. Sieyès, p. 51. Four editions of *What is the Third Estate?* were printed in 1789.
60. Sieyès speech on the Royal Veto in September 1789, quoted in Murray Forsyth's excellent *Reason and Revolution: The political thought of the Abbé Sieyès*, Leicester, 1987, p. 138; cf. 49–56, 64–5, 139–50, 162–4.
61. Sieyès, p. 113; cf. 107 ff., 146.
62. Forsyth, pp. 187–8, 221–2.
63. Sainte-Beuve, p. 214. On the nation as expressing the unanimous will of the people, see Forsyth, Ch. 3.
64. Quoted from G. G. Van Deusen, *Sieyès: His life and his nationalism*, New York, 1932, pp. 85–6, 95.
65. Quoted by Bastid, p. 84.

66. Quoted in Gusdorf, p. 174; cf. 103, 110, 114–16.

Chapter 2

1. Alfred Cobban, 'The myth of the French Revolution' in *Aspects of the French Revolution*, 1968, 1971 Paladin edn, Frogmore, p. 93; cf. 35, 43–6, 49, 57–63, 108.
2. Stanley Hoffmann *et al.*, *France: Change and tradition*, London, 1963, p. 2; François Furet, *Interpreting the Revolution*, 1978, Eng. edn 1981, Cambridge, Part I.
3. Alfred Cobban, *A History of Modern France*, 1957, revised Penguin edn 1961, Harmondsworth, I, p. 149.
4. Burke, *Reflections*, pp. 195–200; cf. 149, 155, 164.
5. Tocqueville, '*The European Revolution*', p. 111.
6. Germaine de Staël, *Des Circonstances Actuelles qui peuvent terminer la Révolution et des principes qui doivent fonder la République en France*, 1906, 1979 edn by L. Omacini, Paris-Geneva, p. 273. Her biographer wrote of the *philosophes*: 'They were the press, they were public opinion, they were the teachers of kings; no single group of intellectuals ever held such power before or since.' (J. Christopher Hérold, *Mistress to an Age: The life of Madame de Staël*, London, 1959, p. 26.)
7. Cobban, *Aspects*, pp. 101–6.
8. T. Skocpol, *States and Social Revolutions: A comparative analysis of France, Russia and China*, London, 1979, p. 179; cf. 29–32, 163–5, 175, 199–200. See also Barrington Moore, Jun., *Social Origins of Dictatorship and Democracy: Land and peasant in the making of the modern world*, 1966, Penguin edn 1973, Ch. 2, esp. pp. 57, 64; and Stanley Rothman, 'Barrington Moore and the dialectics of revolution: an essay review', *American Political Science Review*, LXIV, 1970, pp. 70–1. On 'The classic theory of the bourgeois revolution', see D. M. G. Sutherland, *France 1789–1815: Revolution and Counterrevolution*, London, 1985, pp. 12–18; and Albert Soboul, *The Parisian Sans-Culottes and the French Revolution, 1793–4*, Oxford, 1964, Introduction.
9. The most elaborate exposition of this standpoint, in the wake of Burke, was the Abbé A. de Barruel's *Mémoires pour servir à l'histoire du jacobinisme*, Hamburg, 1803.
10. Burke, pp. 225–31; cf. Cobban, *Aspects*, pp. 18–19, 29–33, 36. See also J. G. A. Pocock's essay 'The political economy of Burke's analysis of the French Revolution' in his *Virtue, Commerce and History*, Cambridge, 1985, Ch. 10.
11. Tocqueville, *The Old Régime and the French Revolution*, p. 20; cf. Part 3, Ch. 1 *passim*.
12. Germaine de Staël, *Considérations*, vol. I, p. 1.
13. Tocqueville, '*The European Revolution*', pp. 42, 45. See also Sutherland, pp. 22–33.
14. Keith M. Baker, Introduction to *The Political Culture of the Old Régime*, Oxford, 1988, p. xviii; cf. Ch. 22 by Mona Ozouf in the same volume.

15. Tocqueville, pp. 82, 84; cf. 48–90.
16. Tocqueville, p. 76.
17. Tocqueville, p. 85 and Cobban, *Aspects*, p. 99. On the institutional aspects of the early phase of the Revolution, see Jacques Godechot, *Les Institutions de la France sous la Révolution et l'Empire*, 1951, 2nd edn 1968, Paris, Books 1 and 2.
18. Of the numerous works on the 1789 Declaration prompted by the revolutionary bicentenary, see particularly Stéphane Rials, *La déclaration des droits de l'homme et du citoyen*, Paris, 1988; and Marcel Gauchet, *La Révolution des droits de l'homme*, Paris, 1989.
19. Tocqueville, *The Old Régime*, p. 7.
20. Sutherland, pp. 94–9, 210–17, 231, 282–3, 383.
21. Tocqueville, *The Old Régime*, p. 41; cf. 42–51. On 'federalism' in the French Revolution, see Sutherland, pp. 176–89.
22. Quoted in Cobban, *Aspects*, p. 115 in his essay on 'Local government during the French Revolution'.
23. Burke, *Reflections*, p. 62; cf. 61–4, 216, 219, 221, 232–3.
24. Bastid, *Sieyès*, pp. 90–4.
25. Bastid, p. 121 for the views of Robespierre in 1791, who then believed in such a compromise. See also Cobban, *History of Modern France*, I, p. 180.
26. Cobban, *Aspects*, p. 141; cf. 25 and his *History of Modern France*, I, p. 161.
27. R. R. Palmer, *Twelve Who Ruled*, Princeton, 1941, p. 60; cf. Godechot, pp. 359–71.
28. Palmer, p. 56; cf. 43 and Sutherland, p. 167; cf. 133, 137, 147–8.
29. Rials, pp. 39, 97; and Sutherland, p. 132. See also Furet, 'La monarchie et le règlement électoral en 1789'; and Ran Halévi, 'La monarchie et les élections: position des problèmes' in Baker (ed.), *The Political Culture of the Old Regime*.
30. Cobban, *Aspects*, p. 140; cf. 141, 145, 158.
31. Cobban, p. 142; cf. N. Hampson, *Will and Circumstance*, Ch. 11, *passim*.
32. Palmer, p. 128; Godechot, pp. 294, 297–300.
33. Speech by Robespierre of 5 Nivôse (Christmas 1793) quoted in Palmer, p. 264; cf. 265. More generally, on 'The political ideas of Maximilien Robespierre during the period of the Convention', see the essay by Cobban in *Aspects*, Ch. 9.
34. Palmer, pp. 255, 277; cf. 306. For a vehement statement of the 'totalitarianism' thesis applied to the Jacobins, see Talmon, *The Origins of Totalitarian Democracy*, especially Part 1, Ch. 3 and Part 2, *passim*. The classic study is C. Brinton, *The Jacobins*, New York, 1930.
35. Palmer, p. 128.
36. Cobban, *History of Modern France*, I, p. 213; cf. 171, 212–34. On 'Revolutionary justice' see Godechot, pp. 375–88.
37. Quoted by Hampson, 'From regeneration to terror: the ideology of the French Revolution' in O'Sullivan (ed.) *Terrorism, Ideology and Revolution*, p. 62.
38. Barrington Moore, *Social Origins of Dictatorship and Democracy*, p. 100.
39. Cobban, *History of Modern France*, I, p. 234. Napoleon was appointed General by Robespierre and arrested after his Thermidor overthrow.

40. Germaine de Staël, *Des Circonstances Actuelles*, p. 3; cf. 42–4, 129.
41. Germaine de Staël, p. 170; cf. 160, 167–9. See also 'Note on property', *ibid.*, pp. 45–8 and 152.
42. Germaine de Staël, pp. 111, 189; cf. Godechot, pp. 458–9 and Cobban, *History of Modern France*, I, pp. 242–3.
43. Cabanis, *Oeuvres Philosophiques*, Paris, 1956 edn, II, p. 474 quoted in Thomas E. Kaiser, *The Ideologues: From the Enlightenment to positivism*, Ph.D. dissertation, Harvard; Xerox Microfilm, University of Michigan, p. 270; cf. 58, 102, 178–82, 273.
44. Cabanis, p. 475; cf. 473–4, quoted in Kaiser, pp. 224–5; cf. 94–7, 215–16, 223.
45. F. Picavet, *Les Idéologues*, Paris, 1891, pp. 220–1; cf. 123–4, 408; and Gusdorf, pp. 318–19, 317–27, 360–1; Kaiser, pp. 267–8, 310, 315–17. See also Cabanis, pp. 453–4, 473–4, 477–9 and Martin S. Staum, *Cabanis: Enlightenment and medical philosophy in the French Revolution*, Princeton, 1980, pp. 292–6.
46. Daunou report to the Committee on Public Instruction, in James Guillaume (ed.), *Procès-verbaux du comité d'instruction publique de la Convention Nationale*, Paris, 1891–1906, IV, p. 793, quoted in Kaiser, pp. 300–1; cf. 288–93.
47. Daunou, quoted by Gusdorf, p. 302.
48. The Say quotation is from his Utopia *Olbie, ou essai sur les moyens de réformer les moeurs d'une nation*, Paris, 1799, pp. 97–8. See also Roederer, *Oeuvres*, Paris, VII, 1859, pp. 130, 265–6; and Cabanis, pp. 23–4.
49. Quoted by Jean Roels, *La Notion de Représentation chez Roederer*, UGA Heule, 1968, p. 23; cf. 16. Roederer spent part of the Terror in hiding translating Hobbes' *De Cive, ibid.*, p. 18.
50. Madame de Staël, pp. 161–2, 175–7. See also Sutherland, pp. 249–50, 277–8, 308–9.
51. Tocqueville, '*The European Revolution*', pp. 118; cf. 117–21.
52. Bastid, *Sieyès*, p. 231; cf. 197, 219–29, 234–9, quoting Joseph Bonaparte, *Mémoires et Correspondance*, Paris, 1853, I, p. 77.
53. Quoted by Cobban in *Aspects*, p. 190.
54. Burke, pp. 259–62.
55. Bastid, *Sieyès*, p. 285. For a more recent biography, see Jean-Denis Bredin, *Sieyès. La clé de la Révolution Française*, Paris, 1988.
56. Tocqueville, '*The European Revolution*', p. 147; cf. Tocqueville, *The Old Régime*, p. 209 and Madame de Staël, *Considérations*, II, pp. 324, 377.
57. Quoted by Sutherland, p. 342; cf. Bastid, pp. 255–8, 266.
58. Quoted by Sutherland, p. 360; cf. 339–40, 365.
59. Tocqueville, '*The European Revolution*', pp. 154–5. On the Napoleonic élite, see Sutherland, pp. 385–90.
60. Tocqueville, p. 138.
61. Lord Acton, *Essays on Freedom and Power*, p. 158; cf. Arendt, *On Revolution*, p. 47. See also Jacques Godechot, 'The new concept of nationalism and its diffusion in Europe' in Otto Dann and John Dinwiddy (eds.), *Nationalism in the Age of the French Revolution*, London, 1988, Ch. 2.

62. Sieyès, *What is the Third Estate?*, pp. 124, 126, 128; cf. 58. More generally, see Elie Kedourie, *Nationalism*, London, 1960, Ch. 1 on 'Politics in a new style'.

63. Jean Roels, *Le concept de Représentation Politique au Dix-Huitième Siècle Français*, Louvain-Paris, 1969, pp. 93–7, 118–20, 128–9.

64. Quoted by B. Baczko, 'Le Contrat Social des Français: Sieyès et Rousseau' in Baker (ed.), *Political Culture*, p. 495; cf. pp. 494–506. See also Mariana Valensise, 'La Constitution française', *ibid.*, pp. 441–60; and François Furet, 'Burke ou la fin d'une seule histoire de l'Europe', *Le Débat*, 39, March–May 1986, pp. 57–66.

65. Jean-Jacques Chevallier, *Histoire des institutions et des régimes politiques de la France moderne (1789–1958)*, Paris, 3rd edn 1967, pp. 37–8. See also Buchez and Roux, *Histoire parlementaire de la Révolution française, ou Journal des Assemblées nationales depuis 1789 jusqu'en 1815*, Paris, 1834, II, pp. 16–17.

66. Furet, 'The French Revolution revisited', p. 212; cf. 213, 215.

67. William Doyle, *Origins of the French Revolution*, Oxford, 1980, p. 208; cf. 167, 191, 209–11.

68. Sieyès, *What is the Third Estate?*, p. 182.

69. Peter Campbell, *French Electoral Systems and Elections since 1789*, London, 1958, p. 50; cf. 46–51 and Godechot, pp. 74–6.

70. Burke, *Reflections*, p. 206.

71. Burke, p. 208; cf. 207, 223–4.

72. Campbell, pp. 52–4 and Godechot, pp. 284–8, 458–61.

73. Cobban, *History of Modern France*, I, p. 199; cf. Sutherland, pp. 132, 158, 302, 311–13, 334, 358–9, 365.

74. Furet, 'The French Revolution revisited', p. 201; cf. 218.

75. Tocqueville, '*The European Revolution*', pp. 126, 144.

76. J. McManners, 'The historiography of the French Revolution' in A. Goodwin (ed.), *New Cambridge Modern History*, VIII, 1965, Ch. 2, pp. 622, 629–31.

Chapter 3

1. Isaiah Berlin, 'The hedgehog and the fox', 1953, in *Russian Thinkers*, London, 1978, pp. 77–8.

2. Pierre-Simon Ballanche, *Essais de Palingénésie Sociale*, 1827–9, quoted from his *Oeuvres*, Paris, 1830, III, p. 259.

3. Alphonse de Lamartine, *Souvenirs et Portraits*, Paris, 1874, I, pp. 188–9. For a pen portrait of Maistre by Lamartine, see Jean Rebotton, 'Lamartine and the Maistre family' in Richard A. Lebrun (ed.) *Maistre Studies*, London, 1988, pp. 276–7. The *Considerations* were published anonymously because Maistre was an official of a government that had recently signed a peace treaty with France.

4. Quoted by Dominique Bagge, *Les Idées Politiques en France sous la Restauration*, Paris, 1952, p. 48 note.

5. Jean-Yves Le Borgne, *Joseph de Maistre et la Révolution*, Brest, 1976, p. 43; and Robert Triomphe, *Joseph de Maistre: Etude sur la vie et sur la doctrine*

d'un matérialiste mystique, Geneva, 1968, p. 97 note. Henri de Maistre has published a biography of his ancestor, *Joseph de Maistre*, Paris, 1990. It adds little to our existing knowledge.

6. Quoted in Le Borgne, p. 44; cf. 36–46 on Maistre's pre-revolutionary writings, notably the posthumously published Rousseauist *Discours sur la Vertu* of 1777 and *Le caractère extérieur du magistrat ou les moyens d'obtenir la confiance publique* of 1784. The quotation is from Maistre's *Mémoire sur la vénalité des charges*. For this work and the unfinished *Mémoire sur les Parlements*, also of 1788, see C. de Paillette, *La Politique de Joseph de Maistre d'après ses premiers écrits*, Paris, 1895.

7. J. M. Roberts, *The Mythology of the Secret Societies*, New York, 1972, pp. 295–6; cf. Ch. 6 *passim*. See also Triomphe, pp. 100–15; Le Borgne, pp. 25–31, 47–57; and Richard A. Lebrun, *Joseph de Maistre: An intellectual militant*, Kingston and Montreal, 1988, pp. 53–69.

8. Le Borgne, p. 59.

9. Letter of the Baron de Rubat, published in François Descostes, *Necker écrivain et financier, jugé par le comte Joseph de Maistre*, Chambéry, 1896, pp. 23–4. More generally, see Triomphe, pp. 118–22.

10. *Etude sur la Souveraineté* quoted by Dominique Bagge, *Les Idées Politiques en France*, p. 268.

11. Sainte-Beuve's extended, two-part article on Maistre is in *Revue des Deux Mondes*, 1843, III and the quotation is from p. 375. The view adopted is that advanced by Le Borgne, pp. 61–2 and J. Nicholas, 'La conversion de Joseph de Maistre', *Annales Historiques de la Révolution Française*, January–March 1971, pp. 113–29 in preference to that of Triomphe, p. 133; cf. 136.

12. 'Discours à Madame la Marquise de Costa', *Lettres et Opuscules inédites*, Paris, 1851, 4th edn 1861, II, pp. 141–2, quoted in Le Borgne, p. 70; cf. 66–88. Maistre was the only senator of Savoyard origin to go into exile, to 'begin a new career as a counter-revolutionary propagandist' (Lebrun, p. 36).

13. Joseph de Maistre, *Correspondance diplomatique, 1811–17*, Blanc edn, Paris, 1860, II, p 32. See also Samuel Rocheblave, *Etude sur Joseph de Maistre*, 1922, p. 41.

14. Letter of his friend Comte Costa de Beauregard, *Oeuvres Complètes*, Lyon, 1884–7, IX, p. 11. For other references to Burke, *ibid.*, I, pp. 109, 321 and VIII, p. 533. See also Lebrun, pp. 100–3.

15. Maistre's *Essai sur le principe générateur des constitutions politiques*, Paris, 1814, quoted in F. Holdsworth, *Joseph de Maistre et l'Angleterre*, Paris, 1935, p. 223. See also Maistre's 'Etude sur la Souveraineté' in *Oeuvres Complètes*, I, pp. 497–500.

16. *Essai sur le principe générateur des constitutions politiques*, written in 1809, published in 1814, in Maistre's *Oeuvres Complètes*, I, pp. 241–2; cf. 235, 246–7, 265.

17. *Ibid.*, p. 299; cf. 243–4, 265–6. Rémusat's article 'Du Traditionnalisme' is in *Revue des Deux Mondes*, 18 May 1857, pp. 250–2; cf. 241–70.

18. Maistre, *Fragments* written in 1794–5 and published posthumously in *Oeuvres Complètes*, I, pp. 217–18, quoted in J.-P. Cordelier, *La Théorie Constitutionnel*

de Joseph de Maistre, Paris, 1965, p. 166; cf. 72–94 for a detailed comparison of Burke and Maistre. On his sympathy with the American Revolution, see Triomphe, p. 98.

19. Letter to the future Louis XVIII's favourite d'Avaray of 30 August 1797 in Ernest Daudet edition of *Joseph de Maistre et Blacas: Leur correspondance inédite et l'histoire de leur amitié, 1804–1820*, Paris, 1908, p. 9. For Constant's role in prompting Maistre's *Considérations sur la France*, see the critical edition to this work by René Johannet and Francis Vermale, Paris, 1936, pp. XIX–XXIII; and J.-L. Darcel's introduction to his edition of the *Considérations*, Geneva, 1980, pp. 20, 42, 153 note, 162 note.

20. Letter of Vignet of 1794, *Oeuvres Complètes*, IX, p. 78; cf. Le Borgne, pp. 105–15, 132–3, 157.

21. *Considérations sur la France* in *Oeuvres Complètes*, I, p. 7. Louis-Claude de Saint-Martin's anticipatory work was his *Lettre à un ami ou considérations politiques, philosophiques et religieuses sur la Révolution française*, Paris, 1795. See also Auguste Viatte, *Les sources occultes du Romantisme*, Paris, 1928.

22. Quoted in Pierre Haubtmann, *P.-J. Proudhon: Genèse d'un Antithéiste*, Paris, 1969, p. 161.

23. 'Discours préliminaire' to *Du Pape*, Lyon, 1819, written in 1816–17; and correspondence, *Oeuvres Complètes*, XIV, p. 156; cf. Le Borgne, pp. 175–7, 185–92.

24. *Considérations*, in *Oeuvres Complètes*, I, p. 74.

25. Triomphe, p. 372. See Maistre's *Réflexions sur le protestantisme et la souveraineté* of 1797, published in *Oeuvres Complètes*, VIII, pp. 63–97. More generally, see Le Borgne, pp. 199–206, 219–24, 228–9; cf. 121–8. On the Latin derivation of *homo*, see Hannah Arendt, *On Revolution*, p. 39.

26. Charles Loyseau, *Traité des seigneuries*, Paris, 1608, quoted by Keohane, *Philosophy and the State in France*, pp. 126–7; cf. 84.

27. Quoted by R. R. Palmer, *Twelve Who Ruled: The year of the Terror in the French Revolution*, Princeton, 1941, pp. 34–5.

28. *Oeuvres Complètes*, VII, p. 434; cf. pp. 383–500.

29. Quoted in Palmer, pp. 36, 46–7; cf. 56.

30. Palmer, p. 42.

31. Hannah Arendt, 'The cold war and the West', *Partisan Review*, XXIX/I, Winter 1962, pp. 16, 18. In 1990 it was also occurring in the Soviet Union and Eastern Europe.

32. *Etude sur la Souveraineté*, Book II, Ch. 4, in *Oeuvres Complètes*, I, p. 465; cf. 464–7. On the Greek conception of 'isonomy', see Hannah Arendt, *On Revolution*, p. 22.

33. *Etudes sur la Souveraineté* in *Oeuvres Complètes*, I, 473 and 312–13.

34. *Considérations sur la France*, Paris, 1936 edn, p. 94.

35. See Félicité de Lamennais, *De la Religion considérée dans ses rapports avec l'ordre politique et civil*, Paris, 1825, Ch. 1; and Louis de Bonald, *Démonstration philosophique du principe constitutif de la société*, Paris, 1830.

36. *Etude sur la Souveraineté* in the edn by Jack Lively, *The Works of Joseph de Maistre*, London, 1965, p. 112.

37. *Soirées de St. Petersbourg* in the Lively edn, p. 192. Maistre's eulogy of the executioner was inspired by Sir Henry Jones' translation of the *Laws of Menu*. See Cyprian P. Blamires, *Three Critiques of the French Revolution: Maistre, Bonald and Saint-Simon*, unpublished D.Phil. thesis, Oxford, 1985, pp. 139–41.
38. Hannah Arendt, *On Revolution*, p. 185; cf. 184–6. The Maistre quotation is from the *Soirées de St. Petersbourg*, quoted by Pierre Haubtmann, *P.-J. Proudhon: Genèse d'un Antithéiste*, p. 129.
39. Alexis de Tocqueville, 'The European Revolution', p. 154.
40. Quoted in Fernand Baldensperger, *Le mouvement des idées dans l'émigration française, 1789–1815*, Paris, 1924, II, p. 244. Maistre became a close friend of Blacas, who spent 1804–8 in St Petersburg (Lebrun, p. 190).
41. Maistre, *Lettres à un gentilhomme russe sur l'Inquisition Espagnole*, Paris, 1922, p. 60.
42. See Blamires, pp. 151–2.
43. *Du Pape*, I, p. XIX; cf. C. Latrelle, *Joseph de Maistre et la Papauté*, Paris, 1906, pp. 338–45.
44. *Considérations sur la France* in Lively edn, p. 68. For a statement of the view that Maistre was sympathetic to nationalism, see Francis Bayle, *Les Idées Politiques de Joseph de Maistre*, Lyon, 1944, pp. 39–43, drawing upon Albert Blanc's edition of Maistre's *Mémoires Politiques et correspondance diplomatique*, Paris, 1858, whose author thanks Cavour for his help in publishing a book that was inspired by the Italian government.
45. *Etude sur la Souveraineté* in *Oeuvres Complètes*, I, p. 327; cf. Ch. 4 *passim* and pp. 545–53. Maistre admits in a note on p. 552 that his ideas on nationality are incomplete, 'would take him too far and would anyway be beyond him'. For his high opinion of the French, see 'Caractère et influence de la nation française', one of his posthumously published 'Fragments sur la France' included in his *Oeuvres Complètes*, I, pp. 187–96.
46. Triomphe, p. 26.
47. For Maistre's 1809 report, see *Oeuvres Complètes*, XI, p. 352; and more generally, Le Borgne, pp. 247–9, 274–5, 318. On the irritation of the Sardinian authorities, see Triomphe, p. 212 note; cf. 174–5, 184–5, 191–2, 308–25, 342–7. On his truculent personality, see testimony of his friend Costa de Beauregard, *Un homme d'autrefois*, Paris, 1878, pp. 405–6.
48. Letters quoted by Haubtmann, p. 130 and George Cogordan, *Joseph de Maistre*, Paris, 1894, p. 108. See also Triomphe, pp. 178, 225–41, 330; Le Borgne, pp. 252–4 and *Lettres et Opuscules inédites du Comte Joseph de Maistre*, sixth edn Paris, 1873, II, p. 62.
49. Letter of 24 March 1817, quoted by Lebrun, p. 251.
50. Madame de Staël, *Considérations sur les principaux événemens de la Révolution Française*, Paris, 1818, III, p. 177. Maistre wrote to Bonald on 22 March 1819 that he found Madame de Staël's *Considérations* very provocative and when Bonald wrote his extended refutation in 1818 he affected to regard this pioneering study as 'another novel on politics and society' by the author of *Corinne* and *Delphine*. See Bonald's *Oeuvres Complètes*, Paris, 1864, II,

pp. 593–660. On 'The English image of Joseph de Maistre', see E. D. Watt's article in *European Studies Review*, IV/3, 1974, pp. 239–59.

51. Quoted by John Morley in *Critical Miscellanies*, London, 1886, II, p. 329.
52. Eugène Rodrigues, *Lettres sur La Religion et la Politique*, Paris, 1832 (bound with Saint-Simon's *Nouveau Christianisme*), pp. 191, 203; cf. 200–4. Further references to Maistre at pp. 249–50, 260.
53. Rodrigues, Fifth Letter, p. 171; cf. 174.
54. On the influence of Maistre and Comte on Maurras and his *Enquête sur la Monarchie*, see Bayle, pp. 23–6, 138–40; and Cordelier, pp. 177–83.
55. Maistre, *Etude sur la souveraineté, Oeuvres Complètes*, I, p. 554.
56. Proudhon, *De la Justice dans la Révolution et dans l'Eglise*, quoted by Haubtmann, *P.-J. Proudhon: Genèse d'un Antithéiste*, pp. 123, 131 note.
57. Proudhon, *Idée générale de la révolution*, quoted by Haubtmann, p. 123. The late-nineteenth-century champion of this school, Louis Veuillet, wrote to Maistre's son on 9 February 1847: 'God made me a Catholic. M. de Maistre made me Roman.' Quoted by Lebrun, p. 261; cf. 269.
58. Haubtmann, p. 131; cf. 125–31; cf. K. Steven Vincent, *Pierre Joseph Proudhon and the Rise of Republican Socialism*, Oxford, 1984, pp. 24–6. On reprints, see Mellon, *Political Uses of History*, p. 60 note; and Lebrun, pp. 239–40, 246.
59. Haubtmann, *La Philosophie Sociale de P.-J. Proudhon*, Grenoble, 1980, pp. 186, 188–9, and the appendix 'Comte vu par Proudhon', pp. 183–96.
60. Haubtmann, *P.-J. Proudhon: Genèse d'un Antithéiste*, p. 207, quoting *De la Justice*, II, p. 177. See also Haubtmann, *ibid.*, p. 198.
61. Arendt, *On Revolution*, pp. 66, 76, 65; cf. 68, 70, 87.
62. Triomphe, p. 369.

Chapter 4

1. Frank E. Manuel, *The New World of Henri Saint-Simon*, Cambridge, MA, Harvard University Press, 1956, p. 212; cf. 119–24.
2. Thomas Kaiser, pp. 610ff. On the Newton mania of the late eighteenth and early nineteenth centuries, see Henri Gouhier, *La Jeunesse d'Auguste Comte*, Paris, 1933–41, II, pp. 200–14; cf. 185 and III, pp. 158–9, 170, 230. For an early English example, see the work of a friend and disciple of Newton, J. T. Desaguliers, *The Newtonian System of the World, the Best Model of Government*, London, 1728.
3. P.-C.-F. Daunou, *Essai sur la puissance temporelle des papes et sur l'abus qu'ils ont fait de leur ministère spirituel*, Paris, 1818; cf. Daunou, *Essai sur les garanties individuelles que réclament l'état actuel de la société*, Paris, 3rd edn, 1822, pp. 151–5.
4. *Elémens d'Idéologie*, Paris, 1817 edn, p. 287, quoted in Kaiser, p. 616.
5. *Oeuvres de Claude-Henri de Saint-Simon*, Paris, 1966 edn, I, p. 248.
6. Keith Taylor (ed.), *Henri Saint-Simon (1760–1825): Selected writings on science, industry and social organization*, London, 1975, p. 162, extracted from the second 'Letter to an American' in *L'Industrie*, II, 1817.
7. *Ibid.* p. 163.

8. Manuel, p. 23; cf. Gouhier, II, pp. 67–73.
9. Ronnie Butler, *Balzac and the French Revolution*, London, 1983, p. 17 and Ch. 1 *passim*. See also Marcel Marion, *La Vente des biens nationaux pendant la Révolution*, Paris, 1908.
10. Manuel, p. 39; cf. 26ff. and Gouhier, II, pp. 76–86.
11. Manuel, pp. 49–50 and Gouhier, pp. 89–101, 111–12. On the discussions with Bonaparte, see Antoine-Clair Thibaudeau, *Mémoires sur la Convention et le Directoire*, Paris, 1824, II, p. 338.
12. *Du Système Industriel* in *Oeuvres de Saint-Simon*, III, p. 78.
13. Guizot's review of Montlosier's *De la Monarchie française* in *Archives philosophiques, politiques et littéraires*, III, June 1818, quoted by Pierre Rosanvallon, *Le Moment Guizot*, Paris, 1985, p. 210. See also Manuel, pp. 263–70.
14. Gouhier, III, p. 223 and II, pp. 215–16; cf. 2, 321–3.
15. Gouhier, II, p. 3, quoting *De la Littérature*, Paris, Year VIII, Pt I, Ch. 20.
16. Condorcet, *Vie de Turgot*, London, 1786, pp. 276–7, quoted by Frank E. Manuel, *The Prophets of Paris*, Cambridge, MA, pp. 162, 50. On the Abbé de St-Pierre, see Keohane, pp. 363–73.
17. Baker, *Condorcet*, p. 343; cf. 340–2.
18. Manuel, *The New World of Henri Saint-Simon*, p. 75; cf. 153 and 397–8 note. See also Kaiser, pp. 157–61.
19. Baker, pp. 375–6.
20. Taylor (ed.), *Selected Writings*, pp. 101–2; cf. 113. See also Manuel, *New World*, pp. 124–9.
21. Manuel, *New World*, p. 118; cf. 81. On Condorcet, see Baker, p. 381.
22. Manuel, p. 86; cf. 64, 81–5, 88, 117, 137.
23. Manuel, pp. 53, 56–8, 80; and Gouhier, II, pp. 41, 45, 102, 123–5.
24. *Des Circonstances Actuelles*, p. 32; cf. 26–30.
25. Cheryl Welch, *Liberty and Utility, The French Ideologues and the Transformation of Liberalism*, New York, 1984, pp. 100–1; cf. Destutt de Tracy, *Commentaire sur l'Esprit des Lois* written in 1806, published in English in 1811, 1st French edn 1819, pp. 62–78, 223–4. More generally on the ideologue influence on Saint-Simon, see Manuel, pp. 80–1.
26. Taylor, (ed.), *Selected Writings*, p. 112; cf. 111 from Saint-Simon's 1813 *Memoir on the Science of Man*. See also Gouhier, II, pp. 198–9.
27. Manuel, p. 300; cf. 67–70, 295–302, 309; and Welch, pp. 46–50.
28. Welch, p. 44. See also Kaiser, pp. 499–502.
29. Quoted in Manuel, p. 382 note.
30. See Gusdorf, p. 403 and *Oeuvres de Condorcet*, I, pp. 421–2. See also the call for a 'social science', including political science, by a future *idéologue*, Lacretelle, in vol. IV, p. 749 of the *Encyclopédie Méthodique* of 1781, quoted by Gusdorf, p. 394; cf. 400–1.
31. Welch, pp. 35, 44–5. For the quotation from Cabanis, see *ibid.*, p. 37.
32. *Ibid.*, p. 51; cf. 23.
33. Quoted *ibid.*, p. 31 from *La Décade Philosophique* of 8 July 1795.
34. Quoted by Gouhier, II, p. 42 from *La Décade Philosophique*, XX, 1799, pp. 336–9.

35. Kaiser, pp. 313–14, 634; cf. 322–3.
36. Gouhier, II, p. 344. See Jules Michelet, *Histoire du XIXᵉ Siècle: Le Directoire*, Paris, 1872, pp. 18, 21–2, 181–2.
37. Gouhier, p. 152; cf. 176.
38. Gouhier, III, p. 174–5; cf. 74; II, pp. 345–6; and Manuel, pp. 117, 195, 216, 342.
39. Augustin Thierry, *Considérations sur l'Histoire de France*, reprinted in his *Oeuvres*, Paris, 1878, VII, p. 182, quoted in Douglas Johnson, *Guizot: Aspects of French history*, 1787–1874, London, 1963, p. 325. See also Gouhier, III, pp. 72–9 and Gruner, pp. 103–8; and R. N. Smithson, *Augustin Thierry: Social and political consciousness in the evolution of a historical method*, Geneva, 1972, pp. 15–20 and Chs. 3–5.
40. Gouhier, III, p. 383; cf. 385.
41. Quoted by Gouhier, III, p. 242 note.
42. Friedrich Hayek, *The Counter-Revolution of Science: Studies in the abuse of reason*, Glencoe, 1955, p. 193.
43. Gouhier, III, pp. 199, 226–7, 360–1, 371–2.
44. Quoted by Albert Hirschman, *The Passions and the Interests*, Princeton, 1977, p. 80; cf. 71–80.
45. Hirschman, pp. 83–4, quoting Steuart's *Inquiry*, London, 1767, I, pp. 215, 279.
46. Hirschman, p. 95, quoting the *Philosophie Rurale* from Ronald L. Meek, *The Economics of Physiocracy*, Cambridge, MA, 1963, p. 63.
47. Hirschman, pp. 110–11, quoting *An Inquiry into the Nature and Causes of the Wealth of Nations*, Cannan edn, New York, 1937, p. 595. See also Hirschman, pp. 69, 103–13.
48. Kaiser, pp. 533–4, quoting Jean-Baptiste Say's *Traité d'Economie Politique*, Paris, 1803, I, pp. i–iii and *Oeuvres diverses de J.-B. Say*, Paris, 1848, pp. 368–9, 389–90.
49. Kaiser, pp. 227–34, quoting Roederer, *Oeuvres du Comte P. L. Roederer*, VII, 1859, pp. 130, 265; Cabanis, *Oeuvres Philosophiques de Cabanis*, Paris, 1956 edn, II, pp. 23–4, 366, 462–3, 466; Say in *La Décade Philosophique*, IX, Year 4, p. 42.
50. Ghita Ionescu (ed.), *The Political Thought of Saint-Simon*, London, 1976, p. 122; cf. 121–3, quoting from *L'Industrie*.
51. Ionescu, p. 123. We shall encounter this concept of theft again in Chapter 7 on Proudhon.
52. Ionescu, pp. 126–7. The word 'lawyer' has been substituted throughout for 'jurist'.
53. Quotation from Taylor (ed.) of *Selected Writings*, p. 131; cf. 130–5. For Maistre's views, see *The Pope*, 1819, English edn London, 1850, p. 347; cf. 213 and the conclusion, pp. 346ff. More generally, see Gouhier, III, pp. 81–91.
54. Taylor (ed.), *Selected Writings*, p. 141.
55. Taylor, p. 144, from Saint-Simon's letter to Carnot, who had secured for him the post of Librarian of the *Arsénal*. See Gouhier, III, pp. 100–2. More generally, on the internationalism of Saint-Simon and the Saint-Simonians, see J.-L.

Puech, *La Tradition Socialiste en France et la Société des Nations*, Paris, 1921, Chs. 1 and 2 respectively.

56. Taylor (ed.), *Selected Writings*, p. 34.
57. Quoted in Gouhier, III, p. 206; cf. 208.
58. Gouhier, II, p. 156; cf. 155–9, quoting Saint-Simon's 1808 'Introduction to the scientific studies of the nineteenth century'.
59. Felix Markham (ed.), *Social Organisation, the Science of Man and Other Writings*, Oxford, 1952, pp. 78–9. See Taylor (ed.), *Selected Writings*, pp. 83–5.
60. Manuel, p. 76.
61. Taylor (ed.), *Selected Writings*, pp. 102, 230, the latter from a footnote 'On liberty' to the Preface to *Du Système Industriel*, 1821.
62. Stanley Mellon, *The Political Uses of History: A study of historians in the French Revolution*, Stanford, 1958, pp. 185–8; cf. 153–84 and Pierre Rosanvallon, pp. 157–67, 238–9, 256–7.
63. Quoted in Gouhier, II, p. 313; cf. 314–18.
64. Gouhier, III, p. 333 note; cf. 327–34.
65. This article first appeared in the Saint-Simonian *Le Producteur* in March 1826 but is quoted from the Ronald Fletcher edition of Comte's Early Essays in *The Crisis of Industrial Civilization*, London, 1974, pp. 219, 225; cf. 217ff.
66. *Ibid.*, p. 230; cf. 219–20, 225–6.
67. Auguste Comte, *Système de Politique Positive*, Paris, 1851–4, I, pp. 109–10. On Condorcet, see *ibid.*, I, p. 64 and II, p. 451. On Maistre, see *ibid.*, I, p. 64 and II, pp. 86, 178; cf. Comte's more critical *Cours de Philosophie Positive*, Paris, 1830–42, IV, pp. 5–8, 11–12, 25–9, 34–5, 66ff., 184, 422–3, 582. See also Elie Halévy, *L'Ere des Tyrannies*, Paris, 1938, pp. 43ff.
68. Hirschman, p. 48; cf. 17–19, 37, 41ff.
69. Boswell's *Life of Johnson*, quoted *ibid.*, p. 58; cf. 49–63.
70. Speech to his Lisieux electors in 1841 and again to Chamber of Deputies on 1 March 1843. See Rosanvallon, pp. 134–5.
71. Gruner, p. 91 note; cf. Joseph Barnave, *Introduction à la Révolution Française*, Paris, 1793. The Barnave 1791 quotation is from Rosanvallon, p. 17.
72. Michael James, 'Pierre–Louis Roederer, Jean-Baptiste Say, and the concept of *industrie*', *History of Political Economy*, IX/4, 1977, pp. 457–65; cf. Roederer's *Mémoires sur quelques points d'économie politique*, 1800–1, published in *Oeuvres du Comte P.-L. Roederer*, VII, pp. 41–97. See also Gusdorf, pp. 528–30.
73. Roederer, 'Introduction', *Journal d'Economie publique, de Morale et de Politique*, Year IV, no. 1, p. 3; cf. Thomas Kaiser, 'Politics and political economy in the thought of the ideologues', *History of Political Economy*, XII/2, 1980, p. 147. As well as his pioneering work in economics, Roederer was attracted by 'political arithmetic', like his friend Madame de Staël. See his edited *Collection de divers ouvrages d'Arithmétique politique*, Paris, 1796.
74. Kaiser, 'Politics and political economy', p. 149, quoting Roederer, 'Introduction', p. 9; cf. his *Oeuvres*, VIII, pp. 265–6.
75. Destutt de Tracy, *Commentaire*, p. 357, quoted by Gruner, pp. 101–2; cf. 79, 97. On Tracy's labour theory of value, see his *Commentaire*, pp. 292–4.
76. Jean-Baptiste Say, *Traité d'économie politique*, 1st edn, Paris, 1803, I, pp. i–ii,

xxxiii–iv; cf. Kaiser, 'Politics and political economy', pp. 150–1. Say's *Treatise* was very popular and would have been immediately reprinted except that Napoleon, who had excluded him from the *Tribunat*, forbade it. A new edition had to await Napoleon's exile in 1814. See Charles Gide and Charles Rist, *Histoire des Doctrines Economiques*, Paris, 5th edn 1926, p. 125; cf. 124–36 for more general views on Say's economic theory. It was translated from the fourth edition by C. R. Princeps, Philadelphia, 1821.

77. Bert F. Hoselitz, 'The early history of entrepreneurial theory' in J. T. Spengler and W. R. Allen (eds.), *Essays in Economic Thought*, Chicago, 1960, p. 251; cf. 247–54. See also James, pp. 466–9, who suggests that Say may have been anticipated by Richard Cantillon's *Essai sur la nature du commerce en général*, London, 1755.

78. Welch, p. 83; cf. Tracy, *Elémens d'idéologie*, IV, Paris, 1817, p. 338.

79. Welch, p. 84, quoting Tracy's *Elémens*, IV, p. 341.

80. Welch, p. 90, quoting Tracy's *Elémens*, IV, p. 294; cf. 295.

81. Kaiser, *The Ideologues*, pp. 563–4, 569–73; cf. Tracy, *Elémens*, IV, pp. 319–21.

82. 'Letters from an inhabitant of Geneva to his contemporaries' in Taylor (ed.), *Selected Writings*, pp. 71–7.

83. Quoted by Gouhier, III, p. 137; cf. 114–6 and Ephraim Harpaz, ' "Le Censeur Européen". Histoire d'un journal Industrialiste', Part 1, *Revue d'Histoire Economique et Social*, XXXVII, 1959, pp. 203–4.

84. Saint-Simon, 'On liberalism and industrialism' in *Catechism of the Industrialists*, 1824, which appears in slightly different translations in the Ionescu (pp. 182–3) and Taylor (p. 257) selected editions of Saint-Simon's works. See also Gouhier, III, pp. 35 note, 49 note, 142–3, and Taylor, p. 287.

85. Taylor (ed.), *Selected Writings*, p. 161 note.

86. Kaiser, 'Politics and political economy', p. 143. On the origin of the term 'Industrial revolution', see Manuel, *The Prophets of Paris*, p. 310, presumably from Blanqui's *Histoire de l'Economie Politique en Europe*, 1837, American edn New York, 1880, Ch. 38 *passim*.

87. Ionescu edition of *The Political Thought of Saint-Simon*, p. 128, from 'On what has until now retarded the progress of industry', *L'Industrie*, 1817.

88. Taylor (ed.), *Selected Writings*, p. 158; cf. 159.

89. Taylor, pp. 164–5. As these letters were written between the secretaryships of Thierry and Comte, Gouhier follows Dunoyer in suggesting that Saint-Simon used a young philosophy teacher Maignien to actually write them. Gouhier, III, pp. 131–2.

90. Taylor, (ed.), *Selected Writings*, p. 166.

91. Taylor, pp. 166–8.

92. Harpaz, pp. 188–91, 203–6, 213; and Elie Halévy, *L'Ere des Tyrannies*, pp. 31–40.

93. See Gouhier, III, pp. 143–56, for a discussion of Dunoyer's February 1827 article in the *Revue Encyclopédique*, 'Notice historique sur l'industrialisme' (included in Dunoyer's *Oeuvres*, Paris, 1870, III, notably pp. 178–84); and Saint-Simon's comments in *Catéchisme des Industriels* in 1824, republished in *Oeuvres de Saint-Simon et d'Enfantin*, Paris, 1865–76, XXXVII, pp. 168ff. See also Harpaz,

pp. 194–8, Manuel, pp. 184–90 and Gruner, pp. 89–91, 94–102, 111–22.

94. *Bibliothèque Nationale* MSS, NAF 24605, quoted by Manuel, *New World*, p. 197; cf. 237–9. See also Gouhier, III, pp. 144–9, 156 and Constant's 1826 review of Dunoyer's *L'industrie et la morale dans leur rapport avec la liberté* in Ephraim Harpaz (ed.), *Benjamin Constant Publiciste, 1825–1830*, Paris, 1987, pp. 85, 100–30.

95. John Stuart Mill, *Auguste Comte and Positivism*, London, 1865, p. 196; cf. 141 and 168. For a satire upon Saint-Simon's eulogy of the entrepreneur, see Stendhal's pamphlet *D'un Nouveau Complot contre les Industriels*, 1825, 1972 edn Paris, pp. 10–27, 78–90.

96. P. Duchon, *Mémoires de Laffitte, 1767–1844*, Paris, 1932, quoted by Butler, p. 146; cf. 144. See also Fritz Redlich, 'Jacques Laffitte and the beginnings of investment banking in France', *Bulletin of the Business Historical Society*, 1948, XXII, pp. 137–61; Maurice Lévy-Leboyer, *Les Banques Européennes et l'Industrialisation Internationale dans la première moitié du dix-neuvième siècle*, Paris, 1964, pp. 426, 432 note, 483 note.

97. Manuel, p. 183; cf. 181–2, 192. On the Restoration Stock Exchange, see Bertier de Sauvigny, *La Restauration*, Paris, 1955, p. 312.

98. André Liesse, *Portraits de financiers*, Paris, 1908, p. 274; cf. Gouhier, III, pp. 117–29, 164, and Lévy-Leboyer, p. 483 note. More generally on Laffitte's key innovative role in French banking, see Bertrand Gille, *La Banque et le Crédit en France de 1815 à 1848*, Paris, 1959, pp. 52–5, 109–17, 248–52, 258–9, 276–83, 302–3, 372–3. For a hostile view, see Marcel Chaminade, *La Monarchie et les puissances d'argent (1814–1848)*, Paris, 1933, pp. 161–70.

99. Louis Blanc, *Histoire de Dix Ans, 1830–1840*, Paris, 1841, new edn n.d., I, p. 166; cf. 198, 299–304, 365–6. See also David H. Pinkney, *The French Revolution of 1830*, Princeton, 1972.

100. Blanc, II, p. 304; cf. 126–34, 149–53, 214–21, 303–6. See also Lévy-Leboyer, pp. 483–7; and T. E. B. Howarth, *Citizen King: The life of Louis-Philippe King of the French*, London, 1961, p. 193; cf. 139, 147, 175, 185, 189, 195. For a less hostile view of Laffitte, see Sherman Kent, *Electoral Procedure under Louis Philippe*, New Haven, 1937, pp. 17, 19, 157–8, 166, 237.

101. Arthur L. Dunham, *The Industrial Revolution in France, 1815–1848*, New York, 1955, p. 340; cf. 222 note, 342, 430–1. On Ternaux's industrial activities, see Charles Ballot, *Introduction du machinisme dans l'industrie française*, Paris, 1923, pp. 195–208. See also L. M. Lomüller, *Guillaume Ternaux, 1763–1833: Créateur de la première intégration industrielle française*, Paris, 1978, pp. 27–9, 318, 325, 378–80. On Ternaux and Saint-Simon, see Gouhier, III, pp. 117–9 and Manuel, pp. 256, 289, 330–1, 411 note; cf. 325–7.

102. Madame Sontadé-Rouger, 'Les Notables sous la Restauration', *Revue d'Histoire économique et sociale*, 1960, I, pp. 99–107; cf. Butler, pp. 89, 123–4, 155–7; cf. Kent, Ch. 2 on 'The electorate and the corps of eligibles', under the July Monarchy.

103. Montlosier, *De la Monarchie française*, Paris, 1814, quoted in Manuel, pp. 412–13 note. More generally, see Manuel's Ch. 21, especially pp. 243–9; cf. 72–3, 282–3.

104. *Considérations sur les intérêts du tiers adressés au peuple des provinces*, quoted in Keith M. Baker (ed.), *The Political Culture of the Old Régime*, p. 407.
105. Reprinted from *Le Politique* in Taylor (ed.), *Selected Writings*, p. 190; cf. 188. See also Plato's *Republic*, Dent edn 1976, Book 8, pp. 248, 256, 261. For the d'Argenson and Tracy anticipations see Gouhier, ii, p. 20, and iii, p. 208 note; and for Dunoyer, see Halévy, p. 37 quoting *Le Censeur Européen* of 1817, ii, p. 102.
106. First extract from the *Organisateur, Oeuvres*, ii, pp. 17–26 and Taylor (ed.), *Selected Writings*, pp. 194–7; cf. Gouhier, iii, p. 220.
107. Taylor (ed.), *Selected Writings*, p. 185; cf. 183–4. For Say's attack on the state as entrepreneur, see his *Treatise on Political Economy*, Book i, Chs. 17 and 18.
108. Taylor, p. 209, from *L'Organisateur*, 1820, which Taylor has entitled 'On the replacement of government by administration'.
109. Taylor, pp. 213–14; cf. 211–16 from *Du Système Industriel*.
110. Taylor, p. 237; cf. 231–6, 255.
111. Lévy-Leboyer, pp. 16–17 on the Laffitte industrial finance scheme to set up *La Société Commanditaire de l'industrie* in June 1825 with initial funding of 50 million francs, blocked by the *Conseil d'Etat* insistence on state veto power. More generally, see Gouhier, p. 228 note.
112. Taylor, pp. 202–6, from Saint-Simon's 'Sketch of the new political system', in *L'Organisateur*, 1819. See also Manuel, pp. 312–19.
113. J.-C.-L. Simonde de Sismondi, *Nouveaux principes d'économie politique*, Paris, 1819, 2nd edn 1827, ii, p. 264; cf. i, pp. 92, 200, 333–4; ii, pp. 220, 347.
114. Manuel, p. 254.
115. Saint-Simon, *Nouveau Christianisme*, 1825, in *Oeuvres de Saint-Simon et d'Enfantin*, xxiii, p. 109; cf. 110, 113, 117. Durkheim pointed out that Necker had foreshadowed this phrase in 1775. See Emile Durkheim, *Le Socialisme*, Paris, 1928, p. 85.
116. *The Crisis of Industrial Civilization*, p. 104, from 'A brief appraisal of modern history' which first appeared in *L'Organisateur* in 1820.
117. E. H. Carr, *Studies in Revolution*, London, 1950, p. 4.
118. Carr, pp. 1–2; cf. 5–11.
119. Manuel, p. 2; cf. 1.
120. See the critical review of the literature arguing that Saint-Simon was a socialist by Blamires, pp. 450–63, who on pp. 455–6 also presents the Volgin argument from *Sen-Simon, izbrannye soehineniya*, Moscow–Leningrad, 1958. See also Gouhier, ii, p. 346 and iii, pp. 227–8.
121. Manuel, pp. 1, 113; cf. 5–6, 347. See also George Lichtheim, *A Short History of Socialism*, London, 1970, Fontana edn 1975, pp. 52–4 and Taylor (ed.), *Selected Writings*, pp. 52–5.
122. Gruner, p. 144; cf. 141 quoting Abel Transon, *De la Religion Saint-Simonienne*, Paris, 1830, p. 50. See also Welch, pp. 171–2 and Sebastien Charléty, *Histoire du Saint-Simonisme, 1825–1864*, Paris, 1931, Ch. 2.
123. Gruner, p. 145; cf. 126, 146–8.

124. Frederick Engels, *Socialism: Utopian and Scientific*, 1880, in K. Marx and F. Engels, *Selected Works*, Moscow, 1962, II, p. 151; cf. I, p. 652; Hayek, *The Counter-Revolution of Science*, pp. 133, 137, 229–30.
125. Kumar, p. 304; cf. 39–44, 303–5, 328.
126. J. E. S. Hayward, 'Solidarist syndicalism: Durkheim and Duguit', *Sociological Review*, VIII/1, July 1960, p. 21; cf. 22.
127. Paul Carnot, *Hippolyte Carnot et le Ministère de l'Instruction Publique de la IIᵉ République*, Paris, 1948, pp. 22–5, 57–63; and Vincent Wright, 'L'Ecole nationale d'administration de 1848–1849: un échec révélateur', *Revue Historique*, CCLV/1, January–March 1976, pp. 21–42. See also Guy Thuillier, *L'ENA avant l'ENA*, Paris, 1983, especially Ch. 4, 'L'échec de l'Ecole de 1848', but also pp. 34–75.
128. Quoted by James H. Meisel, *The Myth of the Ruling Class: Gaetano Mosca and the élite*, 1958, 1962 edn Ann Arbor, p. 256; cf. 11–12, 29, 192, 255–8, 331, 398.

Chapter 5

1. Benjamin Constant, Preface to *Mélanges de Littérature et de Politique*, 1829, in *Oeuvres*, Paris, Pléiade edn 1957, p. 836.
2. Constant, p. 835.
3. Charlotte T. Muret, *French Royalist Doctrines since the Revolution*, New York, 1933, p. 69; cf. 70.
4. Muret, p. 70; cf. 68–9.
5. Jean-Rodolphe de Salis, *Sismondi, 1773–1842, La Vie et l'Oeuvre d'un Cosmopolite Philosophe*, Paris, 1932, pp. 94–5.
6. Etienne Hofmann, *Les 'Principes de Politique' de Benjamin Constant. La Genèse d'une oeuvre et l'évolution de la pensée de l'auteur (1789–1806)*, Geneva, 1980, II, p. 368; cf. I, pp. 328–32. Vol. II consists of the 'lost' work by Constant which was first published (in an admirably edited edition) in 1980.
7. *Le Cahier Rouge*, in *Oeuvres*, p. 126.
8. Paul Bastid, *Benjamin Constant et sa Doctrine*, Paris, 1966, II, pp. 1061–70; cf. I, pp. 38–9.
9. 'Eloge de Sir Samuel Romilly', 1819, quoted in Marcel Gauchet's selection from the works of Constant, *De la Liberté chez les Modernes*, Paris, 1980, p. 683 note; cf. 449. On Sir James Mackintosh as part of the group of Scottish Philosophic Whigs, see Stefan Collini, Donald Winch and John Burrow, *That Noble Science of Politics: A study in nineteenth-century intellectual history*, Cambridge, 1983, especially pp. 45–6. On Constant's own enthusiasm for Scottish Whig politics, see his comment in *Le Cahier Rouge*, in *Oeuvres*, p. 158. See also Gustave Rudler, *La Jeunesse de Benjamin Constant, 1767–94*, Paris, 1909, pp. 2–5, 58ff., 163–72, 177; and Kurt Kloocke, *Benjamin Constant: Une biographie intellectuelle*, Geneva–Paris, 1984, p. 18–21; cf. 300.
10. Madame de Staël, *Considérations sur . . . la Révolution Française*, I, p. 15; cf. 323–8; and Hofmann edition of Constant's *Principes de Politique*, II, p. 230, repeated in *Réflexions sur les constitutions*, Paris, 1814, Ch. 4, p. 68.

11. Hofmann edn of *Principes de Politique*, II, p. 226.
12. Stephen Holmes, *Benjamin Constant and the Making of Modern Liberalism*, New Haven, 1984, p. 211; cf. Gauchet, pp. 96–103 for the table of contents of Constant's so-called *Fragments*.
13. Kloocke, p. 22; cf. 20, 301, and Rudler, pp. 123, 149–50, 173–80, 265.
14. Hofmann, II, p. 379 note; cf. 370, 374, 379–90. See also Constant's 'De la jurisdiction du gouvernement sur l'éducation' in Gauchet, pp. 572–7, 698–9 note.
15. Hofmann, I, p. 124; cf. Kloocke, pp. 27–8. Constant's essay 'On the perfectibility of the human species' was written in 1805 but not published until 1829 in *Mélanges de Littérature et de Politique*; it is reprinted in Gauchet.
16. Constant, *De la force du Gouvernement*, Paris, 1796, pp. 95–6.
17. Hofmann, I, p. 348; cf. II, p. 435.
18. Holmes, p. 196; cf. 225 and Ch. 7 *passim*, and *Oeuvres*, p. 1613.
19. 'Des Effets de la Terreur', addition to the second edition of Constant's *Des réactions politiques*, Paris, 1797, quoted from the Pozzo di Borgo edition of Constant, *Ecrits et Discours Politiques*, Paris, 1964, I, p. 111; cf. 109, 112.
20. Constant, 'Fragments sur la France' in *Mélanges*, p. 850; cf. 876, 881. See also Hofmann, II, pp. 468–9 on Louis XIV's *Memoirs*.
21. Constant, 'De Madame de Staël et de ses ouvrages' in *Mélanges*, pp. 877–8.
22. Hofmann, II, pp. 491–2; cf. 407, 410–11, 485–6, 628–9. See generally Book 18, Ch. 3 on revolutions.
23. Hofmann, II, p. 494.
24. Hofmann, II, p. 488; cf. 486, 489.
25. Hofmann, II, p. 488.
26. Hofmann, II, pp. 489, 491. See also Madame de Staël, *De la Littérature considérée dans ses rapports avec les institutions sociales*, 1800, 1959 edn Geneva–Paris, II, p. 291; and her *Considérations*, I, pp. 378–80; II, p. 146.
27. Hofmann, II, p. 470; cf. 411–12. As Madame de Staël wrote: 'What particularly characterises English government is the possibility of peaceful improvement . . . the constitution was established by grafting the new onto the old.' *Considérations*, III, p. 221; cf. 226–9.
28. J. Christopher Herold, *Mistress to an Age: A life of Madame de Staël*, London, 1959, pp. 106, 145.
29. Herold, I, p. 44; cf. 39–48.
30. Quoted in Kloocke, pp. 38, 40; cf. 39–46. See also Rudler, pp. 474, 479; and Bastid, II, pp. 693–7, 714–17.
31. Herold, p. 222. Constant appears in the character of M. de Lebensei (*ibid.*, pp. 234–5). She is (in part) Ellénore in *Adolphe*.
32. 'De Madame de Staël et de ses ouvrages' in *Mélanges*, quoted from *Oeuvres*, p. 861.
33. Herold, pp. 5–6.
34. Herold, pp. 78–88. On Necker's admiration of the English constitution, compared to Montesquieu, Delolme and Mounier, see the hagiographic Henri Grange's *Les Idées de Necker*, Paris, 1974, pp. 307–49, especially 331–49.
35. Herold, pp. 101–2.
36. Herold, p. 196. See also Grange, p. 495; cf. 496–7. In addition to their direct

contact, the works of Necker that may have influenced Constant were *Du pouvoir exécutif dans les grands Etats*, n.p., 1792; *De la Révolution française*, Paris, 1797; and *Dernières vues de politique et de finance*, n.p., 1802.

37. Herold, p. 439. The most complete study is Béatrice Jasinski, *L'Engagement de Benjamin Constant: amour et politique, 1794–96*, Paris, 1971.
38. Madame de Staël, *Considérations*, III, pp. 158, 210.
39. *Ibid.*, pp. 166–7; cf. 168.
40. Herold, p. 208; cf. 96, 189, 194–5, 205–6.
41. Herold, p. 221; cf. Kloocke, pp. 15, 16.
42. Quoted by Herold, p. 239; cf. 149, 153, 235, 462.
43. Edouard Herriot, *Un ouvrage inédit de Madame de Staël: Les Fragments d'écrits politiques*, Paris, 1904, p. 75; cf. Kloocke, pp. 67–8, 75; cf. 118 and Béatrice Jasinski, p. 205f.
44. Kloocke, p. 68. Maistre was not the only one to reply to Constant. See Adrien de Lezay, *De la faiblesse d'un gouvernement qui commence et de la nécessité où il est de se rallier à la majorité nationale*, Paris, 1796.
45. Constant, *De la Force*, n.p., 1796, pp. 4–5. In the same year Madame de Staël's *De l'influence des Passions*, I, Lausanne, 1796, p. 28, expressed exactly the same viewpoint. On the political context, see Bronislaw Baczko, 'L'expérience thermidorienne' in Lucas (ed.), *The Political Culture of the French Revolution*, Ch. 18.
46. Constant, *De la Force*, p. 38; cf. 19–21.
47. *Ibid.*, p. 40.
48. *Ibid.*, p. 78.
49. *Ibid.*, p. 82; cf. 83 and Ch. 6 *passim*.
50. *Ibid.*, p. 89; cf. 90–1.
51. *Ibid.*, pp. 102–3.
52. Sutherland, pp. 303–5.
53. *De l'Esprit de Conquête et de l'Usurpation dans leurs rapports avec la civilisation européenne*, 1814, quoted from *Oeuvres*, p. 1057. However, it was derived from Ch. 1 of his unpublished *Principes*. See Hofmann, II, p. 20. The idea that 'the extremes meet' would have been found by Constant in Rousseau's *Contrat Social*, Book III, Ch. 15.
54. Holmes, p. 137; cf. 110, 120. *Des Réactions Politiques* is included in Constant, *Ecrits et Discours Politiques*, Pozzo di Borgo edn. See especially Ch. 1 and Bronislaw Baczko, *Comment sortir de la Terreur: Thermidor et la Révolution*, Paris, 1989, pp. 333–42.
55. Constant, 'Fragments sur la France', part of the 1829 *Mélanges* republished in *Oeuvres*, p. 851.
56. See the introduction by Lucia Omacini to *Des Circonstances Actuelles*, Paris–Geneva, 1979 edn, p. LXVI; cf. LXVIII–IX, LXXXIII. See also Simone Balayé, *Madame de Staël. Lumières et Liberté*, Paris, 1979, p. 67.
57. *Des Circonstances Actuelles*, pp. 179–81, 211–12 notes.
58. *Ibid.*, pp. 162–4.
59. *Ibid.*, pp. 111, 127; cf. pp. 107–12, 172.
60. *Ibid.*, p. 281; cf. 129, 177, 294. She had read and admired Condorcet's 1785 *Essai sur l'application de l'analyse à la probabilité des décisions rendues à*

la pluralité des voix. Ibid., p. 299 note. See also Herold, pp. 188–201. On 'political science', see Madame de Staël's *De la Littérature*, II, pp. 371–84; cf. I, pp. 11–12, 33.

61. *Ibid.*, p. 282.
62. Constant, *Principes de Politique*, 1815, in *Oeuvres*, p. 1137; cf. 1136–8, slightly amended from the earlier Hofmann version in *Principes*, II, pp. 390–1; cf. I, pp. 125, 135–6. On Constant and the *idéologues*, see Pierre Deguise, *Benjamin Constant méconnu*, Geneva, 1966, pp. 70–9; cf. Picavet, p. 573, Gusdorf, p. 330 and Kaiser, p. 190. On ideological determinism in Constant, see *De la Force*, pp. 92–3.
63. Welch, p. 29. See also Gusdorf, pp. 334–5, 550, and Hofmann, I, pp. 224–7.
64. Lynn Hunt *et al.*, 'The failure of the liberal republic in France, 1795–1799: the road to Brumaire', *Journal of Modern History*, L1, December 1979, pp. 735–41, 755–9.
65. Bastid, *Sieyès*, pp. 183–5; cf. 189–91.
66. Quoted by Hofmann, I, p. 164; cf. 151–65; Bastid, *Constant*, I, pp. 133–5; Kloocke, pp. 82–3.
67. Henri Guillemin, *Benjamin Constant muscadin, 1795–1799*, Paris, 1958, pp. 158–61, 178–9. This presents a very hostile picture of Constant during the Directory. The most authoritative work on this period is Jasinski.
68. Cooper, *Talleyrand*, p. 114; cf. 85–118.
69. *Le Mercure britannique*, December 1798, quoted by Guillemin, p. 239.
70. Quoted in Kloocke, p. 91 note; cf. Constant's 'Souvenirs historiques', *Revue de Paris*, 1830, XI, p. 119 and XVI, p. 111. See also Bastid, *Sieyès*, p. 217.
71. Herold, p. 172; cf. 174–5. More generally see Paul Gautier, *Madame de Staël et Napoléon*, Paris, 1902.
72. Germaine de Staël, *Considérations*, II, p. 237; cf. 195–201, 232–6, 244.
73. Hofmann, I, p. 189, quoting *Archives Nationales* 284 AP16, dossier 5.
74. Bentham's *Works*, II, p. 530, quoted by Welch, *Liberty and Utility*, p. 137. For a brief but hostile portrait of Sieyès by Constant in 1815, see *Oeuvres*, pp. 865–6. For more extended comments on the Directory and Sieyès' role in the Brumaire coup, see Constant's 1830 'Souvenirs Historiques' reprinted in Harpaz (ed.) *Benjamin Constant Publiciste*, pp. 174–93.
75. Gusdorf, p. 200.
76. Letter of December 1790, quoted by Rudler, p. 474.
77. Hofmann, I, p. 191; cf. 192–4; Guillemin, p. 279; Bastid, *Constant*, I, pp. 153–4.
78. Constant, *Ecrits et Discours*, I, p. 142; cf. 139–41. See also Hofmann, I, pp. 196–8, 205–16.
79. Constant, *Ecrits et Discours*, I, pp. 148, 152.
80. *Ibid.*, p. 185; cf. 155–89.
81. Quoted in Herold, p. 215; cf. 213–14, 225.
82. Constant, 'Journaux Intimes', 6 January 1803, in *Oeuvres*, p. 226.
83. *De l'Esprit de Conquête et de l'Usurpation* in *Oeuvres*, pp. 1038–9.
84. Hofmann, II, p. 493; cf. *Des Circonstances Actuelles*, p. 204.
85. Hofmann, I, pp. 298–301.
86. See the introduction by Burton R. Pollin to his edition of Constant's translation

of William Godwin, *De la Justice Politique*, Quebec, 1972, pp. 2–27. Godwin's article on the 'Benjamine' appeared in the *Morning Chronicle* of 25 May 1815. See also Hofmann, I, pp. 171; II, p. 363; and Kloocke, pp. 87–93. On Godwin, see George Woodcock, *Anarchism*, Harmondsworth, 1963, especially Ch. 3; and M. Philp, *Godwin's 'Political Justice'*, London, 1986.

87. Hofmann, I, pp. 229–38 and Kloocke, pp. 92–3.

88. R. Barny, 'J.-J. Rousseau dans la Révolution Française, 1787–91', *Annales historiques de la Révolution française*, L, no. 231, Jan.–March 1978, pp. 115–16, quoted in Hofmann, I, p. 314; cf. 250, 304–14, 319–20, 325–8. See also J.-R. de Salis, *Sismondi*, pp. 22–3, 69–73. On the background to the notion of Napoleon as a Rousseauist Emperor, see F. G. Healey, *Rousseau et Napoléon*, Geneva–Paris, 1957.

89. *Oeuvres*, p. 1621, from a chapter added to the fourth edition of *De l'Esprit de Conquête*.

90. Quoted by Jacqueline de La Lombardière, *Les idées politiques de Benjamin Constant*, Paris, 1928, p. 116 from Constant's *Réflexions sur les Constitutions*. See also *Oeuvres*, p. 852.

91. Constant, *Commentaire sur l'ouvrage de Filangieri*, Paris, 1822, I, p. 2. However, he agreed with Montesquieu that 'Where rights have disappeared, privileges are a defence. Despite their disadvantages, they are better than the lack of any countervailing power.' (Hofmann, II, p. 225.) For Madame de Staël's flattering judgement, see her *Lettres à Ribbing*, Paris, 1960, letter of 22 October 1794, p. 181; cf. 174, 180, 342, 353 for other interesting comments on her early view of Constant. On Destutt de Tracy's *Commentary*, see André Jardin, *Histoire du Libéralisme Politique*, pp. 185–7.

92. *De l'Esprit de Conquête*, Ch. 13, p. 1018 and note; cf. 1015, 1020, 1193 note. See also Hofmann, II, p. 389.

93. Hofmann, I, p. 170; cf. 325; and Jean Roussel, *J.-J. Rousseau en France après la Révolution, 1795–1830*, Paris, 1972, pp. 496–509 and Part I on the end of the Rousseau cult, notably pp. 103–12 on the Maistre critique. For an earlier defence of British-inspired institutions against Rousseau, see the Genevan Delolme's *La Constitution anglaise* of 1771.

94. Hofmann, II, pp. 22–3, 30, 49. Partly repeated in the 1815 version of 'Principes', see *Oeuvres*, p. 1103; cf. 1104.

95. *Ibid.*, p. 27; cf. 28 and *Esprit des Lois*, Book 11, Ch. 3.

96. 'Principes de Politique' in *Oeuvres*, p. 1106; cf. 1215–16 and Hofmann, II, pp. 163–4, 619.

97. Hofmann, II, p. 35; cf. 36, 466.

98. *Oeuvres*, p. 1046; cf. 1045–50. See also Constant's famous 1819 lecture 'De la liberté des Anciens comparée à celle des modernes' in Gauchet, pp. 502–6. More generally, see Giovanni Sartori, *The Theory of Democracy Revisited*, Chatham, NJ, 1987, II, Ch. 10 on 'Greek Democracy and Modern Democracy'.

99. *Oeuvres*, p. 1051; cf. Hofmann, II, pp. 438–40, 450–2. See E. Harpaz, 'Mably et ses contemporains' in *Revue des Sciences Humaines*, 1955, pp. 351–66.

100. Speech by Constant in the Chamber of Deputies of 10 March 1820, *Oeuvres*, p. 1629 note.

101. 'Principes de Politique' in *Oeuvres*, pp. 1109–11.
102. *Ibid.*, pp. 1233, 1235; cf. 'Des Réactions Politiques' in *Ecrits et Discours*, p. 74. See also *De la Force*, p. 101.
103. *Ecrits de Discours*, p. 76. Léon Blum gave the same reply to the leftist Marceau Pivert in 1936 when the latter proposed violating legal forms because the Fascists would have done so.
104. *Oeuvres*, p. 1099; cf. *Ecrits et Discours*, pp. 80–1.
105. *Oeuvres*, p. 1105, Ch. 1 of 'Principes' on popular sovereignty.
106. Hofmann, II, p. 460; cf. 461–7 and Holmes, pp. 97–8. However, I disagree with the claim that, unlike Tocqueville and Mill, Constant was *only* concerned with tyranny in the *name* of the majority. Holmes, pp. 95–6. Compare J. S. Mill, *On Liberty*, 1859, Pelican edn 1974, p. 76.
107. 'Principes de Politique' in *Oeuvres*, p. 1113; cf. 1112–14. On the early formulation of the 'pouvoir préservateur', see the quotations by Gauchet, pp. 85–8, from Constant's unpublished 1802 MS.
108. *Oeuvres*, pp. 1112–26, 1171–6, and Bastid, *Constant*, II, pp. 928–55 which discuss the argument of Constant's *Réflexions sur les Constitutions* of 1814. Compare these powers with those of the President of the Fifth Republic in Hayward, *Governing France*, pp. 101–3.
109. Hofmann, II, p. 397; cf. 394, 398 and *Oeuvres*, pp. 1133, 1138–44.
110. Hofmann, II, p. 399. This passage came from his 1802 *Fragments* and was repeated in his *Réflexions sur les Constitutions*, Paris, 1914.
111. 'Principes de Politique' in *Oeuvres*, p. 1177; cf. 1178.
112. Hofmann, II, p. 481; cf. *Oeuvres*, pp. 1239–43, 29–30, 478–9; Gauchet, pp. 432–40, 551–5.
113. Hofmann, II, pp. 76, 67; cf. Constant's *Commentaire sur l'ouvrage de Filangieri*, I, p. 65, repeating the same argument fifteen years later.
114. *Oeuvres*, p. 1109; cf. 1100 and *Ecrits et Discours*, 6 November 1830, III, p. 157.
115. Hofmann, pp. 127–40, 149; cf. *Réflexions sur les Constitutions*, pp. 152–5. See also Joseph Barthélémy, *L'Introduction du Régime Parlementaire en France sous Louis XVIII et Charles X*, Paris, 1904, p. 25.
116. Hofmann, II, p. 53; cf. 463–4 and *Oeuvres*, pp. 836–7.
117. Hofmann, II, pp. 58, 515–16; cf. J. S. Mill, *On Liberty*, pp. 68–9 and *passim*.
118. Letter to his Aunt of 29 May 1795, quoted by Bastid, *Constant*, I, p. 109; cf. Hofmann, II, pp. 93–4 and *Oeuvres*, pp. 1200–1.
119. *Oeuvres*, p. 880.
120. Hofmann, II, pp. 221–2, 238–40 and *Commentaire sur l'ouvrage de Filangieri*, II, 1824, p. 65.
121. Hofmann, II, p. 204; cf. 106.
122. *Ibid.*, p. 201.
123. *Ibid.*, p. 209; cf. 207.
124. Quoted by Murray Forsyth, *Reason and Revolution: The political thought of the Abbé Sieyès*, p. 118, from his 1789 pamphlet on the Rights of Man; cf. Forsyth, Ch. 7 *passim* and pp. 162–4. See also Pierre Rosanvallon, *Guizot*, pp. 95–123.

125. *Oeuvres*, pp. 837, 1146–54; Hofmann, II, pp. 200–1, 211–16. See also Bastid, *Constant*, II, pp. 987–99 and Holmes, pp. 150–3.
126. 'De l'Esprit de Conquête et de l'Usurpation' in *Oeuvres*, pp. 1088–9 note.
127. *Ibid.*, p. 1088; cf. 1619–20 and Hofmann, II, p. 427.
128. 'De Godwin et de son ouvrage sur la justice politique', 1817, republished in *Mélanges* and quoted from Gauchet, pp. 567–8. See also Hofmann, II, pp. 363–4.
129. Hofmann, II, p. 141.
130. *Ibid.*, pp. 275–6; cf. Gauchet, p. 457. Patrice Rolland gives greater weight to economic liberalism in 'Equivoques du libéralisme. A propos de Benjamin Constant' in *Commentaire*, no. 15, 1981, pp. 413–14.
131. Hofmann, II, p. 384.
132. *Ibid.*, pp. 278–9; cf. I, 355–62 and II, 85, 145, 223, 276–314. See also Gauchet, pp. 457–66.
133. *Oeuvres*, pp. 1615–16; cf. 1621–3. More generally, see Herold, pp. 435–6 and Kloocke, pp. 186–8. See also his letter justifying helping Napoleon's enemies in terms of 'modern patriotism' in a letter to Sir James Mackintosh of 27 March 1814 in *Memoirs of the Life of the Rt. Hon. Sir James Mackintosh*, London, 1835, 2nd edn 1836, pp. 275–6. Most of the first part of *De l'Esprit de Conquête* was taken from Book 13 of Constant's 1806 *Principes* and most of the second part, *De l'Usurpation*, from Books 5–6 and 17–18.
134. Barthélémy, pp. 14–17; cf. Gouhier, III, pp. 9, 15, 90–1, 95 note. See also the *Mémoires* of the Baron Eugène de Vitrolles, 1884, 7th edn 1950, I, p. 59.
135. 'De la liberté des brochures, des pamphlets et des journaux considérée, sous le rapport de l'intérêt du gouvernement' in *Oeuvres*, p. 1276 note.
136. Preface to 1819 edn of 'Des Réactions Politiques' in *Ecrits et Discours*, I, p. 221 note. On Destutt de Tracy, see Welch, p. 111.
137. 'On the State of France in 1815' in Sir James Mackintosh, *The Miscellaneous Works*, London, 1846, 1851 edn, pp. 636–7; cf. his *Memoirs*, p. 324. See also Kloocke, pp. 192–6, 203–4.
138. Madame de Staël, *Considérations*, III, p. 141; cf. 142. But see Simone Balayé, p. 222.
139. *Oeuvres*, p. 778; cf. E. de Las Cases, *Mémorial de Sainte-Hélène*, Paris, 1823, 1961, edn, p. 446. See also Barthélémy, pp. 54–7; Bastid, *Constant*, I, pp. 285–6; and Kloocke, pp. 223–4.
140. Constant, *Cours de Politique Constitutionnelle*, I, p. 272; cf. *Oeuvres*, p. 1249. See also Kloocke, pp. 205–10, 227. Sismondi defended Constant in a series of newspaper articles and in *Examen de la Constitution française*, Paris, 1815.
141. Ephraim Harpaz (ed.), *Benjamin Constant et Goyet de la Sarthe: Correspondence 1818–1822*, Geneva, 1973, p. 465.
142. Quoted in Kloocke, p. 247; cf. 248–56.
143. Stendhal, *Lettres de Paris*, Paris, 1825, 1936, 1983 edn, p. 272; cf. 119, 122, 223, 245, 261, 271–5. On Constant's excitement at attending a British parliamentary debate in 1816, see Alfred Fabre-Luce, *Benjamin Constant*, Paris, 1939, p. 271.
144. Barthélémy, p. 184; cf. 185–7 and Chateaubriand, *Mémoires d'Outre-Tombe*,

Paris, 1849, VIII, p. 113; cf. 248, 252. Constant's reply to Chateaubriand was his 1816 pamphlet *De la doctrine politique qui peut réunir les partis en France*, Paris, 1816. For an excellent selection of his political writings see Jean-Paul Clément (ed.), *Chateaubriand Politique*, Paris, 1987.

145. Constant, 'Des Elections Prochaines' included in his *Cours de Politique Constitutionnelle*, II, pp. 330–1; cf. 336–9, 344–6, 387–8.

146. Barthélémy, p. 148; cf. 156–7 and Kloocke, p. 229–30, 237. See also G. Bertier de Sauvigny, 'French politics, 1814–47', Ch. 12 of *The New Cambridge Modern History*, IX, 1965, p. 346.

147. E. Harpaz, *L'Ecole Libérale sous la Restauration*, Geneva, 1968, p. 102; cf. Harpaz, *Benjamin Constant et Goyet de la Sarthe*, p. 256 for 1820 figures and p. 285, where Constant contrasts the 'extremely timid' doctrinaire group of Royer-Collard and Ternaux with his 'Left' group.

148. Letter of 6 November 1820 in Harpaz, *Constant et Goyet*, p. 439; cf. 623, 634. For three *Lettres à MM. les habitants de la Sarthe*, giving an account of his parliamentary activities to his constituents, see Constant's *Cours de Politique Constitionnnelle*, II, pp. 465–91.

149. Quoted in Gauchet, p. 476 from Ch. 8 of *Réflexions sur les Constitutions*.

150. Kloocke, p. 236, quoting an article in *Minerve* of 14 March 1818. See also the collection of texts edited by R. Bourgeois, *Benjamin Constant, L'Affaire Regnault*, Grenoble, 1979.

151. Holmes, p. 32; cf. 31–5 and Kloocke, pp. 74, 78–9, 240–1. See Max Weber, *Gesammelte Aufsätze zur Wissenschaltslehre*, Tübingen, 1922, 1973 edn pp. 190–212.

152. See Pasquale Pasquino, 'Emmanuel Sieyes, Benjamin Constant et le "Gouvernement des Modernes" ', *Revue Française de Science Politique*, April 1987, pp. 214–28. See also Holmes, p. 129; cf. Bastid, *Constant*. II, pp. 733–4.

153. Hofmann, II, p. 421. Book 16 is called not Liberty but 'Authority among the Ancients'.

154. *Ibid.*, p. 436; cf. 419–35; cf. *Oeuvres*, pp. 1044–5. Among those influenced by Constant's typology and more generally was the young Karl Marx. See François Furet, *Marx et la Révolution Française*, Paris, 1986, p. 24; cf. 22, 29, 33–4, 65.

155. 'De M. Dunoyer et de quelques-uns de ses ouvrages', first published in the *Revue Encyclopédique*, February 1826, republished in *Mélanges* and quoted from Gauchet, pp. 559–61.

156. *Commentaire sur l'ouvrage de Filangieri*, II, pp. 123–4.

157. Hofmann, II, p. 424; cf. 433, 435.

158. 'De l'Esprit de Conquête' in *Oeuvres*, p. 994; cf. 1010; cf. *Commentaire sur Filangieri*, II, pp. 60–1.

159. Hofmann, II, pp. 385–6; cf. 387–8.

160. 'Du pouvoir municipal, des autorités locales et d'un nouveau genre de fédéralisme', Ch. 12 of 'Principes de Politique' in *Oeuvres*, p. 1192; cf. 1188–93. See also Ch. 13 of 'De l'Esprit de Conquête, pp. 1018–9; and Madame de Staël, *Considérations*, II, p. 153 and III, pp. 164, 182, 192.

161. 'Principes de Politique', Ch. 17 on religious freedom, in *Oeuvres*, p. 1231; cf.

1217–30 and Hofmann, II, pp. 165–73. See also Bastid, *Constant*, II, pp. 600–55, 754–69 and Madame de Staël, *Des Circonstances Actuelles*, pp. 227–33.

162. François Furet, *La Gauche et la Révolution au milieu de XIXᵉ siècle: Edgar Quinet et la Question du Jacobinisme, 1865–1870*, Paris, 1986, pp. 22–32; cf. Quinet, *Christianisme et Révolution Française*, Paris, 1845.

163. Constant, *Discours à la Chambre des députés*, Paris, 1828, II, p. 620; cf. *Oeuvres*, pp. 858–9.

164. *La Cousine Bette*, 1846, in the Pléiade edition of *La Comédie Humaine* in Balzac's *Oeuvres*, Paris, 1960, VI, p. 229.

165. Fabre-Luce, p. 297. However, see Bastid, *Constant*, I, p. 455; cf. 454.

166. Constant, *Ecrits et Discours*, II, p. 156; cf. 227 note for sources. On Constant's role in 1830, see David H. Pinkney, *The French Revolution of 1830*, Princeton, 1972, pp. 45, 152, 159–60, 189.

167. François Ribadeau-Dumas, *La Destinée secrète de La Fayette ou le messianisme révolutionnaire*, Paris, 1972, p. 395; cf. 399, 414–15.

168. *Mémoires d'Outre-Tombe*, Paris, 1849–50, IX, pp. 303–4.

169. Ribadeau-Dumas, pp. 412–13.

170. Holmes, p. 4. On the funeral, see Louis Blanc, *Histoire de Dix Ans, 1830–40*, II, pp. 174–7, and Pinkney, pp. 337–8. On Blanqui and Constant's funeral, see Ch. 8.

171. De Salis, *Sismondi*, p. 121; cf. 117–22. See also Rudler, p. 15; Fabre-Luce, pp. 282, 302, 307–8; Bastid, *Constant*, I, pp. 467–8; Rosanvallon, pp. 65–7, 87–9, 152, quoting Guizot's *Mémoires*, II, pp. 144–6. Guizot translated Gibbon's *Decline and Fall of the Roman Empire* in 1812 after Constant turned down the offer.

172. Quoted by Hampson, *Will and Circumstances*, p. 176.

173. Edouard Laboulaye's new edition of Constant's *Cours de politique constitutionnelle* was published in Paris in 1861 and again in 1872. See also his *L'Etat et ses Limites*, Paris, 1863, esp. pp. 124–33, from a pamphlet separately published with the Constantian title 'La liberté antique et la liberté moderne'.

Chapter 6

1. Alexis de Tocqueville, *Oeuvres Complètes*, IV, *Correspondance Anglaise*, I, Paris, 1954, pp. 37–38, letter dated 22 March 1837 to his English translator, Henry Reeve.

2. André Jardin, *Alexis de Tocqueville, 1805–1859*, Paris, 1984, pp. 9, 14; Ch. 2 *passim*; 102, 218–19, 268–79. See also George W. Pierson, *Tocqueville and Beaumont in America*, New York, 1938, pp. 403–13. For anticipation by Chateaubriand of Tocqueville's ideas on the French Revolution's continuity with the *Ancien Regime* and on the inevitability of democracy and equality, see Clément, *Chateaubriand Politique*, pp. 50, 53, 90, 99–100.

3. Tocqueville, *O.C.*, XIII, *Correspondance d'Alexis de Tocqueville et de Louis de Kergorlay*, I, Paris, 1977, p. 418, letter dated 10 November 1836.

4. 'De Tocqueville on democracy in America', *Collected Works of J. S. Mill*, XVIII, 'Essays on politics and society', Toronto, 1977, p. 57. This review of the first

volume of *Democracy in America* was originally published in the *London Review* in October 1835.

5. Tocqueville, *O.C.*, XIII, *Correspondance Tocqueville–Kergorlay*, II, p. 233; cf. 230, letter dated 15 December 1850.

6. Melvin Richter, 'Comparative political analysis in Montesquieu and Tocqueville', *Comparative Politics*, I, January 1969, pp. 130, 137, 156, 158–9.

7. Emile Durkheim, *Montesquieu et Rousseau*, Paris, 1953, p. 46.

8. Melvin Richter, 'The uses of theory: Tocqueville's adaptation of Montesquieu' in Richter (ed.), *Essays in Theory and History: An approach to the social sciences*, Cambridge, MA, 1970, pp. 75, 87.

9. Tocqueville, *Democracy in America*, 1835, Mayer–Lerner edition, New York, 1966, I, Part 1, Ch. 3 *passim*, especially pp. 43, 49; cf. Marvin Zetterbaum, *Tocqueville and the Problem of Democracy*, Stanford, 1967, pp. 139–43; and Jean-Claude Lamberti, *Tocqueville et les Deux Démocraties*, Paris, 1983, pp. 60, 70–1, 87.

10. Letter to Corcelle of 17 September 1853, quoted by Jack Lively, *The Social and Political Thought of Alexis de Tocqueville*, Oxford, 1965, p. 44.

11. Letter to his father, 3 June 1831, quoted by James T. Schleifer, *The Making of Tocqueville's Democracy in America*, Chapel Hill, 1980, p. 40.

12. *Democracy in America*, II, Part 2, Ch. 14, p. 512. Montesquieu's argument is briefly stated in Book 20, Ch. 7 of *De l'Esprit des Lois*, 1748; 1979 edn Paris, II, p. 14. On Tocqueville's inversion of Montesquieu's argument, see Seymour Drescher, *Tocqueville and England*, Cambridge, MA, 1964, p. 127; and Zetterbaum, pp. 131–4; cf. 62–6. See also Tocqueville's *Journeys to England and Ireland*, London, 1958, p. 116.

13. *Democracy in America*, II, Part 2, Ch. 20, pp. 528–31.

14. K. W. Smart, ' "Individualism" in the mid-nineteenth century (1826–1860)', *Journal of the History of Ideas* XXIII, Jan.–March 1962, p. 78; cf. 79–80. On Protestantism as an unstable compromise between catholicism and atheism, see Tocqueville's letter to Kergorlay of 29 June 1831 in *Oeuvres*, XIII/1, pp. 228–31.

15. Tocqueville, *The Old Régime and the French Revolution*, 1858, 1955 edn New York, p. 282; cf. 4–7, 151. See also *Democracy in America*, II, Part I, Chs. 5–6, pp. 408–16; cf. 5, 16–17. More generally, see James Ceaser, 'Alexis de Tocqueville on political science, political culture, and the role of the intellectual', *American Political Science Review*, LXXIX, 1985, pp. 659–62, 667–70; Drescher, p. 14 note; Lively, *Tocqueville*, pp. 38, 72–96, 183ff.; Lamberti, pp. 14, 190–1, 202–9, 270.

16. Letter of 30 August 1829 to Gustave de Beaumont, in *O.C.*, VIII/1, *Correspondance Tocqueville–Beaumont*, Paris, 1967, p. 80. See also Edward T. Gargan, *De Tocqueville*, London, 1965, pp. 26–32; Furet, *Interpreting the French Revolution*, pp. 135–9; Jardin, *Alexis de Tocqueville*, p. 81; and Augustin Thierry, *Considérations sur l'histoire de France* in his *Oeuvres*, IV, Paris, 1864, p. 120.

17. Pierre Rosanvallon, *Le Moment Guizot*, p. 319; cf. 59–60, 181–5. See the analysis at the start of Guizot's *Du Gouvernement de la France depuis la*

Restauration et du ministère actuel, Paris, 1820, pp. 1–3, which Rosanvallon (p. 203) describes as a 'bourgeoisie manifesto'. See also F. Guizot, *Histoire de la civilisation en Europe*, 1840, Paris, 1985 edn, pp. 171–2, 182–3; and Furet, *Interpreting the French Revolution*, pp. 135–9.

18. Larry Siedentop, 'Two liberal traditions' in Alan Ryan (ed.), *The Idea of Freedom: Essays in honour of Isaiah Berlin*, Oxford, 1979, pp. 161–2; cf. 156–60.
19. Rosanvallon, pp. 51, 171.
20. Rosanvallon, p. 179.
21. Lamberti, p. 50; cf. Gargan, *De Tocqueville*, pp. 28–9.
22. Lamberti, pp. 162–4, 261–2; cf. Guizot, *Mémoires pour servir l'histoire de mon temps*, Paris, 1867, VIII, p. 521 and Rosanvallon, p. 84. See also François Furet, *Marx et la Révolution Française*, Paris, 1986, pp. 66–9, 110–12, 117–19.
23. Lamberti, p. 167. More generally, see Roger Langeron, *Un conseiller secret de Louis XVIII: Royer-Collard*, Paris, 1956, especially pp. 38ff. and 242–4. See also R. Pierre-Marcel, *Essai Politique sur Alexis de Tocqueville*, Paris, 1910, pp. 278–85.
24. Lamberti, p. 171 note, quoting Tocqueville's *O.C.*, XI, *Correspondance Tocqueville–Royer-Collard*, Paris, 1970, p. v.
25. From Royer-Collard's 1831 speech on the need for a hereditary peerage, included in Pierre Manent (ed.), *Les Libéraux*, Paris, 1986, II, p. 131.
26. Amable de Barante, *La vie politique de Royer-Collard*, Paris, 1861, II, p. 131; cf. Siedentop, pp. 163–7 and J.-C. Lamberti, *La notion d'individualisme chez Tocqueville*, Paris, 1970, pp. 11–18.
27. Harold Laski, 'The political theory of Royer-Collard', Ch. 4 of his *Authority in the Modern State*, New Haven, 1919, p. 291; cf. 289–303. Laski exaggerates Royer-Collard's pluralism. See also Manent, II, p. 124 and Jardin, *Histoire du Libéralisme Politique*, pp. 253–5, 262.
28. Lamberti, *Tocqueville et les deux démocraties*, p. 181; cf. 169–83.
29. Schleifer, pp. 98–9; cf. 148. See also Laboulaye's introduction to Constant's *Cours de Politique Constitutionnelle*, I, p. VII; Roland Pierre-Marcel, *Essai Politique sur Alexis de Tocqueville*, Paris, 1910, pp. 180–1; and Furet, *Interpreting the French Revolution*, p. 135 and note. See also Bastid, *Constant*, pp. 1100–11 and especially Lamberti, *Tocqueville et les deux démocraties*, on concealing his debt to Constant, pp. 15, 75–6, 102–3, 108, 312; and Condorcet, the *Idéologues* and Madame de Staël, pp. 214–15, 312.
30. Isaiah Berlin, *Four Essays on Liberty*, Oxford, 1969, p. 126; cf. XLVI–VII, 124; and Lively, *Tocqueville*, pp. 10–11, 98 note; but see 223–8 and particularly Lamberti, *Tocqueville et les deux démocraties*, pp. 75–83, 106–7, 224–5, 310–11, and Siedentop, pp. 168–70. However, for a passage of Tocqueville's 1836 article published in Mill's *London and Westminster Review* which is close to Constant's conception of modern freedom, see 'Etat Social et Politique de la France avant et depuis 1789' in *Oeuvres*, II/1, p. 62.
31. Lamberti, *La notion d'individualisme chez Tocqueville*, p. 34; cf. 28–40, 56, 81.
32. *Democracy in America*, I, Part 2, Ch. 3, p. 168. More generally, see Lamberti, *Tocqueville et les deux démocraties*, pp. 93, 104–5, 117–21, 124–5, 146–8, 213–16.

33. Tocqueville, 'Mon Instinct, Mes Opinions', November 1841, quoted in Antoine Rédier, *Comme disait M. de Tocqueville*, Paris, 1925, p. 48.
34. *Oeuvres*, XI, *Correspondance Tocqueville–Royer-Collard*, letter of 27 September 1841, p. 108.
35. Letter of 16 September 1842, quoted by Pierre-Marcel, p. 338.
36. Letter of 24 July 1836 to Stoffels, quoted at length by Lamberti, *Tocqueville et les deux démocraties*, p. 159; cf. 160–2. See also Lamberti, *La notion d'individualisme*, pp. 19–28.
37. June 1835 letter to J. S. Mill in Tocqueville's *Correspondance Anglaise, Oeuvres*, VI, p. 294.
38. Tocqueville, 'Etat Social et Politique de la France avant et depuis 1789', in the uncut French version of the 1836 article in the *London and Westminster Review*, published in the *Oeuvres* edition of *L'Ancien Régime et la Révolution*, II/1, p. 35; cf. 33–6, 65–6.
39. *The Old Régime*, p. 1; cf. 20–1, 192; cf. *European Revolution*, p. 164.
40. *Ibid.*, p. 120; cf. X, 208; his *European Revolution*, pp. 99, 102–3 and Lamberti, *Tocqueville et les deux démocraties*, pp. 250–5.
41. *The Old Régime*, pp. 207–8.
42. Guizot, *Histoire de la civilisation en Europe*, p. 173; cf. 171–88.
43. Guizot, p. 239; cf. 296–8.
44. *The Old Régime*, pp. 32, 60; cf. Part 2, Chs. 2–5 *passim*.
45. Quoted by Schleifer, p. 149, who dates the note from 1833.
46. *Democracy in America*, I, Part 2, Ch. 6, p. 218; cf. 217–19.
47. *Ibid.*, II, Part 1, Ch. 2, p. 398. See also Zetterbaum, pp. 107–23, 147–57.
48. Letter to Gobineau of 5 September 1843, quoted in Zetterbaum, p. 151 note. See also Drescher, *Tocqueville and England*, pp. 153–68. On the importance of national pride, see *Correspondance Anglaise*, Letters to J. S. Mill in 1840–1, *Oeuvres*, VI, pp. 330–1, 335.
49. *European Revolution*, pp. 169–70, as retranslated by Zetterbaum, p. 150.
50. *The Old Régime*, Part 3, Ch. 1, pp. 139–40.
51. *Ibid.*, p. 147; cf. 145–6, 150, 205.
52. Tocqueville, 'Etat Social et Politique de la France', pp. 57–8.
53. *The Old Régime*, p. 163; cf. 158–66.
54. *Ibid.*, p. 159.
55. Letter to Henry Reeve, 3 February 1840, in *Correspondance Anglaise, Oeuvres*, VI, pp. 52–3.
56. *The Recollections of Alexis de Tocqueville*, 1893, 1959 edn New York, p. 67.
57. Quoted by Jardin, *Histoire du Libéralisme Politique*, p. 239. Royer-Collard's cynical verdict on the leader of 'Resistance' to revolutionary change was: 'Mr. Casimir-Périer was ignorant and brutal. These two virtues saved France.' Quoted *Ibid.*, p. 292.
58. Sherman Kent, *Electoral Procedure under Louis-Philippe*, 19.
59. Letter to Stoffels of 26 August 1830, quoted by Edward Gargan, *Alexis de Tocqueville: The critical years, 1848–51*, Washington, DC, 1955, p. 11.
60. Quoted by Jardin, *Histoire . . .*, p. 327; cf. 318–29. See also Kent, pp. 27, 50, 54–6, 72–3 and Ch. 9 *passim* on corrupt electoral practices.

61. Denys Cochin, *Louis-Philippe*, Paris, 1918, p. 103.
62. *Recollections*, pp. 3, 2; cf. 4–8, 66–7. More generally see Lamberti, *Tocqueville et les deux démocraties*, pp. 48–54.
63. *Recollections*, p. 9.
64. Quoted by Jack Lively, *The Social and Political Thought of Alexis de Tocqueville*, p. 139; cf. 2–4, 134–41; and Lamberti, *Tocqueville*, pp. 158–67.
65. Letter to Reeve of 7 November 1840, in *Correspondance Anglaise, Oeuvres*, VI, pp. 63–4; cf. 37.
66. *Recollections*, p. 11. On the 'New Left' parliamentary group in 1846–7, see Jardin, *Tocqueville*, pp. 379–83. On Proudhon's onslaught on private property, see Chapter 7 above, pp. 180–1.
67. *Recollections*, p. 10. The full text, under the title 'Of the middle class and the people', was published in vol. IX, pp. 515–19 of Beaumont's edition of Tocqueville's *Works*.
68. *Recollections*, pp. 12–13.
69. National Assembly speech of 12 September 1848, quoted by Gargan, *Tocqueville: The critical years*, pp. 118–19 from vol. IX, pp. 549, 552 of Beaumont edn of the *Works*.
70. *Recollections*, p. 106; cf. 105.
71. *Ibid.*, pp. 150, 107, 159.
72. Letter of 21 July 1848 to Stoffels; quoted by Gargan, *Tocqueville: The critical years*, pp. 86–7; cf. 69, 81 note, 89–90.
73. *Democracy in America*, p. LXXXVIII.
74. *Recollections*, pp. 188–90; cf. Jardin, *Tocqueville*, pp. 396–7 and Gargan, pp. 98–9, 115.
75. Speech on 25 May 1848 at the constitutional committee, quoted from the minutes by Gargan, p. 100. See also *Recollections*, pp. 193–6.
76. *Recollections*, pp. 224–5.
77. Gargan, p. 140; cf. 129–71, *Recollections*, Part 3, especially Ch. 4; and Jardin, *Tocqueville*, Ch. 23.
78. This passage was prepared for Tocqueville's presidential address to the Academy of Moral and Political Sciences on 3 April 1852 but was left out. Quoted by Gargan, p. 237 from Beaumont's edition of Tocqueville's *Works*, IX, p. 647. The address is to be found on pp. 116ff. See also his letter to Kergorlay of 15 December 1850 in *Oeuvres*, XIII/11, p. 230.
79. Written in 1852 and quoted by John Lukacs in the introduction to Tocqueville's *European Revolution*, p. 22; cf. *Recollections*, pp. 184–5 and Drescher, pp. 173–5.
80. Letter to Beaumont on 29 January 1851 in *Oeuvres*, VIII/II, p. 369. For Tocqueville's measured portrait of Louis-Napoleon, see *Recollections*, pp. 226–9.
81. Letter to Reeve on 9 January 1852 in *Correspondance Anglaise, Oeuvres*, VI, p. 133.
82. Drescher, p. 1.
83. Letter of 14 December 1851 quoted by Jardin, *Tocqueville*, p. 437.
84. Furet, *Interpreting the French Revolution*, p. 147.
85. J. S. Mill, 'Essays on politics and society', *Collected Works of J. S. Mill*, p. 167;

cf. 163–7, from his review of the second volume of *Democracy in America* which appeared in the *Edinburgh Review*, October 1840, LXXII, pp. 1–47.

86. *Ibid.*, p. 159; cf. 188–9. For some of the many discussions of what Tocqueville meant by 'democracy' and his attitude towards it, see Lively, *Tocqueville*, pp. 49–52, 104–9; Schleifer, pp. 10–12, 265–73; and Lamberti, *Tocqueville et les deux démocraties, passim*, especially pp. 28–35, 133–5.

87. Tocqueville letter to *Times*, 11 December 1851, denouncing Louis-Napoleon's *coup d'état*, published in *Correspondance Anglaise, Oeuvres*, VI, p. 128; cf. 119–29. See also his letters to Nassau Senior of 27 July 1851 quoted by Drescher, *Tocqueville in England*, p. vii and to Mrs Austin of 29 August 1856 in *Correspondance Anglaise*, p. 191. More generally, see Drescher, pp. 202, 214–15, 223.

88. *European Revolution*, p. 102.

89. *Democracy in America*, I, Part 2, Ch. 6, p. 220.

90. Letter to Eugène Stoffels of 5 October 1836, quoted in Lively, *Tocqueville*, p. 118. For the quotation from 1839 election address, *ibid.*, p. 115.

91. Quoted by Manuel, *The New World of Henri Saint-Simon*, p. 281, citing *Bibliothèque Nationale* MS NAF 24607.

92. Letter to Chabrol on 9 June 1831, published as Appendix 4 of the Mayer-Lerner edition of *Democracy in America*, p. 731; cf. 732–3.

93. Quoted in Schleifer, p. 128. See also his letter of 29 June 1831 in *Correspondance d'Alexis de Tocqueville et de Louis de Kergorlay*, I, pp. 234–5.

94. *Democracy in America*, I, Part 2, Ch. 7 *passim*. See also Schleifer, pp. 192–8, 217, 223.

95. Mill's review of *Democracy in America* in 'Essays', pp. 156, 175–9.

96. *Democracy in America*, p. 227.

97. *Ibid.*, pp. 529–31.

98. Constant, *Ecrits et Discours*, p. 140, speech of 6 April 1829.

99. Letter to Reeve on 15 November 1839 in *Correspondance Anglaise, Oeuvres*, VI, p. 48; cf. letter to J. S. Mill, *ibid.*, pp. 294 (June 1835) and 326–7 (14 November 1839).

100. *Democracy in America*, I, Part I, pp. 154–5 and Ch. 8 *passim*. For a more sanguine view, see Siedentop, pp. 167–8, 172.

101. Quoted in Schleifer, p. 105; cf. 106–17.

102. Hérold, *Mistress to an Age*, p. 195.

103. *European Revolution*, p. 113.

104. Obituary on Tocqueville, included in Laboulaye, *L'Etat et ses Limites*, Paris, 1863, p. 156; cf. 138–201.

105. Tocqueville, *Voyages en Angleterre, Irelande, Suisse et Algérie*, of his *Oeuvres*, V, Paris, 1958, pp. 63–4; cf. 29–31, 36–7. Tocqueville returned to the contrast between the English aristocracy and French nobility in *The Old Régime*, Part 2, Ch. 9, pp. 82–4, 88–9.

106. *Voyages*, p. 82; cf. 36–42, 80–2, 89–90.

107. *Ibid.*, pp. 58–9. See also letter to J. S. Mill, June 1835 in *Oeuvres*, VI, p. 294; cf. Drescher, *Tocqueville in England*, p. 98 and Drescher, 'Tocqueville's two Démocraties', *Journal of the History of Ideas*, XXV/2, April–June 1964, pp. 207–9.

108. Letter of 29 June 1831 to Kergorlay in *Oeuvres*, XIII/I, p. 234.
109. *Voyages*, p. 35; cf. 31–5, 49, 69, 83–4; cf. Drescher, *Tocqueville in England*, pp. 76–81.
110. Unpublished preparatory note for vol. II of *Democracy in America*, quoted by Schleifer, pp. 176, 182; cf. 178, 185.
111. Douglas Johnson, *Guizot*, p. 226.
112. *The Old Régime*, pp. 167–8; cf. 201–2.
113. *European Revolution*, p. 121.
114. *The Old Régime*, pp. XIV, 96.
115. *Democracy in America*, pp. 265–6, 398, 408–16, 516–17, 652–3. See also the interesting discussion in Lively, pp. 184–92.
116. *Democracy in America*, pp. 166–7; cf. Lively, pp. 143–6.
117. *European Revolution*, p. 129.
118. *Voyages*, p. 68; cf. 70.
119. *Democracy in America*, p. 94; cf. I, Part 1, Ch. 6 *passim*. More generally, see Drescher, p. 83–7 and Lively, pp. 167–76.
120. *The Old Régime*, p. 286; cf. 175, 285.
121. *Democracy in America*, p. 254; cf. 249–54. See also R. Pierre-Marcel, p. 223 note.
122. Quoted by Gargan, *Tocqueville: The critical years*, p. 117. More generally, see Drescher, pp. 144–50.
123. *Recollections*, pp. 78–81.
124. Preface to Claudio Jannet's *Les Etats-Unis Contemporains*, Paris, 1876.
125. *Collected Works of J. S. Mill*, XVIII, p. 156. See also Tocqueville's letter to Mill of 3 December 1835 in *Oeuvres*, VI, pp. 302–3.
126. Joseph Barthélémy, *Traité de Droit Constitutionnel*, Paris, 1933, p. 46. See also Prévost-Paradol, *Essais de Politique et de Littérature*, Paris, 1863, II, pp. 64–83.
127. Letter to Eugène Stoffels of 28 April 1850, quoted by both Mayer, pp. 78–9 and Lively, p. 211 in slightly different translations. For a different version, see *Recollections*, pp. 68–9. See also *Democracy in America*, p. 677 and more generally Lamberti, *Tocqueville et les deux démocraties*, pp. 264–5, 298–9, 304–6.
128. *European Revolution*, p. 166.

Chapter 7

1. Proudhon, *Correspondance*, 14 vols., Paris, 1875, I, p. 52. More generally, see George Woodcock, *Pierre-Joseph Proudhon: A biography*, London, 1956, Ch. 1 *passim*; Pierre Haubtmann, *P.-J. Proudhon: Genèse d'un Antithéiste*, Paris, 1969, pp. 28–30; and K. Steven Vincent, *Pierre-Joseph Proudhon and the Rise of French Republican Socialism*, Oxford, 1984, pp. 15–23, 48–61.
2. Proudhon, *Les Confessions d'un Révolutionnaire*, Paris, 1849, Rivière edn 1929, pp. 173, 338.

3. Proudhon, *Correspondance*, II, p. 305, letter of 8 April 1848.
4. Diary entry for March 1846, quoted by Haubtmann, *La Philosophie Sociale de Proudhon*, Grenoble, 1980, p. 178; cf. 177.
5. Proudhon, *De la Justice dans la Révolution et dans l'Eglise*, Paris, 1858, Rivière edn 1930–5, II, p. 241. See also his *Système des Contradictions Economiques ou Philosophie de la Misère*, Paris, 1846, Rivière edn 1923, I, p. 159.
6. Aaron Noland, 'Proudhon and Rousseau', *Journal of the History of Ideas*, XXVIII/1, Jan.–March 1967, pp. 35, 37.
7. Proudhon, *Idée Générale de la Révolution au XIXᵉ siècle*, Paris, 1851, Rivière edn 1923, p. 187; cf. p. 88. For the nineteenth-century onslaught on Rousseau, see especially Jacques Julliard, *La Faute à Rousseau*, Paris, 1985, *passim* and pp. 133–7 on Proudhon as l'anti-Rousseau'.
8. *Idée Générale*, p. 191; cf. 188–9, 198.
9. *Ibid.*, p. 187; cf. 195–9.
10. *Ibid.*, p. 194 and Julliard, p. 137.
11. *Idée Générale*, p. 238; cf. Noland, p. 49.
12. *Carnets de P.-J. Proudhon*, Paris, 1974, IV, p. 260; cf. 259, note dated 22 May 1851.
13. *Confessions d'un Révolutionnaire*, Paris, 1849, Rivière edn 1929, p. 348; cf. 351; *Idée Générale*, pp. 229–31, 320; *Carnets*, IV, pp. 261–2, 280–2. For later attacks on Jacobinism and defence of the Girondins as the authentic French revolutionaries, see *De la Justice*, I, 299; II, p. 155; IV, pp. 157–63; and *Du Principe Fédératif et de la nécessité de reconstituer le parti de la Révolution*, Paris, 1863, 1921 Bossard edn p. 184. See also Daniel Guérin, *Proudhon oui et non*, Paris, 1978, based partly on Proudhon's unpublished notes on the French Revolution from the Besançon Municipal Library, especially pp. 21–34, 77–107, 137–8. On Proudhon's affinities with Michelet, whose lectures he attended in 1838–41, see Pierre Haubtmann, *Proudhon, 1849–55*, Paris, I, pp. 118–20.
14. Quoted in Guérin, p. 34; cf. 35, 42.
15. *Confessions*, pp. 90–1.
16. *Ibid.*, p. 82.
17. *Idée Générale*, p. 94.
18. *Ibid.*, p. 203.
19. Letter of February 1869, quoted in Vincent, p. 32.
20. Quoted by Haubtmann, *Proudhon . . . Antithéiste*, p. 130; cf. 131. See also *De la Justice*, I, p. 261.
21. See the interesting discussion in Richard Vernon, *Citizenship and Order: Studies in French political thought*, Toronto, 1986, Ch. 2 on 'God and the state: Maistre and Proudhon', especially pp. 55–8, 66–9, 75–6. For the Maistre and Proudhon references to revolutionary legislation, see respectively *Oeuvres Complètes*, I, pp. 76–7 and *Idée Générale*, 1868 edn p. 137.
22. *De la Justice*, I, p. 458; cf. 323, 326, 382–4, 394, 402ff., 458–60; II, pp. 12ff., 275; II, p. 516; IV, pp. 391–3. On Hobbes (mentioned over fifty times) and Maistre (thirteen times), see Proudhon's *La Guerre et Paix*, pp. 30–1; cf. 111ff.
23. *Confessions*, pp. 340–1; cf. criticism of Saint-Simon as seeking change from above, p. 82.

24. *Carnets*, IV, entry for 10 April 1851, p. 247; cf. 244–8 and Haubtmann, *Proudhon, 1849–55*, I, pp. 111–13 and pp. 132–4 for detailed references.
25. *Idée Générale*, p. 395 and note; cf. 195–9, 202, 237, 385–6, 390. On Proudhon's initial misapprehension that Leroux shared his views, after having read his major works in mid-1840, see Proudhon's *Deuxième Mémoire*, 1841, Lacroix edn 1867, pp. 309–13 and *Correspondance*, I, p. 239.
26. Letter of 7 September 1853 to Prince Napoleon-Jérome, *Correspondance*, V, pp. 240–1; cf. 195. See also M. Wallon, *Les Saint-Simoniens et les chemins-de-fer*, Paris, 1908.
27. Proudhon, *Manuel d'un Spéculateur à la Bourse*, Paris, 1854, conclusion, quoted in Haubtmann, *Proudhon, 1849–55*, I, p. 410; cf. 405–9. See also the attack on Saint-Simonian industrial feudalism in *De la Justice*, III, pp. 13, 503 and IV, pp. 459–61.
28. Letter of 2 May 1841, *Correspondance*, I, pp. 324ff., quoted by Robert L. Hoffman, *Revolutionary Justice: The social and political theory of P.-J. Proudhon*, Urbana, 1972, p. 75.
29. *Qu'est-ce que la Propriété?*, 1840, 1966 Garnier–Flammarion edn, pp. 299–300.
30. *Correspondance*, III, p. 267; cf. *Carnet*, III, p. 387.
31. *De la Justice*, III, pp. 168, 176–7, 295; cf. I, pp. 388, 395.
32. Woodcock, p. 13. Proudhon's main acknowledgement of intellectual debt to Fourier is in his *De la Création de l'Ordre dans l'Humanité*, 1843, a work he later regarded as a failure.
33. Hubert Bourgin, *Fourier*, Paris, 1905, pp. 549–70.
34. *Du Principe Fédératif*, p. 222 note; cf. *De la Justice*, II, pp. 71–2 and *Avertissement aux Propriétaires*, 1841, 1867 Lacroix edn, p. 54ff.
35. Proudhon, *De la Création de l'Ordre dans l'Humanité*, Paris, 1843, Rivière edn 1927, paras. 377, 381, 390. On Say, see *Correspondance*, IV, p. 243.
36. *De la Justice*, IV, pp. 384, 453.
37. Proudhon, *Intérêt et Principal*, Paris, 1850. On the controversy seen from Bastiat's standpoint, see P. Ronce, *Frédéric Bastiat, sa vie, son oeuvre*, Paris, 1905, pp. 184–96.
38. *Qu'est-ce que la Propriété?*, Lacroix edn 1867, pp. 127–33; cf. 124ff.
39. Vincent, p. 294. On Proudhon's reading, see *ibid.*, p. 53 and Haubtmann, *Proudhon, sa vie et sa pensée*, pp. 171–8, 1079–92.
40. See Keohane, p. 48, quoting Pasquier, *Les Recherches de la France*, Paris, 1611, pp. 975–6.
41. Quoted in Woodcock, p. 45. Brissot's *Recherches philosophiques sur le droit de propriété et sur le vol*, Chartres, 1780.
42. *L'Histoire de Juliette ou les prospérités du vice*, 1792 in *Oeuvres Complètes du Marquis de Sade*, Paris, 1967, VIII, p. 212, quoted by Robert L. Hoffman, *Revolutionary Justice*, p. 47; cf. 45–6.
43. *Confessions d'un Révolutionnaire*, p. 323; cf. 97–101.
44. See the letter from Adolphe Blanqui to Proudhon on 1 May 1841, which was published in later editions of *Qu'est-ce que la Propriété*, 1966, Flammarion edn p. 46. See also Chapter 8, note 62 below.
45. Karl Marx and Frederick Engels, *The Holy Family*, Moscow, 1956, p. 46.

46. The 1846 judgement comes in a letter of 28 December 1846 to Annenkov published as an appendix to Karl Marx, *The Poverty of Philosophy*, 1847, 1956 Moscow edn, p. 193. The 1844 judgement comes from *The Holy Family*, pp. 58–9.

47. See Haubtmann, *Marx et Proudhon*, Paris, 1947, pp. 63ff. See also the partial English version in Hoffman, *Revolutionary Justice*, pp. 95–6; cf. 85–105 and David McLellan, *Karl Marx: His life and thought*, London, 1973, p. 159; cf. 154–5, 160.

48. Karl Marx, *The Poverty of Philosophy*. The 1956 Moscow edition appends (pp. 194–202) a letter to J. B. Schweitzer on 24 January 1865 in which Marx gave his final – extremely hostile – views on Proudhon, having just received the news of his death.

49. *Système de Contradictions Economiques ou Philosophie de la Misère*, 1846, Rivière edn 1923, II, p. 31. For Proudhon's marginal notes on Marx's *Poverty of Philosophy*, see *ibid.*, pp. 415–23. More generally, see Pierre Haubtmann, *Marx et Proudhon: Leurs rapports personnels, 1844–47*, Paris, 1947.

50. *Carnets*, Paris, 1960, I, pp. 196, 198, 272; cf. 176–8.

51. *Ibid.*, 1961, II, p. 98; cf. 83, 90–1, 305, 308, 315, 323.

52. *Ibid.*, II, pp. 353, 369; cf. 344–9; Proudhon, *Mélanges*, Paris, 1868, II, pp. 6–8.

53. *Qu'est-ce que la Propriété?*, 1966 edn, p. 395; cf. 298–9.

54. Letter of 2 February 1842 to Bergmann, *Correspondance*, II, p. 13.

55. *Idée Générale*, pp. 99–100.

56. Letter to Langlois of 14 August 1851, *Correspondance*, IV, pp. 83–4.

57. *Idée Générale*, p. 157.

58. Respectively in letter of 18 May 1848 in *Correspondance*, II, p. 330 and Alfred Darimon, *A Travèrs une Révolution*, Paris, 1884, p. 40. Darimon, a close collaborator of Proudhon's during the Second Republic, provides in this book a superb Proudhonian perspective on the 1848 Revolution.

59. *Confessions d'un Révolutionnaire*, pp. 170, 204; cf. 169, 187, 190.

60. 'Toast à la Révolution', from *Le Peuple*, 17 October 1848, reprinted in *Confessions d'un Révolutionnaire*, pp. 401, 406.

61. *Ibid.*, pp. 215–16.

62. *Mélanges*, III, p. 178; cf. Haubtmann, *Proudhon, 1849–55*, Paris, 1988, I, pp. 22–3, 125.

63. Vincent, *Proudhon*, p. 173; cf. Woodcock, p. 120. See also *Correspondance*, II, pp. 250, 256 and 272 on his pre-1848 journalistic plans.

64. Woodcock, pp. 123, 136.

65. Haubtmann, *Proudhon, 1849–55*, I, p. 23.

66. *Ibid.*, p. 52; cf. 33–6; cf. Raoul Labry, *Herzen et Proudhon*, Paris, 1928, pp. 85–9, 107.

67. Haubtmann, *Proudhon, 1849–55*, I, pp. 47, 65–8, 88.

68. Letter of 1841, *Correspondance*, VI, p. 313. L. Hiernaux, *Organisation du crédit au Travail*, Paris, 1884, pp. 191–2. See also Proudhon's *Carnets*, I, pp. 74–87, 90–3, 114–15, 126–7, 176–85, 189–93, 211–14. On his 1848–9 polemic with the Fourierists over Proudhon's plagiarism, see *Mélanges*, I, pp. 222, 276. In his *Banque d'Echange* of 1848, Proudhon admitted that his key idea was not new.

See vol. VI of the Lacroix edition of the *Oeuvres Complètes*, p. 246; cf. 243.

69. *Carnets*, I, p. 81; cf. 237, 290–7, 362.

70. *Organisation du crédit et de la circulation et Solution du Problème Social*, 1848, reprinted in vol. VI of the Lacroix edition of *Oeuvres Complètes*, 1868, pp. 112–27; cf. 178–88.

71. M. Aucuy, *Les Systèmes Socialistes d'Echange*, Paris, 1908, pp. 120–30.

72. *Le Représentant du Peuple*, 4 May 1848, p. 1.

73. Darimon, pp. 93–4; cf. 94–7, 114–15.

74. *Le Peuple*, 15 April 1849, p. 2; cf. *Mélanges*, II, pp. 80–3 and Jean Gaumont, *Histoire Générale de la Coopération en France*, Paris, 1924, I, p. 246 note.

75. *Confessions d'un Révolutionnaire*, p. 186; cf. 187, 196–8, 247–66.

76. Haubtmann, *Proudhon, 1849–55*, pp. 49, 243–77, 287, 394–5 note.

77. *New York Daily Tribune*, 21 April 1840, p. 2. Dana wrote a series of articles for this newspaper on the People's Bank.

78. Letter of 7 June 1849, *Correspondance*, II, p. 380; cf. *Idée Générale*, p. 96.

79. *Confessions d'un Révolutionnaire*, p. 244–5; cf. 280.

80. *Ibid.*, pp. 271, 278, 281, 309.

81. *Ibid.*, p. 364.

82. *Ibid.*, p. 298; cf. 297–302, 329–30; *Correspondance*, III, p. 264.

83. Entry of 13 November 1850 quoted by Haubtmann, *Proudhon, 1849–55*, p. 97; cf. 89–101.

84. *Ibid.*, p. 100.

85. *Ibid.*, pp. 102–8.

86. *Ibid.*, p. 64; cf. 52–3.

87. Aimé Berthod, introduction to *Idée Générale*, p. 9; cf. 8–17.

88. *Idée Générale*, p. 93.

89. *Ibid.*, p. 96; cf. 94.

90. *Ibid.*, p. 186.

91. *Ibid.*, p. 351; cf. 211–14.

92. Diary entry for 3 December 1851, quoted by Haubtmann, *Proudhon, 1849–55*, p. 138.

93. *Ibid.*, p. 139; cf. Victor Hugo, *Histoire d'un Crime*, Paris, 1877, Nelson edn, n.d., pp. 168–70.

94. Haubtmann, *Proudhon, 1849–55*, p. 141; cf. 143–4.

95. *Ibid.*, pp. 338–9. On the 'heroic Baudin' see Proudhon, *La Révolution sociale démontrée par le Coup d'Etat du Deux Décembre*, 1852, Rivière edn 1936, p. 166. On the need to educate the people, *ibid.*, p. 296.

96. Letter to Chaudey quoted by Haubtmann, *Proudhon, 1855–65*, p. 308.

97. *Correspondance*, IV, p. 217, letter of 23 February 1852, to Madier-Montjau.

98. *Ibid.*, p. 217; cf. 196, 216 and *La Révolution sociale*, p. 152.

99. Letter of 28 February 1852 to Marc Dufraisse, *Correspondance*, IV, pp. 223–4; cf. *La Révolution sociale*, p. 159.

100. *Correspondance*, IV, p. 224.

101. *Carnets*, IV, pp. 77, 113, 175, 195, 210, 229; cf. III, pp. 357–9.

102. *Correspondance*, III, p. 123, letter to Prefect of Police Carlier.

103. Diary quoted by Guérin, *Proudhon*, p. 43; cf. *Correspondance*, III, pp. 15–19.

104. *Correspondance*, III, pp. 62, 68.

105. *Ibid.*, V, p. 241.

106. Proudhon, *La Révolution sociale*, pp. 88–102, 299–346; cf. *Correspondance* V, pp. 153–65 and VI, pp. 185–90, 196–8 and Haubtmann, *Proudhon, 1849–55*, pp. 341–51, 415–18.

107. Diary notes of 30 March 1852 and 13 April 1852, quoted in introduction to *La Révolution sociale*, pp. 10, 70. On Louis-Napoleon's Saint-Simonian links, see T. A. B. Corley, *Democratic Despot: A life of Napoleon III*, London, 1961, pp. 17, 27, 44–7, 66, 87, 114–15, 120.

108. *La Révolution sociale*, pp. 127–8.

109. *Ibid.*, p. 135; cf. 74–5, 107–8, 160, 293–4.

110. *Ibid.*, introduction, p. 82, quoting diary entry of 8 October 1852.

111. Haubtmann, *Proudhon, 1849–55*, p. 337.

112. Diary quoted by Hoffman, *Revolutionary Justice*, p. 199.

113. *De la Justice*, I, p. 284.

114. *Confessions d'un Révolutionnaire*, p. 354; cf. 358.

115. *Qu'est-ce que la Propriété?*, 1966 edn, pp. 299–300.

116. *Idée Générale*, p. 434.

117. Haubtmann, *Proudhon, 1849–55*, p. 203.

118. *De la Justice*, III, p. 270; cf. Haubtmann, *Proudhon, 1855–65*, p. 339.

119. *Idée Générale*, p. 334; cf. 261–8, 326–7; *Confessions d'un Révolutionnaire*, pp. 232–40 and Haubtmann, *Proudhon, 1849–55*, pp. 204–8.

120. *Confessions d'un Revolutionnaire*, p. 216 note, added after the first edition; cf. pp. 217, 230–1.

121. *Ibid.*, p. 372; cf. *Idée Générale*, p. 184; cf. 183.

122. *Du Principe Fédératif*, Paris, 1921 edn, p. 117; cf. 115–16, 173–4 and letter to Blanc of 8 April 1848 in *Correspondance*, II, p. 306–8; cf. 317.

123. *Manuel d'un Spéculateur à la Bourse*, 1854, 1857 edn, pp. 46ff.

124. Letter to Villiaumé of 24 January 1856, *Correspondance*, VII, pp. 8–21.

125. *De la Capacité Politique des Classes Ouvrières*, 1865, Rivière edn Paris, 1924, p. 116.

126. *La Révolution sociale*, pp. 124–5. See also Hoffman, pp. 310–24.

127. Haubtmann, *Proudhon, 1855–65*, pp. 295–9; cf. 282. See also Proudhon's brochure *Les Démocrates assermentés et les Réfractaires*, Paris, April 1863, and *Correspondance*, XIII, pp. 35, 45–6. More generally on the Second Empire's electoral manipulation of universal suffrage, see Theodore Zeldin, *The Political System of Napoleon III*, London, 1958, especially pp. 83ff., and Bernard Le Clère and Vincent Wright, *Les Préfets du Second Empire*, Paris, 1973, pp. 60–71.

128. Maxime Leroy refers to Reynaud's article in the 1832 *Revue Encyclopédique* in his introduction to the Rivière edition of Proudhon's *Capacité Politique*, pp. 15–16.

129. *Ibid.*, p. 5.

130. Henri Michel, *Propos de Morale*, Deuxième Série, Paris, 1904, p. 98 and I. Tchernoff, *Le Parti Républicain au coup d'état et sous l'Empire*, Paris, 1906, pp. 185–6; Haubtmann, *Proudhon, 1855–65*, pp. 368–71; Woodcock, p. 261.

131. *Capacité Politique*, pp. 409–17 for the text of the *Manifeste des 60* and details

of the signatories. See also J.-L. Puech, *Le Proudhonisme dans l'Association Internationale des Travailleurs*, Paris, 1907, pp. 153–4; I. Tchernoff, *Le Parti Républicain*, pp. 406–10.

132. Introduction to *Capacité Politique*, p. 11. On Tolain see *La Grande Encyclopédie*, Paris, 1885, XXXI, pp. 143–4, and H. Robert, G. Cougny and E. Bourloton, *Dictionnaire des Parlementaires Français, 1789–1889*, Paris, V, p. 428. See also the pro-Proudhonian novelist and journalist Jules Vallès' comments on Tolain in his *L'Insurgé*, Paris, 1886, 1950 edn, pp. 89, 91.

133. *Quelques Vérités sur les Elections de Paris*, Paris, 1863, p. 33. See also Alexandre Zévaès, 'Les conditions ouvrières et révolutionnaires sous le Second Empire' in *La Révolution de 1848*, XXIX, Sept.–Nov. 1932, pp. 137–9.

134. Haubtmann, *Proudhon, 1855–65*, p. 372, quoting Proudhon's letter to Chaudey of 22 February 1864. The counter-*Manifesto of the 80* is appended to the Rivière edition of the *Capacité Politique*, pp. 418–19.

135. Haubtmann, *Proudhon, 1855–65*, pp. 374–5 and *Correspondance*, XIII, pp. 247–66 for his lengthy *Lettre aux ouvriers* of 8 March 1864. See also *Capacité Politique*, pp. 87–90, 232–3.

136. *Capacité Politique*, p. 65; cf. letter to Eugène Noel of 16 August 1864, *Correspondance*, XIV, p. 30.

137. Letter to Chaudey of 1 June 1864 in *Correspondance*, XIII, p. 294.

138. *Idée Générale*, p. 203.

139. Proudhon, *Jésus et les Origines du Christianisme*, posthumously ed. Havard, Paris, 1896, p. 94, quoted in Haubtmann, *Proudhon, 1849–55*, p. 209; cf. 210–13.

140. *Idée Générale*, pp. 187–9, 195–6, 205–6, 238, 268. See also Haubtmann, *Proudhon, 1849–55*, pp. 189–201.

141. *Confessions*, pp. 61–2; cf. 373.

142. Letter of 20 August 1864, quoted in the Charles-Brun 1921 edition of *Du Principe Fédératif*, Paris, p. 202 note.

143. *Proudhon Antithéiste*, p. 13; cf. 148.

144. *Ibid.*, p. 34; cf. 32–37, 114–15.

145. *Ibid.*, p. 35 note.

146. *Contradictions Economiques*, Rivière edn, I, p. 384, quoted in Vincent, *Proudhon*, p. 105; cf. 111, 117. In 1825, the Restoration Parliament passed a law punishing sacrilege with death, although it was never applied.

147. Haubtmann, *Proudhon, 1855–65*, pp. 82–102; cf. 15–21, 151–3.

148. Haubtmann, *Proudhon, 1849–55*, p. 260; cf. *Confessions*, p. 315, 357–62 and *Principe Fédératif*, pp. 158–67, 274–5.

149. Haubtmann, *Proudhon, 1855–65*, pp. 58–70, 221–4, 268–70; and Proudhon, *La Pornocratie ou les Femmes dans les Temps Modernes*, Paris, posthumously published in 1875.

150. Letter of 27 June 1861 to Suchet, *Correspondance*, XI, p. 131; and Haubtmann, *Proudhon, 1855–65*, p. 182.

151. Sorel, *The Illusions of Progress*, 1908, 1969 English edn, Berkeley, p. 140; cf. 141–3. Proudhon refers to *Democracy in America* in a footnote in *Qu'est-ce que la Propriété?*, 1966 edn, p. 73.

152. *Correspondance*, XII, p. 220, letter of 2 November 1862 to Millet.
153. *Idée Générale*, p. 151; cf. 152; cf. *Confessions*, pp. 83, 220–2.
154. *Idée Générale*, p. 331; cf. 314–15, 328.
155. *Ibid.*, p. 320.
156. *Ibid.*, p. 327.
157. *Ibid.*, p. 333. Reported in *Confessions*, p. 234 and *Capacité Politique*, p. 198. See also *Révolution Sociale*, p. 133.
158. *Idée Générale*, p. 322; cf. *Confessions*, p. 370. See Alan Forrest on 'Federalism' in Lucas (ed.), *The Political Culture of the French Revolution*, Ch. 16.
159. For Proudhon's remark, see *Principe Fédératif*, Rivière edn 1959, p. 331.
160. *Ibid.*, p. 345.
161. *Confessions*, p. 78.
162. *De la Justice*, II, p. 288; cf. p. 161 and Haubtmann, *Proudhon, 1849–55*, p. 217; cf. 134 note. On the change in the late 1850s to greater modesty and federalism, see Gaëtan Pirou, *Proudhonisme et Syndicalisme Révolutionnaire*, Paris, 1910, pp. 198–218.
163. *Principe Fédératif*, p. 327.
164. *Ibid.*, p. 345.
165. *Ibid.*, p. 326; cf. 319.
166. *Ibid.*, p. 335; cf. 366 and note. On the Saint-Simonian advocacy of a United States of Europe, see J.-L. Puech, *Tradition Socialiste en France et la Société des Nations*, Paris, 1921, Ch. 2.
167. Vernon, *Citizenship and Order*, pp. 94–5; cf. 81–102 and Vincent, *Proudhon*, pp. 215–19. For a contrasting emphasis on the links between Tocqueville and Proudhon, see Preston King, *Fear of Power: An analysis of anti-statism in three French writers*, London, 1967, pp. 43–6, 60, 105.
168. *Principe Fédératif*, p. 285; cf. 286.
169. *The Principle of Federation*, Vernon abridged edn, p. 74; and *Principe Fédératif*, p. 361.
170. *Capacité Politique*, p. 286; cf. 285–92.
171. *The Principle of Federation*, pp. 68–9 and *Principe Fédératif*, pp. 355–6; cf. Haubtmann, *Proudhon, 1855–65*, pp. 288–93, 330–2, 340–1. See also Proudhon's unfinished, posthumous *Contradictions Politiques*, 1870, Rivière edn 1952, pp. 235–47; and *Correspondance*, XII, pp. 275–8, letter of 5 February 1863 to the minister of the interior.
172. *Confessions*, 1851 postscript, p. 346 and letter to Michelet of 23 March 1856, *Correspondance*, XIV, p. 183; cf. letter to Beslay of 7 April 1860. *Ibid.*, X, pp. 8–9.
173. *Idée Générale*, p. 332; cf. *Correspondance*, III, p. 289, letter of 2 June 1850 to Dufraisse.
174. Haubtmann, *Proudhon, 1849–55*, p. 380, quoting the diary entry for 28 October 1854.
175. *Ibid.*, p. 382, quoting entry for 16 September 1855.
176. Haubtmann, *Proudhon, 1855–65*, pp. 161–2; cf. 182 and *Correspondance*, IX, pp. 16–17, 36, 89, 104, 112, 224ff., 572; X, 83–5, 110–11 and XII, p. 333.
177. On his debt to Hobbes and Maistre, see especially *La Guerre et la Paix*, 1861,

Rivière edn 1927, pp. 30–1, 111ff. On Vico and Hegel, *ibid.*, pp. LXXVIII–IX, 51, 106–7, 202.

178. *Contradictions Economiques*, II, pp. 289–90; cf. I, p. 328.
179. *Guerre et Paix*, p. 507; cf. 500ff. and Haubtmann, *Proudhon, 1855–65*, pp. 207–16, 254–5.
180. *Idée Générale*, 1851 edn, pp. 270–5; *Capacité Politique*, pp. 157–8; *Principe Fédératif*, pp. 549–51.
181. Letter to Beslay quoted in Pirou, *Proudhonisme*, p. 283.
182. Quoted in Nicholas Brian-Chaninov, *Guerre et Paix de Léon N. Tolstoy*, Paris, 1931, p. 30; cf. 33. See also Raoul Labry, *Herzen et Proudhon*, pp. 199–200. Isaiah Berlin attributes greater influence to Maistre, *Russian Thinkers*, London, 1978, pp. 58–9, 65 note. Proudhon refers to Tolstoy's visit in his letter to Chaudey of 7 April 1861, *Correspondance*, X, p. 341.
183. Quoted by Haubtmann, *Proudhon, 1855–65*, p. 361; cf. 187–9, 192–203, 246–7, 323–8.
184. *Le Censeur*, 1815, III, p. 43 and IV, p. 42, quoted in Gouhier, *La Jeunesse d'Auguste Comte*, III, p. 17.
185. *Le Peuple*, 17 October 1848 and *Idées Révolutionnaires*, Paris, 1849, p. 255, published as an appendix to the Rivière edition of *Confessions*, p. 399; cf. 400–2 and Berthod, introduction to *Idée Générale*, pp. 17–19.
186. *Confessions*, pp. 94, 111; cf. 110–13.
187. Marx and Engels, *Selected Works*, I, pp. 110, 117.
188. *Ibid.*, pp. 22–3 from *The Class Struggles in France*, 1848–1850.
189. E. E. Fribourg, *L'Association Internationale des Travailleurs*, Paris, 1871, pp. 2, 71–4, 84. Office du Travail, *Les Associations Professionnelles Ouvrières*, Paris, 1903, I, pp. 232–3 and II, p. 108 and note. More generally, see J.-L. Puech, *Le Proudhonisme dans l'Association Internationale des Travailleurs*, Paris, 1907, especially pp. 43–51, 120–33, 224–6.
190. Letter of 4 April 1862, *Correspondance*, XIV, p. 219; cf. *Guerre et Paix*, Bruxelles, II, Ch. 10, pp. 310–11.
191. Hoffman, pp. 332–41. For Proudhon's influence upon Brousse, see David Stafford, *From Anarchism to Reformism: A study of the political activities of Paul Brosse, 1870–90*, London, 1971, pp. 39–41, 53–5, 62; cf. 16–17.
192. See three works by J. Barberet, *Les Grèves et la loi sur les coalitions*, Paris, 1873, pp. 78–81, 113–14, 119, 132–45; *Le Mouvement Ouvrier à Paris de 1870 a 1874*, Paris, 1874, pp. 26, 48, 57–8, 88–117, 125, 142; *La Bataille des Intérêts*, Paris, 1879, pp. 14–15, 258–9, 264–75, 310ff. and 331–72. More generally see M. R. Kelso, 'The inception of the modern French labour movement, 1871–79', *The Journal of Modern History*, VII/2, June 1936, pp. 173–93.
193. Stafford, *From Anarchism to Reformism*, p. 330 note.
194. Letter from Marx to Engels on 20 July 1870, quoted in V. R. Lorwin, *The French Labor Movement*, Cambridge, MA, 1954, p. 13 note.
195. Jacques Julliard, *Fernand Pelloutier et les Origines du Syndicalisme d'Action Directe*, Paris, 1971, pp. 205–10; cf. 44, 61–72, 229–30, 237, 288, 383.
196. Bernstein's preface to the 1903 French edition of *The Suppositions of Socialism and the Problems of Social Democracy*, quoted by Annie Kriegel, 'Le

syndicalisme révolutionnaire et Proudhon' in *Le Pain et les Roses: Jalons pour une histoire des Socialismes*, Paris, 1968, p. 44 note; cf. 34–50. See also E. H. Carr, *Studies in Revolution*, London, 1950, Ch. 3.

197. James H. Meisel, *The Genesis of George Sorel*, Michigan, 1951, pp. 94–8; cf. Sorel, 'In defence of Lenin', Appendix 3 of his *Reflections on Violence*, 1908, Collier edn 1961, New York, p. 285; cf. 207–8, 216–18.

198. *Matériaux d'une théorie du prolétariat*, completed in 1914, 1st edn 1919, 3rd edn 1929, Paris, p. 416; cf. 394. The appendix 'Proudhonian Exegeses', pp. 415–40 was added in June 1920.

199. *Ibid.*, p. 449; cf. 394, 422, 424–5, 434–48; Pirou, pp. 228, 376–83 and Meisel, pp. 206–12.

200. Meisel, p. 248; cf. 219, 236–40, quoting Sorel's 'Ultime Meditazione' in *Nuova Antologia*, Sept.–Oct. 1928, p. 307. On federalism as a myth, see Sorel, *Introduction à l'économie moderne*, Paris, 1911, pp. 152–3. Proudhon's views are frequently quoted and discussed in this work. See also *The Illusions of Progress*, notably the chapter added in 1920 on 'The advance towards socialism', pp. 210–14. There are numerous references in *From Georges Sorel: Essays in socialism and philosophy*, New York, 1976. See particularly the introduction, pp. 17ff.

201. Joseph Paul-Boncour, *Le Fédéralisme Economique*, Paris, 1900, 2nd edn 1901, p. 16; cf. 221–2, 261 and Paul-Boncour, *Entre Deux Guerres*, Paris, 1945, I, pp. 62–3.

202. Bouglé *et al.*, *Proudhon et Notre Temps*, Paris, 1920. See also C. Bouglé, *La Sociologie de Proudhon*, Paris, 1911; Maxime Leroy, *Histoire des Idées Sociales en France*, Paris, 1954, III, Ch. 16; G. Gurvitch, *Proudhon, sa vie, son oeuvre*, Paris, 1965 and *Revue d'Histoire Economique et Sociale, 1956*, XXXIV/1, p. 80.

203. *Holmes–Laski Letters*, London, 1953, I, pp. 81–2; cf. 80, 83, 97.

204. Herzen, *My Past*, II, p. 119; III, pp. 212, 214, 227.

205. Labry, *Herzen et Proudhon*, pp. 70, 78–81, 89; cf. 36, 64–9, 85–6, 160–1, 217–18, 238–43.

206. Haubtmann, *Proudhon, 1849–55*, p. 214; cf. 32–6; George Woodcock, *Anarchism*, Harmondsworth, 1962, pp. 182, 184, 207. See, more generally, *ibid.*, Chs. 5 and 10.

207. George Lichtheim, *Marxism in Modern France*, New York, 1966, pp. 14–15.

208. *Confessions*, p. 355. Proudhon was one of the influences on Robert Michels in his influential critique of mass democracy in *Political Parties*, London, 1915, pp. 38, 238–9, 404 of the Dover edition.

Chapter 8

1. Quoted in Maurice Dommanget, *Blanqui et la Révolution de 1848*, Paris, 1972, p. 117.

2. Proudhon, *Lettres au Citoyen Rolland*, Paris, 1946, p. 85.

3. Quoted in Alain Decaux, *Blanqui l'Insurgé*, Paris, 1976, p. 478.

4. Edward S. Mason, 'Blanqui and communism', *Political Science Quarterly*, XLIV/4, 1929, p. 498; cf. 509, 525.

5. Georges Lefebvre, *The Directory*, French edn 1937, English edn 1965, London, p. 32.
6. H. Draper, 'Marx and the dictatorship of the proletariat', *Cahiers de l'Institut de Science Economique Appliquée*, September 1962, no. 129, pp. 6–7, 10–11.
7. R. B. Rose, *Gracchus Babeuf: The first revolutionary Communist*, London, 1978, p. 4.
8. J. L. Talmon, *The Origins of Totalitarian Democracy*, London, 1952, Sphere edn 1970, Part III *passim*.
9. *Ibid.*, p. 173.
10. Quoted by Rose, p. 100; cf. 71, 77, 105–7. His advocacy of direct democracy was inspired by the Rousseauist Marquis de Girardin's *Discours sur la nécessité de ratification de la loi par la volonté générale*, Paris, 1791.
11. Rose, p. 218; cf. 215–17, 237, 343.
12. *Ibid.*, p. 335; cf. 142, 172–7, 190–8, 336.
13. Appendix 7 in Philippe Buonarroti, *Babeuf's Conspiracy for Equality*, French edn 1828, English translation 1836 by Bronterre O'Brien, London, pp. 315–16. See also David Thomson, *The Babeuf Plot: The making of a republican legend*, London, 1947. For a good brief summary, see Sutherland, *France 1789–1815*, pp. 295–8.
14. G. P. Maximoff, *The Political Philosophy of Bakunin*, Glencoe, 1953, p. 277.
15. Elizabeth L. Eisenstein, *The First Professional Revolutionary: Filippo Michele Buonarroti (1761–1837)*, Cambridge, MA, 1959, p. 3. She is not using the phrase 'permanent revolution' in Proudhon's sense of an *unending* revolution but in the sense of an *unended* revolution.
16. *Ibid.*, pp. 8–10, 17–26.
17. Quoted *ibid.*, p. 37; cf. 44–5.
18. *Ibid.*, p. 49. See also J. M. Roberts, *The Mythology of the Secret Societies*, New York, 1972, pp. 234–6.
19. Eisenstein, p. 50.
20. Buonarroti, *Babeuf's Conspiracy*, p. 102 note.
21. *Ibid.*, p. 117; cf. 189–96.
22. Quoted in Eisenstein, p. 92; cf. 90.
23. *Ibid.*, pp. 67–8. The review appeared on 4 April 1829 and the author was Charles de Rémusat.
24. Alan Spitzer, *The Revolutionary Theory of Louis Auguste Blanqui*, New York, 1957, pp. 128–9; cf. 112 and M. Dommanget, 'Buonarroti et Blanqui' in Dommanget *et al.*, *Babeuf et les Problèmes du Babouvisme*, Paris, 1963, pp. 242–3, 277.
25. Michel Ralea, *L'Idée de Révolution dans les Doctrines Sociales*, Paris, 1923, pp. 218–22.
26. Dommanget, *Les Idées Politiques et Sociales d'Auguste Blanqui*, Paris, 1957, p. 3; cf. appendix, pp. 404–7 for the full details.
27. Spitzer, p. 144.
28. *Ibid.*, p. 119.
29. Decaux, pp. 17–24, 33, 37, 42; cf. Samuel Bernstein, *Auguste Blanqui and the Art of Insurrection*, London, 1971, pp. 14–17. Blanqui's father, on his post-Thermidor release from prison, published a brochure warning against

dictatorial authority governing in the name of democracy: *Réflexions sur le gouvernement démocratique et les ecueils qu'il faut éviter*. It does not appear to have influenced his son!

30. Blanqui, 'Notes on Robespierre' (1850) published in his *Oeuvres Complètes*, I, *Ecrits sur la Révolution*, Paris, 1977, pp. 315–16, 322; cf. 309–26. See also Dommanget, *Idées Politiques*, pp. 308–13.

31. Spitzer, p. 125. Blanqui wrote part of the introduction to the eulogy of *Les Hébertistes*, Paris, 1864, by his disciple Gustav Tridon. See also Bernstein, pp. 270–3.

32. Quoted in Palmer, *Twelve Who Ruled*, p. 129.

33. Patrick H. Hutton, *The Cult of the Revolutionary Tradition: The Blanquists in French politics*, 1864–93, Berkeley, 1981, p. 2; cf. 6, 162.

34. Decaux, p. 47; cf. 44–51.

35. Hutton, pp. 17, 22.

36. Dommanget, *Idées Politiques*, p. 94, quoting a manuscript in the *Bibliothèque Nationale* (BN).

37. B. Croce, *History of Europe in the Nineteenth Century*, London, 1934, p. 93. See more generally Roberts, *Mythology of the Secret Societies*, pp. 283–94, 300–2.

38. Spitzer, pp. 131–2. See also Alan B. Spitzer, *Old Hatreds and Young Hopes*, Cambridge, MA, 1971, pp. 291–2 and *passim*.

39. Dommanget, *Auguste Blanqui: Des Origines à la Révolution de 1848: Premiers Combats et Premiers Prisons*, Paris, 1969, pp. 36–8.

40. Dommanget, *Blanqui*, p. 57; cf. Decaux, pp. 47–54, 97.

41. Lord Elton, *The Revolutionary Idea in France, 1789–1871*, London, 1923, 2nd edn 1931, p. 107; cf. 86–8.

42. François Furet, *La Gauche et la Révolution au milieu du XIXᵉ Siècle: Edgar Quinet et la Question du Jacobinisme, 1865–1870*, Paris, 1986, pp. 13, 17.

43. Printed in *Courier*, 24 May 1827, quoted by Bagge, *Idées Politiques*, pp. 88, 27.

44. L.-A. Blanqui, *Aux Etudiants en Médecine et en Droit*, Paris, 1830, reprinted in Blanqui, *Textes Choisis*, Paris, 1971, p. 104.

45. Quoted in Dommanget, *Blanqui*, pp. 73–5; cf. Bernstein, p. 43.

46. Spitzer, *Blanqui*, p. 135, quoting from *The Times*, 28 April 1879.

47. Dommanget, *Idées Politiques*, p. 122 quoting a BN manuscript.

48. Blanqui, *Critique Sociale*, Paris, 1885, I, p. 196; cf. 'Les Sectes et la Révolution', *ibid.*, pp. 112–16, and Bernstein, pp. 205, 354.

49. Letter to Charles Fauvety of 5 July 1852, quoted from BN manuscript by Dommanget, *Idées Politiques*, p. 139.

50. Letter to Maillard, 6 June 1852, included in *Textes Choisis*, p. 130.

51. *Ibid.*, p. 140.

52. Blanqui, 'Qui fait la soupe doit la manger', *ibid.*, p. 103; cf. 15–16, 98–103.

53. BN manuscript quoted by Dommanget, *Idées Politiques*, p. 122; cf. *Critique Sociale*, I, pp. 199–200. While Blanqui had some friendly contacts with Auguste Comte, he rejected the clerical–conservative implications of positivism. *Ibid.*, pp. 141–2; cf. *Critique Sociale*, I, pp. 200–1.

54. François Pillon, 'Le Socialisme d'Auguste Blanqui', *Critique Philosophique*,

Nouvelle série, 1888, II, p. 61; cf. Dommanget, *Idées Politiques*, pp. 72–88, 103–6 and *Critique Sociale*, I, pp. 3ff., 69–71, 135–42, 221ff; II, pp. 34, 244.

55. Quoted in Dommanget, *Idées Politiques*, pp. 99, 101: first from Blanqui's newspaper *La Patrie en Danger*, October 1870, and second from *Critique Sociale*, II, p. 360; cf. 359.
56. Quoted in Dommanget, *Idées Politiques*, p. 142; cf. 131, 134, 143, 220.
57. *Critique Sociale*, I, p. 74.
58. Letter of 26 November 1848 in Blanqui, *Oeuvres Complètes*, I, p. 339.
59. *Critique Sociale*, II, p. 316.
60. *Ibid.*, pp. 314–15.
61. *Ibid.*, II, pp. 148ff. See also Spitzer, *Blanqui*, pp. 108–110.
62. *Critique Sociale*, I, p. 212; cf. I, pp. 69, 200. See also Jacques Grandjonc, 'A propos des relations des frères Blanqui entre eux et avec P.-J. Proudhon: quelques documents oubliés ou inédits' in Maurice Agulhon *et al.*, *Blanqui et les Blanquistes*, Paris, 1986, pp. 13–27.
63. Amable de Barante, *Des Communes et de l'aristocratie*, Paris, 1821, 2nd edn, p. 16.
64. Chateaubriand, *Etudes Historiques*, Paris, 1831, p. 1.
65. Quoted in Rosanvallon, *Guizot*, p. 294 note; cf. 295–8.
66. Eisenstein, p. 105; cf. 99–104. See also Louis Blanc, *Histoire de Dix Ans*, IV, pp. 182–3.
67. Eisenstein, pp. 105–9. Teste significantly reissued Etienne de la Boétie's subversive masterpiece *De la Servitude Volontaire* in 1836.
68. Eisenstein, p. 117; cf. 109–16 and Bernstein, pp. 57–8. See also Georges Weill, *Histoire du Parti Républicain en France*, 1814–70, Paris, 1928 edn, pp. 34–7.
69. Dommanget, *Blanqui*, p. 92; cf. 85–6 and Bernstein, p. 48. The friend was Adélaide de Montgolfier.
70. Quoted *ibid.*, p. 112.
71. Quoted in Maxime Leroy, *Les Précurseurs Français du Socialisme*, p. 393.
72. *Textes Choisis*, p. 71. An English translation is available in Paul E. Corcoran (ed.), *Before Marx: Socialism and communism in France*, London, 1983, pp. 36–46.
73. Quoted in Dommanget, *Blanqui*, p. 101.
74. *Textes Choisis*, pp. 72, 77; cf. 78–9.
75. *Ibid.*, p. 85. The poet Heine's report on Blanqui's speech appeared in the *Augsburger Zeitung* of 10 February 1832 and was republished in his *De la France*, Paris, 1830, pp. 47–8.
76. *Textes Choisis*, p. 87.
77. *Ibid.*, pp. 89–91.
78. Dommanget, *Idées Politiques*, p. 250; Dommanget, *Blanqui*, p. 111.
79. Dommanget, *Idées Politiques*, p. 28.
80. Spitzer, *Blanqui*, p. 143; cf. 93–102.
81. *Textes Choisis*, p. 95.
82. *Ibid.*, p. 173. Jules Vallès, the future Communard, dedicated the second volume of his autobiographical novel *Jacques Vingtras* 'To those who having studied Greek and Latin have died of hunger'.

83. *Textes Choisis*, p. 132; cf. 131, 133–4. See also Mason, pp. 505–8.
84. Spitzer, *Blanqui*, pp. 162–3; cf. 164–6, 170–1. On Blanqui's contempt for political institutions, see the quotations from his article in the *Libérateur* of February 1834 in Dommanget, *Blanqui*, pp. 132–3.
85. *Critique Sociale*, II, p. 208.
86. Quoted in Dommanget, *Idées Politiques*, p. 177; cf. 173 and Bernstein, pp. 62–3.
87. *Critique Sociale*, II, p. 206.
88. *Ibid.*, p. 200; cf. 157–8, 174.
89. Quoted in Dommanget, *Idées Politiques*, p. 183; cf. 159.
90. Eistenstein, p. 148; cf. 155 and Dommanget, *Idées Politiques*, p. 206. See also the testimony of Ledru-Rollin's secretary in 1848, A. Delvau, *Histoire de la Révolution de Février*, Paris, 1850, p. 318.
91. Raspail quoted in Dommanget, *Blanqui*, p. 156; cf. 146–7 and Decaux, pp. 165–6.
92. Louis Blanc, *Histoire de Dix Ans*, V, pp. 372–3; Bernstein, pp. 70–6; Alexandre Zévaès, *Une Révolution Manquée: L'Insurrection du 12 Mai 1839*, Paris, 1933, pp. 42–6; Dommanget, *Blanqui*, pp. 149–50, 163–4, 168–74.
93. Bernstein, pp. 79–81; Dommanget, *Blanqui*, pp. 180–3.
94. Dommanget, *Idées Politiques*, pp. 371, 394; Dommanget, *Blanqui*, pp. 200–1, 238.
95. Quoted in Paz, pp. 45–6.
96. Quoted in Dommanget, *Blanqui*, p. 186; cf. 187–8.
97. Bernstein, p. 71; cf. 59, 69–70.
98. *Ibid.*, pp. 88–93 and Dommanget, *Blanqui*, pp. 196–205. For extended accounts of the insurrection, see Louis Blanc, *Histoire de Dix Ans*, V, pp. 374–89 and Zévaès, *Une Révolution Manquée*, pp. 63ff.
99. Dommanget, *Blanqui*, pp. 307–16, 221–2, 126–7; and Decaux, pp. 210–14. The sketch by David d'Angers is reproduced on p. 209 of Decaux.
100. Spitzer, *Blanqui*, pp. 10, 157–8.
101. Dommanget, *Auguste Blanqui et la Révolution de 1848*, Paris, 1972, pp. 71–90 and Dommanget, *Un drame politique en 1848*, Paris, 1948. For a critical review of Dommanget's arguments, see Decaux, pp. 339–44. Dommanget's pro-Blanqui line is supported by Bernstein, pp. 158–64; Blanqui's reply to the accusation is available in his *Oeuvres Complètes*, I, pp. 175–95.
102. Decaux, pp. 334–47 and Maurice Paz, *Un Révolutionnaire Professionnel, Blanqui*, Paris, 1984, Part 2 *passim*, especially pp. 91–125. For Charles de Remusat's testimony, see his *Mémoires de ma vie*, III, Paris, 1960, pp. 306, 390. On Duchâtel, see the entry in the *Dictionnaire de Biographie Française*, XI, Paris, 1967, p. 1182.
103. Letter from Proudhon to Langlois, 7 January 1851, in his *Correspondence*, IV, pp. 8–9. Blanqui's physical courage in the 1839 insurrection seems not to have been great according to Langlois, citing numerous testimonies. See Weill, *Histoire du Parti Républicain*, p. 133 note.
104. Gustave Geoffroy, *L'Enfermé*, Paris, 1897, 1926 edn, II, p. 9; cf. 8 and Dommanget, *Blanqui*, pp. 264–5, 285–7, 307–11, 331–3 on the 1840–7 period.
105. Maurice Dommanget, *Histoire du Drapeau Rouge: Des origines à la guerre de*

1939, Paris, 1967, pp. 25, 30–32; cf. 18–38 and Louis Blanc, *Histoire de la Révolution de 1848*, Paris, 1880 edn, I, pp. 117–19.

106. Proudhon, *Solution du problème social*, Paris, 1848, pp. 28–9; cf. 30–2; cf. Dommanget, *Drapeau Rouge*, pp. 74–158. For a savage assessment of Lamartine's role in the 1848 Revolution, see Tocqueville, *Recollections*, Ch. 6, pp. 117–19.

107. *Textes Choisis*, p. 110.

108. Quoted by Dommanget, *Blanqui et . . . 1848*, p. 7; cf. 4–6 and Bernstein, pp. 136–8.

109. *Textes Choisis*, pp. 109–10.

110. Louis Blanc, *Histoire de la Révolution de 1848*, Paris, 1870, I, pp. 134–5.

111. Alphonse de Lamartine, *Histoire de la Révolution de 1848*, Paris, 1849, II, p. 150; cf. Dommanget, *Blanqui et . . . 1848*, pp. 25–33, 110–14. More generally, see Suzanne Wassermann, *Les clubs de Barbès et de Blanqui en 1848*, Paris, 1913; and A. Lucas, *Les clubs et les clubbistes*, Paris, 1851.

112. Quoted in Dommanget, *Blanqui et . . . 1848*, p. 234.

113. Quoted *ibid.*, p. 286; cf. 49.

114. *Textes Choisis*, pp. 113–14.

115. Quoted in Dommanget, *Blanqui et . . . 1848*, p. 23; cf. 58–67, 123–32 and Decaux, pp. 311, 359.

116. Bernstein, p. 171; cf. 148–52 and Dommanget, *Blanqui et . . . 1848*, pp. 142–5.

117. *Critique Sociale*, I, pp. 206–7 quoted in Dommanget, *Blanqui et . . . 1848*, p. 232.

118. Lucien de la Hodde, *Histoire des sociétés secrètes et du parti républicain*, Paris, 1850, p. 121.

119. *Oeuvres Complètes*, I, pp. 298, 305; cf. 233–306; Dommanget, *Blanqui et . . . 1848*, pp. 157–86. On the role of Aloysius Huber, see Dora B. Weiner, *Raspail: Scientist and reformer*, New York, p. 211 note. Proudhon publicly defended Blanqui in *Le Représentant du Peuple*, of 28 May 1848 but he disapproved of his role. See *Confessions d'un Révolutionnaire*, p. 146; cf. 131–44.

120. Marx, 'The class struggle in France, 1848–50' in Marx and Engels, *Selected Works*, I, pp. 160, 162.

121. Tocqueville, *Recollections*, pp. 150–1.

122. *Ibid.*, pp. 159, 170.

123. Marx, 'Class struggles', p. 163.

124. Tocqueville, *Recollections*, p. 130.

125. Victor Hugo, *Choses Vues*, 1887, Paris, 1957 edn pp. 178–9. For a less hostile pen portrait by a Communard, see Jules Vallès, *Jacques Vingtras*, 1885, Paris, 1950 edn, III, p. 171.

126. Quoted in Franco Venturi, *Roots of Revolution*, London, 1960, p. 30; cf. 28, 62.

127. Marx, 'Class struggles', pp. 222–3; cf. 254.

128. H. Draper, 'Marx and the dictatorship of the proletariat', *Cahiers de l'Institut de Science Economique Appliquée*, no. 129, September 1962, p. 30; cf. 31–7.

129. *Ibid.*, p. 63; cf. 46–69 and Charles Da Costa, *Les Blanquistes*, Paris, 1912, p. 4. As against Dommanget, *Idées Politiques*, Ch. 7 and Bernstein, pp. 300–3,

Hutton, pp. 8–10 stresses, like Draper, the contrast between Blanquism and Marxism.

130. 'Avis au Peuple' of 25 February 1851 in *Textes Choisis*, p. 124.

131. 'A propos des clameurs contre l'avis au peuple' of April 1851 in *Textes Choisis*, p. 127. More generally, see Bernstein, pp. 216–23.

132. Dommanget, *Idées Politiques*, p. 6, quoting Louis Combes, *Portraits révolutionnaires: Blanqui*, Paris, 1872, p. 1.

133. Blanqui MS quoted by Spitzer, pp. 45–6.

134. Blanqui MS quoted by Dommanget, p. 196; cf. *Critique Sociale*, II, p. 116, 154 and *Textes Choisis*, p. 171.

135. *Critique Sociale*, I, pp. 178, 184, 189, 203; II, pp. 69–70, 146–7; and Dommanget, *Idées Politiques*, pp. 198–202, 220.

136. *Critique Sociale*, I, p. 205; cf. Dommanget, *Idées Politiques*, pp. 183–4, 271–303.

137. 'Le Communisme, avenir de la société' in *Textes Choisis*, p. 172; cf. 150–2.

138. Da Costa, *Les Blanquistes*, pp. 7–8, 10–11, 16, 21; David R. Watson, *Georges Clemenceau: A political biography*, London, 1974, pp. 23–5.

139. Spitzer, *Blanqui*, p. 140; cf. *Critique Sociale*, II, pp. 129ff., 166–7, 227.

140. *Critique Sociale*, II, p. 146; cf. 129–36, 144–5, 165 and *Textes Choisis*, pp. 180–94.

141. *Critique Sociale*, II, p. 174. More generally, see Bernstein, pp. 287–95, 303–8.

142. Spitzer, *Blanqui*, p. 112; cf. 13.

143. 'Instruction pour une prise d'armes' in *Textes Choisis*, p. 214; cf. 215–20. See also Dommanget, *Idées Politiques*, pp. 326–39, 359–64.

144. Article on 'L'Affaire de La Villette' in *La Patrie en Danger*, 16 September 1870, in *Textes Choisis*, p. 197; cf. 196–200.

145. Bernstein, pp. 325–8 on the 31 October 1870 coup. See also Geoffroy, II, pp. 99–108, Da Costa, pp. 35–7 and Spitzer, pp. 145–152–6.

146. *La Patrie en Danger*, 8 September 1870.

147. Quoted in Dommanget, *Idées Politiques*, p. 228; cf. Geoffroy, II, pp. 113–14.

148. Quoted from *La Patrie en Danger*, November 1870 in Dommanget, *Idées Politiques*, p. 226; cf. 227–8.

149. Decaux, pp. 567–76.

150. Hutton, *Cult of the Revolution*, p. 92; cf. 60–2, 71–97. There are numerous accounts of the Paris Commune both in French and English. One may consult, for example, Roger L. Williams, *The French Revolution of 1870–1871*, London, 1969, especially pp. 124–40; Stewart Edwards (ed.), *The Communards of Paris*, 1871, London, 1973, especially pp. 26–42; and Stewart Edwards, *The Paris Commune*, London, 1971.

151. Spitzer, *Blanqui*, p. 179; cf. 14.

152. Quoted by Decaux, p. 479.

153. Engels' 1891 introduction to 'The civil war in France' in *Selected Works*, I, p. 482; and Hutton, p. 115; cf. 102–4, 114–17.

154. Decaux, pp. 606–21 and Jean T. Joughin, *The Paris Commune in French Politics, 1871–1880: The history of the amnesty of 1880*, New York, 1956, pp. 160–6, 246–59, 266–9, 384–9, 415–19.

155. Hutton, p. 16.
156. Maurice Paz, 'Clemenceau, Blanqui's heir: an unpublished letter from Blanqui to Clemenceau dated 18 March 1879' *Historical Journal*, xvi/3, 1973, pp. 613, 615; cf. 604ff. Geoffroy, ii, pp. 188–98, says the letter was never sent. More generally, see Decaux, pp. 486–8, 554–5, 606; and D. R. Watson's 'Clemenceau et Blanqui', Ch. 10 of Agulhon *et al.*, *Blanqui et les Blanquistes*, pp. 173–8.
157. See the text of *Aux Communeux*, in Da Costa, p. 48; cf. 44–51.
158. Bernstein, pp. 356–7.
159. Da Costa, p. 69.
160. Article in *Le Socialiste*, 21 January 1890, quoted by Jolyon Howarth, *Edouard Vaillant*, Paris, 1982, p. 77; cf. 29–37, 68–70; cf. Hutton, pp. 149–69, 171.
161. Howarth, *Vaillant*, p. 188. On Vaillant's Proudhonism, see *ibid.*, pp. 35, 170, 216–17. On Vaillant's role in promoting trade union unification, see *ibid.*, pp. 196–203; Julliard, *Pelloutier*, pp. 129–30; and Howarth, 'Edouard Vaillant, le Socialisme et le Mouvement Syndical, 1888–1907', *Nouvelle Revue Socialiste*, nos. 12–13, 1975, pp. 96–116.
162. Wolfe, 'Leninism' in Milorad M. Drachkovitch (ed.), *Marxism in the Modern World*, Stanford, 1965, p. 61; cf. 56–62.
163. Eduard Bernstein, *Evolutionary Socialism: A criticism and affirmation*, 1st English edn 1909, 1961 edition, New York, pp. 143–44, 147; cf. 153–61.
164. *Karl Marx and Friedrich Engels Correspondence, 1846–1895*, London, 1934, p. 437.
165. *Ibid.*, p. 438.
166. Quoted by Venturi, pp. 422, 428; cf. 390–417, 778, 780.
167. 'What is to be done?' in James E. Connor (ed.), *Lenin on Politics and Revolution: Selected writings*, New York, 1968, pp. 66–8; cf. 73.
168. *Ibid.*, p. 78; cf. 75–7.
169. Wolfe, 'Leninism', p. 86; cf. 85 and his introduction to Rosa Luxemburg, *The Russian Revolution and Leninism or Marxism*, 1961, pp. 12–14.
170. Leon Trotsky, 'Our political tasks' in Robert V. Daniels (ed.) *A Documentary History of Communism*, London, 1987, i, pp. 21, 22.
171. Wolfe, 'Leninism', p. 65; cf. 87–8.
172. Mason, 'Blanqui and communism', p. 525; cf. 527.
173. Rosa Luxemburg, p. 88; cf. 86–7, 95.
174. *Ibid.*, 90–1.
175. *Ibid.*, pp. 101, 107; cf. 99–108.
176. Lenin, 'On dual power', 9 April 1917 in Daniels (ed.) i, pp. 59–60; cf. Lenin, 'Marxism and insurrection', 13–14 September 1917 in V. I. Lenin, *Selected Works*, London, 1968, pp. 357–9.
177. Luxemburg, pp. 69–70; cf. 60–2, 67–8.
178. *Ibid.*, pp. 76–7; cf. 71–2.
179. *Ibid.*, pp. 77–8.
180. Text in Annie Kriegel (ed.), *Le Congrès de Tours*, Paris, 1964, pp. 114, 117; cf. 100ff.
181. *Ibid.*, pp. 125–6.
182. *Ibid.*, pp. 128–9. Emphasis added.

183. *Ibid.*, p. 130; cf. 129.
184. Leon Trotsky, *The History of the Russian Revolution, 1929–30*, Max Eastman translation, London, 1965, p. 1020; cf. 1021–2.
185. *Ibid.*, p. 1025.

Chapter 9

1. Review of a reprint of Mignet's *Histoire de la Révolution Française* in Prevost-Paradol, *Essais de Politique et de Littérature*, II, Paris, 1863, pp. 25, 29; cf. 26–8.
2. *Bagehot's Historical Essays*, Norman St. John-Stevas edn, London, 1971. p. 429; cf. 403–21. These essays originally appeared in January–March 1852 in the *Inquirer*, signed Amicus.
3. Walter Bagehot, *The English Constitution* (1867), London, Nelson edn, n.d., pp. 50, 53, 55.
4. Bagehot, 'Why an English liberal may look without disapproval on the progress of imperialism in France', first published in *The Economist*, 6 June 1874 and reprinted in Bagehot's *Historical Essays*, pp. 447, 451.
5. Stanley Hoffmann, 'Paradoxes of the French political community' in Hoffmann *et al.*, *France: Change and tradition*, London, 1963, p. 15; cf. 1–17.
6. Michel Winock, *La fièvre hexagonale: Les grandes crises politiques, 1871–1968*, Paris, 1987, p. 54; cf. 53, 92–3.
7. 'The Last Revolution' is the title of Ch. 8 of Elton, *Revolutionary Idea in France*. See especially pp. 153, 168–9. The other quotations are from François Furet, *La Révolution, 1770–1880*, Paris, 1988, p. 489.
8. Furet, *La Révolution*, pp. 493–4.
9. Testimony of Charles de Rémusat in his *Mémoires*, IV, Paris, 1962, p. 351, quoted in Pierre Guiral, *Adolphe Thiers ou de la Nécessité en Politique*, Paris, 1986, p. 249; cf. 39, 123–4; *Bagehot's Historical Essays*, p. 416.
10. The letter of 12 December 1846 from Tocqueville to Gustave de Beaumont, quoted by J. P. T. Bury and R. P. Tombs, *Thiers 1797–1877: A political life*, London, 1986, pp. 147, 219; cf. 126, suggests that their differences may be due partly to the fact that whereas Tocqueville had studied the successful American Republic, Thiers' view of democracy was influenced by his study of the Renaissance Florentine Republic and how it degenerated into Medici despotism.
11. Bury and Tombs, pp. 52–3, 207–8. A leading Communard, Jules Vallès, described Thiers by anticipation in a February 1871 article as a 'parrot-headed vulture'. (Quoted in Guiral, p. 376.)
12. Quoted in Bury and Tombs, p. 234; cf. 118. Thiers, of course, did not believe in God! On Thiers' sacrifice of liberalism to repression in the 1830s, see Guiral, pp. 90–9.
13. *Discours parlementaires de M. Thiers*, Paris, 1879–89, VII, pp. 608–9. Emphasis added.
14. *Ibid.*, p. 685, quoted in Bury and Tombs, p. 123.
15. On Talleyrand's 1829 comments, see Henri Malo, *Thiers 1797–1877*, Paris, 1932, p. 113, who reports Thiers as saying: 'Charles X will leave by the same road as James the Second.'

16. Letter of 8 July 1850 from Thiers to Count Stroganoff, quoted in Bury and Tombs, p. 128.
17. *Discours parlementaires de M. Thiers*, IX, p. 40, quoted in Bury and Tombs, p. 126. See also Guiral, pp. 86, 142. In 1830 Constant had given Sieyès the credit for declaring that the constitutional monarch 'should choose but not govern'. See Harpaz (ed.), *Benjamin Constant Publiciste*, p. 175.
18. Maurice Deslandres, *Histoire Constitutionnelle de la France: L'Avènement de la Troisieme République: La Constitution de 1875*, Paris, 1937, p. 55; cf. 3–4, 21–5.
19. *Ibid.*, p. 138; cf. 133–53, quoting de Falloux's *Mémoires d'un royaliste*, II, Paris, 1888, p. 494. For the Chambord quotation, see Jean-Marie Mayeur, *Les débuts de la IIIᵉ République, 1871–1898*, Paris, 1973, p. 15.
20. *Annales*, 1873, XVIII, p. 43, quoted in Bury and Tombs, p. 299. For a contemporary view of Thiers' role in 1872, see Bagehot's introduction to the 1872 edition of *The English Constitution*, pp. 51–5.
21. Madame de Staël, *Des Circonstances actuelles*, pp. 69–71.
22. J. Pradon, 'L'Ecole du *Correspondant*' in *Revue Internationale d'Histoire Politique et Constitutionnel*, April–June 1955 (special issue on 'Les sources Intellectuelles de la Constitution de 1875'), pp. 106–7; cf. 99ff. and F. Furet, *La Révolution*, p. 495.
23. Odile Rudelle, *La République Absolue, 1870–1889*, Paris, 1982, pp. 18–32. The classic description of the Broglie–Thiers political duel and its aftermath is Daniel Halévy's *La Fin des Notables*, Paris, 1930, and *La République des Ducs*, Paris, 1937. He describes Thiers saying of Broglie in the Chamber: 'Look at the hands, the restless hands, they are Constant's hands, the spit image of Constant.' (*La Fin des Notables*, p. 155; cf. 156 and Chs. 9 and 12 *passim*.)
24. Deslandres, pp. 263, 325–33, 446–8. On the term of presidential office, see Emile Littré, *De l'Etablissement de la Troisième République*, Paris, 1880, pp. 289–90, 303–13.
25. Quoted in Rudelle, p. 36; cf. 35–8. See also Mayeur, pp. 32–4.
26. D. Halévy, *La République des Ducs*, p. 259; cf. Ch. 7 *passim*. On Dupanloup, see *ibid.*, pp. 199, 204–12, 238–40.
27. John Lemoinne, quoted by Halévy, *ibid.*, p. 298. On Thiers' role in 1877, see *ibid.*, pp. 305, 311–13.
28. Ferry speech of 12 June 1877, quoted in Rudelle, p. 56.
29. Rudelle, p. 68; cf. 63, 66–9.
30. *Ibid.*, pp. 69–70.
31. Michel Vovelle, 'La Marseillaise' in Pierre Nora (ed.), *Les Lieux de Mémoire*, I, *La République*, Paris, 1984, p. 118; and Christian Amalvi, 'Le 14-Juillet', *ibid.*, pp. 423–9. Broglie forbade the commemoration of 14 July in 1873. (Mayeur, p. 28; cf. 47–8.)
32. Vovelle, p. 99. On the recognition of the *Internationale*, composed in 1888, by the Socialist Second International in 1910 as the workers' anthem, see *ibid.*, p. 122.
33. Furet, *La Révolution*, p. 517.
34. Rosanvallon, *Guizot*, pp. 17, 28, 36–7, 101 note.

35. Quoted *ibid.*, p. 363.
36. Gambetta's speech of 9 October 1877 in *Discours*, *VII*, Reinach edn, Paris, 1880–5, pp. 282–3, quoted by Rosanvallon, pp. 364–5; cf. 348–55, 363 note.
37. E. de Laboulaye, *La Parti Libéral: Son programme et son avenir*, Paris, 1863, p. xi; cf. 120, 316. See also his *Lettres Politiques: Esquisse d'une constitution républicaine*, Paris, 1872, especially letters 5 and 8. More generally, see Jean de Soto, 'Edouard de Laboulaye' in *Revue Internationale d'Histoire Politique et Constitutionnel*, April–June 1955, pp. 114–50.
38. Letter of 24 January 1863 to the former Saint-Simonian Michel Chevalier, quoted by Pierre Guiral, *Prévost-Paradol (1829–70): Pensée et Action d'un Libéral sous le Second Empire*, Paris, 1955, p. 519. On Saint-Simon's last secretary Leon Halévy, see Alain Silvera, *Daniel Halévy and His Times*, Cornell, 1966, pp. 6–10.
39. Guiral, p. 8; cf. 146–7, 160, 164–71, 749–51.
40. *Ibid.*, pp. 691–702; cf. Albert Thibaudet in *Nouvelle Revue française*, 1 March 1931, pp. 430–1.
41. Anatole Prévost-Paradol, *Essais de Politique et de Littérature*, Paris, 1859, p. 201.
42. Prévost-Paradol, *La France Nouvelle*, Paris, 1868, Book I, pp. 15–17 and Chs. 4–6 *passim*. On Paradol's Anglomania, see Guiral, pp. 115–16, 209–10, 494–7. Guiral published a new edition of *La France Nouvelle*, Paris, 1981, together with some additional extracts.
43. *Essais de Politique*, I, pp. 217–18.
44. *Ibid.*, pp. xliii–iv; cf. xxii–ix, xxxviii–ix and Guiral, pp. 489, 497–501 on Paradol's link with Thiers.
45. *Ibid.*, pp. xlv–vi; cf. xxxiii.
46. *Ibid.*, p. xlvii; cf. *La France Nouvelle*, pp. 295–6. Daniel Halévy claimed that this book had been read by all members of the National Assembly of 1871–5. (*La République des Ducs*, p. 161 note.)
47. Littré, *Etablissement de la Troisième République*, p. 142.
48. *Ibid.*, pp. 195–7; cf. viii–x, 466–73, 485ff. See also Claude Nicolet, *Idée Républicaine en France, 1792–1924: Essai d'histoire critique*, Paris, 1982, pp. 200–17.
49. Littré, *Etablissement*, p. 143; cf. 256, 517–19, 578.
50. Stéphane Rials, *La déclaration des droits de l'homme et du citoyen*, pp. 229–33.
51. Guy Thuillier, *L'ENA avant L'ENA*, p. 105; cf. 124–9 and Christophe Charle, *Les Elites de la République, 1880–1900*, Paris, 1987, pp. 44–51; cf. 27.
52. Thuillier, pp. 130–9 and Pierre Favre, *Naissances de la science politique en France, 1870–1914*, Paris, 1989, pp. 39–40, 44.
53. Emile Boutmy and Ernest Vinet, *Quelques idées sur la création d'une faculté libre d'enseignement supérieur*, Paris, 1871, pp. 15–16. On Boutmy's view of his mentors Taine and Laboulaye, see his essays on *Taine, Scherer, Laboulaye*, Paris, 1901.
54. Ezra Suleiman, *Elites in French Society: The politics of survival*, Princeton, 1978, pp. 52–3; cf. Ch. 2 *passim*.
55. Favre, p. 49; cf. Thuillier, pp. 150–7. Boutmy wrote frequently on Britain. He

was the author of substantial works on *Le développement de la constitution et de la société politique en Angleterre*, Paris, 1887 and *Essai d'une psychologie du peuple anglais au XIXᵉ siècle*, Paris, 1901.

56. Preface to F. Furet (ed.), *Jules Ferry fondateur de la République*, Paris, 1985, p. 9.

57. *Ibid.*, p. 10; cf. Nicolet, pp. 75–9, 115, 128–9.

58. Speech of 20 March 1881, quoted in Rudelle, p. 78 note. See also Pierre Barral, *Les Fondateurs de la 3ᵉ République*, Paris, 1968, pp. 7–8, 12–18, 45–6; Furet, *La Révolution*, pp. 502–3; Winock, pp. 86–8.

59. Louis Legrand, *L'influence du Positivisme dans l'oeuvre scolaire de Jules Ferry*, Paris, 1961, pp. 105–11, 120–5, 136, 184–94; Jean-Michel Gaillard, *Jules Ferry*, Paris, 1989, pp. 130–61; Nicolet, pp. 228–47; Furet, *La Révolution*, pp. 459–60.

60. Letter of 12 May 1879 quoted by Philippe Guilhaume, *Jules Ferry*, Paris, 1980, p. 83; cf. 46–54; François Furet, *La Gauche et la Révolution*, pp. 78–83; Furet, *La Révolution*, p. 21; Gaillard, p. 124.

61. Ferry, *Discours et opinions*, Paris, 1893, I, pp. 558, 562–3, quoted from Furet, *La Révolution*, p. 460; cf. Barral, pp. 312–20.

62. Quoted in Gaillard, p. 175; cf. 176.

63. Letter to his brother of 16 April 1875, quoted *ibid.*, p. 276; cf. 277, 619 and Rudelle, pp. 94–7.

64. Letter of 12 July 1889, quoted by Raoul Girardet, 'Jules Ferry et l'image d'une République à fonder' in Furet (ed.), *Jules Ferry fondateur de la République*, pp. 248–9; cf. 24–7.

65. Gaillard, pp. 63–5. On the Protestant ministers in the Waddington government, see the chapter by Richard in André Encrevé and Michel Richard (eds.), *Les Protestants dans les débuts de la Troisième République, 1871–85*, Paris, 1979, pp. 200–17.

66. Gaillard, pp. 339, 425–35, 443. On the attempt to reconcile democracy and science, see Célestin Bouglé, *La Démocratie devant la Science*, Paris, 1904.

67. Furet, *Le Gauche et la Révolution*, p. 114. Ferry's most recent biographer, Gaillard (pp. 652–3), subscribes to the view that the 1880s saw the end of the French Revolution.

68. Letter to his wife in Paul Cambon, *Correspondance*, Paris, 1940, I, p. 261, quoted by Mayeur, p. 166.

69. *Année Politique 1888*, p. 188 quoted in Rudelle, p. 230; cf. 164–93, 218–24, 230–5. More generally on Boulangism, see Winock, Ch. 3.

70. See J. E. S. Hayward, 'Solidarity: the social history of an idea in nineteenth century France', *International Review of Social History*, IV/2, 1959, pp. 261–84; 'The official social philosophy of the French Third Republic: Léon Bourgeois and solidarism', *ibid.*, VI/1, 1961, pp. 19–48; and 'Educational pressure groups and the indoctrination of the radical ideology of solidarism, 1895–1914', *ibid.*, VIII/1, 1963, pp. 1–17.

71. On 'Le Tour de France par deux enfants: Le petit livre rouge de la République', see Jacques and Mona Ozouf's chapter in Pierre Nora (ed.), *La République*, pp. 291–321; Gaillard, pp. 467–70; and Daniel Halévy, *La République des Ducs*,

pp. 336–9. See also J. E. S. Hayward, ' "Solidarity" and the reformist sociology of Alfred Fouillée, *The American Journal of Economics and Sociology*, XXII/1–2, January 1963, pp. 205–22 and April 1963, pp. 303–12.

72. Léon Bourgeois, *Solidarité*, Paris, 1896, *L'Education de la Démocratie*, Paris, 1897 and *Pour la Société des Nations*, Paris, 1910.

73. Ernest Gellner, *Nations and Nationalism*, Oxford, 1983, p. 124; cf. 125.

74. *Ibid.*, pp. 11, 55; cf. 63–4, 101, 111.

75. *Ibid.*, p. 34.

76. Conor Cruise O'Brien, 'Nationalism and the French Revolution' in Geoffrey Best (ed.), *The Permanent Revolution: The French Revolution and its legacy 1789–1989*, Fontana, 1988, p. 19; cf. 18–30.

77. *Ibid.*, pp. 43–4; cf. 46.

78. Blanqui article in *La Patrie en Danger*, 25 November 1870, quoted by Jean Dubois, *Le Vocabulaire Politique et Social en France de 1869 a 1872*, Paris, 1962, p. 350; cf. 90.

79. Ernest Renan, *Nouvelle Lettre à Strauss*, 1871, quoted in H. Peyre, *Renan*, Paris, 1869, pp. 86–7.

80. Ernest Renan, *Qu'est-ce qu'une Nation?*, Paris, 1882, p. 18; cf. 13–17.

81. *Ibid.*, p. 27; cf. 7–9.

82. *Ibid.*, p. 28; cf. 29.

83. Eugen Weber, *Peasants into Frenchmen: The modernization of rural France, 1870–1914*, London, 1977, pp. 485, 112.

84. *Ibid.*, p. 486; cf. 9, 72 and Ch. 7 *passim*. See also Jack Hayward, *The One and Indivisible French Republic*, London, 1973, pp. 17–19. A similar line of argument to Weber's view of French unification as a process of administrative colonization is taken in Jack Hayward, 'Institutionalized inequality within an indivisible Republic: Brittany and France', *Journal of the Conflict Research Society*, I/1, 1977, pp. 1–15.

85. Weber, p. 493. Charles Tilly in 'Revolutions and collective violence', p. 544, argues that France's modernization phase should be located in the mid-nineteenth century.

86. Hoffmann, 'Paradoxes', p. 1.

87. *Ibid.*, p. 61; cf. 60ff.

88. Henri Mendras, *La Seconde Révolution Française*, 1965–84, Paris, 1988, p. 20. See earlier versions in Mendras, 'An optimistic view of France', *The Tocqueville Review*, I/1, Fall 1979, pp. 24–63; 'Une figure de la France', in Henri Mendras (ed.), *La Sagesse et le Désordre: France 1980*, Paris, 1980, pp. 15–61, and Gérard Pavy, 'Le retournement de l'année 1965', *ibid.*, pp. 63–77.

89. André Tardieu, *Le souverain captif*, Paris, 1936, pp. 211, 232, quoted in Winock, pp. 204–5; cf. 132–5, 388–9; and Tardieu's *La Réforme de l'Etat*, Paris, 1934. On Tardieu, see Malcoln Anderson, *Conservative Politics in France*, London, 1974, pp. 56–8. See also Michael Sutton, *Nationalism, Positivism and Catholicism: The politics of Charles Maurras and French Catholics, 1890–1914*, Cambridge, 1982; and more generally René Remond, *The Right Wing in France from 1815 to de Gaulle*, Philadelphia, 1966, especially Ch. 7. For a latter-day attempt to repeat Maurras' 1900 *Enquête sur la Monarchie*, see Pierre Pujo,

La Monarchie aujourd'hui, une nouvelle enquête, Paris, 1988.

90. Magraw, pp. 306–17. See also Jacques Julliard, *Clemenceau, briseur de grèves*, Paris, 1965; and George Lichtheim, *Marxism in Modern France*, New York, 1966, Chs. 1 and 2.
91. Hoffmann, *Decline or Renewal? France since the 1930s*, New York, 1974, p. 122; cf. Ch. 5 on 'The ruled: protest as a national way of life', *passim*.
92. Crozier, *The Bureaucratic Phenomenon*, 1968, English edn London, 1964, p. 287.
93. Quoted in Raymond Aron, *The Elusive Revolution*, London, 1969, p. 88. See Michel Crozier, *On ne change pas la société par décret*, Paris, 1979, and his *Etat modeste, Etat moderne*, Paris, 1987.
94. Three publications can be selected from the mass of writing inspired by the 1968 events: Philippe Bénéton and Jean Touchard, 'Les interprétations de la crise de mai–juin 1968', *Revue Française de Science Politique*, xx/3, June 1970, pp. 503–43; Hoffmann, 'Confrontation in May 1968', Ch. 6 of *Decline or Renewal?*; and Winock, Ch. 8 devoted to the last of the eight crises that make up his scrutiny of *La fièvre héxagonale*.
95. Pierre Mendès France, *A Modern French Republic*, London, 1962. On the Resistance period, see Andrew Shennan, *Rethinking France: Plans for renewal, 1940–1946*, Oxford, 1989, pp. 111–18, 139.
96. Shennan, p. 120; cf. 118–24. See also Jacquier-Bruère, *Refaire la France*, Paris, 1945, Debré's pseudonymous book (written in collaboration with Emmanuel Monick); and his *La Mort de l'Etat Républicain*, Paris, 1947.
97. Gordon Wright, *The Reshaping of French Democracy*, London, 1950, *passim*; and Shennan, pp. 124–40.
98. De Gaulle's Bayeux speech is quoted from the translation in Martin Harrison's *French Politics*, Lexington, MA, 1969, p. 25. For the full French text of de Gaulle's key constitutional speeches at Bayeux (16 June 1946) and Epinal (29 September 1946) see his *Discours et Messages*, ii, Paris, 1970, pp. 5–11, 26–33.
99. Quotation from Debré's 27 August 1958 speech to the Conseil d'Etat as partially translated in Harrison, p. 32; cf. 31–3.
100. Michel Debré, *Au Service de la Nation*, Paris, 1963, pp. 196–8, translated in Harrison,. pp. 46–8. For de Gaulle's explanation, see his *Mémoires d'Espoir*, Paris, 1971, ii, pp. 18–20. See also, Odile Rudelle, 'Le Général de Gaulle et l'élection directe du Président de la République', in Olivier Duhamel and Jean-Luc Parodi (eds.), *La Constitution de la Cinquième République*, Paris, 1985, pp. 101–25.
101. Mitterrand's speech in the decisive debate on 1 June 1958 that settled the fate of the Fourth Republic, quoted from Olivier Duhamel, *La Gauche et la Ve République*, Paris, 1980, p. 45; cf. 37, 46, 52.
102. Léo Figuères, 'Non au plébiscite!', *Cahiers du communisme*, July 1958, p. 994, quoted in Duhamel, p. 99; cf. 93, 97, 105.
103. Duhamel, p. 472; cf. 145, 155, 169.
104. *Ibid.*, p. 254. Emphasis in the original. See also, pp. 247–60, 543–7.
105. *Ibid.*, p. 342; cf. 338, 343.

106. 'Un entretien avec M. François Mitterrand', *Le Monde*, 2 July 1981.
107. Charles de Gaulle, *Lettres, Notes et Carnets*, Paris, 1980, II, p. 214, quoted by Odile Rudelle, *Mai 1958: De Gaulle et la République*, Paris, 1988, p. 38; cf. 17, 43.
108. Odile Rudelle, 'Lieux de Mémoire Révolutionnaire et Communion Républicaine', *XXᵉ Siècle*, no. 24, October–December 1989, p. 5. However, de Gaulle's foreign minister from 1958 to 1968, Maurice Couve de Murville, regarded the Revolution as ending with the representative regime of the Third Republic. See his remarks in Marie-Laurence Netter, *La Révolution française n'est pas terminée*, Paris, 1989, p. 212.
109. Quotation from de Gaulle's 12 July 1945 broadcast (*Discours et Messages*, Paris, 1970, I, p. 582) in Rudelle, *Mai 1958*, p. 48; cf. 23, 29, 53, 65 note, 288. See also Charles de Gaulle, *Mémoires d'Espoir*, Paris, 1970, I, p. 23. Mitterrand's acerbic diatribe, *Le Coup d'Etat permanent*, Paris, 1964, is now a period piece. More generally, see Maurice Duverger *La Monarchie Républicaine*, Paris, 1974. Debré used the term 'republican monarch' in the pseudonymous work (with E. Monick) by Jacquier-Bruère, *Refaire la France*, Paris, 1945, p. 122.
110. François Furet, '1789–1917: aller et retour', the first article in the special commemorative issue of *Le Débat*, no. 57, November–December 1989, p. 10; cf. 8 and Furet, 'Réflexions sur l'idée de tradition révolutionnaire dans la France du XIXᵉ siècle' in *Pouvoirs*, no. 50, September 1989, pp. 12–13.
111. Furet in *Le Débat*, November–December 1989, pp. 5, 16.
112. On Clemenceau's 'La Révolution française est un bloc', see Marie-Laurence Netter, *La Révolution française n'est pas terminée*, Paris, 1989, pp. 97–105, 218–21. However, opinion polls in 1987 and 1989 indicated that only 19 per cent as against 57 per cent of the public and 16 per cent against 82 per cent of history teachers thought there was one and not several revolutions in the French Revolution. See SOFRES, *L'Etat de l'Opinion, 1990*, Paris, 1990, p. 98.
113. Furet in François Furet, Jacques Julliard and Pierre Rosanvallon, *La République du Centre: La fin de l'exception française*, Paris, 1988, p. 222; cf. Furet in *Le Débat*, p. 4.
114. Netter, p. 245; cf. 23–5; pp. 55–6; cf. 107–8.
115. 'Gauche–Droite: La révolution tranquille', SOFRES poll reported in *Le Point*, 27 November 1989, pp. 62–5. More generally, see Alain Duhamel, 'Le consensus français' in *L'Opinion Française en 1977*, Paris, 1978, pp. 87–115.
116. 'La Révolution française et la monarchie', SOFRES, *L'Etat de l'Opinion: Clés pour 1988*, Paris, 1988, pp. 191–200.
117. CSA poll, 17–24 November 1989, reported in *Le Monde*, 29 December 1989.
118. On the discussion of the 1946 Declaration of Rights, see Gordon Wright, *The Reshaping of French Democracy*, London, 1950, pp. 135–42, 156–61, 199–200. More generally, although with particular reference to the 1789 Declaration, see Marcel Gauchet, *La Révolution des droits de l'homme*, Paris, 1989, pp. vi–xi, 9, 199–201, 316.
119. Jean-Pierre Machelon, *La République Contre les Libertés?*, Paris, 1976, pp. 29–49, 64.

120. Emile Acollas, *Philosophie de la Science Politique et Commentaire de la Déclaration des Droits de l'Homme de 1793* (*sic*), Paris, 1877; Gaston Jèze, 'Valeur juridique des Déclarations de droits et des garanties des droits', *Revue du Droit Public*, 1913, pp. 685–8. On Duguit and Hauriou, as well as the rival views of Esmein and Carré de Malberg, see references in Nicolet, pp. 350–5.

121. Stéphane Rials, 'Une doctrine constitutionnelle française?' in the special issue of September 1989, no. 50 of *Pouvoirs*, '1789–1989: Histoire Constitutionnelle', p. 95; cf. 81ff. See also Gilles Le Beguec, 'Les Français et leurs Constitutions', *ibid*., pp. 116–20.

122. William Doyle, *The Oxford History of the French Revolution*, Oxford, 1989, pp. 396, 388; cf. 389–90.

123. Napoleon's comment was reported by Roederer and quoted by Prévost-Paradol in his *Essais de Politique*, I, p. 198; cf. 196.

124. *Pouvoirs*, no. 50, p. 123.

125. *Ibid*., p. 124. On the gradual and pragmatic abandonment of revolution by the Left, see Olivier Duhamel, *La Gauche et la Vᵉ République*, pp. 472–87.

126. Mignet, quoted by Bury and Tombs, p. 149.

127. Guy Hermet, *Le Peuple contra la Démocratie*, Paris, 1989, pp. 71–3, 80–3. See also Alain Lancelot's classic study of *L'Abstentionnisme électoral en France*, Paris, 1968 for turnout figures from 1815, pp. 12–18 and more generally Part 1 of Daniel Gaxie (ed.), *Explication du Vote: Un bilan des études électorales en France, 1985*, 2nd edn, 1989.

128. Philippe Braud, *Le Suffrage Universel contre la Démocratie*, Paris, 1980, p. 70; cf. 63–7.

129. For a recent exploration of this theme, see Robert Dahl, *Democracy and its Critics*, New Haven and London, 1989. See also the essay on 'Droits de l'Homme et politique' in Claude Lefort, *L'Invention Démocratique*, Paris, 1981, especially pp. 61–83.

130. Previously unpublished article of 1939 by Jean Guéhenno, printed in *Le Monde*, 15 July 1989, p. 10. Jean Guéhenno is best known for his book *Caliban Parle*, Paris, 1928.

INDEX